Students with Learning Disabilities or Emotional/ Behavioral Disorders

Anne M. Bauer
University of Cincinnati

Charlotte H. Keefe
Texas Woman's University

Thomas M. Shea
University of Southern Illinois Edwardsville

Merrill
Prentice Hall

Upper Saddle River, New Jersey
Columbus, Ohio

Library of Congress Cataloging-in-Publication Data

Bauer, Anne M.
   Students with learning disabilities or emotional/behavioral disorders/Anne M. Bauer,
Charlotte H. Keefe, Thomas M. Shea.
       p. cm.
   Includes bibliographical references and index.
   ISBN 0-13-021225-3
       1. Learning disabled children—Education. 2. Emotional problems of children. 3.
Behavior disorders in children. I. Keefe, Charlotte Hendrick II. Shea, Thomas
M. III. Title.

LC4704 .B42 2001
371.94—dc21   00-058425

Vice President and Publisher: Jeffery W. Johnston
Executive Editor: Ann Castel Davis
Editorial Assistant: Pat Grogg
Production Editor: Sheryl Glicker Langner
Photo Coordinator: Anthony Magnacca
Design Coordinator: Diane C. Lorenzo
Production Service: York Production Services
Cover art: SuperStock
Cover Designer: Thomas Borah
Production Manager: Laura Messerly
Director of Marketing: Kevin Flanagan
Marketing Manager: Amy June
Marketing Services Manager: Krista Groshong

This book was set by York Graphic Services. It was printed and bound by R. R. Donnelley
& Sons Company. The cover was printed by Phoenix Color Corp.

Photo Credits: pp. xx, 104, 182, 210, 342, 394 by Barbara Schwartz/Merrill; pp. 15, 64,
138, 172, 352, 380 by Anthony Magnacca/Merrill; pp. 30, 50, 58, 88, 123, 146, 236,
250, 275, 325, 366 by Scott Cunningham/Merrill; pp. 74, 264, 300 by Anne
Vega/Merrill; p. 214 by Todd Yarrington/Merrill; and p. 334 by Tom Watson/Merrill.

10 9 8 7 6 5 4 3 2
ISBN 0-13-021225-3

This book is dedicated to
Riley, Demian, Tarie, CJ, Sarah, and Mickey
a.m.b

My family
c.k.

Dolores, Kevin, Jane, and Keith
t.m.s.

Preface

"Things are changing too quickly. I can't seem to keep up. Children are changing. Families are changing. Schools are changing. And society is changing." (Jean H., teacher)

"I was hired to teach girls and boys with learning disabilities. But every child in my caseload presents social and behavioral problems, as well as learning problems." (Hector L., teacher)

"There is not one student in this room who doesn't have a learning disability, and they're all classified as emotionally/behaviorally disordered. It is really frustrating trying to meet all their needs." (Debra H., teacher)

In our everyday interactions with general education and special education teachers in community schools and university classrooms, we hear these or similar comments over and over again. Teachers such as Jean, Hector, and Debra are not unique. They have thousands of colleagues who daily face the challenges of instructing students with learning disabilities and emotional/behavioral disorders. Their task is difficult.

Jean H. is correct. Things are changing rapidly. Children are bringing more and more complex problems and issues through the classroom door. Teachers must confront and help their students resolve these problems and issues. Society, as those of us from the previous generation knew and experienced it, is vastly different today. Changes are occurring in the family, neighborhood, school, the development and management of knowledge, personal and societal values and standards, transportation, commerce, and the conduct of local, national, and international affairs.

Schools are changing. The small intimate neighborhood school has given way to the large, impersonal community school. Teachers are no longer neighbors and friends, but professionals frequently living outside of the community they serve. Student populations are multicultural, multiracial, and multilingual and include learners with disabilities or at risk for disabilities, who are being increasingly included in general education classrooms and schools.

Academic standards in the general education classroom are more demanding with the advent of state-wide testing. The imposition of higher standards has increased demands on teacher time. As a consequence, teachers have less time and energy to attend to those students who deviate from the norm academically or behaviorally, or who can't keep up with their more talented peers.

The extended, traditional nuclear family with father, mother, children, grandparents, aunts, and uncles has changed to a broad array of parenting structures, such as the neolocal nuclear family of mother, father, and children often living many miles from relatives, single-parent families, foster families, and blended families. The impact of poverty on families has increased. More mothers must work outside the home to sustain the family economically during the childrearing years. More fathers are absent from home.

The children in our classrooms and schools present a broad range of racial, cultural, linguistic, religious, economic, and social characteristics. There are more and more children of poverty and children who are maltreated, abused, and neglected in our schools. The number of children presenting learning disabilities and emotional/behavioral disorders has increased dramatically during the past twenty-five years, and continues to increase annually.

Students with Learning Disabilities or Emotional/Behavioral Disorders responds to a small part of the many and diverse problems confronting general education and special education teachers who are challenged by children and youth with learning disabilities and emotional/behavioral disorders. It offers an integrated perspective to understanding working with students with learning disabilities or emotional/behavioral disorders. We recognize the contribution of various conceptual models to the understanding of these students. In addition, we emphasize that learning disabilities and emotional/behavioral disorders are complex issues, and must be understood within the context in which they occur.

The first section of the text introduces students with learning disabilities or emotional/behavioral disorders. Chapter One provides an overview of learning disabilities and emotional/behavioral disorders, followed by a description of the nature of assumptions regarding learning disabilities and emotional/behavioral disorders (Chapter Two). Chapter Three continues with a description of the developmental contexts in which students develop. In Chapter Four we present biological issues and a discussion of temperament, followed by a discussion of the cognitive, language, and social-emotional characteristics of students with learning disabilities or emotional/behavioral disorders (Chapter Five).

In Chapter Six, family factors that put students at risk for learning disabilities or emotional/behavior disorders and family involvement are discussed. School and classroom issues and strategies follow in Chapter Seven. In Chapter Eight, issues related to cultural diversity and gender and identification as learning disabled or emotionally/behaviorally disordered are presented.

In subsequent chapters we explore how students are identified and placed in special education (Chapter Nine) and how learning and behavior changes are supported for individuals (Chapter Ten) and for an entire class or school (Chapter Eleven). Chapter Twelve describes inclusive environments. In Chapter Thirteen, we discuss adolescents and adults with learning disabilities or emotional/behavioral disorders. The text concludes in Chapter Fourteen with a description of preventive efforts.

Special thanks to Ann Davis, who supported this project, and Pat Grogg, whose smile we could feel through the telephone. Also, thanks to our reviewers who made this a better text with constructive comments and criticisms: Jeffrey P. Bakken, Illinois State University; Kathleen Briseno, College of DuPage (IL); Maryann Dudzinski, Valparaiso University (IN); Barbara K. Given, George Mason University (VA); Carol Moore, Troy State University (AL); and Susan Sperry Smith, Cardinal Stritch University (WI).

Anne M. Bauer
Charlotte H. Keefe
Thomas M. Shea

◆◆

Discover the Companion Website Accompanying This Book

The Prentice Hall Companion Website: A Virtual Learning Environment

Technology is a constantly growing and changing aspect of our field that is creating a need for content and resources. To address this emerging need, Prentice Hall has developed an online learning environment for students and professors alike—Companion Websites—to support our textbooks.

In creating a Companion Website, our goal is to build on and enhance what the textbook already offers. For this reason, the content for each user-friendly website is organized by topic and provides the professor and student with a variety of meaningful resources. Common features of a Companion Website include:

For the Professor—

Every Companion Website integrates **Syllabus Manager™,** an online syllabus creation and management utility.

- **Syllabus Manager™** provides you, the instructor, with an easy, step-by-step process to create and revise syllabi, with direct links into Companion Website and other online content without having to learn HTML.

- Students may logon to your syllabus during any study session. All they need to know is the web address for the Companion Website and the password you've assigned to your syllabus.

- After you have created a syllabus using **Syllabus Manager™,** students may enter the syllabus for their course section from any point in the Companion Website.

- Class dates are highlighted in white and assignment due dates appear in blue. Clicking on a date, the student is shown the list of activities for the assignment. The activities for each assignment are linked directly to actual content, saving time for students.

- Adding assignments consists of clicking on the desired due date, then filling in the details of the assignment—name of the assignment, instructions, and whether or not it is a one-time or repeating assignment.

- In addition, links to other activities can be created easily. If the activity is online, a URL can be entered in the space provided, and it will be linked automatically in the final syllabus.

- Your completed syllabus is hosted on our servers, allowing convenient updates from any computer on the Internet. Changes you make to your syllabus are immediately available to your students at their next logon.

For the Student—

- **Topic Overviews**—outline key concepts in topic areas
- **Electronic Bluebook**—send homework or essays directly to your instructor's email with this paperless form
- **Message Board**—serves as a virtual bulletin board to post—or respond to—questions or comments to/from a national audience
- **Web Destinations**—links to www sites that relate to each topic area
- **Professional Organizations**—links to organizations that relate to topic areas
- **Additional Resources**—access to topic-specific content that enhances material found in the text

To take advantage of these and other resources, please visit the *Students with Learning Disabilities or Emotional/Behavioral Disorders* Companion Website at

www.prenhall.com/bauer

Contents

3   **Developmental Context   58**

4   **Biological Factors and Temperament   74**

5 Cognitive, Language, and Social-Emotional Characteristics   104

10 Supporting Learning and Behavior Change   264

1

An Introduction to Learning Disabilities and Emotional/Behavioral Disorders

TO GUIDE YOUR READING

After you complete this chapter, you will be able to answer these questions:

- What are some general characteristics of students with learning disabilities and emotional/behavioral disorders?

- How did services to address learning disabilities and emotional/behavioral disorders evolve?

- How many children are identified as having learning disabilities and emotional/behavioral disorders?

◆◀ *Matthew is the youngest of Elizabeth and Frank's three children. Elizabeth works part-time outside the home as a critical-care nurse, and Frank is a credit manager for a large regional distributor. Matthew is in the second grade, and both his parents and his teachers have concerns about his behavior and learning.*

Elizabeth and Frank do not recall anything remarkable during Elizabeth's pregnancy with Matthew, or his delivery. They both were pleased to have another child, and had hoped for a boy as their first two children were girls. Both parents found Matthew to be a very difficult child. He was fussy and hard to comfort. Matthew was colicky, and did not sleep through the night until he was six months old. His sleep patterns remain a problem. Matthew usually falls asleep around 11:00 p.m., even though he is to be in bed and quiet at 9:30, and he is up and running again at 6:30 a.m.

Matthew was very active as a toddler and preschooler. He was a frequent visitor at the emergency room, where his complaints ranged from a dog bite (because he pulled and yanked on the neighbor's dog's ears), to eating a nickel, to falling off a fence he was climbing. In preschool, he was referred for consultation because he bit other children. He had a difficult time during group activities. And, during "choice time," he moved quickly from activity to activity rather than engaging in one activity for a reasonable period of time. So he could be managed, he was moved to a classroom with several adult supervisors, including a "volunteer grandma" who spent a great deal of time with him. During that period, because Matthew's sisters frequently talked with him at home, his language skills blossomed and he began to recognize a few written words.

Matthew's transition to kindergarten was difficult. Though he had many of the prerequisite academic skills, Matthew was perceived as immature. He had difficulty in groups, and often wandered about the room while the other students worked at learning centers. He appeared impulsive. For example, if a classmate built a large tower with blocks, he would suddenly spring forward and knock it down. The other students began to avoid Matthew because his play was boisterous and rough. The kindergarten teacher was hesitant to refer Matthew to first grade, but did so because he was sight reading some words.

For first grade, Matthew was placed in a highly-structured first grade classroom. His mornings usually began well, but by 10:30 a.m., his impulsivity and inability to complete tasks without supervision interfered with both his learning and that of his classmates. The first grade teacher used the "STAR" strategy with Matthew: she put a star at his seat, on his desk, over his cubbie, and sometimes, on his hand. Matthew was taught that when he saw the star, he was to "Stop, Think, and then React." The result was limited, as Matthew remained very physical with the other children, and spent much of his recess "on the bench." A home-school communication system was initiated, but Matthew rarely had good days which could be positively reinforced at home. Elizabeth and Frank began to feel frustrated when they received the "laundry lists" of Matthew's inappropriate behaviors sent home from school. ("Today, Matthew was out of his seat four times during reading group, poured his milk on Nate's lunch, refused to share the ball at recess, and knocked down two students on the way to his cubbie.") His parents repeatedly asked questions about Matthew's academic learning, but were told that the primary concern was his behavior. By March of that school year, Elizabeth and Frank were alarmed that

Matthew couldn't copy a simple "thank you note" they had printed out for him to send to his grandparents. He was unable to recall the spelling of "Matthew," and could only write "Matt" to sign the note. At the end of the year, even though he was promoted to second grade, Elizabeth and Frank indicated that they wanted Matthew evaluated. In their view, Matthew was a bright child, but his behavior was becoming more and more difficult to manage, and it had become apparent to them that he was unable to perform the academic tasks his sisters were able to accomplish at the same age.

It is now the beginning of second grade. The school psychologist and other members of the student assistance team have observed and discussed Matthew and have implemented several interventions. They assigned a "study-buddy" to Matthew, and, additionally, twice a week, Matthew has a sixth-grade tutor to help him complete his work. Unfortunately, observations by his teacher and the school psychologist continue to show Matthew to be impulsive, distractible, and disruptive to his classmates. At times, he even appears dangerous in his play and risk-taking behavior. He continues to struggle with completing the same written work his peers accomplish with minimal support. The multifactored evaluation team has completed their assessment, and will be meeting with Elizabeth and Frank to determine if Matthew is eligible for special education services.

REFLECTION *Reflect on your own school experience. Can you remember a classmate, who, because of his or her interactions with others, evoked concern on behalf of a teacher? Or, a classmate who, for some reason, just didn't seem to process information like everyone else? How did the teachers react? How did your classmates react?*

Introduction

In this chapter, we begin our study of learning disabilities and emotional/behavioral disorders with a discussion of the diverse characteristics of these students. We will discuss the evolution of services for children with these disabilities. And, we'll describe the number of students currently identified as learning disabled and emotionally/behaviorally disordered, and how they are currently being served.

General Characteristics of Students with Learning Disabilities and Emotional/Behavioral Disorders

Each of us can close our eyes and create a mental picture of students with learning disabilities and emotional/behavioral disorders. We may imagine the hyperactive first grader who was always "in trouble" for not sitting still or not doing his or her work, the third grader who seemed to be one question off in responding to the teacher and who struggled to read, the bully who taunted us in the fourth grade, the seventh grader who was always alone, or the sad sophomore who attempted suicide.

Matthew's case illustrates the complexity of learning disabilities and emotional/behavioral disorders. Does Matthew demonstrate an emotional/behavioral disorder? Could he be identified as learning disabled? Does he have some combination of the two disabilities?

To be identified as having a disability, and to determine his or her eligibility for special education service, a student must meet very specific criteria (Reschly, 1996). Because definitions of disabilities and special education identification and classification processes vary across states and provinces, students with identical characteristics may be identified as learning disabled or emotionally/behaviorally disordered in one state or province, but not in another. Plus, a student classified as disabled in one state or province may be reclassified when he or she moves from that jurisdiction to another.

Disabilities that have clear, medical bases are usually recognized by the child's physician or parents soon after birth, or by preschool age, and usually, the child is then entered into services. However, the majority of students with disabilities are initially referred for evaluation by a teacher or parent due to academic or behavioral problems that become evident in school. Milder forms of disability exist on a broad continuum, and there is no clear demarcation between the student who has, and the students who does not have, the disability. According to Reschly (1996), the system currently used to identify students as disabled is stigmatizing and unreliable. It provides little correlation between categorization and treatment, honors obsolete assumptions about students and learning, and includes a disproportional number of students who are African-American or Latino.

This text discusses students with learning disabilities and emotional/behavioral disorders. Because the needs and issues related to "high incidence disabilities," (mental retardation and communication disorders) are different from those related to learning disabilities and emotional behavioral disorders, we have not included them.

Differentiating the characteristics of students who have learning disabilities and emotional/behavioral disorders is as difficult as determining their eligibility for classification in either category. Rosenberg (1997) states that learning disabilities are viewed, most often, as a distinct category of disability. However, he contends that there is no agreed-upon conceptual criteria to guide an operational definition of learning disabilities, and that medical, psychological, linguistic, reading, and special education research all underscore the heterogeneity of the category. Rosenberg suggests that professionals who emphasize learning disabilities as occurring independent of other disabilities "run the risk of promoting a limited, or unidimensional, view of the complex interacting factors influencing a student's academic and social performance" (1997, p. 243).

Another complication emerges because schools are reluctant to identify children as having emotional/behavioral disorders. Lopez, Forness,

MacMillan, and Bocian (1996) examined the congruence between the classifications of children as attention deficit disordered, learning disabled, or emotional/behavioral disordered. They found that the majority of children referred were receiving special education services under the category of learning disabled. Comparisons of students' test performances revealed that students with attention deficit hyperactivity disorder and emotional/behavioral disorders did not differ from other at-risk students on intelligence or achievement, but did differ on social skills measures. According to the authors, these results demonstrate that many students with attention deficit hyperactivity disorder and emotional/behavioral disorders are being inappropriately placed in learning disabilities programs.

The overlapping characteristics of learning disabilities and emotional/behavioral disorders pose a significant challenge to teachers and schools when trying to classify students. Rock, Fessler, and Church (1997) contend that, depending on the study, 24 to 52 percent of students with learning disabilities have significant social, emotional, and behavioral problems. Studies of children and adolescents with emotional/behavioral disorders report that between 38 and 75 percent of these learners also could be identified as learning disabled. Substantial numbers of students who are identified as either learning disabled or emotionally/behaviorally disordered move back and forth between these categories during their school careers. Rock and associates attribute these fluctuations in classification to either overlapping symptoms of learning disabilities and emotional/behavioral disorders, or problems in identification procedures. Students with both learning disabilities and emotional/behavioral disorders tend to (a) experience the poorest outcomes from special education services, (b) be at the highest risk for leaving school, and (c) exhibit significantly poorer outcomes as adults.

Students who demonstrate both learning disabilities and emotional/behavioral disorders have far greater challenges than those who have only one disability (Rock and associates, 1997). First, learners who have both disabilities have greater problems successfully responding to instruction. Behavioral problems interfere with teaching and learning, and teachers may be inadequately prepared to meet the needs of students who present these challenging behaviors. Additionally, instruction for these students may be inconsistent due to interruptions for crisis intervention or administration of medication. Second, students with both learning disabilities and emotional/behavioral disorders may have problems in compensation and adaptation. Students with learning disabilities often learn to compensate, i.e., use instructional and management strategies, or adapt modifications to enhance learning. However, students with learning disabilities and coexisting emotional/behavioral disorders have difficulty with flexibility and adaptability. Students with both disabilities may also find frustrating the amount of practice required to learn a task. Finally, students with both learning disabilities and emotional/behavioral disorders may have a negative self-concept that could affect their academic achievement. Social skills problems may create additional barriers to learning (Rock and associates, 1997).

In this section, general characteristics of students with learning disabilities and emotional/behavioral disorders are described. Generalizations about groups of students are always difficult and inherently faulty. Because of the great variations in identifying students with learning disabilities and emotional/behavioral disorders, and the problems in differentiating between these two groups, it is challenging to provide general characteristics for the students who are the focus for this text. Though there are some similarities among students in these groups, characteristics of individuals within each group vary more than they resemble each other. As you read, remember that there is great diversity among students identified as having learning disabilities or emotional/behavioral disorders. Think of the characteristics presented as simply one way to describe students who are referred to as having learning disabilities or emotional/behavioral disorders.

More Boys than Girls Are Identified

Controversy over the discrepancy between the number of boys and girls who are referred, evaluated, and ultimately receive special education services is not new. More than twenty years ago, Gregory (1977) reported gender bias in school referrals. In his study, he requested 140 teachers to read hypothetical case studies of elementary school children described as (a) reading disabled, (b) withdrawn, (c) gifted with mild behavior problems, (d) math disabled, or (e) aggressive. In some cases, the teachers were told the children were male, in others they were told the children were female. Teachers had to decide from the case studies whom they would refer for evaluation. Boys with identical profiles as girls were more likely to be referred for evaluation, except for children with reading disabilities. He concluded that a male child with problems is more likely to be referred than a female child with identical problems.

Gender issues in the identification of learners with disabilities exist in several disability areas. Problems with identification have been noted in the areas of learning disabilities, emotional/behavioral disorders, and attention deficit hyperactivity disorder. These differences may be related to the sociology of clinical identification of some disabilities (Eme, 1992), and expectations that girls will do poorly in mathematics, or that boys will need strong literacy skills for the workplace. Girls with learning disabilities may be underidentified; putting them at risk for academic, social, and emotional challenges (Shaywitz & Shaywitz, 1988).

Eme (1992) reports that the most commonly cited gender ratio in learning disabilities is 3.5 to 5 males to one female. Eme contends that the way students are identified as learning disabled may lower the number of girls identified. In a study on referral, Mirkin (1982) contrasted two models of referral for learning disabilities: a teacher referral system and a system in which reading, spelling, and written expression were measured on a weekly basis. Under the teacher referral system, Mirkin found that 80 percent of the students referred were male. Using the system which employed weekly measures, only 65 percent of the students referred were male. Behavior appears to have influenced teacher referrals for girls. In the teacher referral model, girls referred were rated as having more behavioral problems than those identified in the continuous measurement referral system. Among boys, the students referred using both models had similar behavior. Teachers were more likely to refer children for evaluation and services for learning disabilities if they had attention problems and hyperactive or disruptive behavior, rather than academic underachievement. In these studies, because more males than females manifested disruptive behaviors, teachers referred more males, who then received more services for learning disabilities.

Payette and Clarizio (1994) examined the gender of students referred for evaluation for learning disabilities in a large sample (344 students). They reported that being female and less academically able were the characteristics of those declared eligible for services as learning disabled, even without a severe discrepancy between tested achievement and tested intelligence.

Teachers refer boys more often than girls for assistance prior to referring them for special education evaluation, particularly when behavior problems are involved (DelHomme, Kasari, Forness, & Bagley, 1996). Green, Clopton, and Pope (1996) reported three factors that led to the significantly higher referral of boys. First, teachers appear to have been more likely to believe that boys needed referral because boys tended to have the types of problems (externalizing) that teachers regard as being more in need of services. Second, teachers are generally less likely to regard a child with problems as needing referral if that child is doing well academically (a pattern more common for girls). Third, teachers are less likely to believe that girls need referral because they are more optimistic that girls with problems will improve as they mature.

Four times as many boys as girls are identified as emotionally/behaviorally disordered (Singth, Landrum, Donatelli, Hampton, & Ellis, 1994; Wagner and others, 1991). In a large national sample of adolescents, only 21 percent of the students identified as emotionally/behaviorally disordered were female (Cullinan, Epstein, & Sabornie, 1992). Boys far outnumber girls among students identified and served as emotionally/behaviorally disordered in public school programs, and among students both identified as emotionally/behaviorally disordered in public schools and receiving mental health services outside of the schools (Caseau, Luckasson, & Kroth, 1994).

Though more boys are identified for services as emotionally/behaviorally disordered in the public schools, Caseau, Luckasson, and Kroth (1994) found that girls outnumbered boys among students not identified as emotionally/behaviorally disordered by the public schools, but receiving mental health services outside of school. It appears that, unlike boys, girls were more likely to have serious problems with depression, family conflict, suicidal ideation, and suicide attempts. Apparently, these girls had problems severe enough to warrant identification as emotionally/behaviorally disordered at home and in the community, but not of the type that would warrant identification at school. The girls who did receive services in public schools exhibited acting-out behaviors similar to those of boys.

Research suggests that for a girl with learning disabilities to receive services for learning disabilities, she must be older and more severely impaired than her classmates who are boys (Vogel, 1990). When girls are identified, referred, and diagnosed as having learning disabilities in school systems, and found eligible to receive services, they (a) are significantly lower in intelligence, (b) are more severely impaired, and (c) have a greater aptitude–achievement discrepancy than their male counterparts. Vogel (1990) concluded that girls experiencing learning difficulties are less likely to receive help because:

- There is a mismatch between girls' problems and the screening instruments and referral forms due to little research about girls with learning disabilities (research results on samples of boys with learning disabilities are generalized to girls);
- To be identified, referred, and diagnosed, girls must be significantly lower in intelligence, more severely impaired, or have a larger discrepancy between their ability and achievement; and
- Teachers are more likely to refer boys than girls even when girls have identical problems.

Attention deficit hyperactivity disorder is often presented as a disorder found among young boys. However, as indicated earlier, the discrepancy between boys and girls identified as having attention deficit disorder may reflect the variation in activity levels between boys and girls. Social judgments regarding hyperactivity, attention, or engagement may influence the under-referral of girls with this challenge. Berry, Shaywitz, and Shaywitz (1985) reported that girls identified as having attention deficit disorders were found to have more severe cognitive and language impairments than their male counterparts. Girls identified with attention deficit disorder without hyperactivity were significantly older than boys at the age of referral. Girls with learning disabilities involving severe deficits, and boys with learning disabilities with behavioral problems, were more likely to be identified. Shaywitz and associates concluded that girls with learning disabilities who are not hyperactive will be identified, but only at a later age than their male peers with learning disabilities, even though they have similar or more severe cognitive deficits.

James and Taylor (1990) report findings consistent with those of Shaywitz and associates that girls with hyperactivity have a lower tested intelligence quotient and significantly higher rates of language disorders and neurological problems than boys. James and Taylor found that evidence of neurological factors were not present as frequently in boys as in girls, and, in fact, there was a group of boys who had near normal brain functioning, but were hyperactive. They suggest that a significant number of boys become hyperactive through the same factors that determine the acceptable range of activity and attention in the general population. Chandola, Robling, Peters, Melville-Thomas, and McGuffin (1992) found no support for gender differences in neurological factors of hyperactivity. Prenatal and perinatal factors may be important in terms of cause, but there are no differential effects between the sexes. Indeed, Shaywitz, Shaywitz, Fletcher, and Escobar (1990) found an equal proportion of boys and girls with attention deficient hyperactivity disorder. Because the ways in which girls demonstrate attention deficit disorder may involve more problems with attending and day dreaming, and because the social expectations for academic learning for girls are not consistently high, they may be underidentified as having attention deficit disorder. Because girls exhibit more passive behaviors such as sitting and daydreaming, they are less likely to be identified than their boisterous, physically active male peers. However, both boys and girls are at risk for academic underachievement, and, because girls are less likely to be identified, they are less likely to be helped.

Difficulty in School Achievement

Ability/ Achievy

By definition, both students with learning disabilities and students with emotional/behavioral disorders are identified by failing to achieve in school in comparison to what is judged to be their potential. Traditional perceptions of students with learning disabilities are (a) that they have average or above average intellectual ability, and (b) that their achievement and performance is not commensurate with their cognitive ability. However, these perceptions may not match today's population of school-identified students with learning disabilities. For example, in a longitudinal study of students identified as learning disabled, Wagner and associates (1993) reported the mean tested intelligence scores in the low average range.

Morse, Cutler, and Fink's (1964) early work suggested that students identified as emotionally/behaviorally disordered had above-average cognitive ability. More recent studies, however, indicate that these students exhibit average or lower-than-average measured cognitive abilities when compared to their typical peers (Coleman, 1986). Students with more severe behavioral disorders exhibit intelligence quotients in the mentally retarded range (Freeman & Ritvo, 1984).

Some students may have low achievement, but are not typically considered learning disabled because their school achievement seems comparable to their cognitive ability. The distinction between students with learning disabilities, and those with low achievement, can be difficult to ascertain, and there has been debate concerning the similarities and differences (e.g., Algozzine, Ysseldyke, and McGue, 1995; Kavale, Fuchs, and Scruggs, 1994; Kavale, 1995). For example, a study by Ysseldyke and associates (1982) compared students with learning disabilities and students identified as low achieving, and found that 95 percent of the scores on psychoeducational measures were in a similar range. Ysseldyke (1982) argued that these two groups were not different. Though both Algozinne and associates (1995) and Kavale (1995) agree that students with learning disabilities are the lowest achievers in school, Kavale argues that they are qualitatively different from other students who are low achievers. He contends that the concept of learning disability, which includes a specific, discrete problem, rather than a generalized failure, is no longer used. In a later study by Gresham and MacMillan (1996), students with learning disabilities could be distinguished from a group who were low achieving.

As a group, students identified as learning disabled by schools have a tendency to be judged unsuccessful by the traditional performance markers such as progression from grade to grade and graduation from high school. There has not been extensive research on grade retention of students with learning disabilities, but available research indicates that these students are retained at a rate higher than typical students (Kavale, 1988; McLeskey & Grizzle, 1992; McKinney, Osborne, & Schulte, 1993). Common characteristics of students with learning disabilities, such as tested performance below grade level, immaturity, and social/behavioral problems, are factors which influence the likelihood of retention (McLeskey, Lancaster, & Grizzle, 1995). Research findings are consistent in that indicating a high school dropout rate for students with learning disabilities of approximately 30 percent or more (e.g. Levin, Zigmond, and Birch, 1985; Zigmond & Thornton, 1985; Reiff & deFurr, 1992; Wagner, Blackorby, Cameto, Hebbeler, & Newman, 1993).

During the 1989–90 school year almost half (44.6 percent) of students in high school identified as emotionally/behaviorally disordered in the United States failed one or more courses in the previous year of high school, far more than students with communication disorders (35 percent), or learning disabilities (34.8 percent) (U.S. Department of Education, 1992). The reading achievement of students identified as emotionally/behaviorally disordered has been reported to be significantly below (1.5 to two grade levels) that of their peers in elementary school, and even poorer by the time they reach high school (3.5 grade levels) (Coutinho, 1986).

Students identified as emotionally/behaviorally disordered receive lower grades than any other disability group, and are retained at grade level more often. In addition, they fail minimum competency examinations more frequently than students with other disabilities. Of those students identified as emotional/behavioral disordered taking minimum competency tests (22 percent were exempted), 63 percent failed some part of the examination (U.S. Department of Education, 1994). High School students identified as having emotional/behavioral disorders have a mean grade point average of 1.7 (on a 4-point scale), compared with all students with disabilities of 2.0 and all students of 2.6 (Wagner and others, 1991).

Students identified as having emotional/behavioral disorders are the most likely of all students with identified disabilities to leave school. The number and percent of students identified as having emotional/behavioral disorders, 14 years and older graduating with a high school diploma or certificate, decreased from 8.82 percent in the 1988–89 school year to 7.84 percent in 1992–93. Fifty percent of students identified as having emotional/behavioral disorders drop out of school, and most leave school by the tenth grade. Fifty-eight percent leave school without graduating (Wagner, 1991). Among students identified as having emotional/behavioral disorders, 42 percent graduate as compared to 56 percent of all students with disabilities, and 71 percent of all students (Wagner and others, 1991).

The National Longitudinal Transition Study of Special Education Students (NLTS, U.S. Office of Education, 1992) reported that dropping out of school is the culmination of a cluster of school performance problems, including high absenteeism and poor grade performance. In a study of students identified as having emotional/behavioral disorders, using students' school records and parent interviews, NLTS found that 41.7% graduated, 49.5% dropped out, 3.5% aged out (became too old to attend), and 5.3% were suspended or expelled. With the exception of students with multiple disabilities, the graduation rate for students identified as emotional/behavioral disordered is the lowest of all the disability groups. The dropout rate for that same group is the highest among the disability groups, with students with learning disabilities being the closest with a dropout rate of 32.3 percent. In addition, students identified as having emotional/behavioral disorders are most likely to be suspended or expelled. Students identified as having emotional/behavioral disorders had the highest rate of absenteeism (17.7 days) and the highest likelihood of failing a course (43.9%) (U.S. Office of Education, 1992).

For students with learning disabilities, in the 1985–86 or 1986–87 school year, 3 percent left school because they aged out or because of attendance, 4 percent were suspended or expelled, and 61 percent graduated in comparison to 71 percent of the general school population (Wagner, 1990).

Language Problems or Communication Disorders

Research supports the argument that most students with learning disabilities have language difficulties (Gibbs & Cooper, 1989; Kuder, 1997). Language plays an important role in reading, thinking, socialization, and classroom interaction. Difficulties comprehending and using language are likely to contribute to a variety of unrecognized problems that children with learning disabilities encounter (Kuder, 1997).

vocabulary

A small percentage of students with learning disabilities receives speech and/or language services (American Speech-Language-Hearing Association, 1989a; 1989b; Donahue, 1986; Ganschow, Sparks, & Sudman, 1990; Gibbs & Cooper, 1989). A survey of 961 school psychologists indicated that a large majority (68 percent) of them had minimal training in assessment of speech and language disorders; more than 60 percent of this group referred only one to ten percent of the students with, or suspected of having, learning disabilities to a speech or language clinician (Ganschow, 1992). Extensive research demonstrates a relationship between language ability and educational performance, specifically reading, writing, and the oral language of education (Gerber, 1993). Language problems are discussed in greater detail in Chapter 5.

Many students identified as emotionally/behaviorally disordered may have learning problems or communication disorders. In one study, 97 percent of the students identified as demonstrating mild to moderate emotional/behavioral disorders fell more than one standard deviation from the mean on an individually administered language test (Camarata, Hughes, & Ruhl, 1988). The pattern of language problems was consistent with the problem pattern of students identified as learning disabled. After studying the communication performance of adolescents identified as emotionally/behaviorally disordered and their nonidentified peers, Rosenthal and Simeonsson (1991) suggested that communication deficits may be a central feature of emotional/behavioral disorders.

Social Skills and Interactions Vary from Peers

Students with learning disabilities or emotional/behavioral disorders usually do not demonstrate the same level of social skills as their peers who are not identified with disabilities. Though unusual social interactions are not always considered in students with learning disabilities, problems in interactions are pervasive among students with emotional/behavioral disorders.

Social skill problems are often linked to problems in communication. Tur-Kaspa and Bryan (1994) assessed the social information-processing skills, receptive and expressive vocabulary, and social competence and school adjustment of students with learning disabilities, students without learning disabilities who were low-achieving, and students without learning disabilities who were average achieving. They found that compared to the average achievers, students with learning disabilities performed less competently, and they displayed a distinct pattern of processing social information. When compared to both low-achieving and average-achieving students, the students with learning disabilities had difficulty encoding social information, and tended to choose incompetent self-generated solutions to social situations. The results suggested that poor academic achievement alone and/or poor expressive and receptive vocabulary skills do not explain the poor social skills of students with learning disabilities.

Among students with emotional/behavioral disorders, the most frequently stated reasons for identification are: (a) poor peer relationships, (b) frustration, (c) low academic achievement, (d) shy and withdrawn behavior, (e) disruptive behavior, (f) fighting, (g) refusing to work, and (h) short attention span. Poor peer relationships was the most frequent reason for referral between both boys and girls (Hutton, 1985).

The social skill problems of students identified as emotionally/behaviorally disordered are the most intense of all students with disabilities. In a full-inclusion setting, Sale and Carey (1995) documented that students with physical disabilities received significantly more "liked-most" nominations than any other group of students. Students with emotional/behavioral disorders, however, had the lowest scores, being the least nominated in positive situations, and the most nominated in negative situations.

Aggression is reported to be pervasive among students identified as emotionally/behaviorally disordered (Ruhl & Hughes, 1985). Epstein, Kauffman, and Cullinan (1985) found the most persistent pattern of behavior reported among the students identified as having emotional/behavioral disorders to be aggression.

Other Demographic Characteristics

There are over two million students identified as having learning disabilities, which represents over half (51.2 percent) of the students served in special education. Among those identified as learning disabled, there is a disproportionately high prevalence of African American students, and a low prevalence of Hispanic students. Both overrepresentation and underrepresentation of students from diverse ethnic, cultural, and linguistic groups among students identified as learning disabled have been suggested. Keogh, Gallimore, and Weisner (1997) suggest that overrepresentation occurs because of early literacy experiences, language, and cultural differences rather than in-child deficits. Underrepresentation may occur when children who have learning disabilities are not referred because their problems are attributed to their language and cultural differences.

Demographic and economic differences may influence who is identified as emotionally/behaviorally disordered (Wagner and others, 1991; Oswald and Coutinho, 1995). In school districts, the amount of per pupil revenue was the strongest single predictor of the rate at which students were identified as having emotional/behavioral disorders. As school district revenue increased, the likelihood of identification increased. In addition, state and local evaluation and multidisciplinary team procedures, and the availability of both a full continuum of placement settings and comprehensive services offered by mental health service providers, may have an impact on identification rates (Oswald & Coutinho, 1995).

One would assume that students admitted to a psychiatric hospital for service would be identified as emotionally/behaviorally disordered by their schools. However, Singth, Landrum, Donatelli, and Ellis (1994), found this was not the case. They reported that only 54 percent of the students receiving inpatient psychiatric services and partial hospitalization were identified as emotionally/behaviorally disordered by their schools. The other 56 percent, students with no identified disability, were served in general education classrooms. Ten percent of the students were found to have other disabilities. The average age of hospital admission was 11.6 years. African American students were overrepresented in the sample, as only 56 percent of the students admitted to hospitalization were Caucasian. Significant issues for these students were alcohol abuse (80 percent), and drug abuse (85 percent).

The overrepresentation of African American students identified as emotionally/behaviorally disordered continues to be a concern for special education professionals. Cultural differences may work against children, and cut both ways. On the one hand, many professionals are unaware of the impact of culture on behavior and may mistake cultural differences for emotional/behavioral disorders. On the other hand, students from diverse cultural, ethnic, or linguistic groups may not be identified as emotionally/behaviorally disordered when they are in need of services. McIntyre (1993) found that students risk being denied special education for emotional/behavioral disorders if they are members of an historically oppressed minority (African American, Hispanic American), or if they are from low-income households. Under the original federal definition (discussed later in this chapter), groups were mislabeled due to cultural differences and home circumstances; under the current definitions, culturally diverse students will be provided extra safeguards against incorrect identification (McIntyre, 1993).

Finally, students identified as emotionally/behaviorally disordered have significant involvement with the juvenile justice system. Twenty percent of students identified as emotionally/behaviorally disordered are arrested at least once before they leave school, and 35 percent are arrested within a few years of leaving school (Wagner and others, 1991).

The Evolution of Services

Services aimed at addressing learning disabilities and emotional/behavioral disorders have evolved from exclusion to inclusion. Throughout history, various guiding theories have supported professionals in their work regarding emotional/behavioral disorders and learning disabilities. As Brendtro and Van Bockern (1994) advise, without a guiding theory, a "try anything" eclecticism prevails, which is, as they suggest, "choosing a potluck meal with a blindfold." Without a theory to guide them, professionals working with these challenging children and youth are likely to fall into "folk psychology," contradict themselves in the methodology they implement, have difficulty functioning as members of a treatment team, and be inconsistent with the children and youth with whom they are working (Brendtro & Van Bockern, 1994). In recent times, however, all of the models for serving students identified as learning disabled or emotionally/behaviorally disordered have become less theory guided and more eclectic. In addition, cross-fertilization has increased across all theory bases, as professionals use whatever appears most effective within their own perception of "learning disabilities" or "emotional/behavioral disorders."

In prehistoric societies, where survival depended on the fitness of each member, those who did not contribute to society were ostracized or killed. Some ancient peoples believed that mental disorders were the result of demonic possession, so they rejected, punished, or killed individuals who varied from their societal norms. In medieval times, individuals identified

Educational services for students with learning disabilities and emotional/behavioral disorders have evolved from exclusion to inclusion.

as having emotional/behavioral disorders were often objects of amusement, or were imprisoned or executed. During this period, the Roman Catholic Church began to foster what was then considered humane care, by providing asylums.

With the emergence of the Renaissance, and a greater belief in the value of human life, there was increased interest in the struggles confronted by individuals with disabilities, including those identified as having emotional/behavioral disorders. Phillipe Pinel (1745–1826) was one of the first physicians to attempt to treat rather than confine persons identified as mentally ill. As chief physician at two mental hospitals in France, the Salpatriere and the Bicetre, Pinel was convinced that mental illness was not the result of demonic possession, but of some sort of brain dysfunction. Consequently, he removed the chains which confined his patients, and discontinued the use of bleeding as a form of treatment.

In the United States, in 1843, Dorothea L. Dix studied and reported on the conditions of the mentally ill in Massachusetts. She argued that persons with mental illness could be properly treated and cared for only in hospitals. That, along with her descriptions of conditions, including the use of chains for restraints, resulted in enlargement of the state hospital in Worcester, Massachusetts, which was, at that time, one of only eight mental hospitals in the United States. Dix worked in other locations, and was responsible for the construction of thirty-two hospitals in the United States, Canada, Europe, and Japan.

The desire to help children who appeared to have typical cognitive and sensory ability, but difficulty acquiring oral and written language skills, also received some attention during the 19th century. Physicians, including Pierre Paul Broca and Carl Wernicke, identified the areas of the brain which controlled language. Their medical emphasis continued with references to "word blindness," and Berlin's introduction of the term "dyslexia" (Hallahan and associates, 1996).

Late in the nineteenth century, a few schools in the United States began to make formal provisions for students identified as emotionally/ behaviorally disordered. In New Haven, Connecticut, in 1871, the public schools established classes for students exhibiting unmanageable behaviors. Classes for "unruly boys" were formed in New York City's public schools in 1874. These were, in fact, the first public school special education classes (Kanner, 1970). In terms of learning disabilities, Doris (1993) reports that in the early 1900s groups of children were separated from the compulsory, graded educational system, so that the general education classes could run smoothly. A small number of children were reported as having extreme or pathological cases of reading disability. During the succeeding decades, the narrow category of reading disability expanded to include other educational difficulties.

The first scientific study of childhood psychosis was published in 1838 by Jean Etienne Esquirol (1774–1840), in *Des Maladies Mentales.*

It was not until the works of Lauretta Bender and Anna Freud in the 1920s and 1930s that children with severe emotional/behavioral disorders were systematically studied. During the 1930s Bender, working as a senior psychiatrist at Bellevue Hospital in New York City, studied the role of brain pathology in the development of childhood schizophrenia and other forms of emotional/behavioral disorders in children. She developed the Bender-Gestalt test to measure visual-motor maturation, and applied it to the screening and measurement of brain dysfunction in children (Bender, 1938). In 1927 Anna Freud published *Introduction to the Techniques of Child Analysis,* an elaboration of the work of her father, Sigmund Freud, on ego defenses and identification. From this effort, the psychodynamic perspective of working with students identified as having emotional/behavioral disorders arose. Her work stimulated others, including Erik Erikson (1963) who elaborated on the psychodynamic perspective and added the element of the impact of society and culture on the individual.

W. R. Bender's (1995) perceptual motor theory was grounded in Kirk Goldsteins's work with World War I veterans who had sustained head injuries. Goldstein found that many of his subjects had lost their ability to read, and had difficulty with tasks which included figure-ground relationships and reversing letters. Goldstein's work influenced Alfred Strauss and Heinz Werner to introduce the concept of minimal brain damage. Strauss and Werner proposed a subtype of mental retardation which they called endogenous retardation. This subgroup included children with an assumed brain injury who exhibited characteristics such as disturbances in perception, figure-ground, perseveration, and emotional disorders. Terms such as perceptually handicapped, minimally brain-injured, and minimal brain dysfunction came into prominence.

The work of Strauss and Werner influenced individuals such as William Cruickshank, Ray Barsch, Marianne Frostig, Gerld Getman, and Newell Kephart (Hallahan and others, 1996). During this period, specific perceptual-motor tests were developed to diagnose specific perceptual deficits. Perceptual-motor training was developed on the assumption that specific exercises such as walking on a balance beam, paper-and-pencil activities to improve eye-hand coordination, and reproducing rhythms would generalize to benefitting academic achievement. These instruments and remedial practices underwent critical scrutiny, and their use was found not to be effective in teaching academic skills (Hallahan and others, 1996).

In 1963, a group of parent organizations for children with learning problems assembled at a national conference in Chicago. At this conference, Samuel Kirk first used the term "learning disabilities." Kirk later stated that he had never intended "learning disabilities" as a category of disability, and cautioned parents against utilizing it as a label (Kirk, 1976). Parents, however, adopted the term, and the Association for Children with

Learning Disabilities (now called the Learning Disabilities Association of America) was formed in 1964 (Smith, 1998). In 1968 "specific learning disability" became a federally designated disability category (Hallahan and associates, 1996).

During the early 1960s, Nicholas Hobbs (1982) developed "Project Re-Ed," as a cooperative program of George Peabody College for Teachers, and the states of Tennessee and North Carolina. The objective of Project Re-Ed was to provide therapeutic support for the learner identified as emotional/behavioral disordered, and his or her family and community. In these residential programs, school work was adapted to meet the student's individual needs, and the school setting was used to socialize the child to more productive ways of interacting. These small schools, typically no more than forty children in five classrooms, provided short term services, with the child returning home each weekend to reconnect with family and community. School personnel were assigned to work with the children's family and community.

In the mid 1960s, a group of researchers began applying the learning principles identified in the laboratory and based in the learning of animals to methods for learning or changing behavior in children. Skinner (1965) proposed that responses which were followed by pleasurable consequences (reinforced) could be strengthened, and those followed by unpleasant consequences would be weakened. David Premack (1965) applied this work to activities, and demonstrated that an individual may be willing to do something relatively unpleasant if the activity is followed soon thereafter by a pleasurable activity. Bandura (1969) emphasized the role of vicarious learning, and modeling to promote the development of competent behavior. As a result of these and similar efforts, behavior modification and other behavior therapy techniques emerged as the primary means of addressing emotional/behavioral disorders during the 1970s, and much of the 1980s.

As behavior modification became more pervasive, issues emerged regarding the external nature of its interventions. Many expressed concern that behaviors were controlled, rather than replaced by more productive behaviors and learned interactions. Problems of generalization arose. In addition, research was beginning to demonstrate the situational nature of emotional/behavioral disorders, and the role of cultural mismatch in the identification of students identified as having emotional/behavioral disorders. As a result, practice evolved away from the rigid application of behavioral principles as the primary emphasis of programming; efforts often incorporated learning principles, counseling interventions, and medication in the meeting of the complex needs of students identified as emotional/behavioral disordered. As we move toward the inclusion of students identified as emotionally/behaviorally disordered in the general education setting, a learner may indeed be engaged in interventions from various conceptual bases. An individual student may have a behavior contract (behavior modification), use medication to increase his or her ability to focus (biophysiological), as well as receive psychotherapy (psychodynamic).

Orientation of this Text

In this text, we use a social systems perspective to facilitate the integration of several perspectives for working with students identified as learning disabled or emotionally/behaviorally disordered. Through consideration of the learner's personal characteristics, and the settings in which the learner functions, an integrated effort to support his or her learning of effective ways of interacting is enhanced. A detailed discussion of the social systems perspective is provided in Chapter 2.

The Size of the Population

Bogdan and Kugelmass (1984) suggested that our current special education practice is based on four assumptions: (a) a disability is something an individual "has," (b) differentiating individuals with and without disabilities is both useful and objective, (c) special education is a logical, co-ordinated system of services provided to individuals labeled disabled, and (d) progress in special education is made by improving diagnosis, intervention, and technology. Skrtic (1991) suggests that the real problem in special education is the unconscious acceptance of these assumptions. The Individuals with Disabilities Education Act (IDEA) and its amendments, which mandate free, appropriate public education for all students with disabilities, support the notion that disabilities are things people have, that it is useful to call people disabled, and that special education is a rational system that helps people overcome their disabilities.

In efforts to support these assumptions, special education has attempted to appear as a science. Denti and Katz (1996) suggest that special education has borrowed the credibility of scientific terminology, diagnosis, and medical research to establish a complex set of labels and a body of discourse accessible only to the "in group." Individuals with disabilities, their families, and certainly the general public, are not privy to the "research" which is presumed to support labels such as learning disabled or emotionally/behaviorally disordered. In the medical model, problems are always the individual's problems, and the student as a social being who constructs his or her own meaning is generally not a consideration. This attempt to retain the aura of a "discipline" forces the field to avoid the central normative issues of social health, the competencies related to social health, and the traits developed by students who are successful.

Determining how many students are identified as learning disabled or emotionally/behaviorally disordered is complex. The issue of "how many" and where they are served must include a discussion of assumptions about school. Dudley-Marling & Dippo (1995) describe three assumptions about schooling which are relevant to understanding how many students are identified as learning disabled or emotional/behavioral disordered. They suggest that, as a society, we assume:

1. Compulsory schooling is justifiable, reasonable, and beneficial. Education provides opportunities for every citizen to be what he or she wants to be.

2. Each child comes to school with a unique intellectual endowment. With effort, an "average" student can do well; without effort, even a gifted student may do poorly.

3. Competition is good and natural. The value of competition in school is affirmed by the use of normative evaluation, school placement, and admission to college. Competition is viewed as a natural way to motivate learners and the best way to prepare students for life. In a meritocracy, competition determines who is entitled to the rewards of schooling (choice of occupation, college).

In view of these assumptions, Dudley-Marling and Dippo (1995) suggest that learning disabilities is a category which explains why children who have adequate intelligence and effort do not succeed in school. In addition, it places the responsibility of school failure within the individual student, and it allows schools to be free of considering their own failure based on factors such as race, class, culture, gender, and ethnicity. Learning disabilities provide a solution to a problem created when middle- to upper-middle-class parents want extra support for their children, but do not want to have it in existing school programs that might block aspirations for college, or occupation of choice.

The Number Identified

An accurate count of the number of students identified as learning disabled or having emotional/behavioral disorders is, again, a complex issue. Lopez, Forness, MacMillan, and Bocian, (1996), studying a group of students identified as having attention deficit hyperactivity disorder, provide an example of the confusion regarding identification and placement that may occur. They examined the match between students classified as having attention deficit hyperactivity disorder, a psychiatric diagnosis, and emotional/behavioral disorders, and the actual classroom placement decisions regarding these students. Evaluations of 150 second through fourth graders referred to school study teams resulted in the classification of 43 of the students as having attention deficit hyperactivity disorder, and twelve as having emotional/behavioral disorders. However, the majority of these students were receiving special education services under the category of learning disability, while few qualified as eligible under the category of emotional/behavioral disorders. Comparison of the students' performances on a battery of tests revealed that the students identified as having attention deficit hyperactivity disorder and emotional/behavioral disorders did not differ on intelligence or achievement, but did differ on social skills measures when compared to other at-risk students who did not demonstrate behavior problems. They argue that these data demonstrate that many students who are identified as having attention deficit hyperactivity disorder and emotional/behavioral disorders are being inappropriately placed in special education programs for students with learning disabilities. Schools are apparently reluctant to use the label "emotional/behavioral disorders," or place students in programs for those identified as emotionally/behaviorally disordered.

Lambros, Ward, Bocian, MacMillan, and Gresham (1998) concur that there is a muddle of identifying criteria, and that it is difficult to sort learning disabilities and emotional/behavioral disorders. They suggest that the low-reported incidence of emotional/behavioral disorders (less than 1 percent) is inaccurate, and that a figure of seven percent of all students may be more accurate. They contend that many students with emotional/behavioral disorders are classified only as having learning disabilities. Identification of emotional/behavioral disorders is not being made until the child's later school years, and thus the child is being deprived of appropriate services. They assert that multi-method, empirically-based, and multi-gated assessment strategies must be used to avoid this confusion.

The official counts of students served as learning disabled or emotionally/behaviorally disordered are provided by local educational agencies and states and territories to the United States Department of Education, and are presented in *Annual Reports to Congress.* Each year, a report is made to Congress regarding the number of students served in each federally-recognized category. According to the U.S. Office of Education (1999), during the 1996–97 school year, 2,676,299 children were served for learning disabilities. The children thus identified comprised 51.1 percent of all students receiving special education services. During the same period, 447,426 students were served for having emotional/behavioral disorders, representing 8.6 percent of all students served in special education. The rate of increase for students identified with learning disabilities was 37.8 percent over the past ten years; the rate of increase for students identified with emotional/behavioral disorders was 20.1 percent over the past ten years. The percent of students receiving special education services for learning disabilities or emotional/behavioral disorders varies according to the students' ages.

The Twentieth Annual Report to Congress (U.S. Department of Education, 1999) continues to show an overrepresentation of children and youth in special education from diverse cultural, ethnic, or linguistic groups. That report suggested that poverty, rather than race/ethnicity, may account for some of the overrepresentation of minorities in special education programs. It also suggested that without attention to poverty and its effects on students, simply changing the assessment process will not eradicate the disproportionate representation. Though males and females comprise equal proportions of the school-aged population, about two-thirds of all students receiving special education services are male. This discrepancy is most evident among students in secondary schools, where 73.4 percent of the students identified as having learning disabilities are male, and 76.4 percent of students identified as having emotional/behavioral disorders are male (U. S. Department of Education, 1999).

In a state-by-state analysis of data reporting the placement of students identified as emotionally/behaviorally disordered, Coutinho and Oswald (1996) found that during the most recent four-year period for which data were available, small changes were observed in the national pattern of placement in regular classes, resource rooms, separate classes, and separate facilities. The national placement pattern for students with emotional/behavioral disorders differed from that of other disabilities, with placement in separate facilities more common for those students than for students with learning disabilities, mental retardation, or all disabilities combined. Considerable state-by-state variation was observed for each placement setting. Though many individual states increased or decreased the percentages served through a particular placement option, overall, these changes were masked by the relatively unchanging national pattern of placement of students. Variables other than student, teacher, and local program characteristics were observed to relate significantly to placement in regular classes, separate classes, and separate facilities. Higher per pupil revenues and per capita income were positively correlated to placement in more restrictive settings.

The outcomes for students identified as having emotional/behavioral disorders are unsettling: youths with emotional/behavioral disorders have the highest arrest rate three to five years out of school, and the highest school dropout rate of all other disability groups (Wagner, 1993). Mattison and Felix (1997) traced the educational careers of students eight years following their placement in special education for children with emotional disturbance during elementary or secondary school. They made an effort to distinguish the characteristics of the course of the students' identification as having emotional/behavioral disorders. They reviewed the duration of services, placement, and educational disposition at the time of discontinuation of special education services. The 78 elementary students averaged slightly more than four years of services for emotional/behavioral disorders, and a majority experienced placement in special education classrooms both in general education schools and in separate centers serving students with emotional/behavioral disorders. The 95 secondary students identified as having emotional/behavioral disorders averaged a little over two school years of placement, primarily in separate centers serving students with emotional/behavioral disorders. At follow-up, 75 percent of the younger students had experienced either a successful outcome (57%), or were still in SED programming (27%). In the secondary group, the students were more likely to have an unsuccessful (58.9%) rather than a successful (40.0%) outcome. Secondary students with unsuccessful outcomes were represented primarily by students who dropped out of school (35.8%). Programming for the average student identified as having emotional/behavioral disorders who is placed during elementary school does not appear to be a short-term undertaking, and periods of placement in more intensive or restrictive settings, as well as in a general education school setting, are frequently required. Almost 12 percent of students at follow-up were still in a program for students with emotional/behavioral disorders. At least a quarter of young students identified as having emotional/behavioral disorders were perceived by school district personnel to require prolonged services in order to be able to function sufficiently and thus remain in public school. For secondary students, returning to general education was uncommon, with only fifteen percent making a return.

Summary Points

- The process of determining which students are eligible for special education services and differentiating students who have learning disabilities and emotional/behavioral disorders is difficult.
- Boys are more likely to be identified as having learning disabilities or emotional/behavioral disorders than girls.
- Students with learning disabilities often have difficulties with language and communication. Students with emotional/behavioral disorders may have learning problems or communication disorders.
- Students with learning disabilities or emotional/behavioral disorders usually do not demonstrate the same level of social skills as their peers who are not identified with disabilities.
- Services to address learning disabilities and emotional/behavioral disorders have evolved from exclusion to inclusion. Throughout history, various theories have guided professionals in their work with these students.

Key Words and Phrases

high incidence disability—one of the four disability areas identified in federal law which comprises 90 percent of all students served in special education.

References

Algozzine, B., Ysseldyke, J. E., & McGue, M. (1995). Differentiating low-achieving students: Thoughts on setting the record straight. *Learning Disabilities Research and Practice, 10* (3), 140–144.

American Speech-Language-Hearing Association. (1989a). Issues in learning disabilities: Assessment and diagnosis. *Journal of the American Speech and Hearing Association, 31,* 111–112.

American Speech-Language-Hearing Association. (1989b). Issues in determining eligibility for language intervention. *Journal of the American Speech and Hearing Association, 31,* 113–118.

Bandura, A. (1969). *Principles of behavior modification.* NY: Holt, Rinehart, & Winston.

Bender, L. (1938). *A visual motor gestalt test and its clinical uses.* NY: American Orthopsychiatric Association.

Bender, W. N. (1995). *Learning disabilities: Characteristics, identification, and teaching strategies.* Boston: Allyn & Bacon.

Berry, C., Shaywitz, S., & Shaywitz, B. (1985). Girls with attention deficit disorder: A silent minority? A report on behavioral and cognitive characteristics. *Pediatrics, 76,* 801–809.

Blachman, B. (1994). Early literacy acquisition: The role of phonological awareness. In G. Wallach and K. Butler (Eds.) *Language learning disabilities in school-age children and adolescents* (pp. 253–274). NY: Merrill.

Bogdan, R., & Kugelmass, J. (1984). Case studies of mainstreaming: A symbolic interactionist approach to special schooling. In L. Barton & S. Tomlinson (Eds.), *Special education and social interests* (pp. 173–191). London: Croom-Helm.

Brendtro, L. K., & Van Bockern, S. (1994). Courage for the discouraged: A psychoeducational approach to troubled and troubling children. *Focus on Exceptional Children, 26* (8), 1–14.

Bryan, T. (1991). Social problems and learning disabilities. In B. Wond (Ed.) *Learning about learning disabilities* (pp. 195–231). San Diego: Academic Press.

Camarata, S. M., Hughes, C. A., & Ruhl, K. L. (1988). Mild/moderately behaviorally disordered students: A population at risk for language disorders. *Language, Speech, and Hearing Services in the Schools, 19* (2), 191–200.

Caseau, D. L., Luckasson, R., & Kroth, R. L. (1994). Special education services for girls with serious emotional disturbances: A case of gender bias? *Behavioral Disorders, 20* (1), 51–60.

CEC Today. (1997). Reading difficulties vs. Learning disabilities. *CEC Today, 4* (5), 1, 9, 13.

Chandola, C., Robling, M., Peters, T., Melville-Thomas, G., & McGuffin, P. (1992). Pre- and perinatal factors and the risk of subsequent referral for hyperactivity. *Journal of Child Psychology and Psychiatry, 33,* 1077–1090.

Coleman, M. C. (1986). *Behavior disorders: Theory and practice.* Englewood Cliffs, NJ: Prentice Hall.

Coutinho, M. J. (1986). Reading achievement of students identified as behaviorally disordered at the secondary level. *Behavioral Disorders, 11,* 200–207.

Coutinho, M. J., & Oswald, D. (1996). Identification and placement of students with serious emotional disturbance. Part II: National and State Trends in the Implementation of LRE. *Journal of Emotional and Behavioral Disorders, 4* (1), 40–52.

Crawley, J. F., Parmer, R. S., Yan, W., & Miller, J. H. (1998). Arithmetic computation performance of students with learning disabilities: Implications for curriculum. *Learning Disabilities Research and Practice, 13* (2), 68–74.

Cruickshank, W. M. (1972). Some issues facing the field of learning disability. *Journal of Learning Disabilities, 5,* 380–383.

DelHomme, M., Kasari, C., Forness, S. R., & Bagley, R. (1996). Prereferral intervention and students at risk for emotional or behavioral disorders. *Education and Treatment of Children, 19* (3), 272–285.

Denti, L. G., & Katz, M. S. (1996). Escaping the cave to dream new dreams: A normative vision for learning disabilities. In M. S. Poplin and P. T. Cousin (Eds.) *Alternative views of learning disabilities: Issues for the 21st century* (pp. 59–76). Austin: Pro-Ed.

Donahue, M. (1986). Linguistic and communicative development in learning disabled children. In C. Ceci (Ed.), *Handbook of cognitive, social, and neuropsychological aspects of learning disabilities* (pp. 263–289). Hillsdale, NJ: Erlbaum.

Doris, J. L. (1993). Defining learning disabilities: A history of the search for consensus. In G. R. Lyon, D. B. Gray, J. F. Kavanaugh, & N. A. Krasnegor (Eds.) *Better understanding learning disabilities: New views from research and their implications for education and public policies* (pp. 97–115). Baltimore: Paul H. Brookes.

Dudley-Marling, C., & Dippo, D. (1995). What learning disability does: Sustaining the ideology of schooling. *Journal of Learning Disabilities, 28,* 408–414.

Eme, R. F. (1992). Selective female affliction in the developmental disorders of childhood: A literature review. *Journal of Clinical Child Psychology. 21* (4), 354–364.

Epstein, M. H., Kauffman, J. M., & Cullinan, D. (1985). Patterns of maladjustment among the behaviorally disordered, II: Boys aged 6–11, Boys aged 12–18, Girls aged 6–11, Girls aged 12–18. *Behavioral Disorders, 10,* 125–135.

Erikson, E. H. (1963). *Childhood and society* (2nd ed). NY: W. W. Norton.

Fessler, M. A., Rosenberg, M. S., & Rosenberg, L. A. (1991). Concomitant learning disabilities and learning problems among students with behavioral/emotional disorders. *Behavioral Disorders, 16* (2), 97–106.

Freeman, B. M., and Ritvo, E. R. (1984). The syndrome of autism: Establishing the diagnosis and principles of management. *Pediatric Annals, 13,* 284–296.

Frostig, M. (1961). *The Marianna Frostig Developmental Test of Visual Perception.* Palo Alto, CA: Consulting Psychologists.

Ganschow, L. (1992). Speech/language referral practices by school psychologists. *School Psychology Review, 21* (2), 313–326.

Ganschow, L., Sparks, R., & Sudman, J. (1990). A cause for collaboration in the diagnosis and remediation of students with language learning disabilities. *Learning Disabilities: A Multidisciplinary Journal, 1,* 85–93.

Gerber, A. (1993). *Language-related learning disabilities: Their nature and treatment.* Baltimore: Paul H. Brookes.

Gibbs, D., & Cooper, E. (1989). Prevalence of communication disorders in students with learning disabilities. *Journal of Learning Disabilities, 22,* 60–63.

Gillespie, P., & Fink, A. (1974). The influence of sexism on education of handicapped children. *Exceptional Children, 41* (3).

Gillespie, P., & Heshusius, L. (1981). Mental retardation: A double standard for the sexes. *Equal Play,* Winter/Spring, 16–18.

Green, M. T., Clopton, J. R., & Pope, A. W. (1996). Understanding gender differences in referral of children to mental health services. *Journal of Emotional and Behavioral Disorders, 4* (3), 182–190.

Gregory, M. (1977). Sex bias in school referrals. *Journal of School Psychology, 15,* 5–8.

Gresham, F. M. (1996). Learning disabilities, low achievement and mild mental retardation: More alike than different? *Journal of Learning Disabilities, 29* (6), 570.

Hallahan, D. P., Kauffman, J. M., & Lloyd, J. W. (1996). *Introductions to learning disabilities.* Boston: Allyn & Bacon.

Hobbs, N. (1982). *The troubled and troubling child.* San Francisco: Jossey Bass.

Hutton, J. B. (1985). What reasons are given by teachers who refer problem behavior students? *Psychology in the Schools, 22,* 79–82.

James, A., & Taylor, E. (1990). Sex differences in the hyperkinetic syndrome of childhood. *Journal of Child Psychology and Psychiatry, 31,* 437–446.

Kanner, L. (1970). Emotionally disturbed children: An historical review. In L. A. Faas (Ed.), *The emotionally disturbed child: A book of readings.* Springfield, IL: C. C. Thomas.

Kavale, K. A. (1995). Setting the record straight on learning disability and low achievement: The torturous path of ideology. *Learning Disabilities Research and Practice, 10* (3), 145–152.

Keough, B. K., Gallimore, R., & Weisner, T. (1997). A sociocultural perspective on learning and learning disabilities. *Learning Disabilities Research and Practice, 12* (2), 107–113.

Kephart, N. (1960). *The slow learner in the classroom.* Columbus, OH: Merrill.

Kirk, S. A. (1976). Samuel A. Kirk. In J. M. Kauffman & D. P. Hallahan (Eds.) *Teaching children with learning disabilities: Personal perspectives.* Columbus, OH: C. E. Merrill.

Knitzer, J., Steinberg, Z., & Fleisch, B. (1990). *At the schoolhouse door: An examination of programs and policies for children with behavioral and emotional problems.* NY: Bank Street College of Education.

Kuder, S. J. (1997). *Teaching students with language and communication disabilities.* Boston: Allyn & Bacon.

Lambros, K. M., Ward, S. L., Bocian, K. M., MacMillan, D. L., & Gresham, F. M. (1998). Behavioral profiles of children at risk for emotional and behavioral disorders: Implications for assessment and classification. *Focus on Exceptional Children, 30* (5), 1–15.

Levin, E. K., Zigmond, N., & Birch, J. (1985). A follow-up study of 52 learning disabled adolescents. *Journal of Learning Disabilities, 18,* 2–7.

Lopez, M. F., Forness, S. R., MacMillan, D. L., & Bocian, K. M. (1996). Children with attention deficit hyperactivity disorder and emotional or behavioral disorders in primary grades: Inappropriate placement in the learning disorder category. *Education and Treatment of children, 19* (3), 286–299.

Luebke, J., Epstein, M. H., & Cullinan, D. (1989). Comparison of teacher-rated achievement levels of behaviorally disordered, learning disabled, and non-handicapped adolescents. *Behavioral Disorders, 15,* 1–8.

Lyon, G. R., & Moats, L. C. (1993). An examination of research in learning disabilities: Past practices and future directions. In G. R. Lyon, D. B. Gray, J. F. Kavanagh, & N. A. Krasnegor (Eds.) *Better understanding learning disabilities: New views from research and their implications for education and public policies* (pp. 1–13). Baltimore: Paul H. Brookes.

Mattison, R. E., & Felix, B. C. (1997). The course of elementary and secondary school students with SED through their special education experience. *Journal of Emotional and Behavioral Disorders, 5* (2), 107–117.

McIntyre, T. (1993). Reflections on the new definition for emotional and behavioral disorders: Who still falls through the cracks and why. *Behavioral Disorders, 18* (2), 148–160.

McKinney, J. D., Osborne, S., & Schulte, A. (1993). Academic consequences of learning disability: Longitudinal prediction of outcomes at 11 years of age. *Learning Disabilities Research and Practice, 8,* 18–27.

McLeskey, J., & Grizzle, K. (1992). Grade retention rates among children with learning disabilities. *Exceptional Children, 58,* 548–554.

McLeskey, J., Lancaster, M., & Grizzle, K. L. (1995). Learning disabilities and grade retention: A review of issues with recommendations for practice. *Learning Disabilities Research and Practice, 10* (2), 120–128.

Mirkin, P. (1982). *Direct and repeated measurement of academic skills: An alternative to traditional screening, referral, and identification of learning disabled students* (Report No. 1rld-rrp-7t). Washington, DC: Office of Special Education and Rehabilitation Services.

Morse, W. C., Cutler, R. L., & Fink, A. H. (1964). *Public school classes for the emotionally handicapped.* Washington, DC: Council for Exceptional Children.

Oswald, D. P., & Coutinho, M. J. (1995). Identification and placement of students with serious emotional disturbance. Part I: Correlates of state child-count data. *Journal of Emotional and Behavioral Disorders, 3,* 224–229.

Payette, K. A., & Clarizio, H. F. (1994). Discrepant team decisions: The effects of race, gender, achievement, and IQ on LD eligibility. *Psychology in the Schools, 31* (1), 40–48.

Poplin, M. S. (1996). Looking through other lenses and listening to other voices: Issues for the 21st century. In M. S. Poplin, & P. T. Cousin (Eds.) *Alternative views of learning disabilities: Issues for the 21st century.* Austin, TX: Pro-Ed.

Premack, D. (1965). Reinforcement therapy. In D. Levine (Ed.) *Nebraska symposium on motivation.* Lincoln: University of Nebraska Press.

Reiff, H. B., & de Furr, S. (1992). Transition for youths with learning disabilities: A focus on developing independence. *Learning Disabilities Quarterly, 15,* 237–249.

Reschly, D. (1996). Identification and assessment of students with disabilities. *Future of Children, 6* (1), 40–53.

Rock, E. E., Fessler, M. A., & Church, R. P. (1997). The concomitance of learning disabilities and emotional/behavioral disorders: A conceptual model. *Journal of Learning Disabilities, 30* (3), 245–263.

Rosenberg, M. S. (1997). Learning disabilities occurring concomitantly with other disability and exceptional conditions: Introduction to the Special Series. *Journal of Learning Disabilities, 30*, 242–244.

Rosenthal, S. L., & Simeonsson, R. J. (1991). Communication skills in emotionally disturbed and nondisturbed adolescents. *Behavioral Disorders, 16* (3), 191–199.

Ruhl, K. L., & Hughes, C. A. (1985). The nature and extent of aggression in special education settings serving behaviorally disordered students. *Behavioral Disorders, 10*, 95–104.

Sale, P., & Carey, D. M. (1995). The sociometric status of students with disabilities in a full-inclusion school. *Exceptional Children, 62* (1), 6-19.

Sewartka, T. S., Keering, S., & Grant, P. (1995). Disproportionate representation of African Americans in emotionally handicapped classes. *Journal of Black Studies, 25* (4), 492–506.

Shaywitz, S., Shaywitz, B., Fletcher, B., & Escobar, M. (1990). Prevalence of reading disabilities in boys and girls: Results of the Connecticut longitudinal study. *Journal of the American Medical Association, 264*, 998–1002.

Singth, N., Landrum, T. J., Donatelli, L. S., Hampton, C., & Ellis, C. R. (1994). Characteristics of children and adolescents with serious emotional disturbance in systems of care. Part I: Partial hospitalization and inpatient psychiatric services. *Journal of Emotional and Behavioral Disorders, 2* (1), 13–20.

Skinner, B. F. (1965). *Science and human behavior.* NY: Free Press.

Skrtic, T. M. (1993). The crisis in special education knowledge: A perspective on perspective. In E. L. Meyen, G. A. Vergason, & R. J. Whelan (Eds.) *Challenges facing special education* (pp. 165–192). Denver: Love.

Smith, C. R. (1998). *Learning disabilities: The interaction of learner, task, and setting.* (4th ed.). Needham Heights, MA: Allyn & Bacon.

Stein, S., and Merrill, K. W. (1992). Differential perceptions of multidisciplinary team members: Seriously emotionally disturbed vs. socially maladjusted. *Psychology in the Schools, 29* (4), 320–331.

Strauss, A. A., & Lehtinen, L. E. (1947). *Psychopathology and education of the brain-injured child* (Vol. 1). NY: Gruene and Stratton.

Tur-Kaspa, H., & Bryan, T. (1994). Social information processing skills of students with learning disabilities. *Learning Disabilities Research and Practice, 9*, 12–23.

Tur-Kaspa, H., Wesel, A., & Segev, L. (1998). Attributions for feelings of loneliness of students with learning disabilities. *Learning Disabilities Research and Practice, 13* (2), 89–94.

U.S. Department of Education. (1999). *Twentieth annual report to Congress on the implementation of the Individuals with Disabilities Education Act.* Washington, DC: Author.

U.S. Department of Education, OCR (Office of Civil Rights). (1993, July). *Revised data circulated to individuals who attended the Forum of Disproportionate Participation of Students from Ethnic and Cultural Minorities in Special Education.* Symposium convened by Project FORUM at NASDSE, Alexandria, VA.

Vogel, S. A. (1990). Gender differences in intelligence, language, visual-motor abilities, and academic achievement in students with learning disabilities: A review of the literature. *Journal of Learning Disabilities, 23* (1), 44–52.

Wagner, M. (1991). *Dropouts with disabilities: What do we know? What can we do?* Menlo Park, CA: SRI International.

Wagner, M. (1993). *Trends in postschool outcomes of youth with disabilities: Findings from the national longitudinal transition study of special education students.* Menlo Park, CA: SRI International.

Wagner, M., Blackorby, J., Cameto, R., Hebbeler, K., & Hewman, L. (1993). *The transition experiences of young people with disabilities: A summary of findings from the National Longitudinal Transition Study of special education students.* Menlo Park, CA: SRI International.

Wagner, M., Newman, L., D'Amico, R., Jay, E. D., Butler-Nalin, P., Marder, C., & Cox, R. (1991). *Youth with disabilities: How are they doing? The first comprehensive report for the National Longitudinal Transition Study of special education students.* Menlo Park, CA: SRI International.

Wagner, M., & Shaver, D. M. (1989). *Educational programs and achievement of secondary special education students: Findings from the national longitudinal transition study.* Paper presented at the annual meeting of the American Educational Research Association, San Francisco.

Weinberg, L. A. (1992). The relevance of choice in distinguishing seriously emotionally disturbed from socially maladjusted students. *Behavioral Disorders, 17* (2) 99–106.

Weinberg, L. A., & Weinberg, C. (1990). Seriously emotionally disturbed or socially maladjusted? A critique of interpretations. *Behavioral Disorders, 15* (3), 149–158.

Wright, D., Pilliard, E. D., & Cleven, C. A. (1990). The influence of state definitions of behavior disorders on the number of children served under PL 94-142. *Remedial and Special Education, 1* (5), 17–22.

2

The Nature of and Assumptions Regarding Learning Disabilities and Emotional/Behavioral Disorders

TO GUIDE YOUR READING

After you complete this chapter, you will be able to answer these questions:

- What are the relationships among ideas, actions, and outcomes in work with students with learning disabilities and emotional/behavioral disorders?

- What are some conceptual frameworks used in considering learning disabilities and emotional/behavioral disorders?

- What are the commonly-used definitions of learning disabilities and emotional/behavioral disorders, and how are these related to beliefs about students and learning?

- What is the integrated perspective applied in this text, and what assumptions are made regarding students with learning disabilities or emotional/behavioral disorders?

◆◆ *Following Matthew's assessment and evaluation, the multifactored evalua-*
tion team met regarding Matthew. Elizabeth and Frank, Matthew's current
teacher, the school psychologist, the school principal, an occupational therapist, a
communication specialist, the school's special education team leader, and the
school nurse met to discuss their findings, and Matthew's eligibility for special
education services.

Elizabeth and Frank reiterated their concern that Matthew seemed to be
bright, yet very difficult to manage. They described how Matthew was able to
give the Latin names and their meanings of dinosaurs, each particular dinosaur's
eating patterns, and where the best fossils were found, while still being unable
to write his full name. They admitted that they did more for Matthew than they
did for his high-achieving sisters. In addition, they expressed concern about
Matthew's increasing frustration with school, and his growing fascination with
the more macabre aspects of dinosaur hunting patterns.

Matthew's teacher concurred. Though Matthew had only been in her class a
short time, she was impressed with his general information on a wide range of
subjects related to science. He excelled in science, completing activities with few
behavior problems other than his impatience with the children who worked
slowly. He drew sophisticated conclusions from his "data." He read about as well
as the other students, yet his written expression was not well developed. Al-
though Matthew could spell a few words conventionally, developmentally, his
spelling had not progressed much beyond the precommunicative level. In other
words, he was using alphabetic symbols to represent words, but, generally, there
was no letter-sound correspondence. He was unable to read what he wrote in his
journal. Mathematics was less of a problem, because the teacher created special
worksheets for Matthew which had fewer, better-spaced problems on the page.
This accommodation, fewer questions or problems and more space, worked rela-
tively well in other subjects as well. However, Matthew had yet to complete a full
page in his reading workbook or his speller.

Matthew's teacher's primary concern was his behavior. She felt he was far
more active and distractible than the other students. She expressed that it was
difficult to spend adequate time with Matthew while trying to meet the needs of
the other students. Her greatest fear, however, was that he would harm himself,
or others with his exuberant play or risk-taking behavior. Other students avoided
him in their games because of the physical nature of his interactions. Recently,
Matthew has begun forcing interactions with the other students by grabbing their
belongings and running with them. His teacher reported an incident in which she
found Matthew balancing precariously atop a six-foot-high brick wall behind the
school in order to better observe a squirrel's nest. She concluded that Matthew
was a bright, exuberant, active student, possibly bored with many of the activi-
ties conducted in the classroom, who was very difficult to manage because of his
need for supervision and the academic challenges he presented.

The school psychologist reported data based on observations and documenta-
tion of the actions which preceded and followed Matthew's behavior in the class-
room, as well as information from standardized tests. She discerned a pattern in
Matthew's interactions with the teacher. Matthew would "suck her in" to ex-
tended conversations about his interests, using up significant portions of class
time, and thus, reducing his academically engaged time. Plotting the data of
Matthew's physical outbursts in the classroom, she found that they occurred

most frequently when he and the other students were supposed to be doing seat work or guided practice. She recorded no physical outbursts during science, social studies, and health, when math manipulatives were being used, or when he was reading in a small group with the teacher. Data indicated that Matthew was most physically agitated immediately upon arriving at school, and immediately after the morning and afternoon recesses. The psychologist's opinion was that Matthew had difficulty "shifting gears" during school, after recess, and after riding the bus. Elizabeth and Frank concurred that after arriving home, Matthew was usually "wound up," and that they attempted to manage this behavior by arranging some physical activity as soon as he arrived.

Regarding standardized testing, Matthew's intelligence tested at well above average. According to a standardized comprehensive achievement test, Matthew's scores on the general information subtest were above average, and his scores on the reading recognition and comprehension subtests were within the normal range. Mattthew's math computation skills were also within the normal range. However, his numerical reasoning and problem solving skills exceeded his computation skills. His written communication subtest score fell below average. The school psychologist explained that intelligence and achievement scores usually fall in the same range. A considerable gap (at least 16 points) between the IQ score and achievement scores is called a significant discrepancy. In Matthew's case, the standardized tests indicate a discrepancy in several areas: reading, mathematics computation, and written communication. The school psychologist further explained that Matthew's reading and math scores were average, but they were not commensurate with his intelligence score. On the other hand, his written communication score was below average.

The occupational therapist spoke of Matthew's lack of "post-rotary nystagmus" and poorly developed defensive reflexes. She expressed concern about his sensory integration, and suggested that he would respond well to vigorous brushing of his limbs with a soft brush immediately following periods of strenuous physical activity. She indicated that he did not have well-developed cerebral dominance, which appeared to inhibit his completion of many fine-motor and self-help tasks such as shoe tying or snapping his jeans.

The speech-language pathologist indicated that Matthew had a great deal of difficulty with turn taking and role taking. When asked what she meant, she explained that Matthew didn't take turns in conversation. He interrupted, blurted out, and began his responses before his teacher or peers had completed what they were saying. In role taking, she indicated that Matthew made assumptions in his speech, using pronouns before giving the identifier, launching into a statement without making sure his communication partner knew what he was talking about, and initiating new subjects in conversation. The school nurse, expressing concern about neurological involvement, recommended a neurological assessment. She thought diet control or medication might help Matthew control his physical activity.

The special education teacher described the interventions that had been used with Matthew. The length of his assignments had been adjusted. Matthew had been provided with the opportunity of listening to music through headphones in the back of the room when he had difficulty calming down after recess and lunch. A "study buddy" was assigned to help make sure Matthew was on the right page and had the correct materials. However, she explained that these interventions were not very successful in helping Matthew.

During the professionals' presentations, Elizabeth and Frank sat quietly, amazed at how much, and yet how little, these people knew about their son. Frank stated, "We all seem to have a piece of Matthew, depending on who we are and what we do. We're like the old Chinese folk tale about the blindfolded wise men and the elephant. The one touching a leg says it's a tree; the one grabbing the tail says it's a rope; the one touching the side says it's a boulder. How can we come together and help Matthew?"

REFLECTION *Everyone attending the meeting is very concerned about Matthew. Each one, however, uses a unique lens for viewing him. As you read this chapter, consider the impact that your beliefs about children and behavior have on your interactions in the classroom. How does what you believe shape what you do? What is the impact of your life and professional experience and training on what you do?*

Introduction

In this chapter, four factors essential to understanding learning disabilities and emotional/behavioral disorders and the theoretical perspective applied in this text are discussed. The chapter begins with a study of the interrelationship of theory, intervention, and results of intervention. Next, the conceptual frameworks traditionally applied in the education of students with learning disabilities or emotional/behavioral disorders are presented. An examination of the definitions of learning disabilities and emotional/behavioral disorders, and the relationship of the definitions to the conceptual frameworks follows. The chapter concludes with a discussion of an integrated perspective which allows and encourages appropriate implementation of individualized interventions from each of the traditional perspectives and the assumptions made in this text.

Ideas, Actions, and Outcomes

Rhodes (1972) suggested that in working with students, ideas, actions, and outcomes are interrelated and have significant effects on each other. Ideas, or conceptual frameworks of the etiology of human behavior, are inert abstract constructs unless acted upon. Actions, or the interventions imposed to change behavior, are chaotic unless directed by a conceptual framework. Outcomes, or the results of intervention, are affected by actions taken, or the interventions imposed. Rhodes suggests that a conceptual framework (ideas) directs action (intervention) by providing an analysis of the problem and potential outcomes (results) of intervention. He suggests that the same intervention, implemented by two individuals using different conceptual frameworks, may have vastly different meanings, and lead to vastly different experiences and outcomes for the participants.

A conceptual framework is often referred to as a paradigm. Heshusius (1995) describes a paradigm, in its broadest sense, as an interrelated set of beliefs and values about the nature of reality and the nature of knowledge. Kuhn (1970) originated the use of the term "paradigm" in a study of scientific knowledge. He suggested that a scientific community consists of practitioners of a scientific specialty, who have similar educations, similar professional initiations, read the same technical literature, and draw many of the same lessons from that literature. Kuhn recognizes that there are different "schools of thought" in which different communities of professionals explore the same field from mutually incompatible points of view. Though Kuhn broadened the concept very soon after introducing it (Hoyningen-Huene, 1993), paradigm, in its original sense, is a concrete problem solution that the profession has come to accept. The concept of paradigm emerged from Kuhn's recognition that many historical and contemporary fields operate in research traditions resting on a relatively firm consensus among participating specialists; he labeled these consensual traditions as paradigms (Hoyningen-Huene, 1993).

If we recognize, as suggested above, that ideas, actions, and outcomes are interrelated, it becomes apparent that some sort of theory base, or conceptual framework, must be available to us as professionals. Each of us relates to others based on some personal theory or paradigm produced and maintained by our unique life experiences, as well as our innate human universal behavioral response tendencies. We apply these personal theories to make sense of our social world (Brendtro, Brokenleg, and Van Bockern, 1990). Our thoughts, guided by our feelings, provide motivation and direction to our behavior (Weiner, 1980). Wilbur (1990) refers to St. Bonaventure's three ways of gaining knowledge as forming and sustaining our paradigm: the "eye of the flesh," by which we perceive space, time, and objects; the "eye of reason" by which we perceive the world of ideas, images, logic, and concepts; and the "eye of contemplation," or the world of synthesis and transrational thought. As professionals, we make decisions on behalf of our clients in terms of the general principles and theories that we apply to the particular needs of each individual (Schein, 1992).

In the classroom, our personal theory of human behavior, the interactions between ourselves and others, and the existing emotional/behavioral disorders are combined into what we call "teacher stance." Teacher stance is the teacher's personal posture toward self and others, as well as his or her theoretical orientation and instructional and management methods (McGee, Menolascino, Hobbs, & Menousek, 1987). Teacher stance guides the decision-making and design processes necessary for the planning of instruction. In addition, it permits improvisation which evolves from interactions between learners and instructional and management problems (Bauer & Sapona, 1991).

The methods that a teacher employs make a difference not only in terms of what is learned, but also in how it is learned. Students react differently to teachers' actions based on various paradigms, and no two learners react the same way (Joyce & Weil, 1980). A student who prefers predictability may interact well with a highly-structured, sequentially-oriented teacher; a creative child who prefers a more fluid turn of events may function most effectively under a teacher who offers little formal structure, and encourages individual exploration and initiative in the classroom.

Special education is sometimes described as being in the midst of a "paradigm shift," i.e., in the process of changing from a "student problem" model (the point of view that individuals with disabilities are somehow deficient) to the "growth" or "problem solving" model (a point of view that emphasizes growth). In the "student problem" model, the "problem" is the presence of characteristics which cause performance problems. In the "problem solving" model, the problem is based on a mismatch between expectations and the student's performance. In the student problem model, the problematic characteristics are identified and removed or remediated, so that the student no longer has the problem. In the problem solving model, however, educational solutions are used to increase the match between performance and expectations (Iowa Department of Education, 1990).

Several conceptual frameworks have evolved in the fields of learning disabilities and emotional/behavioral disorders. As discussed in Chapter One, these frameworks have developed throughout history, and each have been the prominent frame of reference during a specific period of time. To work without one of these conceptual frameworks while trying to develop interventions for learners with emotional/behavioral disorders, Brendtro and Van Bockern (1994) suggest, is like choosing what to eat at a potluck dinner while blindfolded.

Educators' perceptions of children and the behaviors they exhibit determine in large part the interventions or treatments selected and imposed. For example, a teacher who perceives a child as primarily determined by the environment will approach the problems of intervention from a radically different point of view from that of a teacher who perceives a child as controlled primarily by intrapsychic or biophysical factors. The teacher who perceives the child as controlled by the environment may change the location of the child's seat, develop additional rules for movement and behavior, or reorganize a lesson format or teaching strategy. The teacher who views the child as controlled by intrapsychic factors may encourage the child to express his or her feelings and emotions, or may encourage the expression of feelings through art, music, or some other expressive medium. The teacher who sees biophysical factors as significant in the child's behavior may provide the child with a highly-structured learning environment that includes repeated drill and practice of lessons, or may refer the child to an appropriate medical practitioner. Or, a teacher will discover and acknowledge the child's abilities, including abilities beyond those which have been tested, and create a learning environment to accommodate the student's learning needs.

Conceptual Frameworks

Though each conceptual framework has continued to develop with a separate tradition and literature, they have all become more eclectic over time, according to Brendtro and Van Bockern (1994). In practice, each framework has become more comprehensive. Cross-fertilization has occurred as practitioners pragmatically apply interventions which have emerged from once pure models. The amount of data supporting these frameworks varies, and some have more historical than current significance. The "student problem" frameworks include the psychodynamic perspective, the biophysical perspective, and the behavioral perspective; the "problem solving" frameworks are the "holistic" model and the ecological model.

A Student Problem Model: The Biophysical Perspective

The biophysical perspective emphasizes an organic origin of behavior. Learning disabilities and emotional/behavioral disorders are viewed as the result of a physical deficit or malfunction, and developmental challenges, which are the cause of the behavior exhibited by the individual.

Schroeder and Schroeder (1982) discussed the two primary subgroups of biophysical theory: (a) deficit and (b) developmental. The deficit subgroup includes theories related to genetics, temperament, neuropsychopharmacology, nutrition, and neurologic dysfunction. Developmental theories include neurological organization, perceptual motor learning, physiological readiness, sensory integration, and development.

Biophysical models on "endogenous retardation" emerged from the work of Alfred Strauss and Heinz Werner. Students with endogenous retardation were those who had assumed brain injury and who exhibited characteristics such as disturbance in perception and figure-ground relations, preservation, and emotional disorders. Terms such as "perceptually handicapped," "minimally brain-injured," or "minimum brain dysfunction," historically were used to describe these children. Individuals such as William Cruickshank, Ray Barsch, Marianne Frostig, Gerald Getman, and Newell Kephart were influenced by this work (Hallahan, et. al., 1996), and efforts to use specific exercises such as walking on a balance beam, paper-and-pencil activities, and reproducing rhythms were implemented to improve academic skills.

Samuel Orton (1925; 1928; 1937) observed that some children with reading problems reversed letters and read groups of letters from right to left. Orton hypothesized that the difficulty was due to a failure to establish unilateral cortical dominance (neither side of the brain in control), and used the term "strephosymbolia." He asserted that at least two percent of the school population suffered from this condition to a degree that could inhibit progress in school (1928). Later, in his well-known book, *Reading, Writing and Speech Problems in Children* (1937), Orton discussed a whole range of developmental disorders including dysgraphia, developmental word deafness, and clumsiness.

Hewett (1968) described a classroom model built on these early beliefs about neurological functioning. The teacher using this perspective identifies the learner's sensory and neurologically-based deficit through extensive observation and diagnostic testing. Once the deficit is identified, the teacher trains the learner to accurately perceive the task and demonstrate motor efficiency, before being given more complex tasks. A classroom operating on biophysical principles will offer structure, routine, and frequent repetitions of sequential learning tasks. Extraneous environmental stimuli are minimized to avoid distraction among learners considered to be neurologically impaired. These early efforts and remedial practices have undergone critical scrutiny, and have been found ineffective in improving academic skills (Hallahan, et al., 1996). Recently, however, understanding of the role of neurotransmitters and brain functioning has expanded, generating renewed interest in the organic origins of learning and behavioral problems.

The biophysical perspective is gaining attention, due to increased information about the relationship between neural processing and behavior. Sylwester (1997) explores the relationship between neurobiology and self-esteem. As the brain processes cognitive activity, several dozen neurotransmitter and hormonal systems are at work. Neurotransmitters, substances produced within one neuron and passing over to the dendrites of the next neuron in the information-transfer sequence, have been the subject of much research and discussion. The neurotransmitter serotonin, for example, reportedly plays an important role in regulating our level of self-esteem, and our position in the social hierarchy in which we live and work. High levels of serotonin are related to high self-esteem and low levels to low self-esteem. High levels are related to smooth behavioral control, and low levels to impulsivity, violence, and suicidal behavior. Sylwester indicates that it is possible to stimulate a serotonin release when conditions are adverse, and the student's self-esteem and serotonin levels are low. One medication, for example, Prozac, produces an increased serotonin level that enhances self-esteem. This positive mood leads to positive social feedback which, in time, allows the natural system to take over. Serotonin levels also increase for a brief period of time by alcohol use, but eventually the brain's store of serotonin is depleted, even further decreasing impulse control and self concept.

The teacher using a biophysical framework, when presented with a student who is out of his or her seat, would decrease the surrounding stimuli, increasing the likelihood that he or she will remain in seat. If such impulsivity fails to decrease, the teacher with a biophysical perspective may request that the student be evaluated for the use of medication.

A Student Problem Model: The Psychodynamic Perspective

The psychodynamic perspective emerged out of the work of Sigmund Freud and, as it relates to children, Anna Freud. In this conceptual framework, behavior is said to be determined by dynamic intrapsychic relationships. A teacher using psychodynamic theory would view the causes of behavior as being within the individual. Early life experiences, especially traumatic experiences, may cause unresolved challenges (conflicts) in the learner's emotional development.

In the classroom, the application of a psychodynamic perspective would be reflected in an accepting atmosphere in which the teacher tolerates and interprets the child's behavior. The clinical teaching model developed by Berkowitz and Rothman (1967) is one of the educational interventions that has emerged from this perspective. In this model, the teacher's actions are based on "need-acceptance." Through this, the teacher fosters the child's individuality, security, and self-respect. Emphasis is on utilizing the child's potential to resolve his or her emotional conflicts, and to support the child's movement toward emotional adjustment. The development of academics, though important, is secondary to helping the child resolve emotional conflicts in a secure, accepting environment.

In the psychodynamic perspective classroom, if the student has been identified as having a problem, such as being out of seat, the teacher would explore with the student why he or she feels the need to be out of seat. The student would be assured that he or she is a valued, important part of the classroom group, even though appropriate in-seat behavior was difficult. The student's feelings about being in seat would be explored and validated. The teacher would then work with the student to prevent the conflict, or resolve the issues related to the student being out of seat.

The psychoeducational perspective, a general term representative of an educational application of psychodynamic theory, is sometimes applied in schools and day treatment centers. It includes a variety of psychological and educational methods (Nichols, 1984; Fink, 1988). This perspective is based on the assumption that cognitive and affective processes are in continuous interaction. In order to support students, the psychoeducational teacher provides a specialized environment, in which every student can be successful at his or her present level. This specialized environment is developed through understanding how each student perceives, thinks, and feels in the setting, and recognizes students' vulnerability to competition, sharing, and testing. In the psychoeducational classroom, teachers listen to the student, and focus on his or her feelings.

A Student Problem Framework: The Behavioral Perspective

Whereas professionals using the psychodynamic and biophysical perspectives focus on *why* learners behave as they do; those using the behavioral perspective focus on *what* behaviors the learner demonstrates and the cues and contingencies needed to increase or decrease those behaviors. The behavioral model suggests that behavior is controlled by stimuli in the immediate environment that impinge on the behavior, and that behavior can be changed by manipulating those stimuli. In a behavioral perspective setting, the teacher manipulates the variables which occur before and after a behavior is exhibited. The statement "what you do is influenced by what follows what you do" (Sarason, Glaser, & Fargo, 1972, p. 10) is an excellent summary of the essence of behavioral theory, specifically in reference to behavior modification.

Practitioners of behavior modification assume that all human behavior (adaptive and maladaptive) is the consequence of the lawful application of the principles of reinforcement. Until recently, behavior modification has been the predominant perspective taught in teacher education programs. The simplicity of the model (identify the behavior, select the reinforcer, provide the reinforcer contingent on the behavior, evaluate the procedure) has made it pervasive in special education programs. However, questions regarding the generalization of behaviors learned in this manner, and the "curriculum of control" (Knitzer, Steinberg, & Fleisch, 1990), have called into question the strict application of behavioral interventions without consideration of the context in which the interventions are applied.

As additional emphasis has been placed on the student's internal control, there has been an increased emphasis on cognitive behavior modification. In cognitive behavior modification, the student uses self-talk to modify his or her behavior. This self-talk behavior modification strategy provides an alternative to extrinsic reinforcers and reinforcement schedules which are not portable from one environment to another. In learning disabilities, cognitive behavior modification emphasizes learning specific strategies or procedures to complete academic tasks, or to practice academic skills.

When confronted with student out-of-seat behavior, a teacher applying the behavioral perspective, would chart the frequency the student leaves the desk and use this as a baseline count. The teacher would then consistently reinforce an incompatible alternative, that is, provide a reward to the student after a specific period in seat. A teacher applying cognitive behavior modification would have the student cue himself to remain in seat, and have him mark on a check sheet whether or not he felt the need to get out of his seat and whether he did get out of seat.

A Problem Solving Framework: The Ecological Perspective

Ecology is the study of the interrelationships between an organism and its environment. As presented in this text, the ecological perspective maintains that the child is an inseparable part of a social system, which is made up of the learner and his or her school, family, neighborhood, and community (Hobbs, 1966). In this perspective, the learning disability or emotional/behavioral disorder is a product of the child's response to the settings in which he or she functions, as these interact with the child's personal traits and experiences.

A teacher applying ecological theory is aware of the impact of the environment on the individual or group, and carefully manages the classroom to provide a supportive environment. In addition, the ecological teacher would remain cognizant of the dynamic, reciprocal relationships that exist between the individual or group and the environment, and manage these behaviors for the benefit of the individual or group.

In the ecological perspective setting, the teacher would analyze the context in which the student leaves his or her seat. After identifying the variables which appear related to being out of seat, the teacher would provide supports in the environment that would increase the likelihood that the student would stay in his or her seat.

An Emerging Problem Solving Approach: The Holistic Paradigm

Change in special education, as in any discipline, is difficult. Heshusius (1995) argues that special education has been particularly resistant to fundamental change in instruction and assessment. Formal "diagnostic data" and "intervention programs" are used for placement and programming decisions. Those practices are based on outdated beliefs inherent in the student problem paradigm, which views the learner as reactive and learning as linear. Rather than a linear model, Heshusius proposes a holistic view which attends to, or focuses on, the complexity, flexibility, and real-life purpose of learning. The holistic framework maintains that the whole is (a) more than the sum of the parts, (b) different from the sum of the parts, and (c) cannot be accounted for or reduced to the sum of the parts. In addition, holism assumes that there is order in all that exists, even within complexity. Change, rather than being an additive, sequential, and linear process, is a transformative, complex interaction at many interdependent levels. The holistic framework assumes that the universe is a self-organizing, self-regulating, inherently goal-directed place, and that students can only make meaning in their own ways. Learning in a holistic framework does not take place inside a person's head, but is largely a result of social and cultural interchanges with persons and symbols. For learning to occur, there must be personal ownership of the problem formulation.

In holistic settings:

- learning is immanently or inherently active, a process of self-organization and self-regulation;
- learning is understanding relationships, and change and progress are transformative;
- much of learning occurs through social exchanges with persons and symbols;
- assessment is the documentation of authentic learning processes and outcomes, focusing on what students do over time in purposeful learning activities;
- errors are essential and positive activities, and should never be punished.

Heshusius suggests that this is a fundamentally different way of thinking and feeling about learning, with regard to self and students.

The application of a constructivist point of view is often linked with holism. In constructivism, knowledge and meaning are generated by the individual; people learn through "making sense" of their experiences. First applied in early childhood education, constructivism is becoming an integrated approach to instruction in meaningful contexts (Harris & Graham, 1996). Constructivist teaching models emphasize scaffolding, where students are provided assistance on an as-needed basis, with a fading of the assistance as their competence increases (Pressley, Hogan, Wharton-McDonald, & Mistretta, 1996). Though early applications of constructivism cast teachers as facilitators who did not directly instruct students, a more expanded position has emerged that provides a continuum of implicit to explicit instruction (Mercer & Jordan, 1996). From a constructist perspective, the teacher's questions have evolved from "What are you doing?" to "What would happen if you tried this?"

Emerging "Problem Solving" Frameworks: Postmodern Approaches

Another emerging framework for special education is a critical, sociopolitical interpretation. With increased acceptance of qualitative research in education, new ways of looking at disability, learning disabilities, and emotional/behavioral disorders are emerging. Among the various aspects of this developing viewpoint is the recognition of subjectivity in research, and the use of an interpretivist inquiry. The methods of empiricist science have been suggested to be inappropriately applied to the study of special education (Gallagher, 1998). The emphasis on interpretivist inquiry is to make sense of an experience through the stories of the participants. Ferguson and Ferguson (1995) identify four themes of interpretivist inquiry. First, interpretivists recognize that reality is constructed and intented, and that the reality we experience is a process of social construction. In other words, if two individuals experience the same event, they may interpret it very differently. Second, interpretivists argue that it is impossible to split subject and object; there is no dualism of subjective-objective or mental-physical. To make sense, both aspects must always be considered simultaneously. Third, just as there is no dualism in subjective-objective, it is impossible to separate "fact" from "value." Rather, the production of social construction is recognized to occur within the context of moral values. Finally, the goal of interpretivist research is to describe, interpret and understand, rather than to describe, predict, and control variables. Instead of asking, "what is disability?" the interpretivist asks, "what is the experience of disability?"

In his deconstruction of special education, Skrtic (1991) maintains that the professional behavior of teachers in school is governed more by institutionalized, cultural norms than by rational, knowledge-based actions. The professional bureaucracy of special education is a performance organization, not a problem-solving organization, so new problems are forced into old pigeonholes. Student disability, then, is an organizational pathology, that results from the ways a school works. Structurally, schools are nonadaptable. Special education removes students from the general education system, thus preventing teachers from confronting uncertainty and limiting challenges that may enhance innovation. A disability is a matter of not fitting the standard program or prevailing paradigm of a professional culture.

Sleeter (1995) applies these arguments specifically to learning disabilities. She argues that "having learning disabilities" explains white, middle- and upper-class childrens' difficulties in a way that designates their intelligence and emotional state as normal. It thus avoids placing any blame on the home or school for the student's failure to learn. By developing the category "learning disability," important questions about education, and the inequities within the educational experience, were avoided. By definition, students with learning disabilities were intellectually normal or superior. This allowed them to enjoy whatever advantages, in the form of higher expectations, that accrued to white, middle-class (or above) students, who came from actively supportive families.

Postmodernists do not merely criticize; they offer a view for the school of the future. Skrtic (1991) posits that the successful school in the twenty-first century will be one that produces liberally-educated young people who can work responsibly and interdependently under conditions of uncertainty. In order to do this, schools must promote a sense of social responsibility in students, an awareness of interdependency, and an appreciation of uncertainty. Schools must achieve these things by developing the students' capacity for experiential learning through collaborative problem solving and reflective discourse within a community of interests.

Commonly Used Definitions

Learning Disabilities

Since its original appearance in 1962, the definition of "learning disabilities" has evolved. Hammill (1990) reports eleven definitions, each of which had a period of prominence or popularity. Of these, four are professionally viable, and the seven remaining are historically significant. Hammill contends that the definition of the National Joint Committee on Learning Disabilities (NJCLD, 1988) should serve as the consensus definition, not only because of its strengths, but because of the weaknesses of the other definitions.

According to Public Law 94-142, the first published federal definition of learning disability, the term "specific learning disability" means:

> . . . a disorder in one or more of the basic psychological processes involved in understanding or in using language, spoken or written, which may manifest itself in an imperfect ability to listen, speak, read, write, spell, or to do mathematical calculations. The term includes such conditions as perceptual handicaps, brain injury, minimal brain dysfunction, dyslexia, and developmental aphasia. The term does not include children who have learning disabilities which are primarily the result of visual, hearing, or motor handicaps, or mental retardation, or emotional disturbance, or of environmental, cultural, or economic disadvantage (U.S. Department of Education, 1977, p. 65083).

To be classified as learning disabled, the law requires that a child not achieve commensurate with his or her age and ability peers in one or more of the listed areas when provided with appropriate learning experiences. In addition, the child must demonstrate a severe discrepancy between achievement and intellectual ability in one or more areas including oral expression, listening comprehension, written expression, basic reading, reading comprehension, mathematics calculation, or mathematics reasoning (U.S. Department of Education, 1977).

Hammill (1990) describes three limitations of the federal definition. First, the use of the term "psychological process" not only lacks specificity, it may be construed as a reference to the once-popular perceptual-motor theory of learning disabilities. Second, no criteria are given for operationalizing the process clause of the central nervous system component. Spelling is included as a specific learning disability in the definition, but it is not mentioned in the criteria. Finally, there is no mention of thinking or cognitive processing disorders.

In 1981, the National Joint Committee on Learning Disabilities (NJCLD), a group comprised of representatives from the American Speech-Language-Hearing Association (ASHA), the Council for Learning Disabilities (CLD), the Division for Children with Communication Disorders (DCCD) and the Division for Learning Disabilities (DLD) of the Council for Exceptional Children (CEC), the International Reading Association (IRA), the Learning Disabilities Association of America (LDA), the National Association of School Psychologists (NASP), and the Orton Dyslexia Society (ODS), proposed the following definition of learning disabilities:

> Learning disabilities is a generic term that refers to a heterogeneous group of disorders manifested by significant difficulties in the acquisition and use of listening, speaking, reading, writing, reasoning, or mathematical abilities. These disorders are intrinsic to the individual and presumed to be due to central nervous system dysfunction. Even though a learning disability may occur concomitantly with other handicapping conditions (e.g., sensory impairment, mental retardation, social and emotional disturbance) or environmental influences (e.g., cultural differences, insufficient-inappropriate instruction, psychogenic factors), it is not the direct result of those conditions or influences (Hammill, Leigh, McNutt, Larsen, 1981, p. 336).

The NJCLD definition was not offered in opposition to the federal definition, but as an improvement on that definition. The NJCLD definition reinforces that learning disabilities may exist at any age, and it deletes the controversial clause "basic psychological processes" (Hammill, Leigh, McNutt, & Larsen, 1981).

Until the passage of Public Law 94-142, learning disabilities was a clinical phenomenon that was of interest primarily to physicians, clinicians, and researchers. With the law came the need to operationalize the definition in order to determine eligibility criteria, and to do so in an equitable way (Zigmond, 1993).

The most prevalent tool for identifying individuals with learning disabilities is the statistical determination of discrepancy between ability (usually measured by a norm-referenced individually-administered intelligence test) and achievement, which is an attempt to measure unexpected underachievement (Lyon and Moats, 1993; Swanson, 1996). There are four major discrepancy models used: (a) deviation from grade level, (b) difference between expected and actual grade-equivalent or age-equivalent scores, (c) difference between ability and achievement using standard score comparisons, and (d) differences between ability and achievement based on regression analysis (Mercer and associates, 1996).

There are several criticisms of discrepancy formulas. The very tests compared may be technically inadequate, the ability-achievement discrepancy may be the wrong comparison, or the symptom (low achievement) may be confused with the problem. In addition, the learning disability could affect an individual's performance on both the aptitude and achievement measures. Finally, the processes and strategies regarding the calculation of discrepancy are ignored, and significant variations are used from state-to-state (Meltzer, 1994; Shaw, Cullen, McGuire, & Brinckerhoff, 1995; Swanson, 1996; Zigmond, 1993).

According to a survey of the departments of education in the fifty states and Washington, D.C., 14 departments of education included a discrepancy component in their definition; 48 included discrepancy in their criteria; and 50 included discrepancy in their definition and/or criteria. In addition, six methods for determining the presence of a discrepancy were reported (Mercer, Jordan, Allsopp, and Mercer, 1996). Although there is criticism about the popular use of a discrepancy formula to identify students as learning disabled, there seems to be a consensus that learning disabilities exist. The challenge is to improve methods for identification.

Any definition is only as good as its application. The discrepancy between definitions of learning disabilities and school practices was described by MacMillan, Gresham, and Bocian (1998). In reviewing students referred to student support teams and certified by the schools as having learning disabilities, they found that less than half evidenced the aptitude-achievement discrepancy required by the state. Examination of individual cases revealed that students were classified as having learning disabilities on the basis of low absolute achievement, regardless of whether a discrepancy existed. Moreover, in cases where a discrepancy was found, but the school did not classify the child as having a learning disability, that child evidenced significantly higher achievement. The students identified by schools as having learning disabilities were an extremely heterogeneous group, and included students with mental retardation, and a number who failed to qualify for any special education services.

Stanovich (1999) argues that the use of a discrepancy formula for identifying individuals with learning disabilities is untenable. He suggests that a more inclusive definition would advance efforts to support these students. Stanovich contends that rather than a clear diagnosis, "learning disabilities" represents negotiation among the social, political, educational, and resource concerns of parents, administrators, teachers, psychologists, and special educators.

The exclusion of other disabilities is another problem with the accepted definitions of learning disability. Rosenberg (1997) argues that in related fields, classification schemes recognize heterogeneity, and they incorporate the possibility of comorbidity with other conditions into identification, diagnosis, and intervention procedures. However, in the field of learning disabilities, the disability is viewed as a distinct category with little attention given to the evidence that learning disabilities coexist with other disabilities. Rock, Fessler, and Church (1997) report an increasing prevalence of students with overlapping conditions of learning disabilities and emotional/behavioral disorders. In their review of the literature, they reported that between 24 percent and 52 percent of children with learning disabilities have significant social, emotional, and behavioral problems. And, between 38 and 75 percent of students with emotional/behavioral disorders report as having learning disabilities. In addition, a substantial number of students with the initial label of emotional/

behavioral disorders were reclassified and served as having learning disabilities, reflecting either overlapping symptoms, or problems with identification procedures.

Other disabilities may be concomitant with learning disabilities. A high incidence of concomitant communication disorders among students with leaning disabilities was reported by Schoenbrodt, Kumin, and Sloan (1997). They suggest that "the child with learning disabilities is likely to struggle from 9 to 5, whereas the child with both a language and learning disability will likely struggle around the clock" (p. 267). Polloway, Patton, Smith, and Buck (1997) suggest that though mental retardation and learning disabilities may occur concomitantly, learning disabilities would be considered the secondary diagnosis. Erin and Koenig (1997) argue that there is a great possibility of under-diagnosis of a learning disability in a student with a visual impairment because, (a) severe visual impairment appears earlier than a learning disability, (b) the concept of visual impairment is easier to understand than learning disability, and (c) a visual impairment may be a more acceptable explanation for a child's failure to achieve in school.

Emotional/Behavioral Disorders

In 1961, Lambert and Bower developed a definition for "emotionally handicapped." This definition was used as the basis for the definition of "seriously emotionally disturbed" in Public Law 94-142, the Education for All Handicapped Children Act. In this law, "seriously emotionally disturbed" is defined as:

(1) . . . a condition exhibiting one or more of the following characteristics over a long period of time and to a marked degree, which adversely affects performance through

a. An inability to learn which cannot be explained by intellectual, sensory, and health factors;

b. An inability to build and maintain satisfactory interpersonal relationships with peers and teachers;

c. Inappropriate types of behavior and feelings under normal circumstances;

d. A general pervasive mood of unhappiness or depression; or

e. A tendency to develop physical symptoms or fears associated with personal and school problems.

(2) The term includes children who are schizophrenic or autistic. The term does not include children who are socially maladjusted unless it is determined that they are seriously emotionally disturbed (Federal Register, 1977, 42, 163).

Learners with autism were excluded from the definition of seriously emotionally disturbed by regulation in 1981 and reclassified as "other health impaired." In 1990, Public Law 101-456 (Individuals with Disabilities Education Act) delineated a separate category of disability for autism.

The use of term "seriously emotionally disturbed" in federal law has caused considerable controversy. The Council for Children with Behavioral Disorders (CCBD) has offered a series of arguments against both the label and the definition used in Public Law 94-142. In 1985, the CCBD argued that the term "seriously emotionally disturbed" should be replaced by the term "behaviorally disordered" because the latter term is less associated with a particular theory or intervention technique. In addition, it was argued that "behaviorally disordered" was far less stigmatizing, more representative of the actual problem, and focused more on the educational responsibility delineated in the law (Huntze, 1985).

One of the authors of the definition on which the federal definition is based, Eli Bower (1982) questioned its use in the context of law. He contends that the clinical aspects of the disability present in the original, research-based definition limit services to learners who are seriously troubled. The differentiations required by the definition are, in his opinion, psychologically and educationally untenable.

The Council for Children with Behavior Disorders, which is the largest educational professional organization related to learners identified as emotionally/behaviorally disordered, has worked consistently to change the definition for over a decade. In 1986, the Executive Committee of the Council for Children with Behavior Disorders issued a position paper urging that the "seriously emotionally disturbed" category be revised by replacing it with an educational definition. The Executive Committee urged that the new definition should focus on the sources of data collection needed to make a decision regarding "behavioral disorders," and should document prior attempts to modify behavior within the general education setting. The Committee also urged that "socially maladjusted" children not be excluded from the definition.

In 1990, the National Mental Health and Special Education Coalition (Editor, 1990) developed a new definition that it promotes as a substitute for the present federal definition. Their definition includes the following points:

- "Emotional/behavioral disorders" are identified when the behavioral or emotional responses of the individual are so different from his or her generally accepted, age-appropriate, ethnic, or cultural norms as to result in significant impairment in self-care, social relationships, educational progress, classroom behavior, or work adjustment.

- Learners with depression, anxiety disorders, attention deficit disorders, or other sustained disturbances of conduct or adjustment are all included in emotional/behavioral disorders.

- Emotional/behavioral disorders are more than a transient, anticipated response to stressors in the individual's environment, and they persist despite individualized intervention and/or modification in the educational environment.

- Multiple sources of data must be used to determine eligibility. The disorder must be exhibited in at least two different settings, at least one of which is educational.

This definition has not yet been included in any federal legislation, even though it has been agreed upon by eleven national organizations. McIntyre (1993) suggests that even though learners who are socially maladjusted would be able to receive services under this definition, other learners from diverse cultural groups still may not receive needed services. He contends that appraising cultural norms is extremely challenging due to ethnocentricity; most individuals fully understand only their own culture, and they find it difficult to understand or appreciate behavior which is culturally different from their own. McIntyre argues that if a culturally-determined behavior interferes with social interaction, or academic success, or creates a danger to others, services should be provided.

The "exclusion clause."   The most controversial aspect of the current federal definition is the exclusion of learners who are socially maladjusted. It is extremely difficult to determine whether learners are emotionally/behaviorally disordered, or socially maladjusted. In one study with a relatively large sample (118 school psychologists, 119 principals, and 108 special educators), the groups disagreed on both behavioral and background descriptors of learners in differentiating emotional/behavioral disorders and social maladjustment (Stein & Merrell, 1992). In another study, students labeled as emotionally/behaviorally disordered and socially maladjusted demonstrated a similar pattern of scores on teacher rating scales (Costerbader & Buntaine, 1999). "Social maladjustment" is not defined in Public Law 94-142, nor have there been any federal policy opinions or court decisions defining the term (Weinberg & Weinberg, 1990).

One of the most prevalent views of the difference between emotional/behavioral disorders and social maladjustment is that learners who are socially maladjusted "choose" their behavior or feelings, while learners identified as having emotional/behavioral disorders do not have control over their behavior or feelings (Weinberg, 1992). This view assumes that certain types of learners, such as those who are delinquent, and those diagnosed as conduct disordered, choose to engage in deviant behavior. Weinberg argues that current empirical evidence on the causes of conduct disorders provides evidence suggesting that at least some of the individuals exhibiting behavior congruent with conduct disorders may not be engaging in that behavior on a completely voluntary basis. These learners, then even though they are acting as if they are "socially maladjusted," would qualify for services if "choice" was used as a criteria.

Forness (1992) suggests that the socially-maladjusted exclusion clause must be considered within the historical context of the need to limit services to learners identified as emotionally/behaviorally disordered, and the current underidentification of these learners. Attending to specific child-centered characteristics, rather than looking at behavior in the learner's developmental context, will not resolve the question of whether the learner is socially maladjusted, or emotionally/behaviorally disordered in a society with little tolerance for "deviant" behavior and "bad kids" (Maag & Howell, 1992).

Our Assumptions

An integrated perspective to understanding the nature and treatment of children and youth with learning disabilities or emotional/behavioral disorders is offered in this text. This approach recognizes the contribution of each of the conceptual models described previously to working with learners identified as emotionally/behaviorally disordered or learning disabled. It emphasizes that behavior cannot be understood as a simple cause and effect relationship, but must be understood in the context in which it occurs.

In this perspective, development is the result of a series of transactions between the individual and the environment. Sameroff (1975) suggests that each action by an individual has an impact on the following

Development is the result of transactions between the individual and the environment.

action by that individual. Consider the example of a junior high school student who blurts out answers without raising his hand or being called on by the teacher. The teacher ignores the answer the student blurted out, and asks him to raise his hand if he wishes to be called on. Frustrated in his effort to respond, the student may then both raise his hand and blurt out the answer. As the teacher becomes increasingly impatient, she may send him to the back of the classroom, where he disengages from the activity.

Rather than saying that the student has difficulty paying attention, which is the usual response to such behavior, if the behavior is taken in context it becomes apparent that the student is not responding as the teacher expects, i.e., meeting the teacher's expectations. Such an approach to the learning disabilities and emotional/behavioral disorders of students is based on several assumptions about learners and their behavior.

Bronfenbrenner (1979) suggests that development is the progressive, mutual accommodation between an active, growing human being and the changing properties of the settings in which the developing person lives. This process is affected by relations between these settings, and by the larger contexts in which the settings are embedded. This is the general premise of this text in relation to emotional/behavioral disorders and learning disabilities. In order to effectively intervene in the learning of students, relationships within and between all of the settings in which these learners act, as well as those settings which impinge upon the learner, must be considered.

The following assumptions emerge when behavior is considered from this perspective:

- The application of a single theoretical perspective is limited. By considering the contexts in which the learner develops, the potential of applying interventions grounded in the various frameworks may be recognized. For example, a learner may have a behavior contract, take medication, and apply strategies for writing essays. The intervention is determined by the demands of the various settings, and the learner's needs in those settings.

- Behavior varies with the situation in which the individual finds himself or herself. A student may behave one way for parents, another way for teachers, and yet another way for the principal.

- Behaviors are sensible, purposeful, and meaningful. Behaviors serve a function for the individual related to his or her intent. A young child with limited verbal skills, for example, may throw his lunch on the floor to effectively communicate, "I don't want anymore."

- "Behaviors" should not be eliminated, but rather shaped toward more conventional, positive and productive conduct. It does little good to decrease a learner's aggression toward other children if he or she is not supported in learning other more positive, productive ways to interact.

- The social acceptability of behavior is dependent on both culture and setting. Fighting, which may be the most essential survival skill for a student on the walk home from school, may be the very behavior which causes suspension or expulsion from school if exhibited in the classroom, hallway, playground, or school bus. The behavioral demands of school are unique, and the school's standards may not be the same as the other environments in which the learner interacts.

In the next chapter, the developmental contexts of students with emotional/behavioral disorders or learning disabilities will be more fully explored.

This text uses a growth rather than deficit paradigm of individuals with disabilities. Whereas the deficit paradigm labels individuals with impairments, the growth paradigm avoids labeling, puts the person first, and views the individual as an intact person who has special needs. Rather than remediating deficits, each student should be provided support to enhance his or her opportunity for success. Armstrong's (1994) assertion is correct, that it is more appropriate to recognize students as individuals who need support, rather than problem children who need to be diagnosed or labeled. An inclusive stance must be taken to support Armstrong's contention that general educators and special educators should work together, rather than in settings which are exclusive and parallel.

Summary Points

In this chapter, the following points were discussed:

- A theory, the interventions derived from it, and the results of those interventions are related and interdependent.
- The traditional conceptual frameworks applied in the education and treatment of learners with learning disabilities or emotional/behavioral disorders include the psychodynamic perspective, the biophysical perspective, the behavioral perspective, and the ecological perspective. Postmodern frameworks are emerging.
- The integrative perspective used in the text is a mechanism that allows the individualization of interventions from each of the traditional perspectives.

Key Words and Phrases

behavioral theory—the perspective that perceives behavior as contingent upon stimuli in the immediate environment.

biophysical theory—the perspective that emphasizes an organic origin of behavior.

conceptual framework (theory, model, perspective)—the cognitive structure from which interventions are derived; beliefs followed as the basis of intervention.

curriculum of control—a structure found in classrooms for learners with emotional/behavioral disorders that emphasizes managing undesirable behaviors rather than teaching desirable behaviors.

development—growth and change which is the result of transactions between the individual and the environment.

ecological theory—the perspective that perceives behavior as a product of the individual's response to his or her social system.

etiology—cause

integrated perspective (social systems perspective)—the perspective that emphasizes that behavior cannot be understood as a cause and effect relationship, but must be viewed in the context in which it occurs.

psychodynamic theory—the perspective that perceives behavior as determined by dynamic intrapsychic relationships.

teacher stance—a teacher's personal posture towards self and others, including theoretical orientation and instructional and management methods.

References

Armstrong, T. (1994). *Multiple intelligences in the classroom.* Alexandria, VA: Association for Supervision and Curriculum Development.

Bauer, A. M., & Sapona, R. H. (1991). *Managing classrooms to facilitate learning.* Englewood Cliffs, NJ: Prentice Hall.

Berkowitz, P. H., & Rothman, E. P. (1967). *Public education for disturbed children in New York City.* Springfield, IL: C. C. Thomas.

Bower, E. M. (1982). Defining emotional disturbance public policy and research. *Psychology in the Schools, 19,* 55–60.

Brendtro, L. K., Brokenleg, M., & Van Bockern, S. (1990). *Reclaiming youth at risk: Our hope for the future.* Bloomington, IN: National Educational Service.

Brendtro, L. K., & Van Bockern, S. (1994). Courage for the discouraged: A psychoeducational approach to troubled and troubling children. *Focus on Exceptional Children. 26* (8), 1–14, 16.

Bronfenbrenner, U. (1979). *The ecology of human development.* Cambridge, MA: Harvard University Press.

Costerbader, V., & Bontaine, R. (1999). Diagnostic discrimination between social maladjustment and emotional disturbance: An empirical study. *Journal of Emotional and Behavioral disorders, 7* (1), 2–10.

Doris, J. L. (1993). Defining learning disabilities: A history of the search for consensus. In G. R. Lyon, D. B. Gray, J. F. Kavanaugh, & N. A. Krasnegor (Eds.) *Better understanding learning disabilities: New views from research and their implications for education and public policies* (pp. 97–115). Baltimore: Paul H. Brookes.

Editor (1990). Coalition finalized definition. *CCBD Newsletter*, August, 1990, 1.

Epstein, M. H., Kauffman, J. M., & Cullinan, D. (1985). Patterns of maladjustment among the behaviorally disordered, II: Boys aged 6–11, Boys aged 12–18, Girls aged 6–11, Girls aged 12–18. *Behavioral Disorders*, 125–135.

Erin, J. N., & Koenig, A. (1997). The student with a visual disability and a learning disability. *Journal of Learning Disabilities, 30* (3), 309–320.

Executive Committee of the Council for Children with Behavioral Disorders. (1987). Position paper on definition and identification of students with behavioral disorders, *Behavioral Disorders, 13*, 9–19.

Federal Register (August 23, 1977), 42 (163), 478.

Ferguson, P. M., & Ferguson, D. L. (1995). The interpretivist view of special education and disability: The value of telling stories. In T. Skrtic (Ed.) *Disability and democracy: Reconstructing (special) education for postmodernity* (pp. 104–121). NY: Teachers College Press.

Fink, A. H. (1988). The psychoeducational philosophy: Programming implications for students with behavioral disorders. *Behavior in Our Schools, 2* (2), 8–13.

Forness, S. R. (1992). Broadening the cultural-organizational perspective in exclusion of youth with social maladjustment: First invited reaction to the Maag and Howell paper. *Remedial and Special Education, 13* (1), 55–59.

Gallagher, D. J. (1998). The scientific knowledge base of special education. Do we know what we think we know? *Exceptional Children, 64* (4), 483–502.

Hallahan, D. P., Kauffman, J. M., & Lloyd, J. W. (1996). *Introduction to learning disabilities.* Boston: Allyn & Bacon.

Hammill, D. D. (1990). On defining learning disabilities: An emerging consensus. *Journal of Learning Disabilities, 23*, 74–78.

Hammill, D. D., Leigh, J. E., McNutt, G., & Larsen, S. G. (1981). A new definition of learning disabilities. *Learning Disability Quarterly, 4*, 336–342.

Harris, K. R., & Graham, S. (1996). Constructivism and students with special needs: Issues in the classroom. *Learning Disabilities Research and Practice, 11* (3), 134–137.

Heshusius, L. (1995). Holism and special education: There is no substitute for real life purposes and processes. In T. Skrtic (Ed.) *Disability and democracy: Reconstructing (special) education for postmodernity* (pp. 166–189). NY: Teachers College Press.

Hewett, F. M. (1968). *The emotionally disturbed child in the classroom.* Boston: Allyn & Bacon.

Hobbs, N. (1966). Helping disturbed children: Psychological and ecological strategies. *American Psychologist, 21*, 1105–1115.

Hoyningen-Huene, P. (1993). *Reconstructing scientific revolution: Thomas S. Kuhn's philosophy of science.* Chicago: The University of Chicago Press.

Huntze, S. L. (1985). A position paper of the Council for Children with Behavioral Disorders. *Behavioral Disorders, 10*, 167–174.

Iowa Department of Education. (1990). Trial sites draft—2/12/90. Des Moines: Iowa Department of Education.

Joyce, B., and Weil, M. (1980). *Models of teaching.* Englewood Cliffs, NJ: Prentice Hall.

Knitzer, J., Steinberg, Z., & Fleisch, B. (1990). *At the schoolhouse door: An examination of problems and policies for children with behavioral and emotional problems.* NY: Bank Street College of Education.

Kuhn, T. R. (1970). *The structure of scientific revolution.* Chicago, IL: University of Chicago Press.

Long, N. J., Morse, W. C., & Newman, R. G. (1976). *Conflict in the Classroom* (3rd ed.). Belmont, CA: Wadsworth.

Lovitt, T. C. (1989). *Introduction to learning disabilities.* Boston: Allyn & Bacon.

Lyon, G. R., & Moats, L. C. (1993). An examination of research in learning disabilities: Past practices and future directions. In G. R. Lyon, D. B., Gray, J. F. Kavanagh, & N. A. Krasnegor (Eds.), *Better understanding learning disabilities: New views from research and their implications for education and public policies.* Baltimore: Paul H. Brookes.

Maag, J. W., & Howell, K. W. (1992). Special education and the exclusion of youth with social maladjustment: A cultural-organizational perspective. *Remedial and Special Education, 13* (1), 47–54.

MacMillan, D. L., Gresham, F. M., & Bocian, K. M. (1998). Discrepancy between definitions of learning disabilities and school practices: An empirical investigation. *Journal of Learning Disabilities, 31* (4), 314–325.

McGee, J. J., Menolascino, F. J., Hobbs, D. C., & Menousek, P. E. (1987). *Gentle teaching.* NY: Human Service Press.

McIntyre, T. (1993). Reflections on the new definition for emotional and behavioral disorders: Who still falls through the cracks and why. *Behavioral Disorders, 18* (2), 148–160.

Meltzer, L. (1994). Assessment of learning disabilities: The challenge of evaluating the cognitive strategies and processes underlying learning. In G. R. Lyon (Ed.) *Frames of reference for the assessment of learning disabilities: New views on measurement issues* (pp. 471–606). Baltimore: Paul H. Brookes.

Mercer, C. D., & Jordan, L. (1996). Constructivist math instruction for diverse learners. *Learning Disabilities Research and Practice, 11* (3), 147–156.

Mercer, C. D., Jordan, L., Allsopp, D. H., & Mercer, A. R. (1996). Learning disabilities, definitions and criteria used by state education departments. *Learning Disability Quarterly, 19* (4), 217–232.

Nichols, P. (1984). Down the up staircase: The teacher as therapist. In J. Grosenick, S. Huntze, E. McGinnis, and C. Smith (Eds.) *Social/affective intervention in behavioral disorders* (pp. 43–66). DesMoines: State of Iowa Department of Public Instruction.

Orton, S. T. (1925). "Word blindness" in school children. *Archives of Neurology and Psychiatry, 14,* 581–615.

Orton, S. T. (1928). Specific reading disability—Strephosymbolia. *Journal of the American Medical Association, 90,* 1095–1099.

Orton, S. T. (1937). *Reading, writing, and speech problems in children.* NY: Norton.

Polloway, E. A., Patton, J. R., Smith, T. E. C., & Buck, G. (1997). Mental retardation and learning disabilities: Conceptual and applied issues. *Journal of Learning Disabilities, 30* (3), 297–308.

Pressley, M., Hogan, K., Wharton-McDonald, R. & Mistretta, J. (1996). *Learning Disabilities Research and Practice, 11* (3), 138–146.

Rhodes, W. C. (1972). Overview of interventions. In W. C. Rhodes and M. L. Tracy (Eds.) *A study of child variance* (Vol. 2). Ann Arbor: University of Michigan Press.

Rock, E. E., Fessler, M. A., & Church, R. P. (1997). The concomitance of learning disabilities and emotional/behavioral disorders: A conceptual model. *Journal of Learning Disabilities, 30* (3), 245–263.

Rosenberg, M. S. (1997). Learning disabilities occurring concomitantly with other disability and exceptional conditions: Introduction to the special series. *Journal of Learning Disabilities, 30,* 242–244.

Sameroff, A. (1975). Transactional models in early social relations. *Human Development, 18,* 65–69.

Sarason, I. G., Glaser, E. M., & Fargo, G. A. (1972). *Reinforcing productive classroom behavior.* NY: Behavioral Publications.

Schein, E. (1972). *Professional education: some new directions.* NY: McGraw-Hill.

Schfoenbrodt, L., Kumin, L., & Sloan, J. M. (1997). Learning disabilities existing concomitantly with communication disorder. *Journal of Learning Disability, 30* (3), 264–281.

Shaw, S., Cullen, J. P., McGuire, J. M. & Brinckerhoff, L. C. (1995). Operationalizing a definition of learning disabilities. *Journal of Learning Disabilities, 28* (9) 287–298.

Schroeder, S. R., & Schroeder, C. (1982). Organic factors. In J. L. Paul & B. Epanchin (Eds.) *Emotional disturbance in children.* Columbus, OH: Merrill.

Skrtic, T. (1991). *Behind special education.* Denver: Love.

Sleeter, C. E. (1995). Radical structuralist perspectives on the creation and use of learning disabilities. In T. Skrtic (Ed.) *Disability and democracy: Reconstructing (special) education for postmodernity* (pp. 153–165). NY: Teacher's College Press.

Stanovich, K. E. (1999). The sociopsychometrics of learning disabilities. *Journal of Learning Disabilities, 32,* 350–362.

Stein, S., & Merrell, K. W. (1992). Differential perceptions of multi-disciplinary team members: Seriously emotionally disturbed vs. socially maladjusted. *Psychology in the Schools, 29* (4), 320–331.

Swanson, H. L. (1996). Classification and dynamic assessment of children with learning disabilities. *Focus on Exceptional Children, 28* (9), 1–20.

Sylwester, R. (1997). The neurobiology of self-esteem and aggression. *Educational Leadership, 54* (4), 75–79.

U.S. Office of Education. (1977, December 29). Assistance to the states for education of handicapped children: Procedures for evaluating specific learning disabilities. *Federal Register, 41* (250), 65082–65085.

Walker, J. E., & Shea, T. M. (1999). *Behavior management: A practical approach for educators.* Englewood Cliffs, NJ: Prentice Hall–Merrill.

Weinberg, L. A. (1992). The relevance of choice in distinguishing seriously emotionally disturbed from socially maladjusted students. *Behavioral Disorders, 17* (2), 99–109.

Weinberg, L. A., & Weinberg, C. (1990). Seriously emotionally disturbed or socially maladjusted? A critique of interpretations. *Behavioral Disorders, 15* (3), 149–158.

Weiner, B. (1980). A cognitive (attribution)–emotion–action, model of motivated behavior: An analysis of judgments of help-giving. *Journal of Personality and Social Psychology, 39,* 186–200.

Wilbur, K. (1990). *Eye to eye: The quest for the new paradigm.* Boston: Shambhala.

Zigmond, N. (1993). Learning disabilities from an educational perspective. In B. R. Lyon, D. B. Gray, J. F. Kavanagh, & N. A. Krasnegor (Eds.) *Better understanding learning disabilities: New views from research and their implications for education and public policies* (pp. 251–272). Baltimore: Paul H. Brookes.

3

Developmental Context

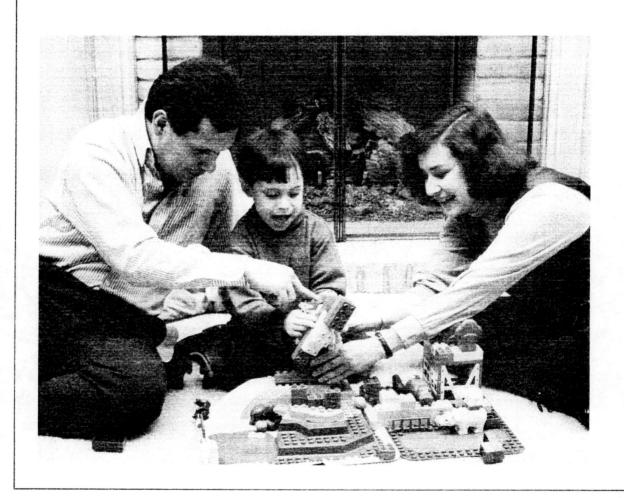

TO GUIDE YOUR READING

After completing this chapter, you will be able to answer these questions:

- What is the social systems perspective?
- What is the transactional nature of development?
- What assumptions regarding learning disabilities and emotional/behavioral disorders emerge if one adopts the social systems perspective?

◆◀ *Micah had his sixth birthday in early August. Later in that same month he began first grade. His teacher, who believed in direct instruction, and who wanted to ensure her students' success on the district's system-wide achievement tests, was concerned about his activity level and inability to complete work. She observed that his fine motor skills were poor, and that he was unable to work independently. The teacher noticed that Micah had a small "sight-word vocabulary," so she assigned him an additional phonics workbook to complete at home with his parents. Concerned about both his academic skills and his behavior, she wanted to refer Micah to the school Student Support Team for intervention, and perhaps evaluation, for special education services. Micah's parents, alarmed that their bright, active child was having "stomach aches" and complaining about school, requested a classroom change. When the principal refused to move him, they withdrew him from the school and put him in a local parochial school.*

◆◀ *Mark had his sixth birthday in early August. Later in that same month he began first grade. His teacher, who believed in developmentally appropriate practice, guided Mark toward the more active learning centers in the classroom which allowed him to be physically engaged. When Mark was frustrated by paper with lines for writing, she provided him with large unlined sheets of paper and told him that he didn't need lines to write stories. She talked with the fourth grade teacher, who provided a study buddy from her class to work individually with Mark on his seatwork and guided practice activities. Mark gradually increased his reading skills, and, by January, his "study buddy" was able to begin to work with another child because Mark was able to complete most of his work independently.*

These two vignettes depict the impact of the social system in which each child was expected to function and develop. Both children have similar issues and abilities. However, because of the way in which the first classroom "worked," the student was pushed toward being identified as having a learning and/or behavior problem. The teacher perceived the challenges Micah presented as *his* problems, rather than *their* problems. Because Micah didn't fit into the classroom program, he was determined to need evaluation by the support team and, possibly referred for special education.

In the second vignette, the child is viewed as a *contributor* to the problem, and was provided a supportive classroom. Mark's activity level was directed toward exploring and learning. His frustrations were met by accommodations on behalf of the teacher. As Lovitt (1996) suggests, the lenses are reversed: instead of focusing on deficits and disabilities, in the second vignette, the focus is on strengths and successes.

REFLECTION   *Reflect on your personal experiences in school. Were you less successful in some settings than others? What variables in those settings challenged you? How did you manage those variables? What roles did your peers, family, or community play in that setting?*

Introduction

The social systems perspective contributes two primary assumptions to our understanding of learning disabilities and emotional/behavioral disorders. First, if we wish to change an individual's behavior, we must initially change the environment in which the individual functions. Second, the individual or the family can be affected by events that occur in settings where he or she is not present. For example, a learner with learning disabilities or emotional/behavioral disorders and his or her family are influenced by their extended family's beliefs about the learning disability or emotional/behavioral disorder, the neighbors' tolerance of differences, the community's mental health policy, and society's perception of "smart," "slow," "good," or "bad," children. This may be true, even if the child himself or herself has very little contact with each of those systems. Unlike other developmental perspectives, the core of the systems perspective is that there is a progressive accommodation (relationship) between the growing organism (the individual) and forces in the larger social and physical environment.

In this chapter, the social systems perspective is presented and discussed in some detail. Each of the contexts within the perspective is exemplified. The second section of the chapter is devoted to an explanation of the transactional nature of development. The chapter concludes with assumptions regarding learning disabilities or emotional/behavioral disorders that emerge if one adopts the social systems perspective.

The Social Systems Perspective

As discussed in the previous chapter, ideas, actions, and outcomes are all interrelated. A conceptual framework must be available in order to work with learners identified as learning disabled or emotionally/behaviorally disordered. As Pagano (1991) suggests, "To act is to theorize." We act as we do because of our beliefs, and we judge others by our beliefs about people and the freedoms and constraints on their actions. The social systems perspective provides such a framework, and is applied in this text.

The social systems perspective regards each individual as developing in dynamic relationships with, and as an inseparable part of, the several social contexts or settings in which the individual either functions directly, or is affected by, throughout his or her life. Bronfenbrenner (1979) viewed this way of looking at the individual as interacting within several nested environments as an "ecology of human development." He used the term "ecology" in its strictest sense, that is, the study of the relationship of humans with their environment. This relationship involves the individual and the environment as both actors and reactors (Thomas & Marshall, 1977). Lesar, Trivette, and Dunst (1995) contend that Bronfenbrenner's human ecology perspective seems especially useful as a framework to guide research and practice for children and adolescents with disabilities, and their families. They suggest that the systems within this perspective uniquely touch people with disabilities and their families. Family members of children and youth without disabilities rarely come into contact with this realm.

In the social systems perspective, development is the continual adaptation or adjustment of the individual within the environment, and is a life-long process. Development is based on each individual's evolution in the environment, his or her relationship to it, as well as the individual's ability to discover, sustain, or change the characteristics of the environment. Learning and development are facilitated by participation in progressively more complex patterns of reciprocal activities with someone with whom the person has developed a strong and enduring emotional attachment. Development takes place when the balance of power gradually shifts in favor of the developing person (Bronfenbrenner, 1979).

Development, then, is the progressive, mutual accommodation (i.e., adaptation and adjustment) between an acting and reacting individual and the constantly changing settings in which the individual functions, as well as the relationships between those settings and the broader contexts in which they are embedded. Using this broad concept of development when discussing behavior, more aspects than those of the immediate setting's environment must be taken into account.

In the social systems perspective, behavior is viewed as the expression of the dynamic relationship between the individual and the environment. Behavior occurs in a setting that includes specific time, place, and objects, as well as previously established patterns of behavior (Scott, 1980). These "previously established patterns of behavior" are the characteristic behavior of an individual that he or she develops over time and brings to the setting where the behavior is occurring.

One major factor in the social systems perspective that impacts on whether an individual is identified as having learning disabled or emotional/behavioral disorders is congruence. Congruence is the "match" or "goodness of fit" between an individual and his or her environment. Individuals judged to be "normal" are those whose behavior is congruent, or in harmony, with the norms, or standards, of their environment. Those judged to be deviant or incompetent are individuals who are not congruent with their environment. These individuals may be either out of harmony with the norms of the environment, or they lack the skills necessary to perform effectively in the environment (Thurman, 1977).

Another important concept in the social systems perspective is that of roles. A role is a set of activities and relations expected of a person occupying a particular position in society, and of others in relation to that person (Bronfenbrenner, 1979). An individual acting in a role tends to elicit perceptions, actions, and interpersonal relationships consistent with the expectations of the role from both the person occupying the role, and others with respect to that person. As the role becomes more established in the institutional structure of society, and a consensus forms regarding the expectations of that role, and the tendency to evoke perceptions, actions, and interpersonal relationships is enhanced. For example, parents are "expected" to keep their children "under control" in a supermarket. The institutionalized role of a "good parent" is one whose child sits in the shopping cart, keeps his or her hands in the cart, and remains quiet and still. The parent whose child is getting in and out of the cart, skidding up and down the aisles on his or her knees, or screaming, evokes a very different set of perceptions, actions, and interpersonal relationships.

The social system perspective is unique in its concern with the ongoing and progressive accommodation between the growing individual and his or her ever-changing, or dynamic, environment. It examines the way these relationships are formed and reconciled by forces from the individual's various impinging social contexts. These social contexts include (a) one-to-one relationships; (b) interactions among contexts; (c) community, work, and school; and (d) society. At the core of these social contexts is (e) the self or the individual. The nested aspect of these contexts is depicted in Figure 3.1, and is discussed in the remainder of this section.

Self

Bronfenbrenner was concerned primarily with ecological contexts outside of the individual. Belsky (1980), however, suggested that using only these contexts failed to take into account the individual differences that each person brings to his or her ecological contexts.

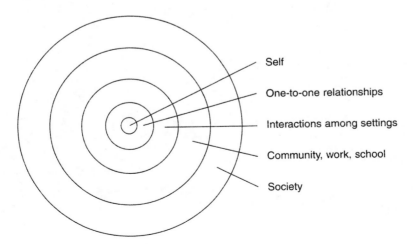

Figure 3.1   Nested Developmental Contexts of the Social Systems Perspective

According to Belsky (1980), the self includes the personal characteristics of each individual. These include the cognitive, communicative, social, physical, and personality characteristics that the individual brings to his or her relationships in ecological contexts. In addition, each individual brings previously learned personal skills, abilities, and competencies for dealing with the environment. For example, the student who is identified as having learning disabilities has individual strengths and weaknesses, ways in which he or she learns best, and personality traits which contribute to his or her learning styles. The student who is identified as having emotional/behavioral disorders also has individual strengths and weaknesses, settings in which he or she is successful, and personality and interaction styles which affect the way in which he or she manages personal behavior.

One-to-One Relationships

All individuals engage in multiple one-to-one relationships or interpersonal relationships. In the home, there are relationships with parents, sisters and brothers, and other individuals. At school, there are relation-

The home is one context in which students engage in multiple one-to-one relationships.

ships with peers, teachers, administrators, and staff. All of these relationships impact on individual functioning and development. Bronfenbrenner (1978) suggests that "in order to develop, a child needs the nurturing, rational involvements of one or more adults in care and joint activity with the child" (p. 773). In other words, "Somebody has got to be crazy about that kid!" (Bronfenbrenner, 1978, p. 774).

In these one-to-one relationships, Bronfenbrenner suggests that learning is facilitated when two individuals regard themselves as doing something together. In addition, greater learning and joint activity takes place when the relationship is characterized by positive feeling; Mutual antagonism interferes with learning. Additionally, the developmental potential of a pair of individuals is enhanced when there are positive feelings and support of the developmental activities from a third person outside of the original pair (Bronfenbrenner, 1979). Social support is of great importance for students with learning disabilities or emotional/behavioral disorders. After studying support patterns among children, Wenz-Gross and Siperstein (1997) found that children with learning problems turned to people in the home more for emotional support, and less for problem solving support, than children without learning problems. Both children with and without learning problems turned to adults outside the home more for emotional support and problem-solving support than for companionship. Peers were also found to be important; both children with and without learning problems turned to peers for companionship, more than for either social support or problem-solving support. Unfortunately, children with learning problems had less positive features in their friendships than children without learning problems. Their friendships had less intimacy, loyalty, and self-esteem, and there was less contact in their friendships. Even though they are viewed negatively by their peers, children with learning problems show similarities in some of their perceptions of support and friendship from those peers. They have people to whom they feel close and who are important to them.

When students have disabilities, they tend to be perceived less positively by their peers. Sale and Carey (1995), using a positive and negative peer nomination technique, found that students with disabilities are socially preferred significantly less, and they have a significantly higher social impact on interactions than their general education peers. Students with emotional/behavioral disorders had the lowest scores when compared to all students with disabilities, as a group. They also had significantly lower scores when compared individually to each of other disability groups.

Caspi, Bem, and Elder (1989) suggest that humans engage in interactional continuity. For example, an individual's interaction style evokes reciprocal, sustaining responses from others during interaction, and, consequently, reinforces the behavior pattern throughout the individual's life whenever relevant interactions are replicated. Individuals who are identified as having learning disabilities or emotional/behavioral disorders may have difficulty with interactional continuity.

Interactions among Contexts

Interactions among contexts may include interactions between school and home, home and service agency, home and church, home and neighborhood, and school and peer group. Bronfenbrenner describes four general kinds of interconnections between settings:

1. multisetting participation, where the same person engages in activities in more than one setting; for example, when a learner spends time both at home and at school;

2. indirect linkage, when the same person does not actively participate in both settings, yet a third party serves as an intermediate link between persons;

3. intersetting communication, by which messages are transmitted from one setting to another using face-to-face interaction, telephone conversations, correspondence or announcements, or chains in the social network; and

4. intersetting knowledge, where information or experience about one setting exists in another.

Bronfenbrenner (1979) suggests that the developmental potential of interrelated settings is increased when the learner does not enter the new setting alone, but enters the new setting in the company of one or more persons with whom he has participated in prior settings, such as when a parent accompanies a child to the first day of school, or playmates begin playing in Little League at the same time. In addition, transitions are enhanced if role demands in the different settings are compatible, and if the individuals engage in mutual trust, a positive orientation, and goals consensus between settings.

This context includes, at a practical level, parent–teacher collaboration and family–community service involvement. Also included are the transitions or movements of an individual between various environments, i.e., the transition from home to school and from school to work. Hanson and Carta (1995) make several recommendations for persons working with the more challenging families, that is, families engaged in substance abuse, child abuse or neglect, poverty, or mental illness. Their recommendations are consistent with a social systems perspective. They suggest that teachers must recognize that the problems children and their families have do not come from a single cause, so single interventions will probably not be effective. These families are so overwhelmed with meeting basic needs that they may not be able to respond to the specific developmental needs of their children. In addition, families living with a multitude of stressors may find it difficult to follow through with plans or programs for their children. In order to support these families, Hanson and Carta (1995) suggest that teachers provide opportunities for positive caregiving transactions. Supporting family members in establishing positive and mutually satisfying relationships with one another holds promise for preventing or relieving stress. Teachers must shift their focus from deficits to emphasis on individual and family strengths, and recognize and encourage informal sources of support.

The Community, Work, and School

Community, work, and school settings affect or are affected by what happens in the other settings in which the individual functions. Such settings do not involve the individual directly. However, events occurring in these settings are affected by, or may affect, the individual. Community, work, and school settings include the availability of special education programs, the goals of educational programs in the community, the school's system-wide disciplinary policies, and so on. Dudley-Marling and Dippo (1996) suggest that having special education services, in fact, fulfills a need for the schools. They contend that special education preserves conventional assumptions about the role of individual potential and effort in school achievement by placing the responsibility of school failure within the student. More specifically, failure is the student's fault, and not the fault of the school or any of its components.

The beliefs of school teachers and administrators may have a significant impact on the education of students with learning disabilities or emotional/behavioral disorders. In a recent survey of teachers' attitudes toward public schools, Langdon (1996) reports that more public respondents (41%) than teachers (35%) say that America is spending about the right amount of money on students with special needs. Three times as many public respondents (47%) as teachers (16%) say that we are spending too little. Seven times as many teachers (36%) as public respondents (5%) say that we are spending too much on students with special needs. These studies suggest that educators may not be willing to support programmatic change for special education students.

School administrators were similarly found unsupportive of students with learning problems. In a study of school administrators in six school districts that had increasing rates of retention in grade, or transitional-grade placements, and increasing incidence of the identification of students as learning disabled, Allington, McGill-Franzen, and Schick (1997) reported that administrators offered a variety of explanations for students with learning difficulties. They offered a number of remedies for these students, almost all of which were outside of the educational programs. The administrators did not offer ideas about altering current general education programs as a potential strategy for addressing the problems of at-risk students. Rather, according to the administrators, many children were having difficulty because they lived in single-parent homes or with parents who had a low level of educational attainment. These administrators also noted the influence of expanded high-stakes testing on the increased identification of learning difficulties in young children. With the pressure to report high achievement, it was easier to identify students as having disabilities. The administrators generally supported the perpetuation of the status quo, and wanted the schools to be allowed to emerge unscathed by the specter of continued failure to educate at-risk children.

Bronfenbrenner (1979) suggests that direct links with powerful individuals in the original setting can positively influence decisions about the needs of the developing person and the efforts of those who act on his or her behalf. In addition, the developmental potential of a setting decreases as there are fewer links in the network chain connecting that setting to settings of power. Cohen (1980) concurs, arguing that supportive families must occur within a context (system) of interrelated, interacting parts. The client or the recipient of the service, and the staff who provide the service, appear in the foreground whenever the system is observed. The background, though, is equally critical to the service delivery process, even though its aspects may be less visible and are sometimes overlooked. Epstein and Elias (1996) provide the example of deinstitutionalization of the mentally ill. They suggest that deinstitutionalization was based primarily on the premise that mentally ill people would adapt to normal communities, while ignoring the fact that accommodation on the part of the communities would also be necessary.

Society

In every society there is a general cultural belief system. A society's cultural belief system, or general social values, is applied to judge individuals whose behavior varies from that of their peers. The direction and growth of an individual are governed by the extent to which opportunities to enter settings conducive to development in various areas are open or closed to that individual (Bronfenbrenner, 1979). Society may close doors to an individual because of his or her behavior, or society's belief about "good children" and "good families."

Denti and Katz (1996) contend that special education has constructed a reality in society which supports society's vision of the purposes of education. The field of special education in our society has acquired an intellectual and institutional life of its own. A culture of special education has emerged with beliefs, values, and rituals passed on to future generations of special educators. Spear-Swerling and Sternberg (1998) state, "If educators wish to help children who are low achievers, they must discard the concept of learning disabilities entirely, in favor of a new way of thinking about children's learning problems . . ." (p. 397).

The Transactional Nature of Development

The social systems perspective assumes that behavior is not linear, i.e., a simple cause and effect relationship. Behavior is viewed as composed of "transactions" among the individual and his or her environment (contexts). Sameroff (1975) contends that the contact between the individual and the environment is a transaction by which each is altered by the other. For example, the behaviors of students in a classroom are influencing their teacher's behavior while the teacher's behaviors are influencing students' behaviors. Teachers with similarly behaving students may vary in their responses towards the students, and thus, cause different developmental outcomes. A child's development cannot be explained entirely by either biological or environmental factors. Rather, developmental and behavioral outcomes are due to the ongoing reciprocal interactions between the individual and the environment (Sameroff & Chandler, 1975).

An example of the way in which teacher–student interaction molds subsequent interaction is provided in Table 3.1. The teacher, Mr. Jones, notices that Susie is not doing her work. She is squirming in her seat and looking around the room. From his desk Mr. Jones tells Susie to get busy on her assignment. Susie looks down and pretends to work. She doesn't complete the assignment and is reprimanded by Mr. Jones.

In a similar situation, the teacher, Miss Mitchell, notices Josh squirming and looking around. She walks over to his desk, bends down so that she is at his eye level and quietly asks Josh if he needs help. Josh says he doesn't understand what to do. Miss Mitchell explains the assignment again in small segments, demonstrating as she explains. They do the first part of the assignment together. Then she asks Josh to verbalize his understanding. When she is satisfied that he understands, she leaves Josh to complete his assignment, which he does successfully.

The transactional model of development forces teachers into social constructivism. In constructivism, each individual is viewed as a trans-

Table 3.1   Teacher–Student Interactions

A.

| Student squirms | → | Teacher tells student to get to work | → | Student looks at assignment | → | Assignment not finished | → | Student reprimanded |

B.

| Student squirms | → | Teacher asks student if he needs help | → | Teacher explains again | → | Student rephrases | → | Student completes work |

active participant, constructing knowledge and information about each interaction. The role of the teacher in social constructivism is that of a capable individual, responsible for learning about the children within his or her care, and utilizing this knowledge to construct developmentally and situationally appropriate practices (Mallory & New, 1994).

Assumptions of a Social Systems Perspective

The social systems perspective provides a framework for this text. The remaining sections of the text describe various aspects of the developmental contexts, including the individual, the family and classroom, and school and society. These sections are based on several assumptions from this perspective about students with learning disabilities or emotional/behavioral disorders.

First, it is assumed that in order to change the student's behavior, the environment must be changed. Even settings in which the individual does not directly engage may have an impact on his or her behavior. For example, stress on a parent's job may increase tension in the home which in turn affects the student's behavior in the classroom.

The social systems perspective also assumes that the nature of the nested context in which the individual is developing is such that linear cause and effect relationships between events and behavior can rarely be identified. The systems perspective recognizes the complexity and multiple variables that impact an individual's behavior.

Just as complex as the development and maintenance of behavior, is the selection of interventions. The systems perspective assumes that there is no "cookbook," "what works with each behavior" listing of interventions. Rather, any development of interventions must involve a careful study of the situation in which the behavior occurs, including all of the personal, temporal, and physical variables within that setting. When asked, "How do you deal with a certain behavior?" the proponent of the systems perspective responds, "It all depends."

These same variables are equally important when developing curriculum and instructional interventions. For example, in order to assist students who are having difficulty with reading, it is not enough to know their grade level scores or skill deficits. It is also important to be knowledgeable about their cultural and community heritage, their interests, their prior knowledge, their socialization experiences, and the contexts in which they succeed or have difficulty. This information is utilized to develop curriculum and intervention strategies that are relevant and accessible to each student.

Though the system perspective is apparently far more complex than linear theories of human development and behavior, it celebrates the incredible diversity among human learners and the uniqueness of each individual. The complexity of each of the issues and characteristics of students with learning disabilities or emotional/behavioral disorders is something you should marvel at as you work through this text.

Summary Points

In the social systems perspective:

- Each individual develops within a series of nested contexts.
- Development is a life-long process of adaptation and adjustment of the individual within the environment.
- Behavior is not linear, but composed of transactions.
- Application of the systems perspective celebrates the incredible diversity among human learners.

Key Words and Phrases

accommodation—adaptation and adjustment

behavior—the expression of the dynamic relationship between the individual and the environment

congruence—match or goodness of fit

constructivism—the belief that each individual learns through interaction with the environment and that as this learning occurs, the individual constructs his or her own knowledge

development—the progressive, mutual accommodation between an acting and reacting individual and the ever-changing settings in which the individual functions, as well as the relationships between those settings and the broader contexts in which they are embedded

ecology—the study of the relationship of humans with their environment

transactions—contacts between two individuals or an individual and the environment by which each is altered by the other

References

Allington, R. L., McGill-Franzen, A., & Schick, R. (1997). How administrators understand learning difficulties. *Remedial and Special Education, 18* (4), 223–232.

Belsky, J. (1980). Child maltreatment: An ecological integration. *American Psychologist, 35,* 320–335.

Bronfenbrenner, U. (1978). "Who needs parent education?" *Teachers College Record, 79,* 773–774.

Bronfenbrenner, U. (1979). *The ecology of human development.* Cambridge, MA: Harvard University.

Caspi, A., Bem, D. J., & Elder, G. H. (1989). Continuities and consequences of interactional styles across the life course. *Journal of Personality, 57* (2), 375–406.

Cohen, S. (1980). Multiple impacts and determinants in human service delivery systems. In R. Turner & H. Reese, (Eds.), *Life-span developmental psychology: Intervention* (pp. 125–148). NY: Academic Press.

Denti, L. G., & Katz, M. S. (1996). Escaping the cave to dream new dreams: A normative vision for learning disabilities. In M. S. Poplin and P. T. Cousin, (Eds.), *Alternative views of learning disabilities: Issues for the 21st century* (pp. 59–76). Austin: Pro-Ed.

Dudley-Marling, C., & Dippo, D. (1996). What learning disabilities does: Sustaining the ideology of schooling. In M. S. Poplin and P. T. Cousin, (Eds.), *Alternative views of learning disabilities: Issues for the 21st century* (pp. 45–57). Austin: Pro-Ed.

Epstein, T., & Elias, M. (1996). To reach for the stars: How social/affective education can foster truly inclusive environments. *Kappan, 78* (2), 157–162.

Hanson, M. J., & Carta, J. J. (1995). Addressing the challenges of families with multiple risks. *Exceptional Children, 62* (3), 102–212.

Langdon, C. A. (1996). The third Phi Delta Kappa poll of teachers' attitudes toward the public schools. *Kappan, 78* (3), 244–250.

Lesar, S., Trivette, C. M., & Dunst, C. J. (1995). Families of children and adolescents with special needs across the life span. *Exceptional Children, 62* (3), 197–199.

Lovitt, T. (1996). Foreword. In M. S. Poplin and P. T. Cousin, (Eds.), *Alternative views of learning disabilities: Issues for the 21st century* (pp. viii–xii). Austin: Pro-Ed.

Mallory, B. L., & New, R. S. (1994). Social constructivist theory and principles of inclusion: Challenges for early childhood special education. *The Journal of Special Education, 28,* 322–337.

Pagano, J. A. (1991). Moral fictions: The dilemma of theory and practice. In C. Witherell & N. Noddings, (Eds.), *Stories lives tell: Narrative and dialogue in education* (pp. 193–206). NY: Teachers College Press.

Sale, P., & Carey, D. M. (1995). The sociometric status of students with disabilities in a full-inclusion school. *Exceptional Children, 62* (1), 6–19.

Sameroff, A. (1975). Transactional models in early social relations. *Human Development, 18,* 65–79.

Sameroff, A., & Chandler, M. J. (1975). Reproductive risk and the continuum of care-taking causality. In F. D. Horowitz, M. Heatherington, S. Scarr-Salaptatek, & G. Siegel, (Eds.), *Review of child development research* (Vol. IV). Chicago, IL: University of Chicago Press.

Scott, M. (1980). Ecological theory and methods of research in special education. *Journal of Special Education, 4,* 279–294.

Spear-Swerling, L., & Sternberg, R. J. (1998). Curing our epidemic of learning disabilities. *Kappan, 79* (5), 397–401.

Thomas, E. D., & Marshall, M. J. (1977). Clinical evaluation and coordination of services. An ecological model. *Exceptional Children, 44,* 16–22.

Thurman, S. K. (1977). Congruence of behavioral ecologies: A model for special education programming. *Journal of Special Education, 11,* 329–333.

Wenz-Gross, M., & Siperstein, G. N. (1997). Importance of social support in the adjustment of children with learning problems. *Exceptional Children, 63* (2), 183–193.

4 Biological Factors and Temperament

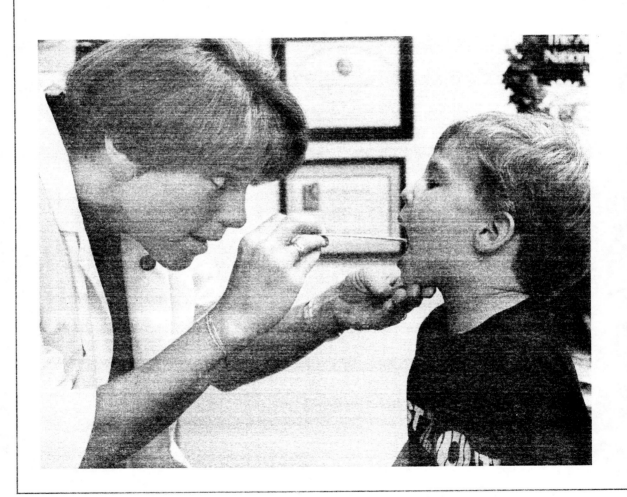

TO GUIDE YOUR READING

After you complete this chapter, you will be able to answer these questions:

- What are some of the biological issues related to learning disabilities or emotional/behavioral disorders?

- What are some of the issues related to temperament and learning disabilities or emotional/behavioral disorders?

- What are some of the more common biological disorders with which students may be identified?

- What are the interventions related to biological disorders?

- What is the role of the teacher in biological intervention?

◆◆ *Sean, who had been receiving special education services intermittently
through his school career, was really struggling in ninth grade. Though he
read well, writing was a difficult, tedious task. He was not able to produce cur-
sive letters smoothly and quickly, and printed all of his notes and assignments.
Note taking in his content area classes of Biology and History was very difficult
for him. In Algebra, he kept at hand a listing of the steps for solving equations
whenever he worked, and did poorly on tests without this support. Sean was doing well in Physical Education, but was very concerned about what would happen when he switched to Health at the end of the semester. His American Literature class was extremely difficult for him; his teacher emphasized the writing
process, yet Sean persisted in applying a five-paragraph essay strategy which he
had learned in seventh grade. Working in cooperative groups was arduous;
Sean's contributions to the discussion or product were consistently concrete and,
in the eyes of both his peers and teacher, immature and unsophisticated.*

*Sean's greatest difficulties, however, took place between and around his
classes. At the beginning of the school year, he was consistently late for home
room because he was unable to sort through his locker for the needed materials.
At first, he dealt with this tardiness by carrying all of his books and materials
throughout the day. His bookbag was extremely heavy, and besides being hard
to carry, the straps would break, the bottom would fall out, or the contents would
spill. Next, he began to pack "before lunch" and "after lunch" bookbags, so that
all he needed to do was grab the right bookbag from his locker in the allotted
minutes. He took both bookbags home, for which his peers taunted him. He continued to carry the two bags, however, explaining that he was tired of getting de-
tentions for being late or not having assignments.*

*Sean had difficulty moving about the building between classes. He always
used the north staircase, even if it was a shorter distance to the south staircase.
He explained that he "didn't know where the rooms were" if he used the other
staircase. Though he had been on medication for attention deficit disorder
throughout elementary school, Sean refused to go to the office to get his medication, stating that it didn't help, and that having to stop to get it got him in trouble
for being late. Sean's school problems are coming to a head. Though he passed
the ninth grade proficiency test, he is in danger of failing Biology and History.*

*At home, Sean's parents describe him as scattered and disorganized, but
having a "heart of gold." He frequently "runs out of clothes" because he fails to
pick up his laundry. He acts as a "foster parent" for kittens from an animal shelter, waking at all hours of the night to feed them with an eye dropper until they
are strong enough to return to the shelter. Sean works part time at a veterinarian's office, cleaning kennels. They describe him as a good worker who has a
way with animals. Sean would like to be a vet, but says he thinks he is too soft
hearted and too disorganized. He knows he needs to do well in school in order to
be admitted to training to become a licensed veterinary technician, but says that
he "just doesn't know what to do." His parents are concerned that he is becoming depressed. He generally sleeps very little, and then he "crashes" for several
days. Last summer he was in a juvenile detention center for a few hours. The
"friends" he was spending time with took a stepparent's car without permission.
When the police pulled them over, the friends ran, leaving Sean sitting in the car.
Since that incident he has become more and more socially isolated, spending his
time with the kittens for which he is caring, and working at the vet's office and*

animal shelter. His parents are very worried about Sean's achievement, depression, and lack of friends.

REFLECTION *Consider the adolescents you have known. Did any of them struggle in school? Were their problems related to achievement? Behavior? Both? Did one problem seem to exacerbate another? Did the problems seem to be a result of learning? A lack of learning? Some neurological reason?*

Introduction

At the core of the developmental contexts is the self—the learner. In recent years, there has been growing evidence that some behaviors may be related to biological variations within the individual. In addition, research has lent credibility to the concept of a temperamental predisposition, suggesting that some children are simply born more difficult to raise and teach than others.

In this chapter, the student and the biological factors which may contribute to learning disabilities and emotional/behavioral disorders are discussed. Issues related to temperament are also explored. The various means of addressing these biological factors, such as medication and diet will be looked at, and the chapter will conclude with a discussion of the role of the teacher in biophysical intervention.

Biological Issues

The consideration of biological issues related to learning disabilities or emotional/behavioral disorders is the basis of the biophysical perspective. This view of the individual emphasizes neurologic and other organic factors as the cause of behavior. If the cause of behavior is organic, then it follows that the ways of dealing with learning disabilities and emotional/behavioral disorders include nutrition, medication, and other medical interventions.

Historically, a relationship between organic neurological differences and learning disabilities has long been sought. Blumsack, Lewandowski, and Waterman (1997) studied the number and type of neurodevelopmental problems reported by students with and without learning disabilities. They reported that students with learning disabilities are significantly more likely than their peers without an identified disability to have neurodevelopmental problems or delays across domains such as language, motor, attention, and social behavior. Though a pattern of neurodevelopmental difficulties was not identified, some specific difficulties, such as following multistep directions, printing the letters of the alphabet, and understanding directions appear to characterize the neurodevelopmental problems of students with learning disabilities.

In terms of soft signs of neurological difference, Deitz, Richardson, Crowe, and Westcott (1996) studied the differences between students with learning disabilities and their typically developing peers matched by age, gender, and ethnicity in maintaining standing balance while the sensory environment is systematically altered. The students with learning disabilities received significantly lower scores on balance in six of the sensory system scales, suggesting that some children with learning disabilities have problems in organization related to balance, which may contribute to their motor problems. Even when students have been identified as both gifted and learning disabled, neurological differences have been noted. McIntosh, Dunham, Dean, and Kundert (1995) reported that students who were gifted and learning disabled had difficulty with tasks related to tactile, kinesthetic, and incident memory tasks.

Recent work in three areas has made significant contributions to the biophysical perspective. First, the study of risk factors has suggested a significant relationship between physical and mental health. Second, studies of families with histories of alcoholism and depression have raised questions of genetic predisposition. Finally, medical technology has provided greater insight into psychoneurology and various brain functions. These factors are discussed in the following sections.

Risk factors.   Preventing children from being at risk for physical and mental health problems begins with the onset of pregnancy (Slavin, 1989). In a longitudinal study, Cherkes-Julkowski (1998) found a relationship between prematurity and learning disability, attention deficit disorder, and language impairment. Physical problems, such as lead poisoning and poor nutrition have been related to children's behavioral problems in school. In the last decade, there have been significant reversals in the general health indicators that affect children. Studies by Baumeister, Kupstas, and Klindsworth (1990) suggested that, without specific prevention efforts, a "biological underclass" of children will emerge whose problems are related to poverty, a lack of prenatal care, and the prevalence of chronic illnesses such as AIDS and Hepatitis B.

The risks to children who live in poverty have been described by Parker, Greer, and Zuckerman (1988) as "double jeopardy." The interaction of both biological factors and poor social support puts children at serious risk for learning disabilities and emotional/behavioral disorders. Children living in poverty are biologically vulnerable due to prematurity, maternal depression, temperamental passivity, and inadequate early stimulation.

Allergies may also affect learning and behavior. According to McLoughlin and Nall (1994), there may be a relationship between allergies and the identification of children as learning disabled or emotionally/behaviorally disordered because of increased absenteeism, learning problems (such as distractibility and difficulty concentrating due to rhinitis, congestion, or headache), and difficulties attending or drowsiness as side effects to medication.

Genetic predisposition.   The term "genetic predisposition" is used to describe the likelihood that a particular characteristic present in parents will be present in their child. Though the particular gene responsible for a trait (characteristic) may not have been identified, it appears that some learning disabilities and emotional/behavioral disorders may be inherited, or "run in families." For example, it is estimated that 30 percent of fathers and 20 percent of mothers of children with attention deficit hyperactivity disorder have the disorder themselves (Copps, 1992). Alcoholism and drug abuse also may be linked to a predisposition or affinity to such addictions (Crabbe, McSwigan, & Kelknap, 1985). The occurrence of schizophrenia, a very-low-incidence disorder, has been studied in families. According to Paul (1980), the children of schizophrenic individuals are far more likely to have schizophrenia, and among identical twins, even those raised apart, there is the same incidence of schizophrenia.

A recent study of twins with learning disabilities in mathematics also lends credence to the potential of genetic predisposition to learning disabilities. Alarc'on, DeFries, Ligh, and Pennington (1997), in examining 40 sets of identical twins and 23 sets of same-gender fraternal twins, found a significant relationship between mathematical disabilities of twins. Multiple regression analysis provided evidence for a significant genetic relationship in mathematics disability.

While some geneticists are searching for the ways in which disorders that appear to be a genetic predisposition are transmitted, others are studying how changes in a single gene can lead to complex behavioral symptoms (Brodsky & Lombroso, 1998). Brodsky and Lombroso use the example of fragile X syndrome, a disorder in which the long arm of the X chromosome is elongated and threadlike. In fragile X syndrome, multiple systems are affected, including the regulation of food intake, cognition, temperament, and behavior. The proteins believed to be responsible for this disorder produce their effects by interacting with other intracellular components. In this way, the disruption of normal development may result after the mutation of a single gene.

Psychoneurology.   The evolution of our understanding of the psychoneurological bases of some learning disabilities and emotional/behavioral disorders can be illustrated by way of example. Copps (1992) describes the evolution of our understanding of Attention Deficit Hyperactivity Disorder (ADHD).

Copps states that the history of Attention Deficit Hyperactivity Disorder began in 1845, when Heinrich Hoffman described "fidgety Phil," the boy who never sat still, as being naughty, rude, and wile (cunning). In

1902, George Still concurred, indicating that such children had a "deficit in moral control." However, he described a biologic deficit in "inhibitory volition" because the children often had competent parents who would not typically have had such "morally defective" children.

Following an outbreak of encephalitis in the 1940s, there were reports of children becoming disruptive, inattentive, and hyperactive as a result of being afflicted with this neurologic disease. These children were referred to as brain damaged or behavior disordered; children who did not have a physically detectable neurologic deficit were said to have minimal brain damage. Despite intensive study of children who demonstrated these behaviors, direct evidence could not be found for minimal brain damage. Because no evidence of damage was detected, and also because the term itself was considered distasteful, the name of this condition was changed to minimal brain dysfunction.

As the symptoms of Attention Deficit Hyperactivity Disorder became increasingly accepted as a dysfunction, rather than a damage, and due to a resurgence of the belief of nurture over nature, poor parenting emerged as a probable cause of this disorder. The response to medication, however, increasingly cast doubt on ineffective parenting, and supported a biological cause.

With increased technology, it became possible to measure the functioning of the brain and levels of neurotransmitters (chemicals in the brain that affect the efficiency with which the brain functions). It became apparent that among individuals with Attention Deficit Hyperactivity Disorder, there is a deficiency or imbalance in several chemical elements, that is, catecholamine, dopamine, and norepinephrine. Though it is not yet clear whether there is a decrease in production or excessive absorption of these neurotransmitters, a significant body of evidence indicates that inefficient transmission of neurological impulses affects the entire attention system of the brain, including attention, inhibition, and motor planning. Viewing Attention Deficit Hyperactivity Disorder in this way, children with the disorder are said to have a deficiency in executive control, which governs the inhibition and monitoring of behavior. These students neurologically have difficulty selecting and maintaining goals, anticipating, planning, completing tasks, and adapting plans.

Similar evolutionary paths are apparent in our understanding of Tourette syndrome, borderline personality disorder, depression, and obsessive/compulsive disorder. These disorders will be discussed in more detail in another section of this chapter.

One construct that frequently emerges in discussions of the psychoneurological bases of learning disabilities or emotional/behavioral disorders is executive function. Executive function regulates, integrates, and coordinates other cognitive functions, such as attention, memory, language, and visual-spatial skills, toward the successful completion of goals (Welsh, 1994). Executive functioning supports successful problem solving and strategizing. Any unique academic task that requires critical think-ing, judgment, planning, or self-monitoring requires executive function skills.

Executive function has important implications for behavior. Welsh (1994), using the available vast research base, suggests that executive functioning skills are mediated in the prefrontal section of the brain. The symptoms demonstrated by adult patients who have received damage to the frontal lobe suggest that this part of the brain is uniquely dedicated to support the executive function activities of insight, anticipation, plan-ning, self-evaluation, and goal directedness (Damasio, 1985; Fuster, 1980).

Attention Deficit Hyperactivity Disorder again provides a good exam-ple of the complexity of the impact of psychoneurological processes and behavior. Studies have demonstrated that in some learners with ADHD, the central nervous system is underaroused (Ferguson & Rappaport, 1983). Decreased cerebral blood flow has been documented in the frontal lobe of learners with attention deficit disorders, and the use of a stimu-lant medication, Ritalin, increased the blood flow to this area of the brain (Lou, Henricksen, & Bruhn, 1984). Ritalin released stored dopamine, a neurotransmitter, from neurons, suggesting that the level of neurotrans-mitters also has an effect on executive function. In a later study, Lou, Henriksen, Bruhn, Borner, and Nielsen (1989) found, more specifically, that the basal ganglia was the locus of the diminished blood flow. The basal ganglia is a structure in the subcortex with many dopamine re-ceptors which connects to the frontal lobe. Neurochemical research (Shay-witz, Cohen, & Bowers, 1983) has indicated that the depletion of dopamine may underlie attention deficits; Ritalin releases stored dopamine, de-creases motor activity, and supports increased attention in many learn-ers with Attention Deficit Hyperactivity Disorder (Barkley, 1977).

Glucose utilization has been related to central nervous system under-arousal and Attention Deficit Hyperactivity Disorder (Pennington, 1991). Among students with emotional/behavioral disorders, glucose underuti-lization has been isolated in the right frontal lobe, and increased utilization in posterior brain regions (Zametkin, Nordahl, Gross, Kiung, Semple, Rum-sey, Hamburger, & Cohen, 1991). So, at least in terms of Attention Deficit Hyperactivity Disorder, the psychoneurological bases of behavior may be a complex interaction of structure, blood flow, and neurotransmitter release.

The role of neurotransmitters in self-esteem and aggression has been explored. The brain uses several dozen neurotransmitters and hormonal systems during information processing. Sylvester (1997) contends that fluctuations in one neurotransmitter, serotonin, play an important role in regulating self-esteem and position in the social hierarchy. High levels of serotonin are related to high self-esteem and high social status, and low levels are related to low self-esteem and low social status. High levels are related to smooth control, and low levels are related to impulsive, reck-less, violent, or suicidal behavior.

Sylvester (1997) suggests that it is possible to stimulate serotonin when conditions are adverse and self-esteem and serotonin levels are low. Administering a medication such as Prozac is one way to increase serotonin levels and enhance self-esteem. Increased self-esteem heightens mood, leading to positive social feedback, allowing the natural system to take over in time. Alcohol, sometimes used by individuals to deal with depression, increases serotonin in the short term, but eventually the store of serotonin is depleted, even further decreasing impulse control.

As more is learned about neurotransmitters and neurological functioning, the relationship between biology and behavior may be strengthened. At this time, as one child psychiatrist put it, linking what we know about the relationship between neurotransmitters and behavior is similar to trying to guess what is going on in a building by counting the number of people coming and going (McConville, personal communication, 1996).

Issues Related to Temperament

An individual's temperament is his or her style; temperament describes how an individual behaves, not what he or she does. Thomas and Chess (1977), described nine factors which compose temperament: activity level, adaptability, approach/withdrawal, attention span and persistence, distractibility, intensity of reaction, quality of mood, regularity, and threshold of responsiveness.

The biological view of temperament was given greater impetus by Buss and Plomin (1984), who argued that to be considered a temperament, a behavioral predisposition must be present in adults, and must be developmentally stable, adaptive, and have a genetic component. Emotionality, activity, sociability, and impulsivity, then, are dimensions of temperament. Temperament consists of the dimensions of an individual's personality that are largely present at birth, exist in most historical ages and most societies, are consistent across settings, and are stable as the individual develops (Plomin, 1983). Temperament is an individual variation that is biological or constitutional, remains with the individual, and is linked to differences in behavioral or expressive style.

Temperament, as an individual variation, can be a significant factor in identification as emotionally/behaviorally disordered. Thomas and Chess (1977) suggest that the "goodness of fit" of the individual's temperament and the environment can be a major factor in problem behavior. For example, a student most comfortable as an observer may have difficulty in the classroom of a teacher who, because of his or her own temperament, prefers active, enthusiastic responses. Temperament may also affect a child's learning by allowing attention and activity to be modulated and directed easily and quickly.

Even among infants, the range of the responses to interaction may be set on a continuum; ten to twenty percent of all infants are described as "easy," an additional ten to twenty percent are described as "testy," and the remainder fall into the intermediate ranges (Brazelton, 1983). Greenspan (1995) describes five different groups of children who are challenging in their interactions. "Highly sensitive" children are those who are often articulate, insightful, and empathic, yet are challenging in their mercurial moods. At school age, the sensitive child may stay on the periphery of interactions on the playground, unable to enter what Greenspan refers to as the "politics" of social interactions. Sensitive children are unusually susceptible to embarrassment and humiliation. These children often have a great variation in their mood, which is confusing to themselves, their peers, and the adults around them.

A second group of children include those Greenspan refers to as "self-absorbed." These children often withdraw, and seem to be content to be passive. Like the highly sensitive child, self-absorbed children stay on the periphery, preferring to stay home or daydream rather than interact with peers. They have great difficulty with interactions, and miss many of the developmental experiences of "getting out there and mixing it up."

The third group, "defiant" children, has a negative response to virtually everything. Defiant children tend to be concrete, and have a strong desire to be organized and in control. They may isolate themselves because other children won't play the way they want to play. They tend to be "all-or-nothing" in their ways of thinking, and have difficulty, for example, competing and remaining friends, or having a brief argument and then becoming "friends" again.

"Inattentive" children, Greenspan's fourth group of children, have difficulty remaining with any activity for a period of time. Inattentive school-aged children have problems with concentration in the classroom because of the vast amount of stimuli occurring simultaneously. For example, these students are unable to listen to the teacher's voice when there are voices in the hall, an airplane is flying overhead, papers are rustling, or the hamster is spinning his treadmill. They are very distractible; the complexities of playground games and classroom relationships are lost on them due to the amount of information they lose as a consequence of their distractibility.

"Active-aggressive" children are described as impulsive and constantly "on the go." According to Greenspan, this pattern of behavior is particularly difficult in families in which there is emotional neglect or physical abuse. The more the child's family is engaged in maltreatment, the more likely the child will be violent. Greenspan describes several characteristics of these children:

- they have experienced little consistent care so they have difficulty caring for others;

- they have difficulty purposefully communicating their intentions and feelings; and

- they tend not to construct internal dialog; rather than speak, they act impulsively.

According to Martin (1992a), there is a limited, though significant, body of research on child characteristics in the social, emotional, and attentional domains (collectively referred to as temperamental characteristics), and the educational process and outcomes for students with disabilities. He reviewed the research on the relationships between temperament and the characteristics of learners with disabilities (Down syndrome, neurological disabilities, learning disabilities, hyperactivity, behavior problems), family interactions, teacher attitudes toward learners (teachability), teacher decision making, and classroom interaction, and presented a model of the effects of temperament on educational outcome, mediated by their effects on parents, peers, and teachers.

In Martin's model, temperament is one of the factors that functions across home and school settings, and affects learning and school behavior. A child's temperament, he suggests, is manifest in classroom behavior, which affects peer attitudes and behavior. Peer attitudes and behavior may have an additional impact on the child's educational outcome because of the increased risk for social rejection (Janke & Lee, 1991). Children who are perceived to have a "difficult temperament" are particularly at risk for social relationship problems (Martin, 1992a).

Another perspective on temperament is provided by Caspi, Bem, and Elder (1989). They explored the "ill-tempered" temperament, which they described as the inability to delay gratification, control impulses, and modulate emotional expression. They found that "ill-tempered boys and girls become ill-tempered men and women, and ill-tempered parents." In their study population, men who were identified as ill-tempered as boys were described as undercontrolled, irritable, and moody as men. These men experienced downward occupational mobility, erratic work lives, and were more likely to divorce. Ill-tempered girls became women who married men with lower occupational status, were more likely to divorce, and were described by their husbands and children as ill-tempered mothers.

Though there may be a relationship between the temperament of parent and child, Martin (1992b) suggests that parents and their children will always differ in temperament in that they are at different developmental stages, share only half of their genetic material, and are responding to different demands. The goodness-of-fit between parent and child is an important determiner of the child's development.

Common Biological Disorders

As indicated previously in this chapter, several disorders have been found to have a biological basis. Among the most common of these disorders are Tourette syndrome, attention deficit hyperactivity disorder, obsessive-compulsive disorder, and depression. Recently, a group of children whose behavior and learning are biologically related to prenatal exposure to drugs and alcohol has been identified.

Tourette Syndrome

Individuals with Gilles de la Tourette disorder demonstrate motor tics (repetitive, recurring, and involuntary physical movements) ranging from eye blinks to complex muscular patterns, and vocal tics including grunts, barks, screams, or throat clearing (Anderson, 1993). These tics occur frequently throughout the day. Generally, tic-free periods are no longer than three months. In about one half of the individuals with Tourette's disorder, the tics usually begin with a single tic such as eye blinking (*DSM-IV*, 1994). Tics occur as early as 2 years of age. Because Tourette is a developmental disability, the tics must occur before the individual is 18 years of age. The "vulnerability" (having a genetic receptivity for developing a condition) to Tourette's syndrome is transmitted in a dominant pattern, and the range by which this vulnerability is expressed could be from Tourette's disorder to motor or vocal tics, Obsessive-compulsive disorder, or attention deficit hyperactivity disorder.

Neuropsychological characteristics have been identified among children with Tourette syndrome. Brookshire, Butler, Ewing-Cobbs, and Fletcher (1994) reported that though students with Tourette syndrome and their peers who did not demonstrate the disorder were similar in academic and cognitive measures, students with Tourette demonstrated poor performance on written arithmetic tasks, and reduced performance on visual motor, expressive language measures, and measures of complex cognition. Harris and Silver (1995) also found these students to have academic difficulties. There were significant problems with spelling and writing for 75 percent of the students in their sample, difficulties in calculation for 50 percent of the students, and problems in word identification and reading comprehension for 25 percent of the students. Visual motor problems were also prevalent in this group.

Burd, Kauffman, and Kerbeshian (1992) reported that in a review of the clinical files of students with Tourette syndrome, slightly one half showed that the student had learning disabilities. Tourette syndrome may be highly disruptive in the classroom, and these students frequently have difficulties in social relationships. For individuals with moderate or severe tics, medication is frequently used.

A relationship has also been reported between neurofibromatosis, another neurological disorder, and learning disabilities. A majority of the students with neurofibromatosis had academic deficiencies related to learning disabilities (Brewer, Moore, & Hiscock, 1997).

Attention Deficit Hyperactivity Disorder

Attention deficit hyperactivity disorder is one of the most frequently diag-nosed and researched disorders among school-aged children. One of the primary questions posed about attention deficit disorder is, "When does normal fidgeting turn into ADD fidgeting, and when does normal difficulty paying attention become ADD difficulty?" (Armstrong, 1996, p. 424.)

Reid, Maag, Vasa, and Wright (1994) examined the educational treat-ment of children clinically diagnosed as attention deficit hyperactivity dis-ordered. Among the children in this large sample, over half were receiving special education services, with most receiving services as emotionally/ behaviorally disordered and learning disabled. The most common special education placement was in general education classrooms with resource room support. Over 90 percent of the students were taking medication.

Though many students with attention deficit hyperactivity disorder may receive services for having learning disabilities, there is great con-troversy about the relationship of attention deficit hyperactivity disorder and learning disabilities. In their review of the literature, Riccio, Gonza-lez, and Hynd (1994) concluded that learning disabilities and attention deficit hyperactivity disorder may have neurological commonalities, and that both groups of children have attention difficulties and language dis-orders. Wiener (1998) reports that a significant proportion of students with learning disabilities also have the symptoms of attention deficit hy-peractivity disorder. Wiener argues, however, that the significance of the comorbidity of attention deficit hyperactivity disorder and learning dis-abilities may be in the nature of the social skills intervention needed. Co-morbidity of attention deficit hyperactivity disorder and learning disabil-ities may be a marker of the severity of the problems the student is experiencing (Forness, Kavale, & San Miguelo, 1998).

A significant amount of research has been done on the relationship between learning disabilities and attention deficit hyperactivity disorders. Stanford and Hynd (1994) compared parent and teacher behavioral rat-ings of groups of students identified as attention deficit disorder with hy-peractivity, attention deficit disorder–inattentive type, and students with learning disabilities on measures of impulsivity, inattention, and social withdrawal. The results indicated that parents and teachers view students with attention deficit disorder with hyperactivity as more disruptive than children with attention deficit disorder–inattentive type or with learning disabilities. Students with attention deficit disorder–inattentive type or learning disabilities were described as more shy and daydreaming. Teach-ers rated students with attention deficit disorders without hyperactivity and students with learning disabilities as being similar on symptoms of withdrawal and impulsivity.

Lazar and Frank (1998) examined the attention, inhibition, working memory, motor learning, and problem solving functions of students identified as having attention deficit hyperactivity disorder, students with learning disabilities, and students with both attention deficit disorder and learning disabilities. They sought to identify whether the functions of the brain's frontal systems varied among these groups of children. Students with learning disabilities and students with learning disabilities and attention deficit disorder had less typical test results and significantly impaired scores when compared with the students who were identified as having attention deficit disorder only. Lazar and Frank concluded that problems in brain frontal system function are not exclusive to attention deficit disorder, but are also present in students with learning disabilities. They suggest that this relationship implies a strong connection between the brain's centers of processing and executive functions.

In a study of placement decisions, Lopez, Forness, MacMillan, and Bocian (1996) examined the congruence between classifications of children with attention deficit disorder and emotional/behavioral disorders, and actual classroom placement decisions. When the students' performance on a battery of tests was compared, students identified as attention deficit disordered and those identified as emotional/behavioral disordered did not differ on intelligence or achievement, but did differ on social skills measures when compared to other at-risk students. Lopez and associates suggest that many students with attention deficit disorders or emotional/behavioral disorders are being inappropriately placed in special education programs due to the reluctance of schools to classify children as emotionally/behaviorally disordered. Instead, they utilize the learning disabilities category.

One of the major controversies regarding the use of medication with students diagnosed with attention deficit hyperactivity disorder involves the impact of medication on learning. Swanson, Cantwell, Learner, and McBurnett (1992), in a study of the clinical effects of medication on behavior and cognition, reported that the effects of stimulant medication on academic performance is minimal compared to its effects on behavior. They found no evidence of beneficial effects of medication on learning or academic achievement. Forness and Kavale (1988) and Forness and others (1992), noting a decrease in classroom performance among children treated with psychostimulants for attention deficit hyperactivity disorder and disruptive classroom behavior, questioned whether the resultant decrease in behavioral problems, or relative gains in attention, are worth the greater loss of learning performance in some children. However, Forness and Kavale (1988) and Forness and others (1992) also noted the potential efficacy for these drugs across a wide range of classroom functioning for many children.

According to Barkley (1990), 2 percent of school-age children receive stimulant medication for attention deficit hyperactivity disorder. However, medication alone does not appear to be the answer for students with attention deficit disorder. Multimethod interventions are emerging. Frankel,

The most positive changes in social skills may occur through a combination of social skills training, working with parents, and medication.

Myatt, Cantwell, and Feinberg (1997) reported that among their students, the most positive changes in social skills occurred through a combination of social skills training, collateral training for parents, and stimulant medication. In another study, Sheridan, Dee, Morgan, and McCormick (1996) provided direct instruction to students on social entry, maintaining interactions, and solving problems, while parents were taught debriefing, problem solving and goal setting. As a consequence, parents' skills improved, students reported improved social skills, and parents and teachers reported a general improvement for most of the students.

The dominant paradigm applied to explain attention deficit hyperactivity disorder has been psychiatric (neurological and biological). As a consequence, according to Maag and Reid (1994), other efforts to explain the disorder, such as a functional approach to assessment and treatment, have been hampered. For the purpose of the student's education, the usefulness of accepted conceptualizations of attention deficit hyperactivity disorder should be judged from an educational perspective, i.e., does the conceptual model have implications for classroom intervention (Maag & Reid, 1994)?

Depression

The characteristics of depression for children are similar to those for adults. A "Major depressive episode" for both adults and children is described as a period of at least two weeks during which there is either a depressed mood or the loss of interest or pleasure in most activities. The *Diagnostic and Statistic Manual of Mental Disorders* (DSM-IV, 1994), notes that in children, depression is often seen as irritation, crankiness, and sadness. The duration of symptoms required for identification is also shorter among children. Children and youth who are depressed have low self-esteem, poor social skills, and are pessimistic.

There have been inconsistent findings from studies of prevalence of depression among students with learning disabilities or emotional/behavioral disorders. In a study of eight- to eleven-year-old children identified as learning disabled, Wright-Strawderman and Watson (1992) found that over a third scored in the depressed range on the Children's Depression Inventory. Females with learning disabilities may be even more likely to demonstrate symptoms of depression (Maag, Behrens, & DiGangi, 1992). Maag and Reid (1994), using four independent measures with students in suburban Omaha, found the prevalence for depression among students with learning disabilities was 10 percent, similar to national estimates for students without learning disabilities, but lower than many previous estimates for students with learning disabilities. Peck (1985) reports that half of the children under age 15 who committed suicide during a three-year period in Los Angeles County were identified as having learning disabilities. Wright-Strawderman, Navarette, and Flippo (1996) suggest that students with learning disabilities, emotional/behavioral disorders, traumatic brain injuries, and students who are gifted and talented may be at risk for depression because they are vulnerable to emotional trauma. These students may have neurological issues that interfere with the development of typical temperament and coping skills, and they may have a negative reaction to caregivers.

Heath and Wiener (1996) compared the nonacademic self-perceptions (including social acceptance, athletic ability, physical appearance, and behavior) of students with and without depression, and with and without learning disabilities, in the fifth and eighth grades. They reported a relationship of self-perception of social acceptance and depression only for students with learning disabilities. However, compared with students who were not depressed and did not have learning disabilities, the students with learning disabilities rated themselves more socially competent. Heath and Wiener suggest that among students with learning disabilities, acceptance by peers may be a protection against depression.

Obsessive-Compulsive Disorder

For many years, obsessive-compulsive disorder was thought to be rare. Recent research by the National Institute of Mental Health (1996), however, suggests that perhaps as many as 2 percent of the population may have obsessive-compulsive disorder. Individuals with this disorder have obsessions (unwanted, intrusive and unpleasant ideas which occur repeatedly) which they manage through compulsions (repetitive behaviors usually involved with counting, listing, or rearranging objects). The most common obsessions are thoughts about contamination, doubts (concerning turning off the stove or locking the door), or a need to have things in a particular order (lining objects up on desks or tables). Common compulsions include hand washing, ordering, checking, or repeating words silently) (*DSM-IV,* 1994).

Individuals with obsessive-compulsive disorder respond well to specific medications, supporting a neurobiological basis of the disorder. The use of positron emission tomography (PET) scanners to study the brains of individuals with obsessive-compulsive disorder has demonstrated unusual neuro-chemical activity in regions known to play a role in other neurological disorders, such as Tourette syndrome (NIMH, 1996).

Children Prenatally Exposed to Drugs and Alcohol

Infants who have been prenatally exposed to drugs and alcohol are at risk for physical, learning, and emotional/behavioral problems. According to Williams and Howard (1993), some of these children demonstrate a marked failure to adapt to the environment, difficulties in appropriate interaction with caregivers, and problems in language, learning, and motor skills. Initial follow-up on infants prenatally exposed to drugs and alcohol suggests that some will suffer long-term behavioral and educational disabilities. However, little empirically documented data concerning the characteristics of exposed children who are in school is available. Though the potential causal mechanisms for neural damage to children who have been prenatally exposed to cocaine are strong, the empirical literature does not support inevitable behavioral and educational disabilities. Though they are similar to other children with neurological challenges, infants who have been exposed to cocaine in utero may have an added disadvantage of a chaotic caregiving environment where the parent focuses more on obtaining and using drugs than on caring for the child. This combination of biological problems and chaotic environment increases the probability that the child will be a "casualty."

Interventions Related to the Biological Disorders

The two primary interventions related to the biological bases of learning disabilities and emotional/behavioral disorders are medication and diet control.

Medication

The use of medication for students with learning disabilities or emotional/behavioral disorders significantly increased in the 1990s (Campbell &

Cueva, 1995). Sweeney, Forness, Kavale, and Levitt (1997) suggest that approximately 2 to 3 percent of all school-age children and adolescents may be on one or more medications at any given time. Among special education students, they estimate that approximately 15 to 20 percent may be on one or more medications.

One of the most important concepts concerning the use of medication as treatment for biologically-based learning disabilities and emotional/behavioral disorders is that medication does not "cure" the disorder; it modifies specific symptoms of the disorder. Though medication can be effective with individuals identified as having learning disabilities or emotional/behavioral disorders, there are several logistical issues which must be given consideration when medication is prescribed. Brown, Dingle, and Landau (1995) suggest that a pervasive problem is assuring that the individual is taking the medication as prescribed. Following medication schedules is complicated by the fact that medication may be prescribed for long periods of time and that the parents and/or child may become ambivalent about its use. When medication is to be administered at school, this responsibility may be affected by school staff and faculty attitudes toward medication and their availability to administer it. In addition, community attitudes and beliefs regarding the appropriateness of using drugs with children may intrude on the parents' decision making about medication.

Evans and Gardiner (1997) suggest that because medication may be administered incorrectly, the decision to use medication should be made after attempts at other interventions and consultation with a psychiatrist. Direct communication among all parties must be established regarding the medication and a plan must be developed for who will administer the medication, as well as how and when it will be administered. In addition, personal responsibility by the student for his or her behavior must be promoted; The student must be alerted to possible changes in his or her personal behavior as a result of the medication. The student may need assistance with explaining his or her medication and its purpose to others, and to be given reminders to take the medication. An evaluation plan should be in place to determine if the medication is having the desired effect. Forness, Sweeney, and Toy (1996) suggest that a professional who is knowledgeable about medication and its effects should be present at the student's Individualized Education Plan meeting.

Medications have been prescribed to help manage the behavior of children and youth since the late 1930s (Wilson & Sherrets, 1979). The treatment and evaluation processes related to the use of medication with children remain complex (Baldwin, 1973). The physician must not only be concerned with the individual child's personal status, but must evaluate the child's environment, the potentially biased evaluations of those associated with the child, and the actual and potential effects of other interventions being applied with the child, e.g., special education services (Shea

& Bauer, 1987). Systematic research regarding the efficacy and safety of pharmacological agents for children has been a recent phenomenon (Brown, Dingle, & Landau, 1994). The available research is limited and, therefore, the use of symptom control medications with children and adolescents must be considered experimental and monitored with great care.

Four classes of medication are used with children and youth who have learning disabilities or emotional/behavioral disorders. These are (a) stimulant medications, (b) antidepressants and mood stabilizers, (c) antipsychotics, and (d) anticonvulsants. Infrequently, some disorders are treated with anxiolytics (e.g., Valium) and adrenergic agents (e.g., clonidine) (Sweeney, Forness, Kavale, & Levitt, 1997; Brown, Dingle, & Landau, 1994).

The most commonly prescribed medications for children and youth with learning disabilities or emotional/behavioral disorders are stimulants. Of these, the two most frequently prescribed are Ritalin and Dexedrine. Dexedrine is used with children who have not responded to Ritalin. The positive effects sought from stimulant medications are: increased control of physical activity; increased goal-directedness; decreased impulsivity and disruptiveness; decreased distractibility; increased attending; improved performance, cognition, and perception; improved motor coordination; improved cooperation; and decreased negative and increased positive behavior. The common side effects of stimulants are: insomnia, decreased appetite, gastrointestinal pain, irritability, clinically insignificant increased heart rate, and paradoxical worsening of symptoms (Sweeney, and others, 1997). The common side effects of the various stimulants are similar, and can be managed by administering the medication early in the day, after meals, and planning times for other doses. An advantage of stimulants is that they are short-term (time) acting drugs, so may be administered during those times when behavior is most problematic (Brown, Dingle & Landau, 1994). Read (1995) reports that in the early 1990s it was predicted that over one million students in the United States would use Ritalin for the treatment of attention deficit disorder. This was an underestimate, however, in that nearly three million children are using Ritalin (Read, 1995). In a study conducted in Wisconsin by Runnheim, Frankenberger, and Hazelkorn, 40 percent of elementary school, 32 percent of middle/junior high school, and 15 percent of high school students with emotional/behavioral disorders identified as attention deficit disordered, were being treated with medication. Teachers reported that the most common medication was Ritalin (66 percent), followed by Dexedrine (11 percent) with the most frequent morning dosage being 10 milligrams. The teachers reported that they believed the medication was effective in reducing the students' inappropriate behavior.

According to Sweeney and others (1997), antidepressants or mood stabilizers are becoming the second most frequently prescribed medication for children and youth. They are administered for depression, attention deficit hyperactivity disorder, obsessive-compulsive disorder, and school phobia. Antidepressants are administered primarily to treat behaviors such as appetite and sleep problems, fatigue, lack of energy, and problems in attention and concentration. Antidepressants may also be used for nocturnal enuresis, sleep walking, night terrors, school phobias, and with individuals identified as having both attention deficit hyperactivity disorder and mood or anxiety disorders. (If the individual with attention deficit hyperactivity disorder has severe side effects, the antidepressant is prescribed with stimulants.) (Brown, Dingle, & Landau, 1994). Four classes of mood stabilizers are available: tricyclic antidepressants, novel antidepressants, lithium, and monoamine oxidase inhibitors. The use and research available with regard to these medications varies greatly.

Antidepressants are usually started at a low dose and adjusted until an optimal effect on target behaviors is attained. Throughout the time during which the antidepressant is used, there should be monitoring of both target behaviors and side effects. The range of effective doses of antidepressants varies across medications, diagnoses, and individual differences including the child's size and metabolism. The known side effects are: cardiac complications, impulsivity, psychosis, mania, seizures, high blood pressure, confusion, insomnia/nightmares, rash, tics, tremors, poor coordination, anxiety, and others (Sweeney and others, 1997).

A less-frequently used group of drugs are antipsychotic/neuroleptic medications or major tranquilizers. The desired positive effects of these medications are: increased calmness, and improved behavior and social functioning. There are, however, a limited number of drug trials with children and adolescents using antipsychotic medication (Brown, Dingle, & Landau, 1994). Among children, antipsychotic medications are most commonly used for such developmental disorders as autism and severe aggression, with target symptoms of overactivity, aggression, hallucinations, delusions, and agitation. Possible side effects of these medications are: nausea, drowsiness, dry mouth and nasal congestion, nervousness, rashes, increased appetite, and weight gain.

There are several other medications that are used less frequently with students with learning disabilities or emotional/behavioral disorders. Antihistamines are sometimes prescribed for children and youth with insomnia. Antianxiety agents are very rarely used because few data on the efficacy and safety of using these drugs with children are available. These medications are reserved for times and occasions when other interventions are insufficient, or inadequate (Brown, Dingle, & Landau, 1994). The use of antianxiety agents is discouraged for individuals with attention deficit hyperactivity disorder because they can produce symptoms of excitation and agitation.

Anticonvulsants are generally not the agent of choice for emotional/behavioral disorders and are typically used only when a child has not responded to other medications (Brown, Dingle, & Landau, 1994). Lithium is an effective treatment of bipolar disorder, depression, and severe impulsive aggression (Bukstein, 1992). Clonidine is effective with mood and activity level in some children with attention deficit hyperactivity disorder who are highly aroused, overactive, impulsive, and defiant. It has also been used as a treatment for Tourette syndrome, anxiety and panic disorders, bipolar disorder, psychosis, agitation, and so on (Sweeney and others, 1997). Medications used with children and youth with learning disabilities and emotional/behavioral disorders are presented and summarized in Table 4.1.

Due to the limited quantity and quality of experimental and clinical research on medications being used with children and youth, there are a variety of unresolved medical, legal, and ethical problems.

Table 4.1   Medications Used with Children and Youth with Learning Disabilities and Emotional/Behavioral Disorders.

Medication	Use	Common Side Effects
Antidepressants Tofranil (Imipramine)	Enuresis, Depression	Sedation, dry mouth, constipation, urinary retention
Elavil (Amitriptyline)	Enuresis	Blurred vision, slowed cardiac conduction
Norpramin (desipramine)	ADHD, Depression	Mild tachycardia, elevated blood pressure
Palemor (Noritriptyline)	ADHD, Depression	Weight gain, orthostatic hypotension
Prozac (fluoxetine)	Depression; obsessive compulsive disorder	Anxiety; diarrhea; drowsiness; nausea; trouble sleeping
Antipsychotics Thorazine (chloropmazine)	Acute psychotic states	Sedation, orthostatic hypotension
Mellaril (thioridazine)	Autism, pervasive developmental disorder	Akathisia motor restlessness, Parkinsonian symptoms, cognitive blunting, photosensitivity
Stelazine (trifluperazine)	Tourette's disorder	Sedation, hypotension, headache, upset stomach, insomnia
Stimulants Dexadrine (dextroamphetamine)	ADHD	Insomina, dysphoria, behavioral rebound
Ritalin (methylphenidate)	ADHD	Loss of appetite, weight loss
Cylert (permoline)	ADHD	Weight loss

Table 4.1 *(Continued)*

Antihistamines Benadryl (Diphenhydramine)	Anxiety, insomnia	Dizziness, oversedation, agitation
Atarax (Hydroxyzine)	Sleep disorders, agitation	Blurred vision, abdominal pain
Inderal (Propanolol)	Aggression	Dry mouth
Antianxiety agents Valium (Diazepam)	Seizures, anxiety disorders, behavioral problems	Substance abuse
Anticonvulsants Phenobarbital	Seizures	Memory and attention problems, hyperactivity
Dilantin (Diphenylhydamtoin)	Seizures	Irritability, aggression, depression
Tegretol (carbamazepine)	Aggression, emotional lability, irritability, seizures	Drowsiness, nausea, rash, eye problems
Depakane (valproic acid)	Mania, seizures	Nausea, weight gain, tremors
Other medications Lithium carbonate	Bipolar disorders, aggression	Stomach upset, tremors, headaches
Catapress (Clonidine)	Tourette's disorders, ADHD, aggression	Sedation

(Brown, Dingle, & Landau, 1994; USP-DI, 1994; Sweeney and others, 1997)

Diet

In 1980, the National Advisory Committee on Hyperkinesis and Food Additives issued a position statement that stated that there is no evidence to support the claim that artificial food coloring, artificial flavoring, and salicylate produce hyperactivity and learning disabilities. The Committee suggested that changes which are observed in children's behavior are related to what is called a placebo effect. Even more recent studies have not demonstrated a link between food ingested and problem behavior (Pescara-Kovach & Alexander, 1994).

The Role of the Teacher in Biological Intervention

The teacher plays an important supportive role to the medical personnel in biological interventions. This supportive role includes (a) referral, (b) collaboration with and reporting of observations, (c) modification of classroom structure and curricular content, (d) obtaining permission to administer medication, and (e) safeguarding and administering medication in the school (Shea & Bauer, 1987).

The teacher is not qualified to refer a child directly to a physician, or to suggest the prescribing of medication. However, the educator may inform the parents of a child's behavior problem. The school may initiate contact with medical personnel on behalf of a particular child with parental consent. It is suggested that an educator not directly involved with the child in the school serve as a contact person or intermediary between the teacher and parents during the referral process (Report of the Conference on the Use of Stimulant Drugs, 1971).

A primary role of the educator in biological intervention is the provision of current and objective feedback to the physician on the observable effects of medication on the child's behavior and learning. As previously discussed, the majority of the present-day symptom-control medications are experimental substances whose effects on a particular child cannot be predicted with exactitude. Consequently, feedback to the prescribing physician will assist in efforts to maximize the positive effects and minimize the side effects of medication. Because teachers are trained observers and are with the child throughout the day, they are in an excellent position to observe the effects of the medication and report, through proper channels, to the physician.

During the biological treatment process, especially during the beginning weeks, the child's behavior and learning styles may change significantly. Thus, it may be necessary for the teacher to modify both classroom structure and curricular content to respond to the child's new needs and behavior. Classroom structure may have to be increased or decreased to permit the child to adjust to "new" behaviors and interests. The curriculum may have to be changed to allow the child to learn the knowledge and skills not learned during earlier, less successful programming.

Professional school personnel must obtain permission to dispense medication in the school when medical personnel (a physician or nurse) are not available during the school day. The school should develop a policy with regard to medication in an effort to improve services and minimize personnel liability (Courtnage, Stainback, & Stainback, 1982). A sample permission form for administering medication in the school is presented in Figure 4.1. This form should be modified in consultation with appropriate school administrative, medical, and legal personnel.

When medication is dispensed in the school, these guidelines should be followed:

1. Permission forms should be obtained and filed in the child's permanent record.

2. Medication should be stored in a central location in a locked cabinet. A refrigerator may be needed for some medications.

Student: _____   Birth date: _____

Address: _____   Telephone: _____

School: _____

Physician's Statement:

1. Name/type of medication:
2. Dosage/amount to be administered:
3. Frequency/times to be administered:
4. Duration of order (week, month, indefinitely):
5. Anticipated reaction to medication (symptoms, side effects):

Physician's signature: Date:

Address: Phone:

Parent Request:

I hereby request and give my permission for the designated school staff member to administer the medication prescribed on this form to my child.

Parent's signature: Date:

Comments:

cc: Physician
     Parent
     School

Figure 4.1   Permission form for administration of medication

3. Medication must be properly labeled with the child's and physician's names. The label should include directions for use.
4. Medications should be logged in and out of the school. Medication should be inventoried daily. One professional member of the school's staff, preferably a nurse, should be appointed to inventory medication and function as a contact person in all communications with parents, physicians, pharmacists, and other medical personnel related to medication.
5. A responsible adult must be present when the child takes his or her medication.
6. A log, to be completed each time a child takes medication, should be maintained in the medication area or the child's record file. A sample

Student: Birth date:

Date	Time	Medication/Dosage	Person Dispensing Medication	Notes

Figure 4.2   Medication log

form is presented in Figure 4.2. The completed forms should be re-tained in the child's file.

Children should not be dismissed from school because medical personnel are not immediately available. Following the above suggestions will prevent this from occurring.

Summary Points

- Emerging research in the areas of risk prevention, genetic predisposition, and psychoneurology have renewed interest in biological issues related to learning disabilities and emotional/behavioral disorders.
- Temperament is an individual's style, and may contribute to identification as learning disabled or emotionally/behaviorally disordered.
- Some common biological disorders with which students may be identified as learning disabled or emotionally/behaviorally disordered include Tourette syndrome, attention deficit hyperactivity disorder, obsessive-compulsive disorder, and depression.

Key Words and Phrases

compulsions—repetitive behaviors usually involved with counting, listing, or rearranging objects

executive function—processes which regulate, integrate, and coordinate various cognitive processes to support goal-directed behavior

genetic predisposition—the likelihood that some particular characteristics present in the parents will be present in their child

neurotransmitters—chemicals in the brain which affect the efficiency with which the brain functions

obsessions—unwanted, intrusive, and unpleasant, repeated ideas

temperament—the dimensions of an individual's personality that are largely present at birth, exist in most ages and most societies, are consistent across settings, and are stable as the individual develops

tics—repetitive, recurring, involuntary movements or sounds

References

Alarc'on, M., DeFries, J. C., Ligh, J. G., & Pennington, B. F. (1997). A twin study of mathematics disabilities. *Journal of Learning Disabilities, 30* (6), 617–623.

American Psychiatric Association. (1994). *Diagnostic and statistical manual of mental disorders (4th ed.)*. Washington, DC: Author.

Anderson, D. J. (1993). Identifying the child with Gilles de la Tourette syndrome. *Preventing School Failure, 32*, 25–28.

Armstrong, T. (1996). ADD: Does it really exist? *Kappan, 77* (6), 424–428.

Baldessarini, R. J. (1985). Drugs and the treatment of psychiatric disorders. In A. G. Gilman, L. Goddman, T. W. Rall, & F. Murad, (Eds.), *The pharmacological basis of therapeutics* (pp. 387–446). NY: Macmillan.

Barkley, R. A. (1990). *Hyperactive children: A handbook for diagnosis and treatment*. NY: Guilford Press.

Baumeister, A. A., Kupstas, F., & Klindworth, L. M. (1990). New morbidity: Implications for prevention of children's disabilities. *Exceptionality, 1*, 1–16.

Blumsack, J., Lewandowski, L., & Waterman, B. (1997). Neurodevelopmental precursors to learning disabilities: A preliminary report from a parent survey. *Journal of Learning Disabilities, 30* (2), 228–237.

Brazelton, B. (1983). *Infants and mothers: Differences in development*. NY: Delacorte.

Brewer, V. R., Moore III, B. D., & Hiscock, M. (1997). Learning disabilities subtypes in children with neurofibromatosis. *Journal of Learning Disabilities, 30* (5), 521–533.

Brodsky, M., & Lombroso, P. J. (1998). Molecular mechanisms of developmental disorders. *Development and Psychopathology, 10*, 1–20.

Brookshire, B. L., Butler, I. J., Ewing-Cobbs, L., & Fletcher, J. M. (1994). Neuropsychological characteristics of children with Tourette Syndrome: Evidence for a nonverbal learning disability. *Journal of Clinical and Experimental Neuropsychology, 16* (2), 289–302.

Brown, R. T., Dingle, A., & Landau, S. (1994). Overview of psychopharmacology in children and adolescents. *School Psychology Quarterly, 9* (1), 4–25.

Bukstein, O. (1992). Overview of pharmacological treatment. In V. B. Van Hassalt & M. Hersen, (Eds.), *Handbook of behavior therapy and pharmacotherapy for children* (pp. 213–232). Boston: Allyn & Bacon.

Burd, L., Kauffman, D. W., & Kerbeshian, J. (1992). Tourette syndrome and learning disabilities. *Journal of Learning Disabilities, 25* (9), 598–604.

Buss, A. H., & Plomin, R. (1984). *Temperament: Early developing personality traits*. Hillsdale, NJ: Erlbaum.

Campbell, M., & Cueva, J. E. (1995). Psychopharmacology in child and adolescent psychiatry: A review of the past seven years. Part II. *Journal of the American Academy of Child and Adolescent Psychiatry, 34* (10), 978–987.

Caspi, A., Bem, D. J., & Elder, G. H. (1989). Continuities and consequences of interactional styles across the life course. *Journal of Personality, 57* (2), 375–406.

Cherkes-Julkowski, M. (1998). Learning disability, attention deficit disorder, and language impairment as outcome of prematurity: A longitudinal descriptive study. *Journal of Learning Disabilities, 31* (3), 194–306.

Copps, S. C. (1992). *The attending physician: Attention deficit disorder.* Atlanta, GA: SPI Press.

Courtnage, L., Stainback, W., & Stainback, S. (1982). Managing prescription drugs in school. *Teaching Exceptional Children, 15* (1), 5–10.

Crabbe, J. C., McSwigan, J. D., & Belknap, J. K. (1985). The role of genetics in substance abuse. In M. Galizio & S. A. Maisto, (Eds.), *Determinants of substance abuse* (pp. 13–54). NY: Plenum.

Deitz, J. C., Richardson, P., Crowe, T. K., & Westcott, S. L. (1996). Performance of children with learning disabilities and motor delays on the Pediatric Clinical Test of Sensory Interaction for Balance (P-CTSIB). *Physical and Occupational Therapy in Pediatrics, 16* (3), 1–19.

Forness, S. R., & Kavale, K. A. (1988). Psychopharmacologic treatment: A note on classroom effects. *Journal of Learning Disabilities, 21* (3), 144–147.

Forness, S. R., Kavale, K. A., & San Miguel, S. B. (1998). The psychiatric comorbidity hypothesis revisited. *Learning Disability Quarterly, 21,* 203–206.

Forness, S. R., Swanson, J. M., Cantwell, D. P., Guthrie, D., & Sena, R. (1992). Response to stimulant medication across six measures of school-related performance in children with ADHD and disruptive behaviors. *Behavioral Disorders, 18,* 42–53.

Forness, S. R., Sweeney, D. P., & Toy, K. I.. (1996). Psychopharmacologic medications: What teachers need to know. *Beyond Behavior, 7* (2), 4–11.

Frankel, F., Myatt, R., Cantwell, D., & Feinberg, D. T. (1997). Parent-assisted transfer of children's social skills training: Effects on children with and without attention-deficit disorder. *Journal of the American Academy of Child and Adolescent Psychiatry. 36* (8), 1056–1064.

Greenspan, S. I. (1995). *The challenging child: Understanding, raising, and enjoying the five "difficult" types of children.* Reading, MA: Addison Wesley.

Harris, D., & Silver, A. A. (1995). Tourette's syndrome and learning disabilities. *Learning Disabilities: A Multidisciplinary Journal, 6* (1), 1–7.

Heath, N. L., & Wiener, J. (1996). Depression and nonacademic self-perceptions in children with and without learning disabilities. *Learning Disability Quarterly, 19,* 34–44.

Howell, K. W., Evans, D., & Gardiner, J. (1997). Medication in the classroom: A hard pill to swallow? *Teaching Exceptional Children, 29* (6), 58–61.

Janke, R. W., & Lee, K. (1991). Social skill ratings of exceptional students. *Journal of Psychoeducational Assessment, 9,* 54–66.

Lazar, J. W., & Frank, Y. (1998). Frontal systems dysfunction in children with attention deficit/hyperactivity disorder and learning disabilities. *Journal of Neuropsychiatry and Clinical Neurosciences, 10* (2), 160–167.

Lopez, M., Forness, S. R., MacMillan, D. L., & Bocian, K. M. (1996). Children with attention deficit hyperactivity disorder and emotional or behavioral disorders in primary grades: Inappropriate placement in the learning disorder category. *Education and Treatment of Children, 19* (3), 286–299.

Maag, J. W., Behrens, J. T., & DiGangi, S. A. (1992). Dysfunctional cognitions associated with adolescent depression: Findings across special population. *Exceptionality, 3,* 31–47.

Maag, J. W., & Reid, R. (1994a). The phenomenology of depression among students with and without learning disabilities: More similar than different. *Learning Disabilities Research and Practice, 9* (2) 91–203.

Maag, J. W., & Reid, R. (1994b). Attention-deficit hyperactivity disorder: A functional approach to assessment and treatment. *Behavioral Disorders, 20* (1), 5–23.

Martin, R. P. (1992a). Child temperament effects on special education: Process and outcomes. *Exceptionality, 3,* 99–115.

Martin, R. P. (1992b). Reflections on "Child temperament effects on special education process and outcomes." *Exceptionality, 3,* 127–131.

McConville, B. (1996). Personal communication.

McIntosh, D. E., Dunham, M. D., Dean, R. S., & Kundert, D. K. (1995). Neuropsychological characteristics of learning disabled/gifted children. *Journal of Neuroscience, 83* (1–2), 123–130.

McLoughlin, J. A., & Nall, M. (1994). Allergies and learning/behavioral disorders. *Intervention in School and Clinic, 29* (4), 198–207.

National Advisory Committee on Hyperkinesis and Food Additives. (1980). *Hyperactivity and food additives.* NY: Nutrition Foundation.

National Institute of Mental Health. (1996). *Obsession Compulsive Disorder: National Institute of Mental Health Decade of the Brain.* Washington, DC: Author.

Parker, S., Greer, S., & Zuckerman, B. (1988). Double jeopardy: The impact of poverty on early child development. *The Pediatric Clinics of North America, 35,* 1227–1240.

Paul, S. M. (1980). Sibling resemblance in mental ability: A review. *Behavior Genetics, 10* (3), 277–290.

Peck, M. L. (1985). Crisis intervention with chronically and acutely suicidal adolescents. In M. L. Peck, N. L. Farberow, and R. E. Litman (Eds.). *Youth suicide* (pp. 112–122). NY: Springer-Verlag.

Pescara-Kovach, L. A. & Alexander, K. (1994). The link between food ingested and problem behavior: Fact or fallacy. *Behavioral Disorders, 19,* (2), 142–148.

Plomin, R. (1983). Childhood temperament. In B. Lahey & A. E. Kazdin, (Eds.), *Advances in Clinical Child Psychology* (Vol. 6, pp. 45–92). NY: Plenum.

Read, J. S. (1995, June/July). Ritalin: It's not the teacher's decision. *CEC Today, 2,* 14.

Reid, R., Maag, J. W., Vasa, S. F., & Wright, G. (1994). Who are the children with attention deficit-hyperactivity disorder? A school-based survey. *The Journal of Special Education, 28* (2), 117–137.

Report of the Conference on the Use of Stimulant Drugs in the Treatment of Behaviorally Disordered Young School Children (1971). *Journal of Learning Disabilities, 4,* 523–530.

Riccio, C. A., Gonzalez, J. J., & Hynd, G. W. (1994). Attention deficit hyperactivity disorders (ADHD) and learning disabilities. *Learning Disabilities Quarterly, 17,* 311–322.

Runnheim, V. A., Frankenberger, W. R., & Hazelkorn, M. N. (1996). Medicating students with emotional and behavioral disorders and ADHD: A state survey. *Behavioral Disorders, 21* (4), 306–314.

Shea, T. M., & Bauer, A. M. (1987). *Teaching children and youth with behavior disorders.* Englewood Cliffs, NJ: Prentice Hall.

Sheridan, S. M., Dee, C., Morgan, J. C., & McCormick, M. E. (1996). A multi-method intervention for social skills deficits in children with ADHD and their parents. *School Psychology Review, 25* (1), 57–76.

Slavin, R. E. (1989). Students at risk of school failure: The problem and its dimensions. In R. Slavin, N. Karweit, & N. Madden, (Eds.), *Effective programs for students at risk* (pp. 3–19). Boston: Allyn & Bacon.

Stanford, L. D., & Hynd, G. W. (1994). Congruence of behavioral symptomatology in children with ADD/H, ADD/WO, and learning disabilities. *Journal of Learning Disabilities, 27* (4), 243–253.

Swanson, J. M., Cantwell, D., Lerner, M., McBurnett, K., Pfiffner, L., & Kotkin, R. (1992). Treatment of ADHD: Beyond medication. *Beyond Behavior, 4* (1), 13–16; 18–22.

Sweeney, D. P., Forness, S. R., Kavale, K. A., & Levitt, J. G. (1997). An update on psychopharmacologic medication: What teachers, clinicians, and parents need to know. *Intervention in School and Clinic, 33* (1), 4–21, 25.

Thomas, A., & Chess, S. (1977). *Temperament and Development.* NY: Bruner-Mazel.

USP-DI (United States Pharmaceutical Convention). 1994. *About your medicine: Prozac.* Washington, DC: Author.

Wiener, J. (1998). The psychiatric morbidity hypotheses: A response to San Miguel, Forness, and Kavale. *Learning Disability Quarterly, 21,* 195–201.

Williams, B. F., & Howard, V. F. (1993). Children exposed to cocaine: Characteristics and implications for research and intervention. *Journal of Early Intervention, 17* (1), 61–72.

Wright-Strawderman, C., & Watson, B. L. (1992). The prevalence of depressive symptoms in children with learning disabilities. *Journal of Learning Disabilities, 25* (4), 258–264.

Wright-Strawderman, L. P., Navarette, L., & Flippo, J. R. (1996). Depression in students with disabilities: Recognition and intervention strategies. *Intervention in School and Clinic, 31* (5), 261–275.

5

Cognitive, Language, and Social-Emotional Characteristics

TO GUIDE YOUR READING

After you complete this chapter, you will be able to answer these questions:

- What issues are related to learning styles and identification as learning disabled or emotionally/behaviorally disordered?

- What cognitive and metacognitive issues are related to students with learning disabilities and emotional/behavioral disorders?

- What language and communication issues are related to students with learning disabilities and emotional/behavioral disorders?

- What interpersonal interactions and social skills do students with learning disabilities or emotional/behavioral disorders demonstrate?

◀◆ *Luke's fourth grade teacher, Ms. Renaldo, was very concerned about him. She requested an observation by a peer teacher, Mr. Raj, and had asked that a Student Support Team be assembled to discuss Luke. It was midterm of the first quarter, and Luke had yet to actively participate in class, or, for that matter, speak directly with his teacher. Luke's report cards and portfolio from earlier grades provided information that Luke was a competent student. Ms. Renaldo, enthusiastic to the point of being theatrical at times, felt that Luke was withdrawn, and perhaps depressed. She requested that Mr. Raj, whose interaction style was more reflective and subdued, observe Luke to look at his behavior "through a different pair of glasses."*

Mr. Raj did indeed provide a different view. He observed Luke as a quiet, yet interested observer of the sometimes flamboyant behaviors of his teacher and peers. He noticed that Luke sat and wrote while the other students talked, and that Luke watched when the others blurted out. When the activities required written responses, Luke's were thorough, reflective, and even, at times, witty. During the activities in which Ms. Renaldo and most of the other students reveled, Luke sat there, unsmiling, looking bemused, or even confused.

Mr. Raj was far less concerned about Luke than Ms. Renaldo, and asked her to perform an experiment. He suggested that Ms. Renaldo sit near Luke for a few minutes, and then quietly ask him a question, one-on-one. Mr. Raj felt that Luke was overwhelmed by the activity level in the classroom, and that he may be a watcher rather than a doer. When Ms. Renaldo approached Luke in the subdued manner, he shrugged, but later, he left a note on her desk with a cartoon of the two of them sitting there, Ms. Renaldo large and smiling, with elaborate dangling earrings (her "trademark"), and Luke holding up his hands as if to fend her off. The caption read, "Not so loud! I get it! I get it!" Ms. Renaldo decided to work less diligently at making Luke become involved in the activities, casting him in the role of observer or recorder. Luke began to participate more during class, and provided many insightful responses. By the middle of the second quarter, after the class engaged in activities such as building human pyramids, doing interpretive dances in response to poetry, and putting on theater makeup to express the themes of a story, Ms. Renaldo provided Luke with the role of "commentator." Rather than participating in the activity itself, Luke was the individual who explained the purpose of the activity and summarized the findings. Ms. Renaldo was pleased with the sensitivity of his perceptions, and Luke was pleased not to have to "dance around in a costume."

REFLECTION *How do you react in a group? Are you a student who plunges in, physically engaging in the activity? Are you a student who observes? Are you a student who would rather talk about what is occurring? Or, do you prefer to write? Would you be seen as a "problem" in some classrooms?*

Introduction

As in any description of patterns of characteristics and behavior of a group, when describing students with learning disabilities or emotional/behavioral disorders, one must keep in mind that, as Guild (1994) suggests, "generalizations about a group of people have often led to naive inferences about individuals within the group" (p. 16). The reader is urged to keep in mind that:

- Learners of any particular age vary in their ways of learning.
- Learning styles emerge from both nature and nurture.
- Learning styles are neutral; one learning style is not better than the other, nor are some "good" and others "bad."
- Within a group, differences are as great as similarities (Guild, 1994).

In this chapter, the cognitive, language, and social-emotional characteristics of students with learning disabilities or emotional/behavioral disorders will be explored. The discussion will be built on the assumption that each student is a unique individual, developing within a unique set of developmental contexts.

Issues Related to Learning Styles and Identification

Teachers and researchers often are tempted to link a specific learning style or interaction pattern to identification of a student as learning disabled or emotionally/behaviorally disordered. However, as Sameroff, Selfer, Barocas, Zax, and Greenspan (1987) discuss, no single factor enhances or limits an individual; it is the cumulative effect of multiple risk factors that increases the probability that an individual's emotional and behavioral development will be compromised. A student who prefers a quiet, subdued learning environment may be somewhat less productive with a teacher who is active and physical, yet that alone does not cause an individual to have a learning disability, emotional/behavioral disorder, or other disability.

The Issue of Choice

Weinberg (1992) suggested that students are not considered emotionally/behaviorally disordered because of their beliefs or behaviors. If the student simply disagrees with the normative values and practices of society, then he or she does not demonstrate emotional/behavioral disorders. Rather, emotional/behavioral disorders suggest a lack of freedom, or an inability to choose. The social interactions of an individual identified as emotionally/behaviorally disordered may not be immediately self-manageable by the individual. For example, a child with emotional/behavioral disorders who is withdrawn may desperately want to join the activities at a birthday party, but simply may be unable to enter the group. With prompting, rather than encouragement, the child may become even more withdrawn and threatened. Even though the child wishes he or she were able to enter the group, he or she is unable to choose to do so. Similarly, students with learning disabilities are not "refusing to work," or choosing not to complete their tasks. The least dangerous assumption about students with learning disabilities is, "if they could, they would."

Another, more specific aspect of learning styles relates to how students react at different times of the day. Historically, teachers have completed academic work in the morning, and other activities in the afternoon, because of beliefs about when children are most able to learn. In an ecological analysis, Ysseldyke and Muyskens (1998) found that rather than being dependent on the time of day, student academic behaviors were most often present when the teacher created an environment that included academic activities, active tasks, and individualized instruction. In fact, there was no significant interaction between time of day and student response. In short, when teachers program more individualized instruction time, more activities, and academic tasks, students respond with more academic feedback, and less inappropriate behavior. Environmental factors, then, as well as learning styles, have a high impact on academic responding.

Multiple Intelligences

Learning styles are often described through the concept of multiple intelligences. Gardner (1993) argues that intelligences cannot be conceptualized apart from the context in which individuals live. Rather than taking a unitary view of intelligence, Gardner and Walters (1993) propose that intelligence involves the ability to solve problems, or generate products that are significant to a particular cultural setting or community. This problem-solving skill assists the learner as he or she approaches goal-oriented situations, and helps the learner plan the most appropriate route to the goal. Gardner (1993; Checkley, 1997) offers a list of eight intelligences, which he contends is only preliminary:

- Linguistic intelligence, related to language and communication;
- Logico-mathematical intelligence;
- Naturalistic intelligence, related to the ability to see patterns and sense categories;
- Spatial intelligence, the ability to form a model of the spatial world, and to maneuver and operate using that model.
- Musical intelligence;
- Bodily kinesthetic intelligence, the ability to solve problems or fashion products using the body or parts of the body;
- Interpersonal intelligence, the ability to understand people, motivation, and cooperation;
- Intrapersonal intelligence, the capacity to form an accurate model of oneself, and use that model to operate effectively in life.

Other models of multiple intelligences are emerging. For example, Sternberg (1988) presents a "triarchic model" in which there are three different kinds of intellectual abilities: analytic, creative, and practical. Students who are gifted in each of these different intelligences excel in different activities. Those with strengths in analytic intelligence are strong in analyzing, evaluating, and critiquing. Those who are strong in creative intelligence are good at discovering, creating, and inventing. Students who are strong in practical intelligence are strong in implementing, utilizing, and applying. An expanded list of styles of thinking and learning was presented by Grigorenko and Sternberg (1997), and is shown in Table 5.1.

Hearne and Stone (1995) reviewed research directed toward finding the talents and abilities of students identified as learning disabled, rather than research directed toward locating their deficits. Compared with groups of students who are not learning disabled, research indicates that students with learning disabilities are creative and original, do well in divergent thinking, do as well on measures of musical and visual-artistic talents, and have similar computer skills. Further, in early grades, students with learning disabilities did not differ from peers without identified disability in thematic maturity and vocabulary of written expression. However, mechanical problems did present difficulties. In addition, students with learning disabilities progressed in nontraditional writing programs such as whole language and process writing. Hearne and Stone (1995) suggest that students with learning disabilities may be students who have talents and abilities that do not match the values and expectations of school, and that their learning disabilities possibly have been determined by a deficit-driven model.

Table 5.1 Styles of Thinking and Learning

- Legislative, with strengths in creating, formulating, imagining, and planning;
- Executive, with strengths in implementing and engaging;
- Judicial, with strengths in evaluating and comparing;
- Monarchic, with a preference to address one goal at a time;
- Hierarchic, with the ability to address multiple goals with different priorities at the same time;
- Oligarchic, with the ability to address equally important, multiple goals;
- Anarchic, in which the individual prefers to shun rules, procedures, and formal systems;
- Global, in which the individual deals best with the large picture or abstractions;
- Local, in which the individual prefers details and concrete issues;
- Liberal, in which the student enjoys change and defying conventions;
- Conservative, in which the individual likes traditions and stability;

(Grigorenko and Sternberg, 1997)

Cognitive and Metacognitive Issues

Contemporary research of learning disabilities stems from four major conceptual models: cognitive, cognitive-behavioral, task-analytic, and constructivist (Hallahan, Kauffman & Lloyd, 1996). The cognitive model, sometimes referred to as the information-processing model, emphasizes cognitive activities such as memory, strategies for storage and retrieval, and metacognition. The cognitive-behavior model has adopted features from both cognitive and behavioral research and emphasizes self-awareness and self-control. The constructivist model views learning as a whole where new experiences are integrated with prior learning. The task-analytic model emphasizes actions and behaviors rather than cognitive activities and metacognition. While each model has its unique features, the emphases of the various models overlap somewhat, and agree concerning the acquisition and broad use of strategies (Hallahan, Kauffman, & Lloyd, 1996). While not all students with learning disabilities experience cognitive problems, a significant number of them manifest problems related to cognitive factors, to some degree (Hallahan, Kauffman, & Lloyd, 1996). Some students with learning disabilities may, in fact, be gifted, and face additional challenges for intervention (Robinson, 1999).

In a review of the research of cognition and learning disabilities, Swanson (1999) suggests that since the mid-1970s, variations in cognitive performance of individuals with learning disabilities have been researched from the perspective of strategy development. The term strategy refers to the conscious application of procedures used for storing and retrieving information, and for problem solving.

Using analyses of records of verbalizations of individuals during the problem solving process, Newell and Simon (1972) described cognition as an information-processing system that evaluates alternative solutions. Using this model, Swanson (1988) found that children with and without learning disabilities were comparable in mental processing. Children without learning disabilities, however, seemed to use more task specific strategies, while children with learning disabilities used a more general approach to problem solving. This research suggests that students with learning disabilities may be constrained by their inefficient use of strategies.

The Role of Memory

Students with learning disabilities have memory problems which persist throughout their lives (O'Shaughnessy & Swanson, 1998). When compared to age peers without learning disabilities, O'Shaughnessy and Swanson concluded that students with learning disabilities did not perform as well on memorization of verbal materials as they did on visual-spatial information. Students with learning disabilities had difficulty remembering letters, words, numbers, and unfamiliar terms, and their memory on serial recall tasks was quite poor. The researchers concluded that students with learning disabilities may have difficulty representing, storing, or retrieving verbal information in their memories.

Several models have been used to research the memory processes of children with learning disabilities. Memory is not a unified concept. Shallice (1979) describes the process of memory as involving three distinctive memory stores: working memory, short-term memory, and long-term memory.

Working memory.   Incoming information is held briefly and selected for future processing in working memory. Information held in working memory is either transferred to short-term memory, or is rapidly replaced by incoming information. In working memory, information is simultaneously stored and processed.

Swanson (1988) summarizes working memory from the perspective of Baddeley and Hitch (1974) and Baddeley (1986) as being both a processing and storage system, while short-term memory is more passive, and deals mostly with information storage. Further, working memory is a central executive process that interacts with two passive storage units—the speech-based articulatory unit, and the visual sketch pad. The function of the executive is to coordinate information. According to Swanson, research in the area of working memory indicates: (a) that strategies play less of a role in learning and memory than previously believed, (b) that working memory is an active system directed by a central executive, and can be a focus of instruction, and (c) that working memory processes are related to achievement.

Short-term memory.   Short-term memory is brief and of limited capacity, usually limited to five to nine items. Short-term memory holds segments of information that can be maintained in memory if the information is restructured by a strategy such as rehearsal or item association (Ashbaker and Swanson, 1996). Short-term memory may be unstable and lost unless transferred to long-term memory, the relatively permanent storage of information.

Information in short-term memory can be coded by sound or meaning. Research has indicated that difficulty in short-term memory of individuals with learning disabilities may be related to the lack or inefficient use of the sound code in the student's mind. For example, good readers are bothered when words sound alike because they process words in sound units; poorer readers are not disrupted by sound-alike words. Further, problems in sound coding may characterize younger children with learning disabilities more than older children with learning disabilities. Older students with learning disabilities may use a sound coding system, but demonstrate other memory problems. Research on coding by meaning is inconclusive, but it seems that children with a reading disability rely on semantic coding more than typical readers (Swanson, 1999).

In their meta-analysis of 41 research studies on short-term memory, O'Shaughnessy and Swanson (1998) found that reading students with learning disabilities have weaknesses in immediate recall that are not exhibited by peers with comparable general intelligence without identified disabilities. Unfortunately, they also found that memory problems in students with learning disabilities did not improve with age. They concluded that memory problems of students with learning disabilities are correlated to their reading disabilities, and that group differences show that, in reading, students with learning disabilities not only have memory problems, but are less likely to use strategies to facilitate memory.

Ashbaker and Swans (1996) differentiated short-term memory and working memory as they relate to learning disabilities. They found that students with learning disabilities performed more poorly on both short-term memory and working memory tasks than their peers without identified disabilities. A student's ability on working memory tasks was a primary predictor of his or her reading proficiency. They determined that a focus on short-term memory or working memory in isolation is not adequate for studying the reading performance of adolescents with learning disabilities.

In a series of studies, Swanson (1994a, 1994b) further explored issues of short-term and working memory. Contrasting students with and without learning disabilities, Swanson concluded that short-term memory and working memory are both important to understanding the performance of individuals with learning disabilities in the areas of reading comprehension and mathematics. However, working memory was more important for students without learning disabilities in task completion. Swanson hypothesized that as students without learning disabilities use their working memory to access variables such as the recall of words in a phrase, or for literal comprehension, while students with learning disabilities rely on short-term memory and higher order cognitive processes for those same tasks (Swanson, 1994a). When contrasted to students identified as "slow-learning," underachieving, and typically achieving, students with mathematics learning disabilities improved their verbal working memory during dynamic assessment. The students with learning disabilities demonstrated poorer working memory than typically achieving students, but better working memory than "slow-learners." Because of this, Swanson (1994b) suggests that dynamic assessment may better assess the learning potential of students with learning disabilities.

Long-term memory.   Long-term memory is the permanent storage of information and has unlimited capacity. Storage is accomplished by links, associations and organizational strategies. While there has been little research concerning individuals with learning disabilities, it seems that they select less efficient strategies, perform a less exhaustive search, and utilize self-checking skills less frequently (Swanson, 1999).

Though the various aspects of memory have been studied regarding students with learning disabilities, research has not addressed memory issues of students with emotional/behavioral disorders.

The Role of Metacognition

Learning and remembering use three knowledge systems, according to Brown (1975): (a) knowing, (b) knowing about knowing (metacognition), and (c) knowing how to know. This model recognizes that, (a) different tasks have different memory demands, (b) applying strategies is key to learning and remembering, and (c) strategies change as children develop. Flavell (1976) describes "knowing about knowing" as metacognition, an awareness of one's knowledge and how one thinks. Further, metacognition deals with the self-regulation that is actively used to monitor and solve problems (Scott, 1999). This model led researchers to examine the use of metacognitive strategies of students with learning disabilities. Research on the metacognitive (e.g., monitoring, evaluating, and regulating) skills of students with learning disabilities indicates they are less aware of efficient metacognitive strategies (Swanson, 1999).

According to Swanson (1999), strategies may not explain the cognition of children with learning disabilities, and research does not support that strategy instruction necessarily eliminates differences between children with and without learning disabilities. Strategies are complicated, and they may be affected by motivation, self-attribution, and perceived self-efficacy.

Motivation

Dev (1997) defines intrinsic motivation as "(a) participation in an activity purely out of curiosity, that is, from the need to know more about something . . . ; (b) the desire to engage in an activity purely for the sake of participating in and completing a task . . . ; and (c) the desire to contribute" (p. 12). In terms of intrinsic academic motivation, Wilson and William (1994) reported that, through the use of two measures of social perception, students with learning disabilities perceive school environment and academic learning tasks as two separate factors. Students exhibited more positive attitudes towards the school environment than toward academic learning tasks.

When contrasting students with and without learning disabilities, Pintrich, Anderman, and Klobucar (1994) reported that though students with learning disabilities were less aware of the reading strategies they used, they did not differ from their peers without identified disabilities on self-efficacy, intrinsic orientation, or anxiety. The students with learning disabilities had a somewhat more positive attributional style, and tended to attribute problems in reading to bad luck or not getting assistance. On the whole, students with learning disabilities were likely to attribute both overall success and failure to external factors.

Self-concept

In comparing typically achieving students to students with learning disabilities, Bear and Minke (1996) reported that students with learning disabilities, (a) perceived themselves to be more forgetful and more likely to have difficulty solving problems; (b) showed no indication of perceiving themselves as any less "smart" than their peers, or any less competent in school work; (c) did not perceive themselves as doing as well as their peers in class performance; and (d) judged their classwork favorably. In a subsequent study, Minke, Griffin, and Deemer (1998) explored the ability of students with learning disabilities to focus on positive indicators of academic performance (i.e., grades and teacher comments) while still being aware of their learning difficulties. Students with learning disabilities used teacher feedback as the best indicator of reading satisfaction in the third through the sixth grade, though social comparison with peers contributed significantly during the sixth grade. Perceived teacher feedback, as it related to reading satisfaction, contributed significantly to students' reported self-worth.

Many students with learning disabilities have less positive self-concepts (Abrams, 1986). Learning disabilities may, in themselves, lead to emotional distress due to anxiety, low academic self-concept, and frustrated attempts to cope. These emotional concerns may then intensify the learning disability, pushing the student to escape from school, or have difficulties with home behavior (Gorman, 1999). Variables which may contribute to the self-concept of students with learning disabilities were further explored by Hagborg (1996). Variables such as socioeconomic status, intelligence, achievement, and grades are traditional markers for school success among students without identified disabilities. However, these same variables were found to be less important for students with learning disabilities. Hagborg did not find differences in self-concept related to lower socioeconomic status, age at classification, or extent of participation in special education.

The impact of placement on the self-concept of students with learning disabilities has been explored. Montgomery (1994), in her review of the literature, concluded that students with learning disabilities in segregated special education classrooms tend to have similar global self-concepts as their peers without identified disabilities, while students with learning disabilities in general education classrooms tend to have poorer global self-concepts. In nonacademic domains such as social, physical, affective, and home/family, students with learning disabilities did not differ in self-reports from their peers without learning disabilities, or students who are gifted and talented. When comparing teacher and parent ratings, Montgomery reported that teachers tended to underestimate the self-concepts of students with learning disabilities, and overestimated the self-concepts of high-achieving students. Parents of students with learning disabilities, or high achieving students, tended to match their children's ratings. Smith and Nagle (1995) reported however, that though students with learning disabilities may perceive themselves as less competent than their peers in academic skills, behavior, and social acceptance, these perceptions were not related to the amount of time the students received special education services.

Attention

Though attention deficit hyperactivity disorder was discussed in Chapter Four, due to the biological nature of that disorder, students with attention deficit hyperactivity disorder (inattention, impulsivity, and difficulties in rule-governed behavior) have problems that are cognitive in nature (DuPaul, Guevremont, & Barkley, 1991). Problems with attention also occur in students with a wide variety of other disabilities (DuPaul and Stoner, 1994). Samuels (1987) delineates attention into five areas: (a) overt attention such as looking at the teacher during a lesson, (b) arousal as a state of attentiveness from low arousal during sleep to high arousal that may be caused by stress or agitation, (c) alertness (readiness to perform), (d) vigilance (maintenance of attention or sticking to a task), and (e) selective attention, which is the ability to separate out irrelevant information (e.g., background noise) from a stimulus to focus on relevant information.

Although students with learning disabilities are generally referred for special education services due to academic difficulties, a study by Kavale and Reese (1992) indicated that 13% of their study population were referred for attention problems. For example, research indicates that students with learning disabilities are perceived as being distractible due to difficulty with vigilance and selective attention (Bender, 1995; Pelham, 1981). Further, some students with learning disabilities are considered to be impulsive (Bender & Wall, 1994). They may respond quickly without appropriate reflection. It is difficult to determine the exact nature of the attentional problems because of the lack of reliable and valid measures (Mercer, 1997).

Intelligence

The tested intelligence quotients of students with learning disabilities, as a group, tend to fall in the low–average range (Bender, 1999). There are, however, individuals who are both gifted and have learning disabilities, and who may resent the interventions designed to address their learning disabilities (Robinson, 1999). The tested intelligence quotients of students with emotional/behavioral disorders, as a group, also tend to be in the low–average range, with individual students scoring from the severe mental retardation range to the superior range (Duncan, Forness, & Hartsough, 1995). Although the majority of students with emotional/ behavioral disorders test with a slightly below-average intelligence quotient, a disproportionate number, compared to the normal distribution, score in the low–average and mild mental retardation range, and relatively few fall in the upper ranges (Kauffman, 1997). Prior and Werry (1986) suggest that the tested intelligence quotient appears to be the best single predictor of educational achievement, and the later adjustment, of students with emotional/behavioral disorders.

Language and Communication Issues

Humans interact in a variety of ways, and in turn, these interactions (social transactions) affect those around them. Social transactions can be categorized into three dimensions: language, speech, and communication (McLaughlin, 1998).

Definitions of language usually share several key elements (Nelson, 1998). Language is a socially-shared code that uses a conventional system of arbitrary symbols to represent ideas about the world, and that have meaning to others who know the same code (Nelson, 1998, p. 26). Two taxonomies may be used to describe language (Nelson, 1998). First, the scientific taxonomy, which artificially dissects language into five components: phonology, morphology, syntax, semantics, and pragmatics (McLaughlin, 1998). These categories are useful for both assessment and intervention (Nelson, 1998). The second taxonomy is a set of categories proposed by Bloom and Lahey (1978), and it includes form, content, and use. This categorization is useful when discussing language difficulties with teachers and parents (Nelson, 1998). The two taxonomies can be integrated into three components: (a) form, i.e., phonology, morphology, and syntax; (b) content, i.e., semantics; and (c) use, i.e., pragmatics. Various aspects of language are presented in Table 5.2.

Typically, language is expressed through speech. Nelson (1998) explains that speech is distinguished from language because it is a behavior and can be observed. Language is knowledge that is represented in the brains of people who know the language, but it cannot be observed directly. Communication is the sharing of needs, experiences, ideas, thoughts, and feelings (Wood, 1976). Speech is the oldest and most prevalent means of communication, however, much communication occurs without using speech through other means such as writing, sign language, Morse code, mime, dance, and art (McLaughlin, 1998; Nelson, 1998).

In addition to the linguistic feature of language, there is a sociolinguistic perspective. The sociolinguistic feature refers to socially defined

Table 5.2 Aspects of Language

Phonology	The study of speech sound elements classified at two levels: phones (individual sound productions) and phonemes (groups of similar sounds).
Morphology	The study of the smallest meaningful units of language. A morpheme can be a word or part of a word. A morpheme is: (1) at least one phoneme, though not all phonemes are morphemes (e.g., the word "I"); (2) at least one syllable, though not all syllables are morphemes; and (3) a word, though not all morphemes are words (e.g., past tense indicated by "ed").
Syntax	The study of the sequence and order of words to form phrases and sentences.
Semantics	The study of word meanings and word relations.
Pragmatics	The study of the practical use of language in social interaction. Pragmatics may be considered the heart of communication because it analyzes the speaker's achievement of a practical outcome by using language as a tool.

(McLaughlin, 1998)

linguistic structures and contextual features (Ervin-Tripp & Mitchell-Kernan, 1977). The sociolinguistic perspective tenets include the following:

1. Natural conversations, rather than contrived tasks, are used to learn about the nature of language and communication.

2. Discourse structures, rather than sentences, are treated as the highest level.

3. Social context, beyond the linguistic structure of sentences, is recognized as influencing how language is interpreted.

4. Variability is viewed as a systematic component of linguistic rules, including those of phonology and grammar, and it appears to be related not only to linguistic context, but also to social features such as sex, age, and setting.

5. Language functions are viewed as diverse, rather than merely representational, in that functions are related to cultural and developmental expectations (Ervin-Tripp & Mitchell-Kernan, 1977).

The sociolinguistic perspective helps us recognize the variability of language difficulties exhibited by children, and the importance of context. It also influences assessment and intervention. For example, if a child has difficulty communicating, we should ask whether a child has sufficient reason for communicating. If not, interventions should encourage authentic reasons and facilitate opportunities for communicating. In addition, the language development of children relative to their cultures should be considered. While it may not be possible to have a full understanding of every language and culture, teachers and other professionals should at least recognize that some rules differ in cultures and languages. Bilingualism is an important issue in modern society. A common approach by language specialists and language textbooks is that all children should learn standard English. However, it cannot be assumed that a child's primary language is matched with his or her cultural heritage (Taylor & Payne, 1983). It is imperative, therefore, that language variation should be explained as language difference rather than language disorder.

Language Ability and Communicative Competence

Communicative competence occurs when information is successfully transmitted between persons or groups. Competence requires that the sender's behavior is relevant to the topic or situation, and that there is a particular effect on the receiver (e.g., indication of understanding) (McLaughlin, 1998). Further, communicative competence is comprised of the communicative knowledge that individual members of a cultural group need to be able to interact with one another in both socially appropriate and strategically effective ways (Schultz, Florio, & Erickson, 1982).

Students with learning disabilities.   Studies have examined the differences in syntax, morphology, phonology, semantics, and pragmatics and their relationship to reading, writing, and oral language of education (Gerber, 1993). Students with reading disabilities are likely to be deficient in phonological awareness. Phonological awareness is not only the awareness of sound segments, but includes the ability to manipulate sound segments (Blachman, 1994).

Some children with learning disabilities have difficulty with parts of word endings that are difficult to hear such as the plural "s," or past tense "ed" (Wiig, 1990). As a result, these children may demonstrate morphological difficulties in acquiring rules for grammar such as plurals, possessives, past tense, comparative and superlative forms of adjectives, and prefixes. These difficulties may emerge in oral language, as well as reading comprehension and written expression.

Because of problems with syntax, students with learning disabilities often generate shorter, less complex sentences, and make more grammatical errors (Vogel, 1974; Simms & Crump, 1983). These learners may also experience difficulty in comprehending complex sentences. Again, such specific linguistic difficulties may contribute to problems in reading and writing (Kuder, 1997).

In a review of research concerning semantic problems of individuals with learning disabilities, Gerber (1993) summarizes several of the challenges facing these students. They may have a limited vocabulary, restrictions in understanding word meanings, problems with multiple word meanings, an inability to understand figurative language, a tendency to excessively use nonspecific terms (e.g., stuff), impoverished schematic knowledge, trouble with word retrieval, difficulty understanding and producing questions, and a struggle with processing oral directions. Gerber (1993) points out that there are both delays and problems in the development of enriched word meanings for many individuals with learning disabilities. She suggests that there may be complex relationships between the variations of language problems for these learners. For example, because vocabulary growth is stimulated by reading, it is possible that reading difficulties not only reflect, but also contribute to, semantic deficiencies.

In pragmatic content, students with learning disabilities may have difficulty analyzing and appropriately responding to social situations (Bryan, 1991). Research in this area has focused primarily on the conversational skills of these students (Kuder, 1997). For example, students with learning disabilities may exhibit conversational difficulty by asking fewer open-ended questions, and by giving conversational partners fewer opportunities to discuss a topic in detail (Bryan, Donahue, Pearl, & Sturm, 1981). Further, students with learning disabilities may have difficulty adjusting their own language to that of their conversational partner. For example, they may have difficulty distinguishing appropriate language for a good friend as opposed to a teacher (Bryan & Pflaum, 1978; Donahue, 1981). Because students with learning disabilities may have difficulty expressing themselves clearly to others, adjusting their language to fit their listening audience, and knowing what to do when they do not comprehend what is being said to them (Kuder, 1997), these problems in pragmatics may affect both classroom and social interactions.

The relationship between difficulties in pragmatics and social interactions has been demonstrated by Haratas and Donahaue (1997) through role-playing scenarios. Students with learning disabilities generated fewer total advice statements in role play about siblings' or classmates' problems, and were less likely to agree, and more likely to disagree, with advice offered by others. These students appeared less aware of the metacognitive structure of conversations, and were less likely to propose effective solutions than their peers.

Students with Emotional/Behavioral Disabilities

Critical relationships exist between language facility, emotional functioning, and behavioral regulation (Gallagher, 1999). Several research studies, ratings, and reports suggest that 40–70% of students with emotional/behavioral disorders have language problems (Baker & Cantwell, 1982; Beitman, Nair, Clegg, Ferguson, & Patel, 1986; Gualtieri, Koriath, Van Bourgondien, & Saleeby, 1983; Prizant et al., 1990). These problems may go unrecognized. However, communication difficulties may surface during classroom and social interactions (Keefe & Hoge, 1996). These problems, which impede communicative competence, include listening, following directions, comprehending assignments, conversational skills, an inability to express feelings appropriately, and a reliance on behavioral actions or facial expressions to communicate intent rather than linguistic forms, which these individuals may be incapable of using (Hummel & Prizant, 1993; Kaufman, Swan, & Wood, 1979).

The expressive language characteristics in the conversations of students identified as emotionally/behaviorally disordered has been compared to their peers who have not been identified as such. Students with emotional/behavioral disorders were found to make more errors in relationships, demonstrate poor topic maintenance, make inappropriate responses, and use situationally inappropriate language (McDonough, 1989). Among students identified as demonstrating mild to moderate emotional/behavioral disorders, Camarata, Hughes, and Ruhl (1988) found that 97 percent were a minimum of one standard deviation below the mean on a measure of language ability. Adolescents in psychiatric placement were found to be significantly less effective in communication than their peers not identified with disorders (Rosenthal & Simeonsson, 1991). Students with emotional/behavioral disorders in residential treatment had significant language disabilities (Warr-Leeper, Wright, & Mack, 1994). They also exhibited difficulties with nonverbal communication. In a study of the facial affect cues of adolescents, Walker and Leister (1994) reported that adolescents with emotional/behavioral disorders are generally less accurate than peers not identified with such disorders, in recognizing facial affect cues of happiness, sadness, fear, anger, surprise, and disgust.

Challenges in communicative competence have been suggested to indeed be the basis of many behavioral problems (Carr and Durand, 1985; Vallance, Cummings, & Humphries, 1998). The literature on normal development suggests that as communicative competence increases, behavior problems decrease. Carr and Durand suggest that working with students on communicative strategies could have the effect of replacing behavioral problems. Gallagher (1999) contends all students with emotional/behavioral disorders should be routinely screened for language, and that a team-intervention approach with the active involvement of a communication specialist should be used.

Interpersonal Interaction and Social Skills

Students with disabilities may not have the same social status, or engage in the same social interactions, as their peers. In an inclusive setting, Sale and Carey (1995) used positive and negative peer nominations to study the social status of students with disabilities. Students with disabilities were found to have significantly lower social-preference scores, and significantly higher social-impact scores than their general education peers. Of all the students with disabilities, those with emotional/ behavioral disorders had the lowest scores. In addition, students with emotional/behavioral disorders had the most "least-liked" nominations. In another inclusive setting study, Vaughn, Elbaum, and Schumm (1996) reported that students with learning disabilities and other low-achieving students were less well accepted than their average or high-achieving peers. A study that included students with learning disabilities in sixth and seventh grades, found that these students received the fewest positive votes in a forced-choice sociogram, and girls with learning disabilities received the fewest positive votes, and the most negative votes (Conderman, 1995).

Though they may not have the same social status, students with learning disabilities or emotional/behavioral problems need the same levels of social support as other students. Wenz-Gross and Siperstein (1997) reported that students with learning problems turned to home members more for emotional support, and less for problem-solving support than students without learning problems. Both students with and without learning problems turn to their peers for companionship more than for either social support or help in solving problems. Wenz-Gross and Siperstein found no differences between students with and without learning problems on the negative qualities of friendships. However, students with learning problems had fewer positive features in friendships than students without learning problems. Students with learning problems had less intimacy, loyalty, self-esteem, and contact in their friendships. Even though they were sometimes viewed negatively by peers, students with learning problems have people to whom they feel close, and who are important to them. Wenz-Gross and Siperstein reported that classroom environments which were high in friction and low in cohesiveness negatively influenced the behavior adjustment of both children with and without learning problems.

Both students with learning disabilities and students with emotional/behavioral disorders are viewed as varying from their peers in social interactions. Handwerk and Marshall (1998) reported that students with learning disabilities had the same behavioral problems as students with emotional/behavioral disorders, differing in terms of the severity of problems, rather than types of problems. Smith (1995) suggests, however, that among students with learning disabilities, the failure to demonstrate the appropriate behavior may be more frequent than the presentation or engagement of overtly antisocial behavior. Rather, Smith contends, students with learning disabilities may either have a "skill-based" problem, in which the student has not yet learned the behavior, or a "performance-based" problem, in which the student has acquired the skill, but does not yet perform it at an acceptable level.

Social Competence

Social competence is comprised of (a) positive relations with others, (b) age-appropriate social cognition, (c) absence of maladaptive behaviors, and (d) effective social skills (Vaughn and Hogan, 1994). To better understand the social competence of students with learning disabilities, Vaughn and associates (Vaughn & Hogan, 1994; Vaughn & Haager, 1994) followed a cohort of students with learning disabilities for six years (from kindergarten through fifth grade), and contrasted the students in the group identified with learning disabilities to students identified as low-achieving, average-achieving, and high-achieving. Students with learning disabilities did not differ from students who were low-achieving on any measure of social competence. Students with learning disabilities resembled students who were low-achieving during kindergarten and first grade, and students who were average- and high-achieving in second and third grade. The self-concept of students in all of the groups was similar. Students with learning disabilities differed from average-achieving and high-achieving students in behavioral problems and social skills. Vaughn and Hogan (1994) determined that examining social competence at any one interval is not necessarily a good indicator of a student's social competence over time. Rather, three patterns of social competence development emerge. Some students exhibit consistent competence, some exhibit early problem resolution, and some demonstrate lingering/inconsistent difficulties.

Both students with learning disabilities and low-achieving students have some difficulties with social functioning, but these difficulties are not present in all settings (Haager and Vaughn, 1995). Haager and Vaughn (1995) suggest that there is no clear explanation for lower peer acceptance of students with learning disabilities or low-achieving students, and they hypothesize that negative peer reactions may reflect problems in social skills and behavior, or that teachers' negative perceptions may influence peer evaluation. Students with learning disabilities may also be less well known by their classmates, increasing their problems with social functioning.

In another set of comparisons of student functioning, Tur-Kaspa & Bryan (1995) studied teacher judgment of social competence and school adjustment for students with learning disabilities, low-achieving students, and average-achieving students. Teachers rated younger average-achieving students significantly higher in social competence and school adjustment than students categorized as having learning disabilities or being low achieving. Though there were no significant differences between teacher ratings of the younger students with learning disabilities or low achievement, a higher percentage of students with learning disabilities was considered at risk for social competence and school adjustment problems. Interestingly, no difference in teacher ratings was found between the groups at the seventh/eighth grade level. In terms of student self-perceptions,

Smith and Nagle (1995) reported that students with learning disabilities perceived themselves as less competent than comparison groups with regard to social acceptance.

A definitive statement about the peer acceptance of students with learning disabilities is difficult to make; some are accepted, some are neglected, and some are rejected (Conderman, 1995). In a comparison of social status of sixth and seventh grade students with and without learning disabilities, Conderman (1995) found that, as a group, students with learning disabilities received fewer positive votes, more negative votes, and fewer attractive and athletic votes on a forced-choice sociogram. As a group, girls with learning disabilities received the fewest positive votes, and the most negative votes. However, using two separate social classification systems, about half of the students with learning disabilities held at least an average social status.

Kavale and Forness (1996) used meta-analysis methods to evaluate 152 studies on the social skills of students with learning disabilities. Their findings suggest that about three-fourths of all students with learning disabilities have social skills problems that distinguish them from their peers. The lack of perceived academic competence on the part of the students with learning disabilities may be a significant factor in their social skills problems. According to teachers and peers, perceived academic in-

A lack of perceived academic competence may contribute to social skills problems.

competence seemed to be related to less interaction, reduced acceptance, greater rejection, and lower social status of students with learning disabilities. Negative evaluations may also be related to a perceived lack of communicative competence, and a reduced ability to demonstrate empathic behavior. Kavale and Forness point out that research studies lack information concerning how perception, memory, cognition, and language interact to influence social skills. The origin of social skills problems of students with learning disabilities remains unanswered.

Students with language-based learning disabilities are particularly at risk for problem behaviors according to Vallance, Cummings, and Humphries (1998). In a study of the independent and relative influence of social discourse and social skills on the problem behavior of children with and without identified language learning disabilities, they found that students with language learning disabilities have far more problems with social discourse. Teachers rated these students as having significantly less ability in social discourse and social skills, and more as having problem behaviors, than their peers without identified disabilities. Vallance and associates suggest that the problems in communicative competence of some children with learning disabilities may contribute to their poor social skills, and may be ultimately manifested in more serious emotional/behavioral disorders.

Dimitrovsky, Spector, Levy-Shift, and Vakil (1998) studied the ability of students with learning disabilities to interpret facial expressions. Students without learning disabilities were found to have far better interpretation ability than their peers with learning disabilities. Among the students with learning disabilities, those with verbal deficits had better interpretive ability than those with nonverbal deficits, or both verbal and nonverbal deficits. Older students did better than younger students; no gender differences were noted. Dimitrovsky and associates conclude that students with learning disabilities may be at greater risk for social problems because of their difficulty with this important aspect of social perception. In terms of interpersonal understanding, students with learning disabilities had significantly more difficulty than their peers without identified disabilities (Kravetz, Faust, Lipshitz, & Shalhav, 1999).

Loneliness and Isolation

Difficulty with social situations may also be related to feelings of loneliness and isolation. Tur-Kaspa, Wesel, and Segev (1998) compared the causal attributions of students with learning disabilities for their feelings of loneliness with those of students without identified disabilities. The students with learning disabilities reported significantly more situations in which they felt lonely. Both students with and without learning disabilities had similar levels of an unpleasant emotional state associated with lonesome situations. Different situations triggered loneliness in students with learning disabilities. Students with learning disabilities were more likely to report status as a newcomer, or a lack of social relationships, than their peers without identified disabilities who were more likely to report difficulties in relationships with the opposite sex as triggers for feelings of loneliness. Tur-Kaspa and associates suggest that this difference may indicate a developmental difference between the two groups with respect to social relationships, with students with learning disabilities being less mature. Both groups of students reported social rejection and objective circumstances as situations which triggered the most feelings of loneliness. Students with learning disabilities had significantly higher expectations of feelings of loneliness in the future, though there was no difference between the groups in their sense of being able to control or change unpleasant situations. Students with learning disabilities were rated lower than their peers on sociometric scales, and teachers rated students with learning disabilities as having more externalizing behavioral problems than students without learning disabilities. In a study of preschool children with learning disabilities, Margalit (1998) also reported high levels of loneliness, and fewer reciprocal nominations, on sociometric instruments.

When considering internalizing and externalizing behavior and loneliness, Margalit and Leving-Alyagon (1994) reported that students who only had difficulties in academic areas demonstrated age-appropriate social adjustment. However, students who were identified as lonely with internalizing behaviors had the highest level of self-reported loneliness, and they perceived themselves as having poor social competence and little acceptance from their peers. Lonely students with externalizing behaviors had the lowest self-management skills, and were not accepted by their peers. These students were aware of their social problems and desired friendships, yet were unable to control their frustration and anger.

"Externalizing" problems, such as overactivity, aggression, and impulsivity are, perhaps, the most obvious interpersonal interactions and social skills which discriminate students identified as emotionally/behaviorally disordered from their peers not so identified. Students with these problems are often referred to as "hard to manage" (Campbell & Ewing, 1990). Though overactivity and defiance among two- and three-year-old children may be age-appropriate signs of developmental transition, high levels of overactivity and failing to follow directions may be an indicator of more significant challenges, and the potential to be identified as emotionally/behaviorally disordered, in the future (Campbell & Ewing, 1990; Campbell, Pierce, March, Ewing, & Szumowski, 1994). Family stress, overactivity, and inattention observed of a three-year-old child in a clinical laboratory were found to be good predictors of teacher ratings of hyperactivity and impulse control when the child reaches age nine (Campbell & Ewing, 1990). Adults' reports of hard-to-manage behavior in preschool-age boys often reflect actual interaction patterns of overactivity, impulsivity, noncompliance, and aggression, which are likely to lead to identification of the child as emotionally/behaviorally disordered (Campbell and associates, 1994).

Aggression

Aggression and violent acts have become more frequent in public schools (Myles & Simpson, 1998). Though challenging for teachers and students, aggression typically does not occur without warning. Myles and Simpson (1998) contend that there are usually four stages in aggressive behavior. First, the student becomes frustrated. Second, the student becomes defensive. This is followed by an aggressive act in the third stage. Finally, the student regains self-control.

Using a direct observation procedure, Wehby, Symons, and Shores (1995) found low overall rates of positive social interactions in the daily classroom ecology of aggressive students. Though there were no significant differences in the rates of teacher instructions toward somewhat-aggressive, and highly-aggressive students, the highly-aggressive students received almost three times as many statements regarding the consequences of their behavior than did the somewhat aggressive students. This may be due to the fact that highly-aggressive students engaged in significantly higher rates of teacher-directed yelling, noncompliance, and other physical behaviors than their less aggressive peers. In peer interactions, highly-aggressive students engage in negative verbal behavior and physical aggression approximately ten times more often than their low-aggressive peers. They also received more threats from others. Rates of teacher praise toward highly-aggressive students were found to be very low, and accounted for only a small proportion of antecedents and consequences of the students' aggression.

The peers of boys identified as emotionally/behaviorally disordered characterized them as demonstrating significantly more aggression, disruption, and poor cooperation. Within their social networks, boys identified as emotionally/behaviorally disordered in the third through sixth grades formed social affiliations with groups which, though comprised of both identified and nonidentified students with emotional/behavioral disorders, exhibited higher levels of peer-assessed aggression and disruption. They also exhibited lower levels of peer-assessed cooperation, leadership, and appropriate academic performance than did the members of other social groups in the same classes (Farmer & Hollowell, 1994).

In his review of the literature, Safran (1995) concluded that peers hold negative views of externalizing behavior problems among fellow students. Younger students can identify aggression in their peers as early as the first grade, and social withdrawal is recognized soon thereafter.

Among students identified as emotionally/behaviorally disordered who have attention deficit hyperactivity disorder, social interaction patterns have been described as having high rates of intrusive behaviors, problems in conversation and reciprocity, and poor emotional regulation. These students may be in a "catch 22" circumstance, i.e., positive peer relations play a prominent role in the development of self-control of aggressive impulses, feelings of acceptance and belonging, value, self-esteem, and communication skills. Students identified with emotional/behavioral disorders may not receive, as a consequence of their behavior, the needed positive peer relations that would help them learn to better manage their social behavior (Guevremont & Dumas, 1994).

Passive Aggression

Aggression by students is perceived by teachers to be threatening. However, many teachers indicate that the most difficult students with whom they work are those who are passive-aggressive. Passive-aggressive students resist control by others to the extent that they simply cannot allow themselves to be cooperative (Fisher, Osterhaus, Clothier, & Edwards, 1994). Passive-aggressive students are those who, when confronted by directions or indicators of appropriate behavior, simply do not respond cooperatively. One of the most difficult challenges related to these students is that, even if cooperation is in their best interest, they will not be able to cooperate. Students who are passive-aggressive tend to sabotage reward systems and negative contingencies. Natural consequences are among the most effective strategies for managing their behavior. Students who are passive-aggressive respond best to sincere, spontaneous encouragement of small steps, to choices, and to strong teacher–student relationships.

Young children who are passive-aggressive are often classified in the diagnostic category "Oppositional/Defiant Disorder" (DSM-IV, 1994). Research efforts have been aimed at finding a link between oppositional/defiant disorder and development of conduct disorders in adolescents (Knowlton, 1995). As with students demonstrating passive-aggression, students with oppositional/defiant behaviors have disruptive and short-lived peer relationships, are unwilling to assume responsibility for their personal behavior, and sabotage positive feedback of their behavior. To remedy this behavior, Knowlton (1994) suggests, in addition to providing consistent and clear consequences, controlling through the use of written schedules, relying on "the clock" or "the class or group" for a control mechanism, and offering choices to the learner.

Social Skills

Students with learning disabilities may have difficulty with social persistence following an "unfriendly" experience (Settle & Milich, 1999). Settle and Milich (1999) report that students with learning disabilities felt significantly worse following unfriendly interactions with peers, but conversely were significantly more positive than the peers after a friendly reaction. Some evidence emerged that girls with learning disabilities were more adversely affected by the unfriendly interaction. Settle and Milich suggested that these children showed a learned helplessness response to social failure, making fewer attempts because they felt that such social initiations would be futile.

Though often reported to have deficits in social skills, Brown and Bauer (1994) found that young children with behavioral disorders are at times so intently engaged in social interactions that their teacher perceives them to be disruptive. They suggest that the efforts to connect socially with others often takes precedence for those children over a teacher's efforts to conduct an activity. Students not identified as emotionally/behaviorally disordered also may demonstrate behaviors that are disturbing to their peers, and thus detrimental to social interactions.

An important facet of social interaction is empathy. Schonert-Reichi (1994) compared empathy among young adult males who were identified as emotionally/behaviorally disordered and those who were not identified as emotionally/behaviorally disordered. She reported that of the two groups, teenage males identified as emotionally/behaviorally disordered demonstrated lower levels of empathy, had less frequent contact with friends, and poorer quality relationships. Empathy consistently predicted the quality of relationships of individuals identified as emotionally/behaviorally disordered.

Effect of Behavior

The behavior of students has an effect on their teachers. And, teachers' responses, positive or negative, have an impact on students' futures. Wood (1981) presented a six-step model to trace the progression of a student's "disturbing" behavior. The steps progress from the point at which a teacher becomes aware of the behavior through the point at which the student is labeled as emotionally/behaviorally disordered. The six steps are:

Step 1. The teacher's attention is attracted by the behavior of a student.

Step 2. The teacher decides whether the behavior is pleasing or disturbing. If the behavior is pleasing, the teacher either positively reinforces it, or ignores it. If the teacher finds the behavior disturbing continue to Step 3.

Step 3. Is the teacher disturbed sufficiently to take some action to change or stop the disturbing behavior? If the teacher is sufficiently disturbed to take action, continue to Step 4. This can be the result of accumulated instances of being disturbed. If the teacher is not sufficiently disturbed to take action, his or her awareness of the disturbing behavior usually begins to lessen.

Step 4. The teacher wishes to take some action to bring an end to the disturbing behavior. What alternatives are available? An important factor to be considered is the interpersonal power characteristics of the situation. Based on appraisal of social and political factors, the teacher may decide to do nothing, to act immediately, to seek alliances with others who will support taking action to stop or change the student's behavior, or to escape from the situation through transfer or resignation. Continue to Step 5, if the teacher's decision is to take action either alone or in alliance with others.

Step 5. The teacher's first action is to have the student's behavior labeled publicly as disordered, disruptive, or problematic. Often, at the same time, an additional label suggesting the perceived severity of the problem is attached by those labeling the behavior. This additional label may be: mild, moderate, or severe. Continue to Step 6, if those concerned wish to make, or can make, inferences about the cause of the disordered behavior.

Step 6. The teacher, usually acting in alliance with the social worker, psychiatrist, psychologist, or others who lend political authority to the labeling process, infers that the student's disturbing behavior is a function of past learning and present environmental factors. If this is the case, the preferred label is behaviorally disordered and the preferred intervention is behavioral. And/or, if the teacher infers that the student's disturbing behavior is a function of past experiences and a present inner emotional state, the preferred label is emotionally disturbed, and the preferred intervention is psychodynamic or psychoeducational.

Summary Points

- Learning styles are neutral; no one learning style is better than another.
- Students with learning disabilities or emotional/behavioral disorders are not free within themselves to choose different learning or interactional styles.
- Students with learning disabilities vary from their peers in the efficiency of their working, short-term, and long-term memories.
- Students with learning disabilities and emotional/behavioral disorders vary from their peers in motivation and self-concept.
- Students with learning disabilities and emotional/behavioral disorders vary from their peers in various components of language and communicative competence. These variations may be related to difficulties in social skills and identification of behavioral problems.

- The interactions of students with emotional/behavioral disorders are marked by greater aggression than those of their peers not so identified.
- Student behavior has an effect on the teacher.

Key Words and Phrases

aggression—behavior exhibited with the intent to dominate others

communicative competence—knowledge that individual members of a cultural group need to be able to interact with one another in both socially appropriate and strategically effective ways

extrinsic motivation—engaging in an activity for an externally supplied reward

intrinsic motivation—engaging in an activity for the sake of participation and completion

language—a socially shared code that uses a system of symbols to represent ideas about the world; these symbols are meaningful to others who know the same code

long-term memory—the relatively permanent storage of information

metacognition—being aware of one's knowledge and thinking processes

morpheme—the smallest unit of meaningful language

oppositional/defiant behaviors—responding to direction or indicators of behavior by refusal, or response opposite to that requested

passive-aggression—responding to direction or indicators of behavior with a lack of response or cooperation

phonology—the sound system of language

pragmatics—the use of language in social situations

semantics—the relationships and meanings of words

short-term memory—temporary memory which holds segments of information; information is only maintained in memory if it is restructured by a strategy such as rehearsal or item association

strategy—the conscious application of procedures that are used to store and retrieve information

syntax—the sequence and order of words to form phrases and sentences

working memory—the store of memory which briefly holds information for future processing

References

Abrams, J. C. (1986). On learning disabilities: Affective considerations. *Journal of Reading, Writing, and Learning Disabilities, 2,* 189–196.

American Psychiatric Association. (1994). *Diagnostic and Statistical Manual of Mental Disorders (4th ed.).* Washington, DC: Author.

Ashbaker, M. H., & Swans, H. L. (1996). Short-term memory and working memory operation and their contribution to reading in adolescents with and without learning disabilities. *Learning Disabilities Research and Practice, 11* (4), 106–213.

Atkinson, R., & Shiffrin, R. (1978). Human memory, a proposed system and its control processes. In K. Spence & J. Spence, (Eds.), *The psychology of learning and motivation: Advances in research and theory* (Vol. 2, pp. 85–195). NY: Academic Press.

Baddeley, A. D. (1986). *Working memory.* Oxford, England: Clarendon Press.

Baddeley, A. D., & Hitch, G. (1974). Working memory. In G. H. Bower, (Ed.), *The psychology of learning and motivation* (Vol. 8, pp. 199–239). NY: Academic Press.

Baker, L., & Cantwell, D. P. (1982). Psychiatric disorder in children with different types of communication disorders. *Journal of Communication Disorders, 35,* 45–52.

Bear, G. G., & Minke, K. M. (1996). Positive bias in maintenance of self-worth among children with LD. *Learning Disability Quarterly, 19,* 23–32.

Bear, G. G., Minke, K. M., Griffin, S. M., & Deemer, S. A. (1998). Achievement-related perceptions of children with learning disabilities. *Journal of Learning Disabilities, 31* (1), 92–102.

Beitchman, J. H., Nair, R., Clegg, M., Ferguson, B., & Patel, P. G. (1986). Prevalence of psychiatric disorders in children with speech and language disorders. *Journal of the American Academy of Child Psychiatry, 25,* 523–535.

Bender, W. N. (1995). *Learning disabilities: Characteristics, identification, and teaching strategies.* Boston: Allyn & Bacon.

Bender, W. N. (1999). Learning disabilities in the classroom. In W. N. Bender, (Ed.), *Professional issues in learning disabilities: Practical strategies and relevant research findings.* Austin: Pro-Ed.

Bender, W. N., & Wall, M. E. (1994). Social-emotional development of students with learning disabilities. *Learning Disability Quarterly, 17,* 323–341.

Bloom, L., & Lahey, M. (1978). *Language development and language disorders.* NY: John Wright & Sons.

Brown, A. L. (1975). The development of memory: Knowing, knowing about knowing, and knowing how to know. In H. Reese, (Ed.), *Advances in child development and behavior* (Vol. 10). NY: Academic Press.

Brown, M. S., & Bauer, A. M. (1994). Acting out or acting together? Social community formation and behavior management. *Beyond Behavior, 5* (3), 15–18.

Bryan, T. (1991). Social problems and learning disabilities. In B. Wong, (Ed.). *Learning about learning disabilities* (pp. 195–231). San Diego: Academic Press.

Bryan, T., Donahue, M., Pearl, R., & Sturm, C. (1981). Learning disabled children's conversational skills: The "TV Talk-Show." *Learning Disability Quarterly, 4,* 250–259.

Camarata, S. M., Hughes, C. A., & Ruhl, K. L. (1988). Mild/moderately behaviorally disordered students: A population at risk for language disorders. *Language, Speech, and Hearing Services in the Schools, 19* (2), 191–200.

Campbell, S. B., & Ewing, L. J. (1990). Follow-up of hard-to-manage preschoolers: Adjustment at age nine and predictors of continuing symptoms. *Journal of Child Psychology and Psychiatry, 31* (6), 871–889.

Campbell, S. B., Pierce, E. W., March, C. L., Ewing, L. J., & Szumowski, E. K. (1994). Hard-to-manage preschool boys: Symptomatic behavior across contexts and time. *Child Development, 65,* 836–851.

Carr, E. G., & Durand, V. M. (1985). The social-communicative basis of severe behavior problems in children. In S. Reiss & R. R. Boutzin, (Eds.), *Theoretical issues in behavioral therapy* (pp. 219–254). NY: Academic Press.

Ceci, S. J., Ringstrom, M. D., & Lea, S. E. G. (1980). Coding characteristics of normal and learning-disabled 10-year-olds: Evidence for dual pathways to the cognitive system. *Journal of Experimental Psychology: Human, Learning, and Memory, 6,* 785–797.

Checkley, K. (1997). The first seven . . . and then eight . . . *Educational Leadership, 55* (1), 1997, 57–68.

Conderman, G. (1995). Social status of sixth- and seventh-grade students with learning disabilities. *Learning Disability Quarterly, 19,* 13–24.

Dev, P. C. (1997). Intrinsic motivation and academic achievement: What does their relationship imply for the classroom teacher? *Remedial and Special Education, 18* (1), 12–19.

Dimitrovsky, L., Spector, H., Levy-Shift, R., & Vakil, E. (1998). Interpretation of facial expressions of affect in children with learning disabilities with verbal or nonverbal deficits. *Journal of Learning Disabilities, 31* (3), 286–293.

Donahue, M. (1986). Linguistic and communicative development in learning disabled children. In S. Ceci, (Ed.), *Handbook of cognitive, social, and neuropsychological aspects of learning disabilities* (pp. 263–289). Hillsdale, NJ: Erlbaum.

Duncan, B. B., Forness, S. R., & Hartsough, C. (1995). Students identified as seriously emotionally disturbed in day treatment: cognitive, psychiatric, and special education characteristics. *Behavioral Disorders, 29,* 238–252.

DuPaul, G. J., Guevremont, D. C., & Barkley, R. A. (1991). Attention-deficit hyperactivity disorder. In T. R. Kratochwill & R. J. Morris, (Eds.), *The practice of child therapy* (2nd ed., pp. 115–144). NY: Pergamon.

DuPaul, G. J., Stoner, G., Willy, W. D., & Putnam, D. (1991). Interventions for attention problems. In G. Stoner, M. R. Shinn, & H. M. Walker, (Eds.), *Intervention for achievement and behavior problems* (pp. 685–713). Silver Spring, MD: National Association of School Psychologists.

Ervin-Tripp, S., & Mitchell-Kernan, C. (1977). Introduction. In S. Ervin-Tripp & C. Mitchell-Kernan, (Eds.), *Child discourse* (pp. 1–23). NY: Academic Press.

Farmer, T. W., & Hollowell, J. H. (1995). Social networks in mainstream classrooms: Social affiliations and behavioral characteristics of students with EBD. *Journal of Emotional and Behavioral Disorders, 2* (3), 143–155, 163.

Fisher, D., Osterhaus, N., Clothier, P., & Edwards, L. (1994). Passive-aggressive children in the classroom: The child who won't do anything. *Beyond Behavior, 5* (2), 9–12.

Gallagher, T. M. (1999). Interrelationships among children's language, behavior, and emotional problems. *Topics in Language Disorders, 19* (2),1–15.

Gorman, J. C. (1999). Understanding children's hearts and minds: Emotional functioning and learning disabilities. *Teaching Exceptional Children, 31* (3), 72–77.

Grigorenko, E. L., & Sternberg, R. J. (1997). Styles of thinking, abilities, and academic performance. *Exceptional Children, 63* (3), 295–312.

Gualtieri, C. T., Korirath, U., Van Bourgondien, M., & Saleeby, N. (1983). Language disorders in children referred for psychiatric services. *Journal of American Academy of Child Psychiatry, 22,* 165–171.

Guevremont, D. C., & Dumas, M. C. (1994). Peer relationship problems and disruptive behavior disorders. *Journal of Emotional and Behavioral Disorders, 2* (3), 164–172.

Guild, P. (1994). The culture/learning style connection. *Educational Leadership,* (May, 1994), 16–21.

Haager, D., & Vaughn, S. (1995). Parent, teacher, peer, and self-reports of the social competence of students with learning disabilities. *Journal of Learning Disabilities, 28* (4) 205–216.

Hagborg, W. J. (1996). Self-concept and middle school students with learning disabilities: A comparison of scholastic competence subgroups. *Learning Disability Quarter, 19,* 117–126.

Handwerk, M. L., & Marshall, R. M. (1998). Behavioral and emotional problems of students with learning disabilities, serious emotional disturbance, or both conditions. *Journal of Learning Disabilities, 31* (4), 327–339.

Hearne, D., & Stone, S. (1995). Multiple intelligences and underachievement: Lessons from individuals with learning disabilities. *Journal of Learning Disabilities 28* (7), 439–448.

Hummel, L. J., & Prizant, B. M. (1993). A socioemotional perspective for understanding social difficulties of school-age children with language disorders. *Language, Speech, and Hearing Services in the Schools, 24.* 216–224.

Kavale, K. A., & Reese, J. H. (1992). The character of learning disabilities: An Iowa profile. *Learning Disability Quarterly, 15,* 74–94.

Kaufman, A. S., Swan; W. W., & Wood, M. M. (1979). Dimensions of problem behaviors of emotionally disturbed children as seen by their parents and teachers. *Psychology in Schools, 16,* 207–217.

Kauffman, J. M. (1997). *Characteristics of emotional and behavioral disorders in children and youth (6th Ed.).* Columbus: Merrill.

Keefe, C. H., & Hoge, D. R. (1996). In-class intervention for students identified as behaviorally disordered. *Intervention in School and Clinic, 31* (4), 218–224.

Knowlton, D. (1995). Managing children with oppositional behavior. *Beyond Behavior, 6* (3), 5–10.

Kravatz, S., Faust, M., Lipshitz, S., & Shalhav, S. (1999). LD, interpersonal understanding, and social behavior in the classroom. *Journal of Learning Disabilities, 32* (3), 248–256.

Margalit, M. (1998). Loneliness and coherence among preschool children with learning disabilities. *Journal of Learning Disabilities, 31* (2), 173–180.

Margalit, M., Leving, S. & Alyagon, M. (1994). Learning disability subtyping, loneliness, and classroom adjustment. *Learning Disability Quarterly, 17,* 297–310.

McDonough, K. M. (1989). Analysis of the expressive language characteristics of emotionally handicapped students in social interactions. *Behavioral Disorders, 14,* 127–139.

McLaughlin, S. (1998). *Introduction to language development.* San Diego: Singular Pub. Group.

Mercer, C. D. (1997). *Students with learning disabilities.* Upper Saddle River, NJ: Merrill.

Montgomery, M. S. (1994). Self-concept and children with learning disabilities: Observer-child concordance across six context-dependent domains. *Journal of Learning Disabilities, 27* (4), 254–262.

Myles, B. S., & Simpson, R. L. (1998). Aggression and violence by school-aged children and youth. *Intervention in School and Clinic, 33* (5), 259–264.

Nelson, N. W. (1998). *Childhood language disorders in context.* Boston: Allyn & Bacon.

Newell, A., & Somon, H. (1972). *Human problem solving.* Englewood Cliffs, NJ: Prentice Hall.

O'Shaughnessy, T. E. & Swanson, H. L. (1998). Do immediate memory deficits in students with learning disabilities in reading reflect a developmental lag or deficit?: A selective meta-analysis of the literature. *Learning Disability Quarterly, 21,* 123–148.

Pintrich, P. R., Anderman, E. M., & Klobucar, C. (1994). Intraindividual differences in motivation and cognition in students with and without learning disabilities. *Journal of Learning Disabilities, 27* (6), 360–370.

Prior, M., & Werry, J. S. (1986). Autism, schizophrenia, and allied disorders. In H. C. Quay & J. S. Werry, (Eds.), *Psychopathological disorders of childhood* (3rd ed., pp. 156–210). NY: Plenum.

Prizant, B. M., Audet, L. R., Burke, G. M., Hummel, L. J., Maher, S. R., & Theodore, G. (1990). Communication disorders and emotional/behavioral disorders in children and adolescents. *Journal of Speech and Hearing Disorders, 55,* 179–192.

Robinson, S. M. (1999). Meeting the needs of students who are gifted and have learning disabilities. *Intervention in School and Clinic, 34* (4), 195–204.

Rosenthal, S. L., & Simeonsson, R. J. (1991). Communication skills in emotionally disturbed and nondisturbed adolescents. *Behavioral Disorders, 16,* 192–199.

Safran, S. P. (1995). Peers' perceptions of emotional and behavioral disorders: What are students thinking? *Journal of Emotional and Behavioral Disorders, 3* (2), 66–75.

Sale, P., & Carey, D. M. (1995). The sociometric status of students with disabilities in a full-inclusion school. *Exceptional Children, 62* (1), 6–19.

Sameroff, A. J., Selfer, R., Barocas, R., Zax, M., & Greenspan, S. (1987). Intelligence quotient scores of 4-year-old children: Social environmental risk factors. *Pediatrics, 79* (3), 343–350.

Samuels, S. J. (1987). Information-processing abilities and reading. *Journal of Learning Disabilities, 20* (1), 18–22.

Settle, S., & Milich, R. (1999). Social persistence following failure in boys and girls with LD. *Journal of Learning Disabilities, 32* (3), 201–213.

Schonert-Reichi, K. A. (1993). Empathy and social relationships in adolescents with behavioral disorders. *Behavioral Disorders, 18* (3), 189–204.

Shallice, T. (1979). Neuropsychological research and the fractionation of memory systems. In L. G. Nilsson, (Ed.), *Perspectives on memory research* (pp. 218–236), Hillsdale, NJ: Erlbaum.

Shaugnessy, T. E., & Swanson, H. L. (1998). Do immediate memory deficits in students with learning disabilities in reading reflect a developmental lag or deficit? A selective meta-analysis of the literature. *Learning Disability Quarterly, 21* (2), 123–150.

Schultz, J. J., Florio, S., & Erickson, R. (1982). Where's the floor? Aspects of the cultural organization of social relationships in communication at home and in the school. In P. Gilmore & A. A. Glatthorn, (Eds.), *Children in and out of school: Ethnography and education* (pp. 88–123). Washington, DC: Center for Applied Linguistics.

Smith, D. S., & Nagle, R. J. (1995). Self-perceptions and social comparisons among children with LD. *Journal of Learning Disabilities, 28* (6), 364–371.

Smith, J. O. (1995). Behavior management: Getting to the bottom of social skills deficits. *LD Forum, 21* (1), 23–26.

Sternberg, R. (1988). *The triarchic mind: A new theory of human intelligence.* NY: Viking.

Swanson, H. L. (1993). Information processing: Analysis of learning disabled children's problem solving. *American Educational Research Journal, 30,* 861–893.

Swanson, H. L. (1994a). Short-term memory and working memory: Do both contribute to our understanding of academic achievement in children and adults with learning disabilities? *Journal of Learning Disabilities, 27* (1), 34–50.

Swanson, H. L. (1994b). The role of working memory and dynamic assessment in the classification of children with learning disabilities. *Learning Disabilities Research and Practice, 9* (4), 190–202.

Swanson, H. L. (1999a). Cognition and learning disabilities. In W. M. Bender, (Ed.), *Professional issues in learning disabilities: Practical strategies and relevant research findings* (pp. 415–460). Austin: Pro-Ed.

Swanson, H. L. (1999b). Learning disabled children's problem solving: Identifying mental processes underlying intelligent performance. *Intelligence, 12,* 261–278.

Taylor, O. L., & Payne, K. T. (1983). Culturally valid testing: A proactive approach. *Topics in Language Disorders, 3* (3), 8–20.

Tur-Kaspa, H., & Bryan T. (1995). Teachers' ratings of the social competence and school adjustment of students with LD in elementary and junior high school. *Journal of Learning Disabilities, 28* (1), 53–64.

Tur-Kaspa, H., Wesel, A., & Segev, L. (1998). Attributions for feelings of loneliness of students with learning disabilities. *Learning Disabilities Research and Practice, 13* (2), 89–94.

Vallance, D. D., Cummings, R. L., & Humphries, T. (1998). Mediators of the risk for problem behavior in children with language learning disabilities. *Journal of Learning Disabilities, 31* (2), 160–171.

Vaughn, S., Elbaum, B., & Schumm, J. S. (1996). The effects of inclusion on the social functioning of students with learning disabilities. *Journal of Learning Disabilities, 29,* 598–607.

Vaughn, S., & Haager, D. (1994). Social competence as a multifaceted construct: How do students with learning disabilities fare? *Learning Disability Quarterly, 17,* 253–266.

Vaughn, S., & Hogan, A. (1994). The social competence of students with learning disabilities over time: A within-individual examination. *Journal of Learning Disabilities, 27* (5), 292–303.

Walker, D. W., & Leister, C. (1994). Recognition of facial affect cues by adolescents with emotional and behavioral disorders. *Behavioral Disorders, 19* (4), 269–276.

Warr-Leeper, G., Wright, N. A., & Mack, A. (1994). Language disabilities of antisocial boys in residential treatment. *Behavioral Disorders, 19* (3), 67–78.

Wehby, J. H., Symons, F. J., & Shores, R. E. (1995). A descriptive analysis of aggressive behaviors in classrooms for children with emotional and behavioral disorders. *Behavioral Disorders, 20* (2), 87–105.

Weinberg, L. A. (1992). The relevance of choice in distinguishing seriously emotionally disturbed from socially maladjusted students. *Behavioral Disorders, 20* (2), 87–105.

Wenz-Gross, M., & Siperstein, G. N. (1997). Importance of social support in the adjustment of children with learning problems. *Exceptional Children, 63* (2), 183–193.

Wilson, D. R., & William, J. D. (1994). Academic intrinsic motivation and attitudes toward school and learning of learning disabled students. *Learning Disabilities Research and Practice, 9* (3), 148–156.

Wood, B. S. (1976). *Children and communication: Verbal and nonverbal language development.* Englewood Cliffs, NJ: Prentice Hall.

Wood, F. H. (1981). The influence of personal, social, and political factors on the labeling of students. In F. H. Wood, (Ed.), *Perspectives for a New Decade: Education's Responsibility for Seriously Disturbed and Behaviorally Disordered Children and Youth.* Reston, VA: Council for Exceptional Children.

Ysseldyke, J. E., & Muyskens, P. (1998). Student academic responding time as a function of time of day. *Journal of Special Education, 31* (4), 411–424.

6 Family Factors

TO GUIDE YOUR READING

After completing this chapter, you should be able to answer these questions:

- What family factors may put children at risk for learning disabilities or emotional/behavioral disorders?

- What are the needs identified by parents of students with learning disabilities or emotional/behavioral disorders?

- What issues are related to family engagement in the education of students with learning disabilities or emotional/behavioral disorders?

- What social services are available to families of children with learning disabilities or emotional/behavioral disorders?

◀◆ *Jessie, a fourth grader, was struggling with the transition from the primary grades. She had difficulty keeping her materials together, and having them ready when class began. She "daydreamed," and rarely responded in class. Her copying from the chalkboard was slow and labored, and she often was unable to write all her assignments into her plan book. At the beginning of the first quarter, her teacher asked a student to be "study buddy" for Jessie, making sure she had everything ready for class and all her assignments written in her plan book. Jessie responded angrily to her buddy's attempts to help, making statements such as "Stop bossing," or, "Get out of my face—do you think I'm stupid or something?" As Jessie's teacher became more and more frustrated with her behavior, she began to send her mother daily notes. These notes weren't efforts of problem solving, but were essentially "shopping lists" of Jessie's behaviors. The notes would say something like, "Today, Jessie failed to complete her plan book, threw her books when she came back from math, and refused to return to her seat after I made several requests."*

Jessie's mother, equally frustrated with these new behaviors from her formerly cooperative daughter, responded two or three times with questions, such as "When do these problems seem to occur most frequently?" or, "Has Jessie been getting her medication on time?". Or, "Has there been a change in the schedule?" This was an effort to prod the teacher into problem solving. These efforts received no response. After two weeks of notes, the mother sent the teacher a note which read, "Last night Jessie spit green beans at her brother, squirted toothpaste all over the sink, and refused to go to bed until I made several requests."

REFLECTION *When confronting a student in the classroom who is challenging, it's often difficult to remember that the student is only in school six hours a day. Those behaviors of concern in the classroom may be manifested at home in a different way. Think of a student in your experience who was very difficult. What would home life be like with this individual? How would you have coped as his or her parent?*

Introduction

Families with members identified as learning disabled or emotionally/behaviorally disordered should be recognized for their strengths. Seligman and Darling (1989) suggest that these strengths are demonstrated by the fact that, despite the challenges of parenting a child with a disability, most families are able to achieve a nearly normal lifestyle, and that most families adapt. When studying this chapter, the reader is urged to keep in mind that families of children with learning disabilities or emotional/behavioral disorders are, in most cases, making the best effort possible to meet the needs of their children.

Family Factors That May Put Children at Risk

Families and parents are instrumental to a child's educational success. Barton and Coley (1992) reported that three factors over which parents exercise authority—student absenteeism, the variety of reading material in the home, and excessive television watching—explain nearly 90 percent of the differences in eighth-grade mathematics test scores across 37 states and the District of Columbia on the National Assessment of Education Progress.

"In order to develop, a child needs the enduring, irrational involvement of one or more adults in care and joint activity with the child. By irrational, I mean, 'Somebody has got to be crazy about that kid.'" (Bronfenbrenner, 1978, p. 519). Throughout his descriptions of the contexts of human development, Bronfenbrenner (1979) emphasizes the potential impact of the family on each student. A family where there is responsibility, reciprocity, and a mutual positive feeling, is more likely to have a positive impact on the child. Brofenbrenner stresses the need for the developing individual to have a strong and enduring emotional attachment to another individual in order to facilitate learning and development. Several factors, then, may have an impact on the student identified as having learning disabilities or emotional/behavioral disorders.

Family composition.   Historically, a substantial number of children spend all or part of their childhood in a one-parent household due to parental death, divorce, or having unmarried parents. Hernandez (1994) reports that 28 to 34 percent of Caucasian children born between 1920 and 1960 lived for a period of time with one or no biological parents. He contends, based on projections of children born since 1980, that 50 percent of these children will live with only one parent for a period of time; among African-American children it may reach 80 percent. These one-parent families are accounted for by proportional shifts in the number of divorces in Caucasian families, and divorce and never marrying in African-American families. Absence of the father contributes to low motivation for achievement, inability to defer rewards, low self-esteem, susceptibility to group influence, and juvenile delinquency, all of which are more marked in boys than girls (Bronfenbrenner, 1970).

Cohen (1993) reports that though the traditional role of fathers is that of economic provider, becoming fathers had a dramatic impact on the lives of his informants far beyond the economic implications of supporting a family. The men interviewed had concerns about being good fathers, and had the lowest level of anxiety about the economic responsibilities of being fathers. Though the men displayed far more involvement in their children's lives than anticipated, they remained the secondary caregiver. Fathers who participate in domestic routines, leisure activities, and learning/enrichment experiences had far more positive attitudes toward their child with a disability (Flynn & Wilson, 1998).

Assumptions are sometimes made about absent fathers from various minority groups who refuse to support their children even when they have the resources to do so. Stier and Tienda (1993) found fathers from these minority groups committed to their children. In their study of absent fathers residing in Chicago's inner city, they found that these men are not marginal to their children's lives; rather, they make great efforts to maintain ties with their children. Among the various groups of absent fathers studied, nearly three-fourths of the African-American men acknowledged an out-of-wedlock child. In addition, about half of all Puerto Rican men, 8 percent of all white men, and 25 percent of the Mexican-American men reported having children outside of marriage. Half of the African-American and one third of the Puerto Rican fathers had dependent children who do not reside with them, whereas less than 20 percent of Mexican-American fathers had dependent children not living them. The nature and level of support given to dependent children varied greatly in regularity and amount. Economic support of any kind is more frequent than direct interaction with children, yet African-American fathers visited their children more than any other category of men. Fathers in each of the cultural groups were not marginal, but made great efforts to maintain ties with their children.

Brofenbrenner (1970) describes the social changes that have occurred in families since World War II as "the unmaking of the American child." He argues that, for the most part, children are no longer brought up by their parents. Rather, de facto responsibility for upbringing has shifted away from the family to other settings in society for several reasons. Families used to be larger, allowing for more natural child care and parent/child support. Children were, in the past, acquainted with a substantially greater number of adults in different walks of life, and were more likely to be active participants in adult settings when they entered them. Currently, children have small circles of friends, often limited to child care settings or telephone contact. Finally, parents simply do not spend as much time with their children as they used to. Bronfenbrenner suggests that if institutions continue to remove parents, other adults, and older youth from active participation in the lives of children, and if the resulting vacuum is filled by the age-segregated peer group, increased alienation, indifference, antagonism, and violence on the part of the younger generation in all segments of our society, including middle-class and affluent children should be anticipated. If children have contact only with their age-mates, there is a reduced possibility for learning culturally established patterns of cooperation and mutual concern. This concern has grown in the thirty years since Bronfenbrenner originally reported these patterns.

Very young, single mothers experience additional stress. Prater (1992) contends that keeping single mothers in school and successful is essential for their children. In her study of ten African-American adolescent mothers at risk of dropping out of school, Prater reports that several structures and strategies supported these mother's efforts to stay in school, and to be supportive of their babies. School-based clinics with family-planning services were needed. In addition, peer-counseling and a network of positive role models were recommended. A high level of teacher insensitivity was reported by the mothers, with little recognition of their unique roles as parenting students. Affordable day care or babysitting services were essential, in that the intergenerational pattern of early pregnancy produced very young grandmothers who did not have the time, desire, or money to stay home and babysit.

Child Maltreatment

In 1996, reports of child maltreatment to child protection agencies exceeded 3.1 million (National Association to Prevent Child Abuse, 1998). About one-third of the children in those reports were confirmed as victims of maltreatment. At least 1,046 died of abuse or neglect—three children every day (National Association to Prevent Child Abuse, 1998).

"Child maltreatment" is an ongoing pattern of behavior in which the individuals involved influence one another and cause disturbances in the caretaking process (Cicchetti, Toth, & Hennessy, 1989). Asen, George, Piper, and Stevens (1989) identified various patterns of abuse which they found helpful in working with families. Although not the primary help-giving professionals in cases of maltreatment, teachers need to be aware of the various kinds of maltreatment because they are mandatory reporters in most states. Asen and associates identified eight patterns of abuse: helpless and help-recruiting, professional, transgenerational, stand-in, distance regulating, transferred, cultural, and denied.

In the helpless and help-recruiting pattern, families seem to have a limited range of skills for dealing with everyday issues, and thus, resort to abuse. In professional abuse, the professional becomes over-involved in the family's problems, and assumes parents' duties and responsibilities. Transgenerational abuse occurs when the grandparents become involved in rearing their grandchildren either by accepting the caregiving role, or as a consequence of sharing their home with their child's family. In some cases, this results in a repetition of the cycle of poor parenting and abuse that occurred when the grandparents were rearing their children. In other cases, the fact that the child's biological parents remain dependent on the grandparents gives the grandparents a second opportunity to parent. In this situation, unresolved problems related to the parents' own childhood may be reactivated.

The fourth pattern of abuse discussed by Asen and associates (1989) is stand-in abuse. If the relationship between the parents is distant, and one parent has a close relationship to the child, then abuse of the child may represent a means of punishing the other parent without undermining the marriage. In times of crisis, the child is singled out and punished, or the child learns to behave in a manner that elicits abuse. In distance-regulating abuse, the child learns that the only way to achieve close physical contact with the mother or father is to behave in such a way as to provoke punishment. The child appears to seek the positive contact that follows the parent's anger and punishment.

Transferred abuse is a complex and difficult pattern to understand. Intense experiences from the parent's past are transferred to the present, and the child becomes the target of the feeling associated with the parent's past experiences. The parent apparently superimposes the past on the present. Cultural abuse is evident when families state that their behavior towards their children is appropriate from the perspective of their cultural origins, even though that behavior is not accepted in the culture in which they presently live, or by authorities within the present culture. The final pattern discussed by Asen and associates is denied abuse, in which the child is injured, but the cause of the injury is denied by the abusing parent.

Forms of maltreatment rarely occur in isolation; the vast majority of maltreated children are subjected to a combination of physical neglect, physical abuse, and verbal abuse (Ney, Fund, and Wickett, 1994). The Child Abuse Prevention and Treatment Act (Public Law 93-247) uses the terms child abuse and child neglect to refer to physical or mental injury, sexual abuse, or neglect of an individual less than eighteen years of age by a person responsible for the child's welfare under circumstances that indicate that the child's health or welfare is harmed or threatened. Reported incidents of child abuse and neglect increased 225 percent from 1978 to 1987 (Alsop, 1990). Children who have experienced maltreatment demonstrate differences in behavior and achievement. Crittenden (1989) reported that maltreated children are often disruptive, defiant bullies who have frequent interpersonal confrontations with peers and teachers. These children may spend more time fighting than learning. Other maltreated children may become so compliant and concerned over meeting others' standards that they rarely experience joy or satisfaction. Overcompliant abused children are so concerned with finding the right answer that they are frequently unable to attend to and manipulate ideas and concepts.

In their study of the long-term impact of the physical, emotional, and sexual abuse of children, Mullen, Martin, Anderson, Romans, and Herbison (1996) reported that a history of any form of abuse was associated with increased rates of psychopathology, sexual difficulties, decreased self-esteem, and interpersonal problems. There was a similarity among the three kinds of abuse and adult outcomes, though there was a trend for sexual abuse to be associated with sexual problems, emotional abuse to low self-esteem, and physical abuse to marital breakdown. However, some of the association between abuse and adult problems was accounted for by the childhood disadvantages from which the abuse often emerged.

Child and parent characteristics are not sufficient to explain child maltreatment (Janko, 1994). The environment may add elements of stress or support to child-caregiver relationships, such as having enough money, food, housing, health care, and the availability of more than one adult to share caregiving responsibilities. Stressors occur within the family, through community resources, and in responses to social policies. As Janko (1994) suggests, a young mother who is learning to parent her challenging baby in the context of brief weekly visits with the child protection worker, while she leads the disorienting life of someone who does not have the psychological and emotional grounding that comes from reliable family and friends, consistent meals, someplace to sleep, and knowing one's belongings are accessible and safe, is under significant stress.

Children and youth with disabilities may be at particular risk for child abuse. Estimates are that as many as 65 percent of children with disabilities are victims of physical, sexual, or emotional abuse. Pearson (1996) suggests that two main issues emerge for teachers working with these students. First, teachers have both the right and the responsibility to report abuse. Second, some classroom practices and policies may leave the teacher vulnerable to accusations of abuse. Though teachers are mandated reporters of child abuse and neglect, there is a low incidence of reporting. Pearson suggests that this underreporting by teachers may be due to a lack of knowledge in diagnosing or recognizing abuse, teachers fear that reporting may make them subject to prosecution, or a fear that they do not have adequate proof.

Often, professionals assume that adults who experienced child abuse or neglect will repeat the pattern in their children. Phelps, Belsky, and Crnic (1998), however, found that adults who have developed a coherent perspective on their negative early attachment relationships do not reenact poor parenting practices with their children. They found that individuals who developed secure perspectives on their negative experiences, even when under conditions of high stress, parented equivalently to the individuals who had consistent, caring relationships, and those who had not resolved their own abuse and neglect. These parents broke the intergenerational cycle and exhibited resilient parenting.

According to Dyson (1996), the experiences of families of children with learning disabilities are not well understood. She reports that much of the writing about these experiences is speculation. Because of the "invisibility" of learning disabilities, the family may exhibit low tolerance towards the child. Parents may also develop false hopes and unrealistic expectations for academic performance. These situations may cause stress and other difficulties in the family.

Family Interaction Patterns

Families with members identified as learning disabled or emotionally/behaviorally disordered often demonstrate great strength in dealing with their children. Most of these families achieve a nearly normal lifestyle and

Family members often demonstrate great strengths in dealing with their children.

adapt to their environment. Seligman and Darling (1989) describe this "normalization" as a typically appearing lifestyle. In some families, however, normalization remains elusive, and other adaptations emerge. The family adaptation patterns that Seligman and Darling describe include, (a) crusadership, in which the family engages actively in efforts to support social change, ranging from campaigns to increase public awareness, to active participation in advocacy groups; (b) altruism, in which families remain active with parents of younger children to help them meet their family's needs; and (c) resignation, in which families become resigned to their "problematic existence" and are isolated from their extended family and other families.

Mlawler (1993) further explored the difficulty of families in adapting as "families with a member with a disability." He argued that in the attempt to help parents become better educational advocates for their children with disabilities, parents and professionals have created an advocacy expectation that runs counter to the philosophy of normalization. He suggested that to truly empower parents, programs that could engage in advocacy along with and on behalf of parents must be developed. These programs should be free, easy to access, and have an available group of independent, uncompromised special educators who serve as experts on behalf of students.

Adherence to a social systems theory prevents us from making any specific cause-and-effect statements regarding family interaction styles and learning disabilities or emotional/behavioral disorders. However, there are family interactions styles that seem to increase the likelihood that a learner will be identified as having these disabilities.

Green (1992) summarized research on an "underorganized" family structure, which is often related to students identified as emotionally/behaviorally disordered. In the underorganized family, parents use global and erratic controls with their children to the extent that consistent behavioral contingencies are not present. Disciplinary responses are based on the parents' needs rather than the children's needs. In underorganized families, conflicts are resolved by threats and counter-threats rather than discussion that leads to closure. Verbal and logical communication is replaced by intense physical action and sound. Family members do not expect to be listened to, and thus resort to yelling. Compliance is insured by the use of force, rather than long-term solutions or negotiated responses. Finally, communication is marked by disconnected interruptions and abrupt topic changes.

In school, the children of "underorganized" families have difficulty focusing attention. Their communication style is disruptive, and it precludes the integration of new information. Behavior is focused on eliciting authoritarian or proximal control from the teacher rather than from achievement, or from engaging in tasks at hand. The families of many learners identified as emotionally/behaviorally disordered follow this underorganized pattern, and are chaotic, disorganized, and less cohesive than the families of peers not identified with these disorders.

A second family structure that Green suggests is the "over organized" family. The over organized family is characterized by parent intrusiveness, over involvement, and protective restrictions. Parents' attempts to control their child result in the child's obsessive worry, performance anxiety, procrastination, passive-aggression, or oppositional behavior. In this pattern, parents take too much responsibility for the child's performance, and the child rebels or takes too little responsibility for achievement.

Green (1992) presents four factors in family interaction patterns that influence the child's school-related behavior. First, the child may have information-processing problems that are maintained by unusual family communication patterns. Second, the child's attention problems may be maintained or amplified by an underorganized family structure with disruptive communication patterns. Third, the child's passive-aggression or performance anxiety may be maintained or amplified by an over organized, rigid, family structure. Finally, a child's lack of effort in school may be maintained or amplified by the family's (a) negative attributions about the child's ability and motivation, (b) blaming the child's success or failure on factors outside of the child's control, (c) casting the identified child into an inferior or problem identity when compared to siblings, and (d) modeling of values that minimize the importance of education and undermine school authority.

Whereas some family structures appear to be putting students at risk for learning disabilities or emotional/behavioral disorders, other family interaction styles may promote the healthy integration of young people into society. Using a sample of 1,000 eighth graders, Epstein (1983) studied the joint impact of family and classroom processes on change in students' attitudes and academic achievement during the transition between middle school and high school. She found that children from homes that provided greater opportunities for communication and decisionmaking exhibited greater independence after entering high school, and they received higher grades. As she contrasted family and classroom processes, family processes were considerably more powerful in producing change than classroom procedures.

In their work with students identified as having serious problems with social interactions, Ramsey and Walker (1988) studied family management practices of male fourth graders with emotional/behavioral disorders. Though they found no differences between these students and their nonidentified peers in the area of parental involvement, significant differences were found in discipline, monitoring, positive reinforcement, and problem solving. They concluded that students identified as having serious social interaction problems were exposed to far more negative and less competent family management practices than their peers.

Lyytinen, Rasku-Puttonen, Poikkeus, Laasko, and Ahonen (1994) concluded, from a review of research studies, that the results of comparisons between families in which there are children with identified learning disabilities and children without identified disabilities have been inconsistent. They summarized the research findings as suggesting that:

- mothers of students with learning disabilities may provide more information and more negative feedback to children when helping them with a problem-solving task;
- mothers of children with learning disabilities may have lower expectations regarding their children's abilities and future achievements; and
- fragmented or ambiguous parental communication may affect the child's conceptual development and interfere with learning.

Lyytinen and associates (1994) report that the relationship between parent communication styles and their child's learning is unclear. Parents may buffer and adapt their communication with their children to address learning problems. Their interractional style (e.g., simple questions, labeling, describing, demonstration) may be a reflection of their child's ability to sustain discourse.

The teaching strategies used by mothers of children with learning disabilities and mothers of normally achieving children on a task resembling a homework assignment were examined by Lyytinen and associates (1994). In this study, the mothers of children with learning disabilities were more dominant, used less cognitively demanding teaching strategies, and were more adult-centered. On the other hand, the mothers of the children who were not identified as having learning disabilities were more successful in motivating and creating a challenging learning atmosphere for their children. These mothers used more time to teach their children. When compared with the children without identified learning disabilities, the children with learning disabilities exhibited less intrinsic motivation, less initiative, and more dependence on their mothers.

Families in which children have been identified as having emotional/behavioral disorders may vary from other families in their interactions. In terms of task orientation, Denham, Renwick, and Holt (1991) found that in preschool children, a mother's warm, but limit-setting parenting allowed the child to appear more confident and emotionally positive. Maternal scaffolding (initial provision of supports with gradual reduction as the child is successful) may influence social/emotional as well as cognitive aspects of development. Denham and associates found that a balance of support and allowance of autonomy allowed children to be more positive. Socially positive girls modeled their mothers' patterns of keeping a social dependency in a friendly way. Boys exhibited less positive social behavior than girls overall. Positive interactions between the mother and child, in fact, predicted appropriate emotional and behavioral competence among peers.

Siblings

Children who have a brother or sister with a learning disability or emotional/behavioral disorder may have to adjust to life with that sibling who, because of his or her behavior, may require a large portion of family time, attention, money, and psychological support (National Information Center for Children and Youth with Disabilities, 1994). The National Information Center for Children and Youth with Disabilities (NICHCY) (1994) suggests that the child's reactions to the sibling with a disability can affect the overall adjustment and development of self-esteem in both children. The nature of the relationships between siblings and family members may be influenced by factors such as the family's resources, lifestyle, and child-rearing practices. In addition, the kind and severity of the disability, number of children in the family, and the age differences between children in the family has an effect on siblings. The coping of siblings can be influenced by the other stress-producing conditions that exist in the family, the kinds of coping mechanisms and interaction patterns that exist within the family, and the kind and quality of the support services available in the community.

NICHCY (1994) suggests that the reactions of siblings are not static. Reactions change in coping with day-to-day realities. Preschool siblings may feel confused, afraid, anxious, angry, and have difficulty understanding the situation. Elementary school-aged children may feel embarrassed or ashamed, worry about catching the disability, or have guilt feelings because they are not disabled. Young adults wonder about the future, and how the people they socialize with, date, and later marry, will accept the brother or sister. The sibling of a child with a disability experiences stress as a family member, frustration at not being able to make themselves understood, unhappiness at being left to play alone, irritation over reminders, withdrawal, anger, or a double standard regarding the behavior of the sibling with the disability.

NICHCY (1994) suggests that families should plan support for their children with disabilities. NICHCY advises families to:

- develop financial plans for future care;
- know their state's laws regarding guardianship and independence;
- provide the siblings without disabilities information about where to access educational, vocational, and medical records of the sibling with disabilities;
- gain an understanding of the legal and eligibility requirements of programs available to the family member with a disability;
- discover the types of community resources available; and
- be aware that, as families grow and develop, the members within it change.

The brothers and sisters of students with emotional/behavioral disorders may not be as seriously affected by their identified sibling as one may assume. Gargiulo, O'Sullivan, and Wesley (1992) found that differences among families may be due to family resources and characteristics that foster positive patterns of sibling adjustment, rather than the presence of the individual identified as having emotional/behavioral disorders, or another disability.

McLoughlin and Senn (1994) suggest that the siblings of school-aged children with disabilities have a primary need for information. Depending on the family, brothers and sisters may be expected to become actively involved in the educational program of a child with a disability. They may be embarrassed, and may need information about how to handle feelings and teasing. In addition, they should have information about day-to-day caregiving needs. As demands are increasingly placed on parents by job and family responsibilities, siblings, particularly older females, may be asked to fulfill some of the needs for day care or babysitting.

A study that compared families of school-aged children with learning disabilities to families of children who were normally achieving revealed that family functioning and sibling self-concept were similar in both groups of families (Dyson, 1996). Further, families with a child with a learning disability may experience greater parental stress associated with academic achievement and behavior at school. One indication was that family routines may be different. However, families of children who were achieving normally and families of a child with learning disabilities both used rules for operating family routines. Families of children with learning disabilities were also found to emphasize personal growth of family members.

Needs Identified by Parents

Using the National Education Longitudinal Study of 1988, Masino and Hodapp (1996) chose students with disabilities and their matched peers without identified disabilities to contrast parent expectations. Despite lower college participation rates among students with disabilities, parent expectations were found to be slightly higher for these students. Masino and Hodapp concluded that parents of children with disabilities and parents of children without disabilities have similar expectations for their children's educational attainment. In another study, however, Whitney-Thomas and Hanley-Maxwell (1996) found differences between the parents of children with disabilities and parents of children without disabilities regarding their vision for their child's future, and their comfort with the transition to adulthood. Parents of students with disabilities manifested greater discomfort and pessimism than did parents of students without disabilities.

Student outcomes may not be the greatest concern for parents. Green and Shinn (1995) reported that parents' satisfaction with special education programs was not related to children's academic performance. Rather, parents were most satisfied when their children received individual attention, when teachers were responsible and friendly, and when their child's self-esteem increased.

Professionals must be careful not to make assumptions regarding the needs of parents of students with emotional/behavioral disorders. Simpson (1988) found a significant difference between teachers' perceptions of parents' needs and parents' expressed needs. He reported that the most widely used and/or requested service by parents is information exchange.

Parents wanted to receive information through informal feedback, progress reports, conferences, and program information. Parents also requested parent-coordinated service programs, counseling, therapy, consultation, consumer and advocacy training, and home program training.

As children grow older, the parents' needs may shift. For example, Alper, Schloss, and Schloss (1995) report that the middle school years pose new challenges to parents. Communication needs increase, with the need to communicate and work with an increasing number of educators and related services personnel. The role of extracurricular activities, which may be difficult for children with disabilities, because of school district restrictions for specific activities, may increase family stress. New problems emerge with scheduling and transportation, and parents sometimes need to spend time and energy to integrate these activities by serving as the organizers (i.e., being scout leaders, youth group coordinators, etc.) As students grow older, the need for greater economic support may emerge. In caring for the students, physical demands increase, with the need for respite care developing. Parents of students begin to want and need information about their child's future.

During the middle school years, the need for advocacy increases. Alper, Schloss, and Schloss, (1995) indicate that four levels of advocacy emerge. In self-advocacy, people speak or act on their own behalf to improve their quality of life. In social support advocacy, or citizen advocacy, people speak out as a means of promoting the general interests of self or others; this advocacy is usually characterized as goodwill. Interpersonal advocacy involves direct interactions by family members, professionals, or others on behalf of the child or youth with disabilities. The final kind of advocacy is legal advocacy, which promotes the legal interests of individual students. This kind of advocacy usually begins when informal, interpersonal advocacy fails.

Students also recognize the importance of family involvement. Morningstar, Turnbull, and Turnbull (1995) report that three areas arose in regard to students' perceptions of family involvement in the transition from school to adult life. First, families played important roles in creating a future vision. Students expressed a preference to live close to families so that they could have continued support. In addition, parents and extended family members helped students shape their aspirations in an informative, almost implicit way. Second, a critical theme of family involvement in the planning process emerged. The majority of students identified certain family members as being able to provide support during the transition process. Parents and extended family members played a potent role in planning. Finally, families had significant influence on self-determination. A number of students were seeking autonomy in making certain kinds of decisions, but they were also seeking ongoing family support. No students indicated a need for support or training in self-determination for themselves or their families.

Family Engagement in Education

The Office of Educational Research and Improvement (1990) reported in their profile of the American eighth grader that approximately 65 percent of the responding parents indicated that they had not talked to school officials about the academic program being pursued by their eighth-grade child. Only 50 percent of the parents had attended a school meeting since the beginning of the school year. Fifty-two percent of the parents said they had never asked about or discussed grades with a teacher or school administrator, and only 29 percent had visited their children's classes.

There are many barriers to parent involvement. Ballen and Moles (1998) suggest that one issue is time. With the rise in situations where both parents work, there is only one parent, or parents are working more than one job, the parents struggle to fulfill their many responsibilities in a limited amount of time. Teachers are also strapped for more time. In addition, parents are unsure of how to help their children, and their experiences with school may cause a reluctance to be involved. There are also cultural barriers, such as language and life experiences, and perspectives that vary from the majority culture in the school. The nurture of families has not been a priority of schools; parents need support if they are to become involved.

Family engagement in the education of their child with learning disabilities or emotional/behavioral disorders must be taken from the perspective of the family as client or consumer. DeChillo and Koren (1995) identified several distinct elements of collaboration from the perspective of family members. Parents reported the need for support and understanding by professionals in their relationships with family members. Families also needed assistance in the practical aspects of getting services for their child. The clear and open exchange of information between families and professionals was perceived as essential, as was flexibility and willingness on the part of professionals to modify or change services based on parental feedback. More than half of the families noted the following barriers to engagement in their child's education: (a) professionals' beliefs that families cause children's disorders, (b) insufficient administrative support for teachers who choose to work with families, (c) child welfare policies that require giving up custody of a child to get service, (d) the inherent power imbalance between professionals and family members, and (e) professionals' lack of knowledge about children's disorders, and their high expectations of families.

Koren and DeChillo (1995) go on to suggest that it is not sufficient to merely provide parents with resources. Rather, it is important to foster a process whereby parents have both control over current resources, and great capability to obtain future resources.

Empowerment of families can occur in three distinct ways: (a) the empowerment of individuals with respect to their own circumstances, (b) the empowerment of individuals with respect to others, and (c) the empowerment of groups in relationship to the larger society. By looking at families from the perspective of empowerment, professionals need to help families handle problems at home within the family, deal with service delivery systems on behalf of their own child, and influence the service delivery system for all children with learning disabilities or emotional/behavioral disorders.

Several practices which are counterproductive when attempting to engage parents in their children's education were identified by Voeltz (1994). A menu approach that forces parents into predetermined roles, over which they have little or no control is one practice that is counterproductive. Another counterproductive practice is the way in which school officials "track," or group parents, as either "concerned parents" who want to be involved in the education of their children, or "unconcerned parents" who do not care to be involved in the education of their children. In addition, the lack of sensitivity to cultural differences alienates rather than engages parents.

Parents may have personal experiences that impact on their participation in their child's school program. Gonder (1998) proposes that parents may not be willing to join the "school team" because they:

- made poor grades as a child;
- are only contacted when there is a problem;
- are afraid they will be accused of being a bad parent because the child is having trouble;
- are afraid the school will say their child is not bright;
- are afraid their child will be treated unfairly;
- lack confidence in their ability to talk with professionals;
- may believe that all public servants are no good and out to get the common folk.

Parents may be intimidated when there are so many school personnel at a conference that they feel outnumbered. In addition, discussing only misbehavior and poor classwork may intimidate parents. Parents may be hesitant to participate when, in their past experiences, their ideas were not incorporated in any action plan. Gonder suggests several strategies to involve parents in their child's education. These strategies are summarized in Table 6.1.

Morrison and Cosden (1997) identify risk and protective factors to help understand the impact of the presence of a child with a learning disability on the functioning of the family. They suggest that the presence of a learning disability is a risk factor that does not predict positive or negative outcomes. However, other risk and protective factors may interact with the presence of the learning disability. The family environment itself

Table 6.1   Ways to Involve Parents

- Call or write before school starts to introduce yourself, and describe some of the projects planned for the year.
- Be positive. Make frequent positive calls, and send positive notes. Begin and end all conversations on a positive note; reiterate the determined plan.
- Have no more than two professionals in a conference with the parents at a given time, and meeting in a neutral location to increase parents' comfort.
- Send a positive note to the parents after the conference.
- Schedule conferences in the evening so parents do not have to leave work or lose pay.
- Arrange for parents to participate in non-intimidating activities.

(Gonder, 1998)

provides both risk and protective factors. Risk factors include the activity level of the child, parental expectations and disappointment with academic performance, lack of flexibility to meet the normal developmental challenges and special needs, overprotection, parent-child enmeshment, and rigidity. Falik (1995) gives examples of these risk factors. An unadaptive reaction to the presence of the learning disability may be that someone external to the family may judge the child as inadequate, through which it is implied that the family is inadequate. Further, the parents' school experiences or feelings about parenting skills may emerge. In addition, the family is usually expected to do something on a time schedule, or take some sort of action that, from the family's perspective, is costly, unfamiliar, or stressful. Several types of resistance can interfere with intervention: resistance to the diagnosis itself, resistance to treatment, over involvement, and pitting one professional against another.

Protective factors include emotional stability, strong parenting skills, flexibility, family cohesiveness, utilization of coping skills, and "goodness of fit" from an ecocultural perspective (Morrison & Cosden, 1997). In other words, a learning disability may be accepted by a family that accommodates the problem and responds with flexible adaptation (Falik, 1995).

Significant challenges confront families of individuals with serious behavior problems. In their study of family perspectives on inclusive lifestyles for people with problem behavior, Turnbull and Ruef (1997) interviewed 127 families of children, youth, and adults with severe behavior problems, such as aggression, property destruction, self-injurious behavior, or pica. In the interviews, most comments were about siblings. Parents reported a lack of bond or close connection between the person with disabilities and his or her siblings. Having a child with severe behavior problems produced far fewer sibling benefits than problems. In addition, families of individuals with severe behavior problems had a difficult time establishing comfortable and connected relationships with the person with problem behavior. Extended family members often implied that a child's behavior problems resulted form poor parental discipline. Families described home routines as challenging and disruptive due to the problem behavior, and that they had difficulty in finding competent care providers. Over half of the families indicated that it was impossible for them to participate in their preferred religious activities as a family unit, and that being excluded from a religious community divided the family. Many of the families described the absence of even one friendship for their child or adult as being disheartening. Whether their children were placed in special or general education classes, the families believed that many teachers lack training and are unwilling to change. The parents did not give priority to community inclusion, not because they thought it was unimportant, but because of time and energy limitations, unavailability of other companionship, and the family's and others' perceptions of worry, fear, and embarrassment. These families reported a tenuous inclusive lifestyle, in which the most pervasive finding was that the families themselves had been the catalyst for any positive action occurring that related to attaining inclusive lifestyle supports.

Successfully engaging parents can have significant impact. Arndorfer, Miltenberger, Woster, Rortvedt, and Gaffaney (1994) describe their efforts using descriptive and experimental analysis of problem behaviors in the homes of five children. The children's parents were actively involved in the descriptive assessment, and they manipulated potential control variables during experimental analysis. The information obtained from each functional assessment method (e.g., behavioral interview, direct observation, experimental analysis) indicated the same function of each child's problem behavior. Based upon the results of the descriptive analysis, hypotheses regarding the function of the challenging behavior were tested. Interventions involving functional communication training were implemented based on the assessment result for the children. The study employed parents in their natural environment, suggested that functional assessment procedures may be useful and/or practical in natural settings, and that parents may have a significant impact on their child's behavior.

The use of the home and natural conditions to engage parents in the education of their children with emotional/behavioral disorders may also have an impact on how willing parents are to participate. Reimers and Wacker (1988) found that the amount of disruption of intervention, and willingness of parents to participate in the intervention, is initially of greatest importance to parents working with the children's behavior in the home. However, once interventions were in place, the effectiveness of the treatment as rated by the parents had the largest influence on acceptability and continuation by the parents.

White and Decker (1996) suggest that many parents who are "hard-to-reach" are self-sufficient, motivated, and involved in their children's education. Parents may have experienced and, with determination, confronted domestic violence, abandonment, illness, and drug use. White-Clark and Decker (1996) provide nine "rules" for teachers to use with hard-to-reach parents:

1. Believe in the importance of parent-centered parental involvement.
2. Embody an ethic of caring, making a sincere effort to understanding the life situations of parents who are not involved in school.
3. Disregard hard-to-reach stereotypes, recognizing that your assumptions change your behavior toward parents.
4. Develop high expectations for all parents, demonstrating to them that their participation is valued.
5. Conceptualize the role of parents as partners, collaborators, and problem solvers.
6. Present clear expectations, roles, and responsibilities which are communicated to parents.
7. Be willing to address personal concerns, actively working on involving parents while maintaining your role as teacher.
8. Understand the purpose and function of the parent involvement program, as well as your place in it.
9. Be willing to work to improve parental involvement, developing creative alternatives.

Cultural diversity and parent engagement. Much attention has been given to engaging families from diverse cultural, ethnic, and linguistic groups in the education of their children. Dauber and Epstein (1993) report that school practices to encourage parents to participate in their children's education are more important than family characteristics like parental education, family size, marital status, socioeconomic level, or student grade. School practices themselves may inhibit the involvement of parents. Freedman, Ascheim, and Zerchykof (1989) suggest several factors that inhibit the involvement of parents from diverse cultural, ethnic, or linguistic groups:

1. School practices do not accommodate the diversity of families served, scheduling events at inconvenient times, providing information in written form, providing impractical information or materials, and school staff consciously or unconsciously conveying the attitude that parents have little to contribute.
2. Time and childcare constraints are inconsistent with the opportunities provided.
3. Parents have had negative experiences with schools.
4. Schools do not support cultural diversity, dealing uncomfortably with parents from various cultural, ethnic, and linguistic groups and communicating only in written English.

5. Families are working to meet their basic needs, which takes primacy over involvement in school.

Cultural, linguistic, and ethnic minority parents often must confront stereotypes regarding engagement in their children's education. Allen, Harry, and McLaughlin (1995) suggest that school systems may not encourage proactive parent involvement, and the "we–they" stance assumed by many professionals may be the factor that breaks down communication. In this study, African-American parents not only participated in homework and behavioral issues regarding their children, but expressed faith in the value of education for success. However, when there was no active communication with the teachers, these parents expressed confusion and distress with the assessment and placement process. McIntyre and Silva (1992) contend that most educators' lack of knowledge regarding both child abuse and culturally different child rearing practices creates fertile ground for misjudging the appropriateness of parents' practices. Teachers who adhere to the disciplinary practices of the majority culture may find themselves viewing culturally different practices as abusive. This use of culturally diverse childrearing practices places parents at greater risk for being reported to agencies in charge of handling abuse and neglect reports.

In their study relating culture and socioeconomic status to professional collaboration, DeGangi, Wietlisbach, Poisson, and Stein (1994) found that professionals reported that they spend more time with families from different cultural backgrounds in identifying their concerns, attempting to understand their needs and customs, and explaining the Individualized Family Service Plan. These professionals also reported that families from lower socioeconomic groups and educational backgrounds were often concerned with basic survival needs, such as housing, clothing, and food, and consequently, deferred to the professional when discussing the Individualized Family Service Plan, had difficulty identifying their child's needs, and were cautious in sharing information. Taylor (1993), however, contends that many families living in poverty are able to solve complex problems related to their own survival in difficult situations, even though they may lack traditional skills.

Harry, Rueda, and Kalyanpur (1999) suggest that teachers should demonstrate cultural reciprocity, whereby an understanding of their own cultural values becomes the point of reference or framework from which to understand different perspectives. If teachers examine the cultural beliefs from which their teaching arises, and look for the cultural underpinnings of their practices, rather than assuming that theirs are the universal values that should be shared by others, relationships with parents from diverse cultural, ethnic, and linguistic groups will be stronger. Discussions specific to working with families from various cultural, ethnic, and linguistic groups are included in Chapter Eight.

Social Services

Lesar, Trivette, and Dunst (1995) argue that the systems perspective seems especially useful as a framework for guiding research and practice in providing social services for children and adolescents with disabilities and their families. The system, a miniuniverse, uniquely touches people with disabilities and their families; family members of children and youth without disabilities rarely come into contact with this universe. Cohen (1980) argues that services for families occur within a system of interrelated, interacting parts. The client and professionals are in the foreground whenever the service is observed. There is, however, an equally critical background of five components, which includes the technology underlying the service, administrative and management personnel, the existing pattern of human services into which the new system is introduced, political and economic conditions, and the feedback among components and the consequences of the feedback on system change. In addition, he argues, human services have a life-cycle during which these five components change.

As a result of his analysis of the outcomes of early intervention practices, and recommendations calling for increased parent engagement in their children's early education, Bronfenbrenner (1975) coined the term "family-centered practices." Dunst and associates (1991) suggest several different types of family-oriented programs:

- Professionally-centered models, with professionals as experts who determine child and family needs;
- Family-allied models, where families are viewed as the agents of professionals; the implementers of interventions that professionals design and determine;
- Family-focused models, where families are seen as consumers of professional services; and
- Family-centered models, in which professionals are instruments of the families, and professionals intervene in individualized, flexible, and responsive ways.

In a study of program models and practices, Trivette, Dunst, Boyd, and Hamby (1995) found that parent and family characteristics did not account for the differences in parents' perceptions of program success. Rather, the nature of the interactions were most important to parents. Their findings suggest that efforts to promote family-centered policies and practices in early intervention and other human services programs will necessitate changes in how programs are organized and operated, and how practitioners view their roles and responsibilities in interactions with children and families. The sources of variations in parents' assessment of help-giving practices were related to differences in program models.

and not parent or family characteristics. Differences in parents' personal control appraisals were found to be almost entirely attributable to a combination of program characteristics and help-giving practices.

Recent changes in social policy are having a significant impact on how human services are delivered to families. Powell, Batsche, Ferro, Fox, and Dunlap (1997) report that several principles emerge when using a family strength-based approach to family support. Programs must have a philosophy based on family strengths, and the personnel staffing the programs work as partners with families in every effort to provide services. Programs need to be family-centered, and their focus should be family-driven. The role of the professional changes to establish a partnership with the family, in recognition that family members have contributions to make, and that there is shared responsibility in the support process. Strength-based approaches require an individualized response to family needs and capabilities, and a broad-based, comprehensive view of family development. Outcomes should be assessed based on family functioning and the quality of life of family members.

Coordinating social services is an additional challenge to families. Koren, Paulson, Yatchmenoff, Gordon, and DeChillo (1997) found that children's age, gender, and ethnicity had no relationship to service coordination, nor did caregivers' income, education, or foster parent status. Unsurprisingly, services were more difficult to coordinate for children with more severe problems. The severity of a student's problem may be associated with service coordination difficulties because of the need for intensive and diverse services. The sheer number of services and providers is likely to have an impact on how readily these elements can be coordinated. Families who were more involved in the services tended to view services as more coordinated.

The nature and extent of support that families with children with emotional/behavioral disorders receive from informal social networks and paid professionals, and the helpfulness of this assistance was explored by Lehman and Irvin (1996). Through a self-administered questionnaire assessing child and family characteristics and the nature of familial support sent to 250 randomly selected families, they found that formal organizations and paid professionals provide more support than informal organizations and unpaid individuals. However, family members were reported as the most helpful for coping with daily challenges. In addition, the greater the number of functions of family service coordination received, the more parents rated themselves as successful in accessing support, and the more satisfied they were with family quality of life.

Poverty.   Garbarino (1992) contends that most children experience poverty not as an isolated event, but as an ongoing condition of their lives. Poverty persists throughout childhood for at least one in five children, with the rate for younger children being even higher. Among the inner-city poor, marginal and submarginal economic resources are combined with personal resources that may be diminished due to violence, academic failure, exploitation, despair, fear, and deteriorated community infrastructure. Violence is pervasive in some communities; in a recent study of the life of preschoolers in an inner-city public housing project, all the mothers cited "shooting" as their greatest fear for their children (Dubrow & Garbarino, 1988).

Homeless children and families present a particular challenge to schools. The Steward B. McKinney Homeless Assistance Act of 1987 defined homeless people as those who, (a) lack a regular and adequate nighttime residence, (b) have a nighttime residence that is a supervised public or private shelter, (c) sleep in an institution that provides temporary residence, or (d) sleep in a public or private place not ordinarily used as a sleeping accommodation for people (Yamaguchi, Strawser, & Higgins, 1997). One-third of the homeless population is comprised of families with children. Many of these children do not attend school. The lack of predictability in the lives of children who are homeless may contribute to behaviors leading to identification as emotionally/behaviorally disordered, and difficulties in achievement may lead to identification as learning disabled.

In regard to learners with emotional/behavioral disorders, there is a special need for comprehensive community services (Soderland, Epstein, Quinn, Cumblad, & Petersen, 1995). Knitzer (1993) argues that the unavailability of appropriate support services in schools, and the lack of collaborative intervention planning among child-serving agencies and professionals has placed serious limitations on the application of effective interventions across settings. In order to increase collaboration, Eber, Nelson, and Miles (1997) suggest "wrap around services." "Wraparound" is a needs driven process for creating and providing services for individual children and their families (Eber, Osuch, & Redditt, 1996). It is not a program or a type of service, but is an approach that involves a commitment to blend and create services for children, their families and their teachers. The wraparound process encourages service planners to think differently about the needs of students and their families, as well as how services can be provided to meet those needs effectively. A unique feature of wraparound is that one integrated plan addresses the needs of the student during and beyond the school day. Wraparound plans include comprehensive services, blended across agencies, that address needs in more than one life domain.

One essential characteristic unique to wraparound is that plans are driven by needs rather than by currently available programs. In contrast to the traditional practice of evaluating student needs based on available educational placements, existing program components and services are analyzed and employed according to their usefulness in meeting student needs. Services are not based on a categorical model, but are accessed or created on the basis of the specific needs of the student, the family,

Table 6.2   Characteristics of Wraparound Services

In wraparound services:

- Supports and services are based on a natural school environment.
- Plans creatively use available resources to meet unique needs, rather than being restricted by how resources are usually organized or utilized.
- Interventions are built on student, teacher, and family strengths.
- Needs of all persons of like age, grade, gender, community, and culture are considered.
- Desired outcomes are generated by parents, teacher, and child expectations.
- The team makes a commitment to unconditional care and assumes responsibility for changing the plan to make it work for the student.

(Eber, Nelson, and Miles, 1997)

and the teacher. The child and family team consists of persons who know the student best, and who can provide active support to that student, his or her family, and the teacher. Extended family members, neighbors, family friends, and mentors are frequently participants in child and family teams. For students served in special education, the school-based portion of the wraparound plan is translated into an individualized education program (IEP). The school plan addresses all components of the school day where proactive supports and interventions are needed. For students with comprehensive needs that involve home and community settings, the school-based wraparound plan is an integrated part of the broader wraparound plan that addresses other life domains. The characteristics of wraparound services are summarized in Table 6.2.

Substitute care.   When families are no longer able to meet their children's needs the children may enter substitute care. The population of foster children has grown both in size and in the complexity of the problems presented, as larger numbers enter those care situations (Schor, 1988). Today, children in foster care have more serious physical and emotional problems than in the past.

Foster care placement is intended to be a planned, temporary service implemented to strengthen families so that they can again care for their children (Schor, 1988). Ideally, if after studying the family and providing appropriate services, uniting the child and the family is impossible, or not in the best interest of the child, parents' rights are terminated, and the child is placed with an adoptive family. There are, however, some children for whom neither reunion with their family nor adoption is feasible. Frequently, these children remain with foster care families in various settings and on a temporary basis until they reach maturity.

The current foster care population is composed of approximately equal numbers of boys and girls. Forty percent of the population are children from minority cultures. Twenty-five percent of the population is disabled. Approximately three-quarters of the children are in foster placements because of maltreatment; most of these children return to their biological families within one year. Twenty percent of these children reenter foster care within a year of discharge. Twenty-five percent of children are likely to remain in foster care after a two-year placement. The American Public Welfare Association (1993) estimated the number of children receiving foster care at two points during fiscal year 1990. During that year, there was an 11.8 percent increase of children in substitute care, with a growth of the overall child population in the country of .36%. For every 1,000 U.S. children, 5.4 were in foster care at the end of fiscal year 1990. Social service agencies are having increased difficulties recruiting and retaining foster care parents.

Children in foster care may have more frequent and serious health care problems than children living with their biological families. Schor (1988) reports that these children tend to be physically smaller than their peers, have more frequent developmental delays, and more serious emotional problems. Students in foster care have significantly greater delays and major deficits in adaptive behavior (Hochstadt, Jaudes, Zimo, and Schachter, 1987). A large number of children in foster care receive special education services. Hill, Hayden, Lakin, Menke, and Amado (1990) concluded that the prevalence of disabilities among children and youth in foster care is about twice that among school-aged children as a whole. George, Voorhis, Grant, Casey, and Robinson (1992) reported that 30 percent of the children in foster care in Illinois, for example, were placed in special education. Of this group, 54 percent of children were identified as having emotional/behavioral disorders. Similarly, Sawyer and Dubowitz (1994) found that almost 30 percent of the children in Baltimore city schools who were in substitute care due to neglect or abuse by their parents were receiving special education services.

Though a high percentage of children in foster care receive special education services; Smucker, Kauffman, and Ball (1996) contend that little is known about the academic and social problems of this population. In their study, searches of school archival records and brief interviews with school personnel were used to obtain measures of school-related problems of four groups of students: those receiving both foster care and special education for emotional and behavioral disorders, foster care only, special education only, or neither. Students in foster care who were receiving special education services were found to exhibit more school-related problems. Students who were only in foster care, or only in special education, did not significantly differ in their school-related problems.

Substitute care is a challenge to both child and family. Normal family developmental processes are disrupted by foster care (Elbow, 1986).

Biological families begin with dependent relationships and progress towards the development of individual identity, as the children assume more and more responsibility for their personal lives. The members of the substitute family begin as independent individuals and progress towards attachments. The process is further limited by the temporary nature of the placement.

The Adoption Assistance and Child Welfare Act of 1980 (Public Law 96-272) was a consequence of national concern for children who were "adrift in foster care" (Seltzer & Blocksberg, 1987). The law emphasized the need to develop plans for the permanent placement of children in need of out-of-home placement whether needed for a short or extended period of time. The idea of permanency planning was described by Laluccio and Fein (1983) as a process of designing and implementing a set of goal-directed activities aimed to help children live in families that offer ongoing relationships with nurturing individuals, and the opportunity to establish lifetime relationships. The process of permanency planning is intended to, (a) protect the child, (b) support stable relationships between child and caregivers, (c) preserve the biological family, and (d) enhance the psychosocial and behavioral adjustment of the child. Selzer and Blocksberg (1987) report a higher rate of adoption from foster care when social service workers and agencies accept the philosophy of permanency planning.

Head Start.   Head Start, from its inception, included parent engagement in several forms: participating on policy councils and boards, working as classroom volunteers, and assuming paid staff positions. As it developed, Head Start mounted additional demonstration programs to broaden parental involvement, including Home Start and Project Developmental Continuity (PDC). Through work with parents, Head Start is a "two generation program," recognizing both parents and their children as participants (Collins, 1993).

Collins (1993) suggests that Head Start is one of the few institutions trusted by individuals who are poor or from diverse ethnic, cultural, or linguistic groups on one hand, and local community leaders and service providers on the other. Since 1972, Head Start has collaborated with state and local education agencies to identify children with special needs. In addition, Head Start provides child health screening, and connects families to programs such as the Special Supplemental Food Program for Women, Infants, and Children (WIC). An increased emphasis is emerging in Head Start regarding creating greater family support through the use of family services coordinators grounded in a "family strengths" model (Gage and Workman, 1994).

The legal-correctional system.   There are four stages in the legal-correctional system for children (Apter & Conoley, 1984). First, "station-house adjudication" is used to describe formal warnings given by police to minors, usually at the police station. Parents are called to pick up their children, and no further action is taken against the child. Petition and authorization, the second stage, is the beginning of the formal court referral process. Court intake staff contact the police, parents, and others to develop information about a specific complaint or violation. Unofficial interventions begin at this step, usually involving a juvenile referee or social worker. During the third phase, which may include detention, hearings, and preliminary examinations, the court engages in a series of evaluations and hearings regarding the case. The juvenile referee may make any number of judgments, including confinement in a juvenile detention facility, day treatment facility, counseling, or community service. During the final stage, the adjudication phase, the child's case goes to court. The child may be "warned and admonished," placed in any number of settings ranging from a group home to foster care, or be put in detention. Probation is frequently used as an alternative.

Summary Points

- Families of children and youth with learning disabilities or emotional/behavioral disorders should be recognized for their strengths. Most of these families function much like other families.

- Family composition and structure may increase the risk of children for learning disabilities or emotional/behavioral disorders.

- Child maltreatment is an ongoing pattern of behavior; children who experience maltreatment vary from their peers in behavior.

- Family patterns such as under organization may be related to students identified as learning disabled or emotionally/behaviorally disordered.

- Successfully engaging parents may have a positive impact on the education of students with learning disabilities or emotional/behavioral disorders.

- Families of students with learning disabilities or emotional/behavioral disorders may be engaged in community services such as substitute care, Head Start, or the legal-correctional system.

Key Words and Phrases

child abuse—physical or mental injury, or sexual abuse, of a child under the age of 18 years by a person responsible for the child's welfare under circumstances that indicate that the child's health or welfare is harmed or threatened

child maltreatment—child abuse and neglect

child neglect—failure to provide for the physical, medical, emotional, or educational needs of a child by an individual responsible for the child's welfare

foster care—substitute care placement that is typically licensed and regulated by state human service agencies

homeless—people who lack a regular, adequate nighttime residence, or have a nighttime residence that is a public or private shelter, institution, or place not designed as a home

pica—eating inedible materials

scaffolding—the initial provision of supports, with gradual reduction as the child is successful

substitute care—the placement of children for rearing with others—not the child's biological parents

References

Allen, N., Harry, B., & McLaughlin, M. (1995). Communication versus compliance: African-American parents' involvement in special education. *Exceptional Children, 61* (4), 364–377.

Alper, S., Schloss, P. J., & Schloss, C. N. (1995). Families of children with disabilities in elementary and middle school: Advocacy models and strategy. *Exceptional Children, 62,* 260–275.

Alsop, R. (1990). *News release: Data on child abuse and neglect.* Denver, CO: American Humane Association.

American Public Welfare Association. (1993). *Characteristics of children in substitute care and adoptive care.* Washington, DC: Author.

Amerikaner, M. J., & Omizo, M. M. (1984). Family interaction and learning disabilities. *Journal of Learning Disabilities, 17,* 540–543.

Apter, S. J., & Conoley, J. C. (1984). *Childhood behavior disorders and emotional disturbance.* Englewood Cliffs, NJ: Prentice Hall.

Arndorfer, R. E., Miltenberger, R. G., Woster, S. H., Rortvedt, A. K., & Gaffney, T. (1994). Home-based descriptive and experimental analysis of problem behaviors in children. *Topics in Early Childhood Special Education, 14* (1), 64–87.

Asen, K., George, E., Piper, R., & Stevens, A. (1989). A systems approach to child abuse: Management and treatment issues. *Child Abuse and Neglect, 13,* 45–57.

Ballen, J., & Moles, O. (1998). *Strong families, strong schools.* Washington, DC: U.S. Department of Education.

Barton, P. E., & Coley, R. J. (1992). *America's smallest school: The family.* Princeton, NJ: Educational Testing Services.

Brofenbrenner, U. (1970). *Two worlds of childhood.* NY: Russell Sage Foundation.

Bronfenbrenner, U. (1975). Is early intervention effective? In M. Guttentag & E. Struening, (Eds.), *Handbook of evaluation research* (Vol. 2, pp. 519–603). Newbury Park, CA: Sage.

Bronfenbrenner, U. (1978). "Who needs parent education?" *Teachers College Record, 79,* 773–774.

Cicchetti, D., Toth, S., & Hennessy, K. (1989). Research on the consequences of child maltreatment and its application to educational settings. *Topics in Early Childhood and Special Education, 9* (2), 33–55.

Cohen, S. (1980). Multiple impacts and determinants in human service delivery systems. In R. Turner & H. Reese, (Eds.), *Life span developmental psychology: Intervention* (pp. 125–248). NY: Academic Press.

Cohen, T. F. (1993). What do fathers provide? Reconsidering the economic and nurturant dimensions of men as parents. In J. C. Hood, (Eds.), *Men, work, and family* (pp. 1–22). Newbury Park, CA: Sage.

Collins, R. C. (1993). Head Start: Steps toward a two-generation program strategy. *Young Children, 48* (2), 25–73.

Crittenden, P. M. (1989). Teaching maltreated children in the preschool. *Topics in Early Childhood Special Education, 9* (2), 16–32.

Dauber, S. L., & Epstein, J. L. (1993). Parents' attitudes and practices of involvement in inner city elementary and middle schools. In N. Chavkin, (Ed.), *Families and schools in a pluralistic society* (pp. 53–72). Albany, NY: State University of New York Press.

DeChillo, N., & Koren, P. E. (1995). Just what is "collaboration?" *Focal Point, 9* (1), 1.

DeGangi, G. A., Wietlisbach, S., Poisson, S., Stein, E., & Royeen, C. (1994). The impact of culture and socioeconomic status on family-professional collaboration: Challenges and solutions. *Topics in Early Childhood and Special Education, 14* (4), 503–520.

Denham, S. A., Renwick, S. M., & Holt, R. W. (1991). Working and playing together: Prediction of preschool social-emotional competence from mother-child interaction. *Child Development, 62,* 242–249.

Dubrow, N., & Garbarino, J. (1988). Living in the war zone: Mothers and children in a public housing project. *Child Welfare, 68,* 3–20.

Dunst, C. J., Johanson, C., Trivette, C. M., & Hamby, D. (1991). Family-oriented early intervention policies and practices: Family centered or not? *Exceptional Children, 58,* 115–126.

Dyson, L. L. (1996). The experiences of families of children with learning disabilities: Parental stress, family functioning, and sibling self-concept. *Journal of Learning Disabilities, 29* (3), 280–286.

Eber, L., Nelson, C. M., & Miles, P. (1997). School-based wraparound for students with emotional and behavioral challenges. *Exceptional Children, 65* (4), 539–555.

Eber, L., Osuch, R., & Reddit, C. A. (1996). School-based applications of the wraparound process: Early results on service provision and student outcomes. *Journal of Child and Family Studies, 5,* 83–99.

Elbow, M. (1986). From caregiving to parenting: Family formation with adopted older children. *Social Work, 31,* 366–370.

Epstein, J. L. (1983). Longitudinal effects of family-school-person interactions on student outcomes. *Research in Sociology of Education and Socialization, 4,* 101–127.

Falik, L. H. (1995). Family patterns of reaction to a child with a learning disability: A mediational perspective. *Journal of Learning Disabilities, 28* (6), 335–341.

Flynn, L. L., & Wilson, P. G. (1998). Partnerships with family members. What about fathers? *Young Exceptional Children, 2* (1), 21–28.

Freedman, S., Ascheim, B., & Zerchykov, R. (1989). *Strategies for increasing the involvement of under represented families in education.* Quincy, MA: Massachusetts Department of Education.

Gage, J., & Workman, S. (1994). Creating family support systems: In Head Start and beyond. *Young Children, 50* (1), 74–77.

Garbarino, J. (1992). The meaning of poverty in the world of children. *American Behavioral Scientists, 35,* 220–237.

Gardner, H. (1983). *Frames of mind: The theory of multiple intelligences.* NY: Basic Books.

Gargiulo, R. M., O'Sullivan, P. S., & Wesley, K. (1992). Sibling relationships involving school children with acquired/congenital and visible/invisible disabilities. *Issues in Special Education and Rehabilitation, 7* (2), 7–23.

George, R. M., Voorhis, J. V., Grant, S., Casey, K., & Robinson, M. (1992). Special education experiences of foster children: An empirical study. *Child Welfare, 71,* 419–437.

Gonder, S. (1998). Parents: Friend or foe? *CEC Today, 4* (67), 12.

Green, R. (1992). Learning to learn and the family system: New perspectives on underachievement and learning disorders. In M. J. Fine & C. Carlson, (Eds.), *The handbook of family-school interventions: A systems perspective* (pp. 157–174). Boston: Allyn & Bacon.

Green, S. K., & Shinn, M. R. (1995). Parent attitudes about special education and reintegration: What is the role of student outcomes? *Exceptional Children, 61* (3), 269–281.

Harry, B., Rueda, R., & Kalyanpur, M. (1999). Cultural reciprocity in sociocultural perspective: Adapting the normalization principle for family collaboration. *Exceptional Children, 66* (1), 123–136.

Hernandez, D. J. (1994). Children's changing access to resources: A historical perspective. *Society for Research in Child Development Social Policy Report, 8* (1), 1–23.

Hill, B. K., Hayden, M. F., Lakin, K. C., Menke, J., & Amado, A.R.N. (1990). State-by-state data on children with handicaps in foster care. *Child Welfare, 69,* 447–462.

Hochstadt, N. J., Jaudes, P. K., Zimo, D. A., & Schachter, J. (1986\7). The medical and psychosocial needs of children entering foster care. *Child Abuse and Neglect, 11* (1), 53–62.

Janko, S. (1994). *Vulnerable children, vulnerable families.* NY: Teachers' College Press.

Knitzer, J. (1993). Children's mental health policy: Challenging the future. *Journal of Emotional and Behavioral Disorders, 1,* 8–16.

Koren, P. E., & DeChillo, N. (1995). Empowering families whose children have emotional disorders. *Focal Point, 9* (1), 1–3.

Koren, P. E., Paulson, R. K., Yatchmenoff, D. K., Gordon, L. J., & DeChillo, N. (1997). Service coordination in children's mental health: An empirical study from the caregiver's perspective. *Journal of Emotional and Behavioral Disorders, 5* (3), 162–172.

Lamminmaki, T., Ahonen, T., de Barra, H. T., Tolvanen, A., Michelsson, K., and Lyytinen (1997). Comparing efficacies of neurocognitive treatment and homework assistance programs for children with learning disabilities. *Journal of Learning Disabilities. 30* (3), 333–345.

Lehman, C. M., & Irvin, L. K. (1996). Support for families with children who have emotional or behavioral disorders. *Education and Treatment of Children. 19* (3), 335–353.

Lesar, S., Trivette, C. M., & Dunst, C. J. (1995). Families of children and adolescents with special needs across the life span. *Exceptional Children. 62* (3), 197–199.

Maluccio, A. N., & Fein, E. (1983). Permanence planning: A redefinition. *Child Welfare, 63,* 197.

Masino, L. L., & Hodapp, R. M. (1996). Parental educational expectations for adolescents with disabilities. *Exceptional Children, 62* (6), 513–623.

McIntyre, T., & Silva, F. (1992). Culturally diverse childrearing practices: Abusive or just different? *Beyond Behavior, 4* (1), 8–12.

McLoughlin, J. A., & Senn, C. (1994). Siblings of children with disabilities. In S. Alper, P. J. Schloss, & C. N. Schloss, (Eds.), *Families of students with disabilities: Consultation and advocacy* (pp. 95–112). Boston: Allyn & Bacon.

Mlawler, M. A. (1993). Who should fight? Parents and the advocacy expectations. *Journal of Disability Policy Studies, 4* (1), 106–109.

Morningstar, M. E., Turnbull, A. P., & Turnbull, H. R. (1995). What do students with disabilities tell us about the importance of family involvement in the transition from school to adult life? *Exceptional Children, 62* (3), 249–260.

Morrison, G. M., & Cosden, M. A. (1997). Risk, resilience, and adjustment of individuals with learning disabilities. *Learning Disability Quarterly. 20,* 43–50.

Mullen, P. E., Martin, J. L., Anderson, J. C., Romans, S. E., & Herbison, G. P. (1996). The long-term impact of the physical, emotional, and sexual abuse of children: A community study. *Child Abuse and Neglect, 20* (1), 7–21.

National Association to Prevent Child Abuse. (1998). *Annual Report to Prevent Child Abuse.* Springfield. IL: Author.

Ney, P. G., Fund, T., & Wickett, A. R. (1994). The worst combinations of child abuse and neglect. *Child Abuse and Neglect, 18* (9), 705–714.

NICHCY (National Information Center for Children and Youth with Disabilities). (1994). *Children with disabilities: Understanding sibling issues.* Washington, DC: Author.

NICHCY (National Information Center for Children and Youth with Disabilities). (1996). *Record Keeping worksheet for parents.* Washington, DC: Author.

O'Connor, S. C., & Spreen, O. (1988). The relationship between parents' socioeconomic status and education level, and adult occupational and educational achievement of children with learning disabilities. *Journal of Learning Disabilities, 21,* 143–158.

Office of Educational Research and Improvement. (1990). *A profile of the American eighth grader.* Washington, DC: U.S. Department of Education.

Pearson, S. (1996). Child abuse among children with disabilities: Implications for special educators. *Teaching Exceptional Children, 29* (1), 34–37.

Phelps, J. L., Belsky, J., & Crnic, K. (1998). Earned security, daily stress, and parenting: A comparison of five alternative models. *Development and Psychopathology, 10,* 21–38.

Powell, D. S., Batsche, C. J., Ferro, J., Fox, L., & Dunlap, G. (1997). A strength-based approach in support of multi-risk families: Principles and issues. *Topics in Early Childhood Special Education, 17* (1), 1–26.

Prater, L. P. (1992). Early pregnancy and academic achievement of African-American youth. *Exceptional Children, 59* (w), 141–149.

Sawyer, R. J., & Dubowitz, H. (1994). School performance of children in kinship care. *Child Abuse and Neglect, 18,* 587–597.

Schor, E. L. (1988). Foster care. *The Pediatric Clinics of North America, 35* (6), 1241–1252.

Seligman, M., & Darling, L. B. (1989). *Ordinary families, special children.* NY: Guilford.

Seltzer, M. M., & Blocksberg, L. M. (1987). Permanency planning and its effects on foster children: A review of the literature. *Social Work, 37,* 65–68.

Smucker, K. S., Kauffman, J. M., & Ball, D. W. (1996). School-related problems of special education foster-care students with emotional or behavioral disorders: A comparison to other groups. *Journal of Emotional and Behavioral Disorders, 4* (1), 30–39.

Soderland, J., Epstein, M. H., Quinn, K. P., Cumblad, C., & Petersen, S. (1995). Parental perspectives on comprehensive services for children and youth with emotional and behavioral disorders. *Behavior Disorders, 20* (3), 157–170.

Stier, H., & Tienda, M. (1993). Are men marginal to the family? Insights from Chicago's inner city. In J. C. Hood, (Ed.), *Men, work, and family* (pp. 23–44). Newbury Park, CA: Sage.

Taylor, D. (1993). Family literacy: Resisting deficit models. *TESOL Quarterly, 27* (3), 550–553.

Trivette, C. M., Dunst, C. J., Boyd, K., & Hamby, D. W. (1995). Family-oriented program models, help giving practices, and parental control appraisals. *Exceptional Children, 62* (3), 237–348.

Turnbull, A. P., & Ruef, M. (1997). Family perspectives on inclusive lifestyle issues for people with problem behavior. *Exceptional Children, 63* (2), 211–227.

Voeltz, D. L. (1994). Developing collaborative parent-teacher relationships with culturally diverse parents. *Intervention in School and Clinic, 29* (5), 288–291.

White-Clark, R., & Decker, L. E. (1996). *The "hard-to-reach" parent: Old challenges, new insights.* Boston, MA: Mid-Atlantic Center for Community Education.

Whitney-Thomas, J., & Hanley-Maxwell, C. (1996). Packing the parachute: Parents' experiences as their children prepare to leave high school. *Exceptional Children, 63* (1), 76–87.

Yamaguchi, B. J., Strawser, S., & Higgins, K. (1997). Children who are homeless: Implications for educators. *Intervention in School and Clinic, 33* (2), 90–97.

7 School and Classroom Factors

TO GUIDE YOUR READING

After completing this chapter, you should be able to respond to the following questions:

- What classroom issues are related to students with learning disabilities or emotional/behavioral disorders?

- What educational services are available for students with learning disabilities or emotional/behavioral disorders?

- What instructional strategies have been effective with students with learning disabilities or emotional/ behavioral disorders?

◆◆ *Though it was only the fourth week of school, Ms. Pat was concerned about Chris. Unlike the other kindergarten students who seemed to live for recess, Chris was always the last in line, and seemed almost afraid to leave the classroom. On the playground, he stood by himself watching the cars go by, and fingered a small car which he kept in his pocket at all times. One day, Ms. Pat asked Chris what he was doing, and he replied, "Just guessing about cars." The other students stopped approaching him to play, and started referring to him as "Chris, the car kid."*

Ms. Pat asked a peer teacher to observe Chris in the classroom. Her observations were fairly consistent with Ms. Pat's observations. During the morning class meeting, Chris would sit outside and to the rear of the class circle, and, frequently, he would gaze out the window. When Ms. Pat would ask him if he wanted to move closer, he would quietly shake his head and say, "too loud." When the other children, or even Ms. Pat, moved near Chris, he would flinch, or quickly move out of the way. During choice time, Chris would choose either a learning center that was not yet occupied, or the one that had the fewest children. He would use the available materials independently rather than with his peers. During project time, however, Chris's work was sophisticated and complex; his wire sculptures, for example, were intricate and creative. He shunned written work, and one of his classmates, who had appointed herself his guardian and tutor, often coaxed him into completing written tasks after she completed her own. During any free time, he would look through children's science books that showed detailed drawings and cross-sections of objects, animals, or buildings. When Ms. Pat asked him if he would like to take one of the books home, he replied, "I can't."

Ms. Pat sent a note home to schedule a conference with Chris's parents. Two women arrived at the conference, one of whom introduced herself as Chris's foster mother, Ms. Lewis. The other was Chris's case worker. The women explained to Ms. Pat that Chris had just entered Ms. Lewis's therapeutic foster home the week before school began. Because of Chris's chaotic past, he was the only foster child placed with Mr. and Ms. Lewis. Chris first entered foster care at three years of age. He had experienced severe abuse and neglect; his mother had been unable to complete treatment for drug and alcohol problems, and Chris's biological father was incarcerated. Recently, the mother's parental rights had been legally terminated. While Chris had entered foster care, his younger brother had been adopted. Unfortunately, Chris's initial foster home was unable to care for him. He was placed in a second home where he was, again, physically abused. Chris's third home was with Mr. and Mrs. Lewis who were committed to working with Chris. Mrs. Lewis indicated that Chris's placement in their home would be long term, and that they would consider permanent adoption.

Ms. Pat was overwhelmed by the information. How could she be concerned about Chris's lack of interest in alphabet worksheets in view of his life experience? Was Chris's behavior related to an emotional/behavioral disorder, a learning disability, or a reaction to a life she couldn't even imagine? What was her role as his teacher?

REFLECTION *For some children, the school and classroom is their most reliable environment, and the teacher is their most responsive adult. In others, the rigidity of the classroom may, in effect, increase behaviors deemed representative of dis-*

abilities. Reflect on your own interactions with children. How can schools support children with learning disabilities or emotional/behavioral disorders? What teacher behaviors or activities may be helpful?

Introduction

One of the key aspects in a definition of either learning disabilities or emotional/behavioral disorders is difficulty in school. Carpenter, Bloom, and Boat (1999) suggest that as teachers make instructional decisions for their classrooms, academic gains become the primary concern. They contend that the teachers also should focus on practices that result in outcomes such as high self-esteem, self-determination, individual empowerment, and joy. In this chapter the classroom issues and services available to students with learning disabilities and emotional/behavioral disorders will be reviewed. Educational strategies will also be evaluated.

Educational Services

Special education traditionally has been the subsystem of the school community system, the program set aside for differences, and a place for children who are different (Rhodes, 1996). Special educational services are provided to students who come to the attention of teachers and parents, and who are referred, evaluated, and labeled learning disabled or emotionally/behaviorally disordered. The purpose of this process is to help students. However, Audette and Algozzine (1997) argue that the referral to placement process is based on several faulty assumptions that may inhibit new ways of looking at students with disabilities in classrooms. The first faulty assumption is that students with disabilities are significantly different from other students. Research, however, has failed to identify consistent differences across various categories of disability. Second, the learning and developmental needs of students with disabilities are assumed to be beyond the capacity of general education personnel, and general educators have been convinced that students with disabilities need services that only specialists can provide.

Third, Audette and Algozzine (1997) describe an assumption that classifications of disability provide precise and useful descriptions of students' learning needs. However, research has failed to identify differences among the efforts of special educators to teach students with different disability classifications. Finally, it is assumed that the mandated processes for determining classifications of disabilities provide a sound and useful basis for designing programs to meet the unique needs of students with disabilities. Yet, truly individualized instruction rarely occurs; students are inserted into established programs.

Placement decisions, then, may not be based on students' needs. Glassberg (1994) found, corroborating the findings of Kauffman, Cullinan, and Epstein (1987), that cognitive, academic, and behavioral factors did not appear to have a dominant role in placement decisions. Rather, age, at time of diagnosis, is most often related to the placement decision. Glassberg found that younger, brighter students tended to be mainstreamed, and older students with more externalizing behaviors tended to be placed in more restrictive settings. Two categories of children emerged with regard to placement decisions. The first group included children who were educated in public school settings, who disrupted or reduced peer and social relationships with or without problem behavior at home, and whose academic achievement is one standard deviation below that of school district age mates. The second group included children who were not educated in public school settings, who avoided peer and social relationships, and who had behavior problems across all settings.

Teachers appear to have diverse opinions about placement alternatives (Martin, Lloyd, Kauffman, & Coyne, 1995). In interviews with teachers, Martin and associates (1995) found that teachers thought that schools are faced with problems they are unable to handle, and that administrative procedures often impede appropriate services. The teachers also reported a lack of collaboration and support among those making placement decisions and those providing services. Teachers indicated that they believed they had little influence in placement decisions.

The "cascade of services" (Reynolds, 1962) is a continuum of services that provides a framework for meeting the individual needs of students with learning disabilities or emotional/behavioral disorders, as well as other students with disabilities. These services range from the least restrictive, that is, the most like general education, to the most restrictive, which include services that do not take place in schools, such as "inpatient" care. The range of services provided in this continuum includes:

- General education classes. The student is placed in a general education classroom, and may or may not be served with supportive services outside of the regular school day.

- General education classrooms with supplementary services. In this setting, the special educator serves as a "support facilitator" (Stainback, Stainback, & Harris, 1989) who, in consultation with the general education teacher, identifies the assistance and supports needed by the student, identifies possible interventions, and facilitates implementation. Students may also be served through a resource room program; Jenkins and Heinen (1989), however, found that students overwhelmingly prefer to receive services in a general education classroom rather than in a resource program.

- Part-time general education/part-time special education placement. In this placement, a student attends both programs depending on his or her needs and curriculum content areas.

- Special-class placement. In special classes, the student typically remains with a single teacher for the entire school day.

- Special schools. In the past decade, the number of students served in special schools has significantly decreased, with a trend toward inclusion of these students in general education schools. Special schools are used to serve the most disabled students.

- Homebound services. Homebound services are usually short-term interventions. This is the most restrictive "outpatient" service in that students have no interaction with other students, and the number of hours of instruction is severely limited, ordinarily to one hour daily, or a few hours weekly.

- Instruction in hospital or residential settings. Students placed in these programs are usually a danger to themselves or others.

IDEA 97 (Individuals with Disabilities Education Act, Public Law 105-17) amends the content of each student's Individualized Education Plan (IEP) to emphasize participation of the student with disabilities in the general education curriculum. IEP goals and objectives must be written with participation in general education in mind. The IEP now must include an explanation of the extent to which the student will not be participating with students without disabilities in the general education classroom, and in nonacademic and extracurricular activities (U.S. Department of Education, 1998). The IEP is further discussed in Chapter 10.

Public Law 94-142 insured that students receive related services, including "transportation and such developmental, corrective, and other supportive services as are required to assist the handicapped child to benefit from special education" (Federal Register, 1977, 121.550). In addition to transportation, students with disabilities must be provided with these services if they are necessary for the student to profit from special education: speech pathology, audiology, psychological services, physical and occupational therapy, recreation, early identification, medical and school health services, counseling and social work services, and parent counseling and training. Public Law 101-476 added rehabilitation counseling to the list of related services. Psychotherapy, as a related service, has remained controversial. Osborne (1984) suggests that if a state requires that psychotherapy be provided by a licensed psychiatrist, then it is an exempt medical service.

Inclusive Education

As indicated earlier, the Individuals with Disabilities Education Act (IDEA, Public Law 105-17, 1997 Amendments) specified that each student's Individualized Education Plan must emphasize participation in the general education curriculum (U.S. Department of Education, 1998). Inclusive programs are those in which students with and without disabilities participate jointly in the same educational curricula, activities, and environments (Janko, Schwartz, Sandall, Anderson, & Cottam, 1997). However, in their surveys and classroom observations, Schumm, Vaughn, Haager, McDowell, Rothlein, and Saumell (1995) found that general education teachers are not likely to develop individualized lesson plans for students with disabilities. At the elementary level, however, teachers are more likely to plan individual assignments, alternative materials, and individualized assessment than at the secondary level.

Students with learning disabilities can expect that teachers, particularly at the elementary level, will consider how to meet their needs within the framework of planning for the class as a whole. In terms of content, Schumm and associates (1995) found that students with disabilities are expected to be responsible for the same content as students without identified disabilities. Students with learning disabilities can expect that teachers will consider how to structure their classrooms so that high levels of peer acceptance exist for all students. Although general education teachers viewed the special education teacher as a valuable resource in planning for students with learning disabilities, communication and collaboration were infrequent. Teachers of students with learning disabilities in their general education classrooms frequently checked to see if the students were following directions or staying on task. In terms of postplanning, teachers tended to reflect about how the class as a whole performed, rather than individual students.

In another study, Fuchs, Fuchs, Hamlett, Philips, and Karns (1995) found that general education teachers vary individually regarding the adaptations they provided students with learning disabilities in their general education classrooms. When the general education teachers were specifically prompted and supported to put specialized adaptations in place, they did so, with fairly high levels of fidelity. Teachers rarely ignored explicit requests to help students with learning disabilities, and implemented multiple concurrent strategies to address learning problems.

In his review of case law, Yell (1995) reports that the courts may evaluate action over inclusion of students with emotional/behavioral disorders differently than other cases of students with disabilities. Yell describes several principles of case law that were derived from the *Daniel R. R. v. State Board of Education* (1989), *Greer v. Rome City School District* (1991), *Oberti v. Board of Education of the Borough of Clementon School District* (1993), and *Sacramento City Unified School District v. Rachial H.* (1994) cases. First, the courts support the concept that students with disabilities have a presumptive right to be educated in inclusive settings. The key to ensuring good faith efforts on the part of the school district to maintain a child with disabilities in the inclusive setting lies in the provision of supplementary aids and services. The Individualized Education Plan remains the proper forum for placement decision-making. Though school districts must have, by case law, a complete continuum of alternative placements available, the needs of classroom peers must be considered in cases of the least restrictive alternative. Schools bear the burden of proof in defending their decisions regarding the educational benefit of a student's placement.

Idol (1994) reported that much of the resistance experienced from general education teachers regarding the inclusion of students with emotional/behavioral disorders was founded in fear. This fear is addressed in a description of the "mindsets" for teacher's working with students with emotional/behavioral disorders offered by Webber, Anderson, and Otey (1991). They suggest that teachers working with students with emotional/behavioral disorders should develop mindsets which include, (a) the attitude that problems have solutions, (b) that small successes should be celebrated, (c) that one should give without expecting thanks or something in return, (d) that there is no reason to be afraid of students, (e) that humor can be found throughout the day, and (f) that one should be realistic.

Differences have been reported between the academic performance and social competence of students with disabilities in inclusive and restrictive placements (Meadows, Neel, Scott, & Parker, 1994). Overall, students with disabilities in inclusive settings had higher reading and written language scores, better work habits, and a higher grade-point average. Their teachers reported that they were more attentive, worked harder, and were better adjusted. Students who remained in self-contained classrooms demonstrated more aggression and less self-control, or were more introverted and withdrawn. The majority of teachers reported that they used the same curricula with all students, and that they used the same criteria to evaluate all students. Teachers participating in the Meadows and associates' study reported that they made minimal classroom modifications for students with emotional/behavior disorders, and that placement in inclusive settings meant a major reduction or complete cessation of individualized programming.

Jenkins and Heinen (1989) found that students with disabilities overwhelmingly prefer to receive services in the general education classroom. However, in an investigation of teachers' perceptions of program options, Harvey (1996) reported that self-contained programs for students with emotional/behavioral disorders were perceived by staff to be superior to inclusive programs in both resources and teaching strategies. Well-established self-contained programs were thought to be superior to newly implemented inclusion programs in resources, teaching strategies, program components, and parent/school relationships. Regardless of program, students with emotional/behavioral disorders were perceived as making moderate progress, and as being moderately aggressive. Teachers did not detect significant differences between student progress in self-contained and mainstreamed programs.

Grade Retention

Often, students with learning disabilities or emotional/behavioral disorders repeat a grade. Grade retention is any school practice that causes a student to repeat a particular grade, or for a student to begin kindergarten or first grade one or more years behind their age peers. McLesky, Lancaster, and Grizzle (1995) studied a focus group of kindergartners a year after their retention. They reported that kindergarten retention did not increase achievement, nor did kindergarten retention benefit immature students or slow students. Negative findings emerged, with parent reports of poorer attitudes toward school, teasing by peers, and perceptions of failure. Long-term results included lower self-esteem, lower achievement, and negative school experiences. Students who were retained were 30% more likely to drop out of high school than their peers. Strong positive parental support was critical if students were to benefit from retention. Factors most often used to determine retention included a failure to master grade level work, and immaturity or delays in the development of social and readiness skills. Due to the similarity of these characteristics to those of students identified as learning disabled, McLesky, Lancaster, and Grizzle contend that retention will not have a positive effect on students with learning disabilities. Rather, if a student with a learning disability is failing in a general education class, they suggest that educators identify the students' needs and the issues involved in the failure.

Students from Diverse Ethnic, Cultural, or Linguistic Groups

McIntyre (1996) suggests that issues of race, class, culture, language, gender, and sexual orientation often impact programming for students with emotional/behavioral disorders. The Council for Children with Behavioral Disorders Task Force for Cultural Issues urged the adoption of the following goals related to providing appropriate services for culturally diverse students with emotional/behavioral disorders (1996):

- Insure that students from diverse cultures are truly exhibiting emotional/behavioral disorders rather than culturally based behavior;
- Provide respectful, culturally appropriate services;
- Implement culturally and linguistically competent assessment procedures;
- Recruit professionals who represent various cultural, ethnic, and linguistic groups;
- Provide preservice and inservice training to professionals in modifications of practice that better address the characteristics of students with emotional/behavioral disorders who are from various cultural, ethnic, or linguistic groups;

- Create a welcoming climate where students from various cultural, linguistic, or ethnic groups feel valued, respected, and physically and psychologically safe;
- Enhance the cultural knowledge base of professionals, clients/students, and the public at large.

Classroom Issues

Students with learning disabilities and emotional/behavioral disorders experience various difficulties in the context of their environments. In the classroom, the context is teacher, students, and "place," including curriculum and materials (Bauer & Sapona, 1991). The components of the classroom ecology are dynamic, and they may enhance or impede a student's success.

The dynamic nature of the classroom ecology presents a challenge to students with learning disabilities or emotional/behavioral disorders. Wilson and Williams (1994) explored students' perceptions of their ability to function within the school environment. Factor analysis suggested that students with learning disabilities perceive the school environment and academic tasks as two separate factors. The students with learning disabilities, as compared to students without identified disabilities, exhibited more positive attitudes toward the school environment than an academic task.

Teacher–Student Relationships

In situations where relations are necessarily unequal, such as in teaching, Buber (1965) maintains that teachers must practice "inclusion." Inclusion in this sense means extending the teacher into the reality in which the student participates. Witherell and Noddings (1991) suggest that teachers can be inclusive by taking the perspective of the student, and allowing students to pursue legitimate projects. Through inclusion, the students and teacher must together construct a caring relationship in which the student responds by fully engaging in the task. School then becomes a place in which teachers and students live together, talk to each other, reason together, and enjoy each others' company (Noddings, 1991). As Brendtro and Brokenleg (1993) contend, teachers need to move beyond the deviance and deficit model. They must work to belong, rather than to further continue the alienation which occurs in climates of control.

Successful programs depend on teachers. Morse (1994) reported a common thread among exemplary teachers: these teachers knew their students, and they had a deep empathy for the stress in their students' lives. As teachers, they worked out what they thought was best for the child even when it caused pain and resistance. All of the exemplary teach-

Teachers must take the perspective of the student, and build a caring relationship.

ers cared deeply. The teacher–student relationship is essential for children who are at risk or considered problems. Morse suggests that the "salient etiological condition" most often mentioned in the histories of these children is the lack of adequate adult caring.

Bacon and Bloom (1994) conducted focus groups with students with emotional/behavioral disorders regarding what teachers need to know to work successfully with them. The results showed that teacher–student relationships were of great concern. The students argued that teachers should demonstrate fairness and respect toward students. They wanted teachers to be able to form relationships with students with emotional/behavioral disorders and have the counseling skills needed to help them. The teacher's personal qualities should support interaction with students with emotional/behavioral disorders.

In another study which "asked the consumers," Crowley (1994) reported that students with emotional/behavioral disorders perceived teachers as helpful when they engaged in flexible academic and behavioral program implementation. The students found teacher rigidity and use of discipline as unhelpful. A pervasive theme of anger toward rigid teachers occurred throughout Crowley's data. To be supportive of students, Curwin (1994) argues that it is essential for teachers to help students "rediscover hope." Teacher behaviors related to "rediscovering hope" are presented in Table 7.1.

In regard to young children, Lago-Delello (1998) assessed classroom dynamics including teacher attitude and perceptions, student academic engagement and perceptions of teacher's expectations, and instructional factors, as well as classroom interactions. The results of this assessment indicated that young children identified as at-risk were experiencing a significantly different reality in the classroom than their peers. The use of collaborative/consultative teaching, task modifications, direct instruction, cooperative learning, and peer tutor programs were suggested to increase students' access to instruction. The reality for middle-school students also varied from that of their peers; students with learning problems experienced more stress, less peer support, greater adult support, yet poorer adjustment in the classroom than their peers without learning problems (Wenz-Gross & Siperstein, 1998).

Unfortunately, there is low retention among teachers of learners with emotional/behavioral disorders. In a study of 96 teachers of learners with emotional/behavioral disorders, over a third indicated that they planned to leave the field during the upcoming year, and ten percent were unsure about their future career plans (George, George, Gersten, & Grosenick,

Table 7.1 Teacher Behaviors to Help Students "Rediscover Hope"

To help students "rediscover hope," teachers should:

- help students believe they are competent;
- present tasks that are not too easy;
- make the subject or topic for instruction personally important to the students;
- actively involve students in the learning process;
- personally demonstrate, in obvious ways, a genuine energy and love of the subject and for teaching;
- communicate to students that classroom activities and goals are real and not gimmicks;
- present lessons that are fun and enjoyable;
- welcome students into school and classroom, helping students feel that they belong in school;
- make personal connections with students; and
- pay attention to and plan for motivation.

(Curwin, 1994)

1995). Teachers who were leaving the profession varied from their "staying" peers by the type of service delivery model in which they worked, the adequacy of the support they received, and the time available to them for developing curricula and completing paperwork.

Teacher Beliefs

Several research studies have looked at the perceptions and beliefs held by teachers about students with learning disabilities and emotional/behavioral disorders. Recently, attention has been focused on the possibility that teacher interactions may be aversive to students with learning disabilities or emotional/behavioral disorders. From this point of view, students' off-task behavior may be interpreted as a result of negative reinforcement (Cipani, 1995). Negative reinforcement, Cipani contends, consists of the contingent removal of an aversive stimulus which results in increased behavior production to escape or avoid the aversive stimulus. In the classroom, students' off-task behaviors are most likely reinforced by escape or avoidance of teacher instruction.

Teachers may also demonstrate negative reinforcement by their interactions with their students. Carr, Taylor, and Robinson (1991) reported that teachers of preschool children with disabilities presented fewer and easier task demands to children with higher rates of disruptive behavior than to children with lower rates of disruptive behavior. They indicated that the teachers' behaviors may have been techniques to avoid student disruptions. The nature of a task may have impact on the student's behavior. DePaepe, Shores, Jack, and Denny (1996) found that students with emotional/behavioral disorders, when presented with difficult tasks, had poorer time on-task, and higher percentages of time engaged in disruptive behavior. Easier tasks produced greater attention and fewer disruptions. In their review of research related to instructional variables and problem behavior, Munk and Repp (1994) found that student choice of task and task variation may reduce problem behaviors. Partial-versus whole-task training, and decreasing task-difficulty may increase the likelihood of fewer disruptions.

The issue of negative reinforcement by Gunter and associates (1994) was further explored. In their study, a student with emotional/behavioral disorders was asked to perform tasks without sufficient information. This condition resulted in higher levels of disruptive behavior and lower probabilities of compliance. The study demonstrated that ineffective instructional strategies (for example, requesting a student to perform a task without necessary information) may be an aversive stimulus from which the child escapes, or attempts to escape, by engaging in disruptive behavior.

Teacher perceptions of students who are labeled "learning disabled" were explored by Clark (1997). She provided teachers with vignettes about hypothetical boys who had failed a test, and included information about the student's ability, pattern of effort, and identification as having or not having a learning disability. When the boys were identified as having learning disabilities, teachers described greater rewards and less punishment, less anger and more pity, and higher expectations of future failure. With an expectation of future failure, teachers, then, may be treating learning disabilities as internal and uncontrollable rather than as something on which they can have an impact.

Simmons, Kameenui, and Chard (1998) also examined teachers' assumptions about learning and students with learning disabilities. When given 100 points to divide among five different factors, teachers assigned 50 percent of the points to internal variables such as academic ability and motivation. Teacher delivery accounted for only 25 percent of the points, time for 16 percent, and only 9 percent for the quality of instructional materials. When asked to modify learning materials, teachers usually changed the delivery of instruction and design of instructional materials. Teachers who believe that internal student variables are more important than their efforts may struggle with a sense of efficacy when confronted by students with learning disabilities or emotional/behavioral disorders.

After following two cohorts of students for three years (one group identified as having learning disabilities and the other not identified as having learning disabilities), Carlisle and Chyang (1996) found that teachers consistently rated students with learning disabilities as having significantly less adequate learning capability, and lower in achievement than their peers without learning disabilities. In comparing student evaluations and expectations with the teachers, they reported that teachers often have higher expectations for students than students have for themselves, and that the students with learning disabilities fall particularly short of teacher expectations.

The efforts of teachers to maintain relationships with their students is challenged by the "deskilling" of teachers through programmed, "teacher-proof" materials, and the emphasis on success with standardized testing (Schubert, 1991). Schubert found, however, that teachers regarded by their peers and students as particularly good somehow resisted pressures to be "deskilled," and:

- maintained a holistic perspective on situational problem solving;
- enjoyed being with students;
- drew insights from student experiences outside of school;
- maintained a sense of mission about the importance of teaching;
- exhibited love and compassion for students;
- exhibited a clear sense of meaning and direction;
- guided their work with a quest for that which is worthwhile and just;
- considered the issue of developmental appropriateness for each situation; and
- were actively involved in self-education.

Students may, through their behavior, increase more positive teacher attention. Alber, Heward, and Hippler (1999), in their study of four middle-school students with learning disabilities, taught the students to show their work to the teachers two or three times per session, and to make statements such as, "How am I doing?" When they utilized this strategy, students received more teacher praise, more instructional feedback, and increased the accuracy of their assignments.

Teacher Language

The prevalence of language deficits in students with learning disabilities or emotional/behavioral disorders highlights a need for examining teachers' instructions to students in relation to students' disruptive behaviors (Harrison, Gunter, Reed & Lee, 1996). Harrison and associates argue that students may experience failure during classroom activities when they are given verbal directions that they do not fully comprehend; they may choose to act-out so that they will be required to leave the room (disengage from the lesson) rather than risk embarrassment from academic failure. Based on the literature, Harrison and associates identified subtle and unintentional stimuli that occur in the reciprocal exchanges of instructional language that may be aversive for students. Students, then, may use disruptive behaviors to escape and avoid teacher instructional language for which they do not have comprehension skills, and therefore find aversive. In response to this form of negative reinforcement, Harrison and associates recommend, (a) assessment of both student and teacher language patterns, (b) consistency of instruction and the use of scripted lessons, and, (c) ongoing teacher self-evaluation of the linguistics of their instruction.

The "Place": Curricula and Materials

Teachers and students do not work in a vacuum. Rather, they work together to address curricula and materials. They participate in evaluations of the learning taking place. In addition, teachers assign students in-class work and homework.

Curriculum design for students with disabilities is a national concern. Simmons and Kameenui (1996) suggest that effective curriculum design incorporates "big ideas," that is, concepts and principles that facilitate the most efficient and broadest acquisition of knowledge across a range of examples in a domain. Curriculum should also provide students with strategies, or ways of solving problems. Mediated scaffolding, in the form of the personal guidance, assistance, and support that a teacher, peer, materials, or task provides a learner should be carefully considered. Integration, both within and across curriculum areas, should be strategic, with care to combine new information with what the learner already knows to produce a more general, higher-order skill. Content should be reviewed to reinforce the essential blocks of information within a content domain.

One consideration for curriculum presented by Simmons and Kameenui (1996) is that of primed background knowledge. Successful acquisition of new information depends largely on the knowledge that the learner brings to the task, the accuracy of that information, or knowledge and the extent to which the learner accesses and uses that information. For students with learning disabilities and emotional/behavioral disorders, priming that background knowledge is necessary to success.

Ellis (1997a, 1997b) suggests that many current accommodations for adolescents with learning disabilities water down the curriculum by reducing opportunities to learn, and by emphasizing memorization of facts. Accommodations are frequently made in three forms: (a) the manner in which students are assessed and graded, (b) the nature of the curriculum is made more basic, and (c) students are assigned to easier tasks. Ellis suggests that when the curriculum is watered down there is an emphasis on memorizing loosely related facts, opportunities to learn content and critical thinking skills are reduced, and the investment in learning is reduced. When the curriculum is "watered-up" rather than "watered-down" there is more emphasis on students' constructing in-depth knowledge, with an emphasis on concepts, patterns, and strategies and relationship understanding. Through "watering up" there is increased reflection, risk-taking, and active participation. More emphasis is placed on social responsibility and collaboration, and academic and social self-esteem are enhanced. Social support is provided for student achievement, and intensive instruction is provided in critical areas.

In a national study of programs for students with emotional/behavioral disorders, Knitzer, Steinberg, and Fleish (1990) reported the presence of a "curriculum of control." This curriculum was evidenced by an emphasis on behavioral management, maintained through elaborate points and levels systems. In these classrooms, maintaining silence and order was emphasized over increasing skills. Though students were referred for poor social interaction skills, no group work was available to students in which they could learn to interact appropriately. Wehby, Symons, Canale, and Go (1998) concurred that though research has demonstrated that there are effective practices for students with emotional/behavioral disorders, classrooms usually reflect an overall lack of systematic programming, negative teacher–student interactions, few praise statements, low rates of instructional interaction, and high rates of reprimand.

Nichols (1992) reports that not only is the curriculum of control dreary, it is counterproductive. The emphasis on management tends to generate the behaviors that placement for students with emotional/behavioral disorders is designed to ameliorate. A "curriculum of control" works best for students who need control the least; the less control an individual has over objective events, the more satisfaction he or she draws from destructive acts.

As opposed to the curriculum of control, Henley (1994) supports a curriculum of "self-control" designed to help students develop the skills they need to cope with social situations in and out of school, and to serve as preventive discipline. Students with emotional/behavioral disorders should be supported in learning to control their impulses when using instructional materials, moving in unstructured space, and making classroom transitions. Students should be taught to assess the social reality of a setting through abiding by rules, organizing materials, accepting feedback, and appreciating feelings. An emphasis should be placed on helping the student cope with the stress of group situations. Teachers should work with students to solve social problems through focusing on the present, learning from past experience, recalling personal behavior, and resolving conflicts. Learning self-regulation is essential if students are to increase their independence, task engagement, and ability to self-evaluate their behavior (Graham, Harris, & Reid, 1992).

Curricula can have an impact on both student learning and behavior. Lamm and Epstein (1992) reported that individuals with severe reading problems often had emotional problems with high levels of anxiety and difficulties in concentration. Students with emotional/behavioral disorders who had reading problems were more aggressive than their peers with emotional/behavioral disorders who did not have reading difficulties (Cornwell & Bawden, 1992). Clarke, Dunlap, Foster-Johnson, Childs, Wilson, White, and Vera (1995) reported that students' behavior could be improved if their interests were incorporated into curricular activities. In their study, after identifying curricular assignments associated with high levels of problem behavior, assignments were modified in accordance with the students' interests while the integrity of the instructional objectives was maintained. These modifications both reduced problem behavior and increased desirable behavior.

Textbooks.   Students with learning disabilities and emotional/behavioral disorders often have difficulty dealing with the textbooks used in general education classrooms. By using advance organizers and preteaching the vocabulary, teachers can increase the likelihood of success for students with disabilities. In addition, some students may require audiotaped textbooks. Students may need explicit instruction regarding the textbook itself, including instruction on the textbook structure. Highlighting information, providing students with a partial outline, and pairing question numbers from study guides with page numbers in the text are useful strategies for students with learning disabilities or emotional/behavioral disorders (Editor, *CEC Today* 1997).

Prentice and Cousin (1993) suggest "moving beyond the textbook," to incorporate art, literature, and drama to help middle-school students with learning disabilities acquire content area concepts and reading skills. They suggest that the teacher begin with student experiences and ideas about a topic, elicit current responses, and brainstorm ideas. Following this opening exercise, the students should seek out the experts, read the content area text, and define the main point of the text. The topics from the text are then analyzed, with the main concepts described. The class then determines how the concepts could be best represented, whether it be through written expression (essay, poetry, fiction), visual arts (clay, painting, drawing, collage, model building), dramatic arts (script writing, reader's theater, mime, or puppets) or trade books. After completing their projects, the students review their initial ideas about the topic. Finally, the students complete self-evaluation.

Test.   Frequently, testing demonstrates what students don't know rather than what they do know, revealing their incompetence rather than competence. Dalton, Tivnan, Riley, Rayson, and Dias (1995) compared test formats for fourth graders with and without learning disabilities. Three different kinds of assessment were compared: visual and verbal multiple choice, constructed diagram, and questionnaire. In addition, a hands-on performance assessment was given to a subset of the students. Students with and without disabilities performed better on the hands-on assessment than on any of the paper and pencil tasks. Students with and without learning disabilities performed better on the constructed diagram as compared to the questionnaire and multiple-choice formats.

One of the most common accommodations for students with learning disabilities and emotional/behavioral disorders in taking tests is to provide extra time. However, several other strategies may provide additional support. Students may need instruction in specific test-taking skills and strategies. Alternative forms of tests may be needed. Clear, readable, and uncluttered test forms must be used. A scribe or a computer may provide support to students in producing their responses. Students should also be given the opportunity to have practice sessions before the actual test (Editor, 1997).

Gajria, Salend, and Hemrick (1994) studied teacher acceptability of testing modifications to students with learning disabilities in general education classrooms. The majority of general education teachers, in grades seven through twelve, indicated that they were aware of test adaptations, but did not use them because they perceived them as ineffective, difficult, or a threat to the academic integrity of their tests. Teachers indicated that they were more likely to use modifications that were applicable to all students, and were less likely to use individualized modifications such as dictating responses, or taking tests in another setting. Teachers indicated that they would be more likely to use modifications if they required little individualization in terms of planning, resources, and extra time.

Class assignments and homework. Rademacher, Schumaker, and Deshler (1996) studied the characteristics of high-quality classroom assignments, and how they are best indicated by teachers, students with learning disabilities, and students without learning disabilities. In their review of the literature, they identified several factors related to the design of effective assignments, including, (a) carefully defined instructional objectives for the task as it related to the topic to be learned, (b) a variety of formats and types of assignments, (c) tasks written to provide a challenge, (d) opportunities for learning and incorporating student choices, and (e) easy to understand and follow instructions. In their actual observation of classrooms, however, they found that teachers initially perform few of the behaviors associated with the assignment characteristics and explanation factors for effective work with students, but that they could be taught to use them in their assignment routines.

Nuzum (1998) contends that clarity about homework is essential, and that the success of homework depends on students' skills and the understanding of assignments, as well as parental expectations and participation. The goals of homework assignments should be made explicit to students. Nuzum suggests that homework assignments should be balanced among seven purposes of, (a) practice, (b) preview, (c) review, (d) discovery, (e) application, (f) problem solving, and (g) creative assignments. Teachers should allow sufficient time to give assignments, and use the assignment as part of the learning process. Efforts should be made to help students organize their homework.

Homework completion is a common problem for students with learning disabilities or emotional/behavioral disorders. The Council for Exceptional Children (1997) has several suggestions to support students with disabilities with assignment completion. They suggest that teachers break tasks into workable and obtainable steps, including clear due dates. Each assignment should include examples and specific steps to accomplish the task. Requirements necessary to complete the assignment should be listed and posted. Teachers should check assignments frequently, and arrange a study buddy for students, if needed. All of the requirements of the completed activity should be clearly communicated to students.

Epstein, Bursuck, Jayanthi, and Sawyer (1998) explored students' ratings of adaptations made by middle-school teachers to support homework completion. Middle-schools students' preferred adaptation would be to have no homework; teachers would give assignments that are finished entirely at school. Students' reasons for this adaptation were that it would provide more time for other activities, and that there would be more help available at school than at home. They also preferred:

- Allowing a small group of students to work together to complete assignments (making learning more enjoyable, making help from peers available);
- Allowing extra credit assignments (a strategy to achieve higher grades);

- Beginning assignments in class with the teacher checking for student understanding (would lead to more accurate answers);
- Reminders about due dates; shorter, more frequent assignments (would facilitate organization).

Two adaptations were least preferred by students with disabilities. The students did not want to have a different assignment than the rest of the class; they felt that it wasn't fair and would negatively affect their self-concept. In addition, they reported feeling left out and less capable when the whole assignment was different. Students also did not want a required assignment book or student plan book, but rather preferred to use their own strategies. Some students reported that using a required assignment book interfered with organization.

Homework is often a point of contention between teachers and students with emotional/behavioral disorders. Sunderland, Bursuck, Polloway, and Foley (1995) found that students with emotional/behavioral disorders have serious problems with homework completion. Teachers identified the difficulties with homework to be distractibility, responding poorly to parents supervising the homework, and procrastination. Parents described procrastination and distractibility as the greatest challenges. Epstein, Polloway, Foley, and Patton (1993) found that among students with disabilities, those with emotional/behavioral disorders had the most pronounced difficulties with homework completion.

Effective Instructional Strategies

Students with learning disabilities or emotional/behavioral disorders require individualized instructional strategies and accommodations. Two styles of pedagogy, critical teaching and scaffolding, have been found to be effective ways to support the learning of these students. In addition, instructional structuring has been related to greater achievement among students with learning disabilities or emotional/behavioral disorders. In this section, specific content strategies and general accommodations for students with learning disabilities or emotional/behavioral disorders are reviewed. Because the research on learning disabilities has traditionally emphasized academic instructional strategies and accommodations, and the research on emotional/behavioral disorders has emphasized behavior and classroom management, much of the information in this section only specifically addresses learning disabilities. These strategies, of course, may be applied with students with emotional/behavioral disorders when appropriate.

Critical Pedagogy

The concept of "critical" pedagogy offers guidance for effective instruction in the classroom for students with emotional/behavioral disorders. "Critical" instruction incorporates students' experiences, background knowledge, and authentic tasks which are meaningful to the students, along with the students' interests, into the teaching/learning process (Goldstein, 1996). Grounded in critical theory, which is an effort to provide the social/cultural context to situations involving change, critical pedagogy emphasizes meaning rather than form, and creativity and divergent thinking rather than correctness. Interactive/dialogue-based teacher–student interactions are utilized rather than teacher-centered instruction. In order to implement this "critical pedagogy," teachers must be well-informed regarding the community's history, the history of the cultural groups of those with whom they are working, and community resources, including people and community centers, that can provide additional information and support to teachers and students.

In addition to traditional social and behavioral interventions, academic instruction may offer strong support for students with emotional/behavioral disorders. According to Swicegood and Linehan (1995), a constructivist approach adopts the position that students' understanding is developmental, socially and culturally mediated, and subjective. The constructivist approach assumes self-regulation, which is a need of students with emotional/behavioral disorders. The implementation of self-regulation strategies, such as self-recording of success in meeting specific teacher expectations, has been found to increase the positive behavior of students with emotional/behavioral disorders (Clees, 1995).

Scaffolding

The term "scaffolding" was initially used by Wood, Bruner, and Ross (1976) to describe the ways in which parents support the problem-solving efforts of young children. Stone (1998) recounts that Vygotsky's (1962) concept of the zone of proximal development has become a foundation for exploring applications of scaffolding. The metaphor of scaffolding which evolved during the 1980's has four key elements. In scaffolding, the adult:

1. Recruits a child in a meaningful and culturally desirable activity just beyond the child's current level of understanding or control.

2. Assesses the child's understanding or skill level so that appropriate support can be provided when needed.

3. Provides a variety of supports (e.g., modeling, pointing, extensive dialogue) depending upon the child's needs.

4. Gradually withdraws the supports so that the responsibility is transferred from adult to child.

Stone (1998) proposes an enriched metaphor of scaffolding, with an emphasis on the communication dynamics and conceptual reorganization involved in teacher-child interaction during instructional activities with students with learning disabilities. Though it is often argued that students with learning disabilities benefit most from a direct approach to instruction, Stone points out that students can benefit from an active, indirect instructional approach, and there is no reason to believe that all learning must take place through direct instruction. Scaffolding may provide such indirect instruction. In addition, Stone suggests that scaffolding may be useful in prevention, recognizing that parents have many opportunities to foster the development of new concepts and strategies.

Scaffolding has been supported as a useful way to refocus attention and efforts in the education of students with learning disabilities (Reid, 1998). Biemiller and Meichenbaum (1998) suggest that scaffolding may be helpful, but students should be placed in situations in which they have increasing responsibility to apply what they learn. They suggest that more competent students may be more likely to receive scaffolding experience, while less competent students do not receive the same opportunities to use metacognitive skills. Teachers may, in fact, moderate instruction to such an extent that these students do not have opportunities for a full scaffolding experience. Palincsar (1998) suggests that the ways in which teachers provide context, activities, and scaffolding to students may increase the effectiveness of instruction.

Scaffolding has not received total support as a metaphor for instruction. Butler (1998) argues that the metaphor is fundamentally flawed, and that there should be an increased emphasis on ways to promote correspondence between instructional activities and our vision of teaching and learning. Donahue and Lopez-Reyna (1998) propose that rather than scaffolding, a "flying buttress" is needed, so that a more permanent support to building new knowledge on an existing foundation becomes an integral and evolving part of the new structure. They argue that some students with learning disabilities may have difficulty with scaffolded instruction because they follow a different agenda, such as camouflaging their lack of comprehension, during instructional discourse. They do not agree that scaffolded instruction always employs cooperative, informative, truthful, relevant, and clear teachers. Others argue that all available research should be applied in drawing conclusions about the efficacy of instructional procedures, and that using scaffolding in itself may be limiting.

Structuring Instruction

Teaching, according to Quinn, Epstein, and Cumblad (1995), is comprised of three sets of activities: those before instruction, during instruction, and after instruction. Before instruction, the teacher must establish a positive learning atmosphere, grounded in a belief that the students are capable of learning. The teacher should assume responsibility for controlling the instructional variables that affect positive learning outcomes, and should convey high yet reasonable expectations for each student's achievement. The classroom space should be organized to reduce disruptive noise, to allow for monitoring and interacting with students, and to promote prosocial student interactions. Also, before instruction, the teacher should establish classroom rules and procedures, and conduct a thorough analysis of student characteristics, task features, and teaching methods. As the teacher considers instructional design, he or she should systematically integrate the information gleaned from assessment with the characteristics of the task to be taught in order to organize maximally effective lessons.

During instruction, Quinn and associates contend that the teacher should manage time carefully, and monitor the level of interaction. "Good teaching" behaviors should be used, including using explicit advance organizers, providing sufficient exemplars, and presenting the material in several ways. The teacher should supply the opportunity for guided and independent practice. After instruction, the teacher should continue to monitor student progress, such as movement toward goals, pacing, amount of practice, patterns of errors, and management of social behavior. In addition, the teacher should evaluate student progress in terms of the instructional content.

It has been demonstrated that peers can be effective instructors of students with learning disabilities or emotional/behavioral disorders. Class-wide peer tutoring is a peer-based strategy in which each student is paired with a partner, and each pair is assigned to a team (Simmons, 1994). The class then works simultaneously on an instructional task. Class-wide peer tutoring increases students' opportunities to respond by providing more frequent interaction between "teacher" (in this case the peer tutor) and student (Arrega-Mayer, 1998). Simmons (1994) studied the relationship of instructional complexity and role reciprocity during class-wide peer tutoring. Students in class-wide peer tutoring settings significantly outperformed their peers who did not receive class-wide peer tutoring on measures of reading fluency. However, when role reciprocity was used, students also significantly improved their comprehension.

Cross-age tutoring (tutoring among individuals of different ages) may be an effective strategy to improve the achievement, social behavior, and self-perceptions of students with learning disabilities or emotional/behavioral disorders. Cockran, Feng, Cartledge, and Hamilton (1993) found that pairing African-American students with emotional behavioral disorders with African-American tutors in a cross-age setting improved both their grades and behavior. In another cross-age peer tutoring program, adults with learning disabilities were successful tutors for adolescents with emotional/behavioral disorders, assisting them in developing problem solving, assertiveness, and self-management skills (Miller, Miller, Armentrout, & Flannagan, 1995).

Peers of students with learning disabilities or emotional/behavioral disorders themselves may be effective behavior change agents. Gaide, Arllen, and Hendrickson (1994) reported that students with emotional/behavioral disorders were effective as partners in peer mediation. Peer confrontation regarding behaviors has also been demonstrated to be effective in increasing positive student behavior (Salend, Jantzen, & Giek, 1992). In peer confrontation, positive peer culture strategies are used to challenge students to change their own behavior. This strategy has been effective in decreasing disruptive behavior in classrooms (Gable, Arllan, & Hendrickson, 1995).

Content Specific Strategies

Literacy Learning

Students' literacy development ranges from novice to expert rather than mastery of selected skills at a particular grade level (Keefe, 1997). Englert and Mariage (1996) suggest that students need to have ways of thinking and ways of talking about literacy. In the sociocultural perspective they suggest, public conversations for students are used to increase self-management, students work to acquire a language-based discourse, individuals participate in a culture in which language is used, and students, as readers and writers, learn how to use cognitive processes to become both users and producers of knowledge. In these classrooms, more effective teachers transfer control to students, and scaffold the performance of students in the zone of proximal development. They adapt activities to provide multiple points of entry into literacy, and involve students in collaborative activity. Teachers, in a literacy community, recognize that the activities and principles are modes of teaching rather than specific curricular events in the school schedule.

Englert, Raphael, and Mariage (1994) describe an integrated literacy curriculum designed to promote literacy in students with disabilities. The Early Literacy Project (ELP) was developed collaboratively by university and school-based researchers. The guiding principles of ELP include: teaching to self-regulation, responsive instruction, building literate communities, literacy in meaningful activities, and an integrated curriculum. Activities composition and comprehension of the whole, connected texts, and specific skills are provided through structured instruction so that all students can be involved in literacy, and teachers can identify the students' entry points (his or her zone of proximal development). Individual accommodations are made in response to each student's zone of proximal development. For example, some students may read a wordless book or compose texts using pictures, random letters, initial letters, blank lines, invented spellings, and conventional spelling. While the teacher accepts work at a student's ability level, the student is encouraged to assume increased responsibility as his or her literacy develops.

In terms of writing, Bernice Wong (1997) reviewed two decades of research on instruction of writing for students with learning disabilities.

Research evolved from an emphasis on spelling and punctuation in the 1970s to a writing-process approach in the 1980s. Current research emphasizes difficulties experienced by individuals with learning disabilities other than spelling and punctuation. In writing, students with learning disabilities had little awareness of the need to plan and revise, and had production problems including a limited awareness of their cognitive processes and text structure during writing.

Wong, Butler, Ficzere, and Kuperis (1997) used a writing strategy with adolescents with learning disabilities and low-achieving students. Students were taught through "thinking-aloud" planning, and by teachers' modeling appropriate questions through interactive dialogues. These dialogues were pivotal in student collaborative planning, and subsequent revision of essays. The evaluation results indicate that the students improved substantially in the quality of their compare-and-contrast essays after training. Improvement was shown in clarity of writing, appropriateness, and organization of ideas involving comparisons and contrasts of topics in the essays. Though students' self-efficacy of writing did not improve, the students reported that they became more aware of how they write, and of areas in which their writing needed improvement.

Keefe, Davis, and Andrews-Beck (1997) observed and categorized the writing behaviors of primary students with mild disabilities in a whole-language classroom. A qualitative analysis revealed that the students were able to develop and productively use metacognitive strategies such as verbal rehearsal, rereading, and questioning. They used external sources of help during the writing process, such as the dictionary, books, environmental prints, pictures, personal previous writings, and peer and teacher assistance. While these learners were only novice writers, observations revealed they engaged in writing, generated ideas, used prior knowledge, and showed some ability to plan, organize, and revise. In addition, the students were able to monitor and correct their writing with regard to both meaning and conventions of writing.

McNaughton, Hughes, and Clark (1994) reviewed 27 studies on spelling instruction for students with learning disabilities. The following activities were found to enhance learning to spell for some students with learning disabilities: (a) limiting the number of words introduced each day, (b) using student-directed and peer-assisted instruction, (c) naming letters aloud during practice, (d) instruction in morphemic analysis, (e) providing immediate error limitation and correction, (f) applying motivating reinforcers, and (g) conducting periodic retesting and review.

In an investigation involving 12 college students with learning disabilities, word processing with an integrated spell checker resulted in significant reduction in spelling errors. Various spell-checker techniques, however, did not enable students to produce a composition with the same level of spelling accuracy as that of peers without identified disabilities.

There is an increasing use of various technologies in the classroom to aid writing. Computer-supported applications for struggling writers include immediate and reliable legible handwriting, increased fluency, efficient editing, and efficient illustration (Hunt-Berg & Rankin, 1994). Research has investigated the efficacy and potential use of various technologies for writing. For example, Bahr, Nelson, and Van Meter (1996) compared two computer-based writing tools: story grammar questions and graphics-based tools. Results indicated that student strengths influenced the benefits of one tool over another. Computer-presented story grammar questions benefitted students with less internal organizational ability. The graphics-based tool benefitted students with strong organizational skills.

Technology has been applied to assist students in spelling and handwriting. Berninger, Abbott, Reed, Abbott, Brooks, Vaughan, & Graham (1998) contrasted using computers and paper-and-pencil methods to improve spelling and handwriting. Results demonstrated that the computer did not offer an advantage in learning to spell for the students who had handwriting disabilities. Students with spelling problems were more successful in using paper and pencil to learn easier words, but learned longer words more easily using the computer. When using word processors with speech synthesis and word prediction capabilities, MacArthur (1998) found that students improved their basic writing skills with that technology. However, using these supports did not increase learning or generalization skills, but rather improved the students' outputs. Teachers must determine whether each student needs to learn basic skills, or to have requirements modified to increase output.

Reading

In a study of the emergent literacy of young children, Katims (1994) conducted a year-long study of preschool children with mild-to-moderate disabilities. The study focused on the influence of curriculum and procedures on literacy development. Curriculum and procedures that support literacy learning include, (a) a literature-rich environment, (b) repeated readings of familiar and predictable books, (c) assisted reading, (d) interactive dialog about books, (e) modeling and demonstration of book handling, and (f) independent interactions with literacy materials.

In their review of twenty years of research, Mastropieri and Scruggs (1997) identified several best practices for promoting reading comprehension for students with learning disabilities. The strongest positive outcomes in reading comprehension were related to teacher-led questioning and self-questioning strategies, followed by text-enhancement strategies. Strategies involving basic skills instruction and reinforcement demonstrated some positive outcomes.

Students with learning disabilities were found, in a study by Carr and Thompson (1996), to be better able to answer inferential questions when they have adequate prior knowledge. However, their ability was not the same as their peers without identified disabilities. Students with learning disabilities should be encouraged to use more strategic behaviors when they have an adequate knowledge base. An "able" as opposed to a "disabled" paradigm will be helpful in discovering conditions for successful learning.

One-to-one instruction in reading is a powerful and often favored intervention for students who demonstrate problems in the earliest stages of reading. It is, however, not always available to the students who most need assistance. Vadasy, Jenkins, Antil, Wayne, and O'Connor (1997) describe an intervention for which a set of lessons was designed to provide individual instruction in phonological and early reading skills to first-grade students. Community tutors delivered lessons after school to 17 students identified as high risk for a learning disability. Their performances were compared to the performances of students in a control condition. These tutors worked one-half hour per day, four days a week, for 267 weeks. Students who were tutored showed significantly more growth on measures of spelling, segmentation, and reading.

Mathematics

Miller and Mercer (1997) summarized issues concerning the mathematics learning of students with learning disabilities. They reported that difficulties in mathematics begin in elementary school, and continue into adulthood. Throughout elementary school, their computation skills may be two to three years behind their peers in some areas, and many secondary students with learning disabilities may only achieve fifth- or sixth-grade proficiency. Miller and Mercer report several factors related to difficulties in mathematics, including learned helplessness, difficulty in information processing, difficulty in selecting the appropriate strategy and evaluating for accuracy, and difficulties with required verbal sequences. In addition, student fear of failure, and low self-esteem regarding mathematics ability, may cause anxiety and confusion. Significantly, poor curricula and instruction may also be instrumental in the students' mathematics difficulties. The typical mathematics curricula revolves almost exclusively around reliance on basal textbooks. Textbooks use a spiraling approach, rapidly introducing numerous skills in a single-graded book, and reintroducing the same skills at higher levels in subsequent graded texts. Skill mastery is difficult due to superficial coverage of many skills. Teachers may choose to move forward through the curriculum before all students have learned the content.

The speed at which students with learning disabilities become proficient in mathematics is a problem. Cawley and Parmer (1996) reported that it takes students with learning disabilities approximately four years to attain what normally achieving students accomplish in one year. In a follow-up study, Cawley, Parmer, Yan, and Miller (1998) examined arithmetic computation of a large sample of typically achieving students and students with learning disabilities. Four trends emerged from their data:

- Normally achieving students demonstrated incremental gains over the years in performance levels, while students with learning disabilities did not.
- Both groups demonstrated a higher percentage correct for items with fewer steps than with those with a greater number of steps. There were more calculation errors rather than faulty procedures in the complex problems.
- Mastery of some operations takes place sooner than others, and there is a different performance across operations.
- The performance of students with learning disabilities lags behind normally achieving students and the discrepancy increases over time in middle school.

Further study indicates that students with learning disabilities demonstrate little growth between the ages of 10 and 12 except in the subsets involving increasingly larger addition items.

Maccini and Hughes (1997) reviewed the literature related to mathematics interventions for adolescents with learning disabilities for the seven-year period of 1988–1995. They found that the majority of interventions focused on basic skills, followed by problem solving, and word stories. Only one study focused on higher-level mathematics (algebraic equations). There is apparently an increase in problem-solving strategies, though most of the studies in the review continue to focus on procedural knowledge, such as facts, computations, and step-by-step procedures.

Accommodations

Placing students with learning disabilities and emotional/behavioral disorders in general education classrooms requires accommodation. The Council for Exceptional Children (Author, 1997) suggests that when making an accommodation, teachers should consider the purpose of the activity which they are adjusting. In addition, teachers should analyze the social skills required by the student to respond to the accommodation, and whether the student is willing to use the accommodation. The cost of the accommodation, in terms of both time and money, should be considered.

Several forms of accommodation may be considered (Council for Exceptional Children, 1997). The teacher could consider changing the instructional grouping or arrangements. He or she may adjust the lesson format, the goals of the lesson, or the planned teaching strategies. Accommodations should be evaluated by asking these questions:

- Does the accommodation increase a student's interactions with his or her classmates?
- Does the accommodation improve a student's ability to be an active participant in the lesson?
- Does the accommodation help the student build skills over time?
- Does the accommodation connect the curriculum and make it relevant to the student's current or future life?
- Does the accommodation reduce the level of abstraction of the materials, or, depending on the student, increase its complexity?
- Does the accommodation match the educator's teaching style to the student's learning style?

Summary Points

- The success of a program for students with emotional/behavioral disorders depends on the teacher to form strong relationships with his or her students.
- Peers with emotional/behavioral disorders may be themselves effective change agents, and work as tutors and peer counselors.
- Teachers' interactions may contribute to the disruptive behavior of their students.
- Students with emotional/behavioral disorders often have language disorders which may affect their classroom interactions.
- Traditionally, programming in classrooms for students with emotional/behavioral disorders has been a "curriculum of control."
- A constructivist approach to academic instruction may provide support to students with emotional/behavioral disorders.
- A "cascade of services" must be available to students with emotional/behavioral disorders.
- Issues of race, class, culture, language, gender, and sexual orientation often impact programming for students with emotional/behavioral disorders.

Key Words and Phrases

cascade of services—a continuum of services that provides a framework for meeting the individual needs of learners

constructivist approach—an approach that assumes a student's understanding is developmentally, socially, and culturally mediated, and subjective

critical instruction—instruction that incorporates students' experiences, background knowledge, and meaningful tasks into the teaching/learning process

cross-age tutoring—tutoring between individuals of different ages

curriculum of control—an emphasis on behavioral management, maintained through elaborate points and levels systems

negative reinforcement—the contingent removal of an aversive stimulus which results in increased behavior production to escape or avoid the aversive stimulus

related services—supportive services required to assist the learner to benefit from special education

References

Alber, S. R., Heward, W. L., & Hippler, B. J. (1999). Teaching middle school students with learning disabilities to recruit positive teacher attention. *Exceptional Children, 64* (2), 253–270.

Arrega-Mayer, C. (1998). Increasing active student responding and improving academic performance through classwide peer tutoring. *Intervention in School and Clinic, 34* (2), 89–94.

Audette, B., & Algozzine, B. (1997). Re-inventing government? Let's re-invent special education. *Journal of Learning Disabilities, 30* (4), 378–383.

Bacon, E. H., & Bloom, L. A. (1994). "Don't ratl' the kids." *Journal of Emotional and Behavioral Problems, 3* (1), 8–10.

Bahr, C. M., Nelson, N. W., & Van Mater, A. M. (1998). The effects of text-based and graphics-based software tools on planning and organizing stories. *Journal of Learning Disabilities, 29* (4), 355–370.

Bauer, A. M., & Sapona, R. H. (1991). *Managing classrooms to facilitate learning.* Upper Saddle River, NJ: Prentice Hall.

Berninger, V., Abbott, R., Rogan, L., Reed, E., Abbott, S., Brook, A., Vaughan, K., & Graham, S. (1998). Teaching spelling to children with specific disabilities: The mind's ear and eye beat the computer or pencil. *Learning Disabilities Quarterly, 21* (2), 106–122.

Biemiller, A., & Meichenbaum, D. (1998). The consequences of negative scaffolding for students who learn slowly—a commentary on C. Addison Stone's 'The metaphor of scaffolding: Its utility for the field of learning disabilities.' *Journal of Learning Disabilities, 31* (4), 365–369.

Bos, C. S., & Anders, P. L. (1990). Interactive teaching and learning: Instructional practices for teaching content and strategic knowledge. In T. E. Scruggs & B. Y. L. Wong, (Eds.), *Intervention research in learning disabilities* (pp. 166–185). NY: Springer.

Brendtro, L. K., & Brokenleg, M. (1993). Beyond the curriculum of control. *The Journal of Emotional and Behavioral Problems, 1* (4), 2–12.

Buber, M. (1965). *Between man and man.* NY: Macmillan.

Butler, D. L. (1998). In search of the architect of learning: A commentary on scaffolding as a metaphor for instructional interactions. *Journal of Learning Disabilities, 31* (4), 374–386.

Carlisle, J. F., & Chang, V. (1996). Evaluation of academic capabilities in science by students with and without learning disabilities and their teachers. *The Journal of Special Education, 30* (1), 18–34.

Carpenter, C. D., Bloom, L. A., & Boat, M. B. (1999). Guidelines for special educators: Achieving socially valid outcomes. *Intervention in School and Clinic, 34* (3), 143–149.

Carr, E. G., Taylor, J. C., & Robinson, S. (1991) The effects of severe behavior problems in children on the teaching behavior of adults. *Journal of Applied Behavior Analysis, 24,* 325–535.

Cawley, J. F., & Parmer, R. S. (1996). Arithmetic computational abilities of students with LD: Implications for instruction. *Learning Disabilities Research and Practice, 11* (4), 230–237.

Cawley, J. F., Parmer, R. S., Yan, W., & Miller, J. H. (1998). Arithmetic computation performance of students with learning disabilities: Implications for curriculum. *Learning Disabilities Research and Practice, 13* (2), 68–74.

Cipani, E. C. (1995). Be aware of negative reinforcement. *Teaching Exceptional Children, 27* (1), 36–40.

Clark, M. D. (1997). Teacher response to learning disability: A test of attributional principles. *Journal of Learning Disabilities, 30* (1), 69–73.

Clarke, S., Dunlap, G., Foster-Johnson, L., Childs, K. E., Wilson, D., White, R., & Vera, A. (1995). Improving the conduct of students with behavioral disorders by incorporating student interests into curricular activities. *Behavioral Disorders, 20* (4), 221–237.

Clees, T. J. (1995). Self-recording of students' daily schedules of teachers' expectancies: Perspectives on reactivity, stimulus control, and generalization. *Exceptionality, 5* (3), 113–129.

Cockran, L., Feng, H., Cartledge, G., & Hamilton, S. (1993). The effects of cross-age tutoring on the academic achievement, social behavior, and self-perceptions of low achieving African-American males with behavioral disorders. *Behavioral Disorders, 18* (4), 292–302.

Cornwall, A., & Bawden, N. H. (1992). Reading disabilities and aggression: A critical review. *Journal of Learning Disabilities, 25* (5), 281–288.

Crowley, E. P. (1993). A qualitative analysis of mainstreamed behaviorally disordered aggressive adolescents' perceptions of helpful and unhelpful teacher attitudes and behaviors. *Exceptionality, 4* (3), 131–151.

Curwin, R. (1994). Helping students rediscover hope. *Journal of Emotional and Behavioral Problems, 3* (1), 27–30.

Dalton, B., Tivnan, T., Riley, M. K., Rawson, P., & Dias, D. (1995). Revealing competence: fourth-grade students with and without learning disabilities show what they know on paper-and-pencil and hands-on performance assessments. *Learning Disabilities Research and Practice, 10* (4), 198–214.

Daniel R. v. State Board of Education, 874 F.2d 1036 (5th Cir. 1989).

DePaepe, P. A., Shores, R. E., Jack. S. L., & Denny, R. K. (1996). Effects of task difficulty on the disruptive and on-task behavior of students with severe behavior disorders. *Behavioral Disorders, 21* (3), 216–225.

Donahue, M. L., & Lopez-Reyna, N. A. (1998). Conversational maxims and scaffolded learning in children with learning disabilities: Is the flying buttress a better metaphor? *Journal of Learning Disabilities, 31* (4), 398–403.

Education for All Handicapped Children Act, Federal Register, Pub. L. No. 94-142, §121–550 (1977).

Effective accommodations for students with exceptionalities. Editor (1997). *CEC Today, 4* (3), 1, 9, and 15.

Ellis, E. S. (1997a). Watering up the curriculum for adolescents with learning disabilities. *Remedial and Special Education, 18* (6), 326–346.

Ellis, E. S. (1997b). Watering up the curriculum for adolescents with learning disabilities–Part 2. *Remedial and Special Education, 19* (2), 91–105.

Englert, C. S., & Mariage, T. V. (1996). A socio-cultural perspective: Teaching ways of thinking and ways of talking in a literacy community. *Learning Disabilities Research and Practice, 11* (3), 157–167.

Englert, C. S., Raphael, T. E., & Mariage, T. V. (1994). Developing a school-based discourse for literacy learning: A principled search for understanding. *Learning Disability Quarterly, 17.* 2–32.

Englert, C. S., Tarrant, K. L., Mariage, T. Y., & Oxer, T. (1994). Lesson talk as the work of reading groups: The effectiveness of two interventions. *Journal of Learning Disabilities, 27,* 165–185.

Epstein, M. H., Bursuck, W. D., Jayanthi, M., & Sawyer, V. (1998). The preferences of middle school: Students for homework adaptations made by general education teachers. *Learning Disabilities Research and Practice, 13* (2), 109–117.

Epstein, M. H., Polloway, E. A., Foley, R. M., & Patton, J. R. (1993). Homework: A comparison of teachers' and parents' perceptions of the problems experienced by students identified as having behavioral disorders, learning disabilities, or no disabilities. *Remedial and Special Education, 14* (5), 40–50.

Forman, E. A., & Kraker, M. J. (1985). The social origins of logic: The contributions of Piaget and Vygotsky. In M. W. Berkowtiz, (Ed.), *Peer conflict and psychological growth* (pp. 23–39). San Francisco: Jossey Bass.

Fuchs, L. S., Fuchs, D., Hamlett, C. L., Phillips, N. B., & Karns, K. (1995). General educators' specialized adaptations for students with learning disabilities. *Exceptional Children, 61* (5), 440–459.

Gable, A. R., Arllen, N. & Hendrickson, M. J. (1994). Use of students with emotional/behavioral disorders as behavior change agents. *Education and Treatment of Children, 17,* 267–276.

Gable, A. R., Arllen, L. N., & Hendrickson, M. J. (1995). Use of peer confrontation to modify disruptive behavior in inclusion classrooms. *Preventing School Failure, 40* (1), 25–28.

Gajria, M., Salend, S. J., & Hemrick, M. A. (1994). Teacher acceptability of testing modifications for mainstreamed students. *Learning Disabilities Research and Practice, 9* (4), 236–242.

George, N. L., George, M. P., Gersten, R., & Grosenick, J. K. (1995). To leave or to stay? *Remedial and Special Education, 16* (4), 227–236.

Glassberg, L. A. (1994). Students with behavioral disorders: Determinants of placement outcomes. *Behavioral Disorders, 19* (3), 181–191.

Goldstein, B. S. C. (1996). Critical pedagogy in a bilingual special education classroom. In M. S. Poplin and P. T. Cousins, (Eds.), *Alternative views of learning disabilities: Issues for the 21st century* (pp. 145–167). Austin: Pro-Ed.

Graham, S., Harris, K. R., & Reid, R. (1992). Developing self-regulated learners. *Focus on Exceptional Children, 24* (6), 1–16.

Graves, A., & Montague, M. (1991). Using story grammar curing to improve the writing of students with learning disabilities. *Learning Disabilities Research and Practice, 6,* 246–250.

Greer v. Rome City School District, 950 F.2d 688 (11th Cir. 1991).

Gunter, P. L., Shores, R. E., Jack, S. L., Denny, R. K., & De Paepe, P. (1994). A cast study of the effects of altering instructional interactions on the disruptive behavior of a child with severe behavior disorders. *Education and Treatment of Children, 17,* 435–444.

Harrison, J. S., Gunter, P. L., Reed, T. M., Lee, J. M. (1996). Teacher instructional language and negative reinforcement: A conceptual framework for working with students with emotional and behavioral disorders. *Education and Treatment of Children, 19* (2), 183–196.

Harvey, V. S. (1996). Educators' perceptions of effectiveness of programs for students with emotional and behavioral disorders. *Behavioral Disorders, 21* (3), 205–215.

Henley, M. (1994). A self-control curriculum for troubled youngsters. *Journal of Emotional and Behavioral Problems, 3* (1), 40–46.

Hunt-Berg, M., & Rankin, J. L. (1994). Ponder the possibilities: Computer-supported writing for struggling writers. *Learning Disabilities Research and Practice, 9,* 169–178.

Idol, L. (1994). Don't forget the teacher. *Journal of Emotional and Behavioral Problems, 3,* 28–33.

Janko, S., Schwartz, I., Sandall, S., Anderson, K., and Cottam, C. (1997). Beyond microsystem: Unanticipated lessons about the meaning of inclusion. *Topics in Early Childhood Special Education, 17* (3), 286–306.

Jenkins, J. R., & Heinen, A. (1989). Students' preference for service delivery: Pull-out, in-class, or integrated models. *Exceptional Children, 55,* 515–523.

Katims, D. S. (1994). Emergence of literacy in preschool children with disabilities. *Learning Disability Quarterly, 17,* 58–69.

Kauffman, J. M., Cullinan, D., & Epstein, M. H. (1987). Characteristics of students placed in special programs for the seriously emotionally disturbed. *Behavioral Disorders, 12,* 175–184.

Keefe, C. H. (1996). *Label-free learning: Supporting learners with disabilities.* York, ME: Stenhouse.

Keefe, C. H., Davis, R., & Andrews-Beck, C. (1997). An analysis of writing strategies of two children with mild disabilities in a whole language classroom. *Journal of Research in Childhood Education, 11* (2), 101–113.

Keough, B., Gallimore, R. & Weisner, T. (1997). Sociocultural perspectives on learning disabilities. *Learning Disabilities Research and Practice, 12* (2), 107–113.

Knitzer, J., Steinberg, Z., & Fleisch, F. (1990). *At the schoolhouse door. An examination of the programs and policies for children with behavioral and emotional problems.* NY: Bank Street College of Education.

Lago-Delello, E. (1998). Classroom dynamics and the development of serious emotional disturbance. *Exceptional Children, 64* (4), 479–492.

Lamm, O., & Epstein, R. (1992). Specific reading impairments: Are they to be associated with emotional difficulties? *Journal of Learning Disabilities, 25* (9), 605–614.

Lenz, B. K., Bulgren, J., & Hudson, P. (1990). Content enhancement: A model for promoting the acquisition of content by individuals with learning disabilities. In T. E. Scruggs & B. Y. L. Wong, (Eds.), *Intervention research in learning disabilities* (pp. 122–165). NY: Springer.

Lieber, J., & Beckman, P. J. (1991). Social coordination as a component of social competence in young children with disabilities. *Focus on Exceptional Children, 24* (4), 1–10.

MacArthur, C. A. (1998). Word processing with speech synthesis and word prediction: Effects on the dialogue journal writing of students with learning disabilities. *Learning Disability Quarterly, 21* (2), 151–166.

Maccini, P., & Hughest, C. A. (1997). Mathematics interventions for adolescents with learning disabilities. *Learning Disabilities Research and Practice, 12* (3), 168–176.

Martin, K. F., Lloyd, J. W., Kauffman, J. M., & Coyne, M. (1995). Teachers' perceptions of educational, placement decisions for pupils with emotional or behavioral disorders. *Behavioral Disorders, 20* (2), 106–117.

Mastropieri, M. A., & Scruggs, T. E. (1997). Best practices in promoting reading comprehension in students with learning disabilities: 1976–1996. *Remedial and Special Education, 18* (4), 197–213.

McIntyre, T. (1996). Guidelines for providing appropriate services to culturally diverse students. *Behavioral Disorders, 21* (2), 137–144.

McLesky, J., Lancaster, M., & Grizzle, K. (1995). Learning disabilities and grade retention: A review of issues with recommendations for practice. *Learning Disabilities Research and Practice, 10,* 120–128.

McNaughton, D., Hughes, C. A., & Clark, K. (1994). Spelling instruction for students with learning disabilities: Implications for research and practice. *Learning Disability Quarterly, 17,* 169–185.

McNaughton, D., Hughes, C. A., & Clark, K. (1997). The effect of five proofreading conditions on the spelling performance of college students with learning disabilities. *Journal of Learning Disabilities, 30* (6), 643–651.

Meadows, N. B., Neel, R. S., Scott, C. M., & Parker, G. (1994). Academic performance, social competence, and mainstream accommodations: A look at mainstreamed and nonmainstreamed students with serious behavioral disorders. *Behavioral Disorders, 19* (3), 170–180.

Miller, R. S., Miller, F. P., Armentrout, A. J., & Flannagan, W. J. M. (1995). Cross-age peer tutoring strategy for promoting self-determination in students with severe emotional disabilities/behavior disorders. *Preventing School Failure, 39* (4), 32–37.

Miller, S. P., & Mercer, C. D. (1997). Educational aspects of mathematics disabilities. *Journal of Learning Disability, 30* (1), 47–56.

Morse, W. C. (1994). The role of caring in teaching children with behavior problems. *Contemporary Education, 65,* 3.

Munk, D. D., & Repp, A. C. (1994). The relationship between instructional variables and problem behavior: A review. *Exceptional Children, 60* (5), 390–401.

Nichols, P. (1992). The Curriculum of Control: Twelve reasons for it, some arguments against it. *Beyond Behavior, 3* (2), 3–5.

Noddings, N. (1991). Stories in dialogue: Caring and interpersonal reasoning. In C. Witherell & N. Noddings, (Eds.), *Stories lives tell: Narrative and dialogue in education* (pp. 157–170). NY: Teachers College Press.

Nuzum, M. (1998). Creating homework success. *Instructor, 108* (3), 86–91.

Oberti v. Board of Education of the Borough of Clementon School District, 995 F.2d 1204 (3d Cir. 1993).

Osborne, A. (1984). How the courts have interpreted the related services mandate. *Exceptional Children, 51,* 249–252.

Palincsar, A. S. (1998). Keeping the metaphor of scaffolding fresh—a response to C. Addison Stone's "The metaphor of scaffolding: Its utility for the field of learning disabilities." *Journal of Learning Disabilities, 31* (4), 370–373.

Prentice, L., & Cousin, P. T. (1993). Moving beyond the textbook to teach students with learning disabilities. *Teaching Exceptional Children, 26* (1), 14–17.

Quinn, K. P., Epstein, M. H., & Cumblad, C. (1995). Academic instruction in day treatment: An integral component of comprehensive community-based programs for children and youth with emotional or behavioral disorders. *Community alternatives: International Journal of Family Care, 7* (2), 23–46.

Rademacher, J. A., Schumaker, J. B., & Deshler, D. D. (1996). Development and validation of a classroom assignment routine for inclusive settings. *Learning Disability Quarterly, 19,* 163–177.

Reid, D. K. (1998). Scaffolding: A broader view. *Journal of Learning Disabilities, 31* (4), 386–397.

Reynolds, M. (1962). A framework for considering some issues in special education. *Exceptional Children, 28,* 367–370.

Rhodes, W. C. (1996). Liberatory pedagogy and special education. In M. S. Poplin and P. T. Cousin, (Eds.), *Alternative views of learning disabilities: Issues for the 21st century* (pp. 135–144). Austin: Pro-Ed.

Rogoff, B. (1993). Children's guided participation and participatory appropriate in a sociocultural activity. In R. H. Wozniak & K. W. Fischer (Eds.), *Development in context: Acting and thinking in specific environments* (pp. 121–153). Hillsdale, NJ: Erlbaum.

Sacramento City Unified School District v. Rachel H. 14 F.3d 1398 (9th Cir. 1994).

Salend, S. J., Jantzen, N. R., & Giek, K. (1992). Using a peer confrontation system in a group setting. *Behavioral Disorders, 17* (3), 211–218.

Schubert, W. H. (1991). Teacher lore: A basis for understanding praxis. In C. Witherell & N. Noddings, (Eds.), *Stories lives tell: Narrative and dialogue in education* (pp. 207–233). NY: Teachers College Press.

Schumm, J. S., Vaughn, S., Haager, D., McDowell, J., Rothlein, L., and Saumell, L. (1996). General education teacher planning: What can students with learning disabilities expect? *Exceptional Children, 61* (4), 335–352.

Scruggs, T. E., & Mastropieri, M. A. (1998). What happens during instruction: Is any metaphor necessary? *Journal of Learning Disabilities, 31* (4), 404–409.

S. Rep. No. 17, 105th Cong., 1st Sess. 1–61 (1997).

Simmons, D. C. (1994). Importance of instructional complexity and role reciprocity to classwide peer tutoring. *Learning Disabilities Research and Practice, 9* (4), 203–212.

Simmons, D. C., & Kameenui, E. J. (1996). A focus on curriculum design: When children fail. *Focus on Exceptional Children, 28* (7), 1–16.

Simmons, D. C., Kameenui, E. J., & Chard, D. J. (1998). General education teachers' assumptions about learning and students with learning disabilities: Design of instruction analysis. *Learning Disability Quarterly, 21* (1), 6–22.

Soderlund, J., Bursuck, B., Polloway, E. A., & Foley, R. A. (1995). A comparison of homework problems of secondary school students with behavior disorders and nondisabled peers. *Journal of Emotional and Behavioral Disorders, 3* (3), 150–155.

Stainback, S. B., Stainback, W. C., & Harris, K. C. (1989). Support facilitation: An emerging role for special educators. *Teacher Education and Special Education, 12,* 148–153.

Steinberg, Z., & Knitzer, J. (1992). Classrooms for emotionally and behaviorally disturbed students: Facing the challenge. *Behavioral Disorders, 17* (2), 145–156.

Stone, C. A. (1998). The metaphor of scaffolding: Its utility for the field of learning disabilities. *Journal of Learning Disabilities, 31* (4), 344–364.

Swicegood, P. R., & Linehan, S. L. (1995). Literacy and academic learning for students with behavioral disorders: A constructivist view. *Education and Treatment of Children, 18* (3), 335–347.

Vadasy, P. F., Jenkins, J. R, Antil, L. R., Wayne, S. K., & O'Connor, R. E. (1997). Community-based early reading intervention for at risk first graders. *Learning Disabilities Research and Practice, 12,* 29–39.

Vygotsky, L. S. (1962). *Thought and language.* Cambridge, MA: MIT Press.

Webber, J., Anderson, T., & Otey, L. Teacher mindsets for surviving in the BD classrooms. *Intervention in School and Clinic, 26,* 288–291.

Wehby, J. H., Symons. F. J., Canale, J. A. & Go, F. J. (1998). Teaching practices in classrooms for students with emotional and behavioral disorders: discrepancies between recommendations and observations. *Behavioral Disorders, 24* (1), 51–56.

Wenz-Gross, M. & Siperstein, G. N. (1998). Students with learning problems at risk in middle school: Stress, social support, and adjustment. *Exceptional Children, 65* (1), 91–100.

Wilson, D. R., & William, J. D. (1994). Academic intrinsic motivation and attitudes toward school and learning of learning disabled students. *Learning Disabilities Research and Practice, 9* (3), 148–156.

Witherell, C., & Noddings, N. (1991). Prologue: An invitation to our readers. In C. Witherell & N. Noddings, (Eds.), *Stories lives tell: Narrative and dialogue in education* (pp. 1–12). NY: Teachers College Press.

Wong, B. Y. L. (1997). Research on genre-specific strategies from enhancing writing in adolescents with learning disabilities. *Learning Disability Quarterly, 20,* 140–159.

Wong, B. Y. L., Butler, D. L., Ficzere, S. A., & Kuperis, S. (1997). Teaching adolescents with learning disabilities and low achievers to plan, write, and revise compare-and-contrast essays, *Learning Disabilities Research and Practice, 12,* 2–15.

Wood, D., Bruner, J. S., & Ross, G. (1976). The role of tutoring in problem solving. *Journal of Child Psychiatry and Psychology, 17.* 89–100.

Yell, M. L. (1995). *Clyde K. and Sheila D. v. Puyallup School District:* The courts, inclusion, and students with behavioral disorders. *Behavioral Disorders, 20* (3), 179–189.

8 Cultural Diversity and Gender

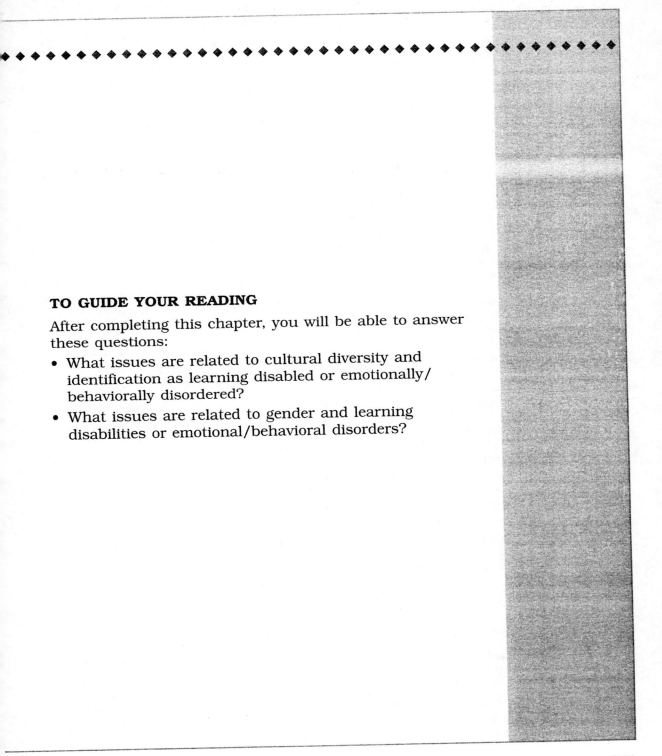

TO GUIDE YOUR READING

After completing this chapter, you will be able to answer these questions:

- What issues are related to cultural diversity and identification as learning disabled or emotionally/ behaviorally disordered?

- What issues are related to gender and learning disabilities or emotional/behavioral disorders?

◆◆ *The Student Assistance Team was having its initial meeting about Daming, a first grader. After three months in the classroom, Daming had yet to speak to Mr. Terrence, the teacher. Daming responded immediately to instructions, and completed all assigned individual work with accuracy. However, in group discussions, she was silent. During cooperative learning activities, she sat quietly and did not participate. On the playground, she would seek out her younger sister MeiMei and the two would sit together watching the other students. Though MeiMei, in kindergarten, would sometimes join her classmates, Daming would remain by the kindergarten class, observing her sister. Mr. Terrence called Ms. Chen, Daming's mother, but was unable to communicate well with her because of Ms. Chen's limited proficiency in English. Mr. Chen sent a note apologizing for any offense that Daming may have committed, and indicated that he had spoken to her about being respectful of the teacher and that he would keep her home if she showed disrespect. Mr. Chen was attending the local university, and was concerned that Daming would not achieve well in American schools.*

Linda Wang, a Chinese-American teacher whom Mr. Terrence had specifically requested as a participant in the team indicated that, when she spoke to Daming in Chinese she found out that the family had only arrived in the United States a week before school began in late August. Daming's father was a graduate student in molecular biology, and her mother, who had been a chemist in China, was seeking admission to graduate school. During the time he was seeking permission to study in the United States, Mr. Chen spoke English with the children, so both Daming and MeiMei became fairly fluent in English, though stilted and formal. Both girls could read English, and MeiMei's reading skills were better than some of her classmates.

The Student Assistance Team was having a difficult time designing interventions or accommodations for Daming. The very behaviors that Mr. Terrence desired were those which would be of great concern to her family. The ability to speak out in class, ask for help, or participate in a group activity were judged disrespectful, or not appropriate, for school by her family, but were necessary for her to achieve in Mr. Terrence's first grade class.

REFLECTION *Should the Student Assistance Team simply help Daming become bicultural? Would they be able to communicate to her family that her "new" behavior was appropriate for her American school, and, in fact, was necessary for her to receive a positive evaluation?*

Introduction

In many communities, there is a significant mismatch between the demographics of the faculty and that of the student body. Yet teachers, who may not share the culture, language, or life experiences of their students, must address their individual needs. Reflect on your culture, language, and life experiences. Are they similar to those of students in a "typical" classroom in your local school district? What issues can arise because of a mismatch? Issues related to cultural diversity and gender as these factors relate to learning disabilities and emotional/behavioral disorders will be explored in this chapter. Both cultural diversity and gender appear to have an impact on who is referred to, determined eligible for, and placed in special education services for students with learning disabilities or emotional/behavioral disorders.

Cultural Diversity and Identification Issues

Racial and ethnic diversity have grown dramatically in the United States in the last thirty years, and this diversity is projected to increase even more in the future. In 1997, 66 percent of the children in the United States where white, non-Hispanic, 15 percent were African-American non-Hispanic, 15 percent were Hispanic, 4 percent were Asian and Pacific Islander, and 1 percent were Native American or Alaska Natives. The percentage of white children has decreased from 74 percent in 1980 to the current level of 66 percent. The number of Hispanic children has increased faster than that of any other racial and ethnic group, growing from 9 percent of the child population in 1980, to 15 percent in 1997. By 2020, it is projected that more than one in five children in the United States will be of Hispanic origin (Forum on Child and Family Statistics, 1998).

There has also been marked growth among children who are not proficient in English. The number of school-aged children who spoke a language other than English at home, or who were not proficient in English, was 12.4 million in 1995, up from 1.25 million in 1979. The percentage of children who speak another language at home varies by region of the country, from 6 percent of children in the midwest, to 16 percent of children in the West. This difference is due to differing concentrations of immigrants and their descendants in the region (Forum on Child and Family Statistics, 1998).

In the classroom, each student and teacher reflects his or her own personal culture. Individual students and teachers tend to react as if their personal cultural norms represent the "natural" way human beings do things. Those who behave otherwise may be judged wrong. This perspective is called ethnocentric, which means that people think their own culture represents the best, or at least the most appropriate, way for human beings to live (Spradley & McCurdy, 1984).

In the literature on learning disabilities and emotional/behavioral disorders, cultural diversity is often discussed in the context of teacher–student interactions in school. Branch, Goodwin, and Gualtieri (1993) facilitate this discussion by providing definitions of several key terms related to the issue of cultural diversity. They describe culture as a patterned way of thinking, feeling, and reacting that has been acquired over time. These patterns are transmitted by symbols, actions, and artifacts that constitute the distinctive achievements of a human group.

Teachers and students each reflect his or her own personal culture.

Diversity is described by Branch and associates (1993) as the quality or condition of being different. Diversity is used primarily for labeling and identifying someone as different, rather than attempting to understand those individuals who are labeled as diverse or different. Identifying a person as belonging to a particular group does not provide information about what things are important to him or her, or the customs he or she practices.

Pluralism (Branch and associates, 1993) is defined as the relative lack of assimilation into society. Groups of people may live separately from the mainstream culture and maintain their own customs, values, and ways of life, or they may migrate to mainstream cultures and become assimilated. In a pluralistic society, people are able to maintain their cultural identities as well as membership in the mainstream culture.

When a population to be served by special education is culturally diverse, all activities and services provided to that population must take into consideration its major cultural characteristics: language, culture, and disability (Garcia & Yates, 1994). Both overrepresentation and underrepresentation of various cultural groups occurs in programs for students identified as learning disabled and emotionally/behaviorally disordered. Oswald, Coutinho, Best, and Singh (1999) investigated the influence of economic, demographic, and educational variables on the identification of students from diverse ethnic, cultural, and linguistic groups as having disabilities. Results indicated that students who are African American were about one and one-half times more likely to be identified as having emotional/behavioral disorders than their peers who were not African American. In a study of the use of public youth services (alcohol and drug treatment, child welfare, juvenile justice, mental health, and public school services for students with emotional/behavioral disorders) in San Diego County, African American and white students were overrepresented across all sectors. Hispanic students were underrepresented across all sectors.

Keough, Gallimore, and Weisner (1997) suggest that there is an overrepresentation of culturally diverse students with learning disabilities because of the nature of their early literacy experiences, language, and cultural differences rather than their in-child deficits. Underrepresentation may also occur because children with real learning disabilities may not receive services if their problems are attributed to their cultural differences. In a study of predictors affecting the placement of minority students in programs for students with learning disabilities, some factors predicted placement in programs for students with learning disabilities across all ethnic groups, while others varied by student ethnicity (Artiles, Aquirre-Munoz, & Abedi, 1998). Similar reasons may account for overrepresentation and underrepresentation among students identified as emotionally/behaviorally disordered. The challenge is to determine the indicators that denote problems due to learning disabilities or emotional/behavioral disorders, culturally based factors, and cultural context.

In their review of twenty-two years of research on learning disabilities, Artiles, Trent, and Kuan (1997) found few studies on ethnic minority students. They found that research on ethnic minority students received attention in the 1970s, decreased in the 1980s, and started to rise again in the 1990s. The studies, most of which compared various ethnic groups, focused on assessment, sensory-perceptual processing, and placement issues. They concluded that the special education community deals with issues related to diversity on a "special occasion" basis (e.g., special issues of journals, keynote addresses at conferences). With little sound research, improved educational outcomes are unlikely. Artiles, Trent, and Kuan suggest that research on ethnic minority students might be influenced by sociopolitical forces, and that articles in the 1970s were more common because of the attention given to social and racial issues in the 1960s. In the 1980s, the political climate reduced support for equity and ethnic minority issues, and during the 1990s there have been more conversations about multiculturalism in academia, popular culture, and the media.

Though each cultural group has distinctive learning-style patterns, the great variation among individuals within each group means that educators must use diverse teaching strategies with all students. Guild (1994) contends that "generalizations about a group of people have often led to naive inferences about individuals within that group" (p. 16). He suggests that there are five components on which researchers in cultural diversity and education concur:

1. Students of any particular age will differ in the ways in which they learn.
2. Learning styles are a function of both nature and nurture.
3. Learning styles, in themselves, are neither good nor bad.
4. Within any group, the variations among individuals are as great as their commonalities.
5. There is cultural conflict between some students and the typical learning experience in school.

Bos and Fletcher (1997) agree, and suggest that there is a need to go beyond traditional variables of ethnicity, gender, and socioeconomic status, because culture is multidimensional and varies among ethnic groups. It cannot be assumed that all members of an ethnic group have the same culture. Professionals need to consider a broad range of variables, including community and family contexts, district and school context, classroom context, and culturally relevant pedagogy.

Adaptive behavior in one culture may be considered maladaptive behavior when exhibited in another culture (Dunn & Tucker, 1993). Both adaptive and maladaptive functioning are vital indicators of the life success of children from various cultural groups. The conflicts generated from the mismatch between various perceptions of behavior may be, in fact, significant predictors of minority children's behavior problems (Dunn & Tucker, 1993).

Hodgkinson (1995) argues that the ways in which individuals have been identified by the U.S. Census are "whimsical, changeable, and unscientific" (p. 173). He contends that skin color and race, citizenship and race, and the definition of "Hispanic" are all conceptual nightmares. Hodgkinson estimates that if a box labeled "multiracial," meaning any racial-ethnic mixing for the previous four or more generations, was added to the next census, as many as 80 percent of African American individuals, and a majority of Americans in general, would check the box. The current African American population of 30 million could decline in the 2000 Census to about three million; Asian Americans, most of whom are now marrying non-Asians, and Native Americans, who are producing more children in mixed marriages than in marriages involving two Native American parents, could virtually disappear from the demographic landscape. Hispanics could become either the largest racial minority, or they could disappear, depending on how many consider themselves mixed, or how Hispanic race is defined. Hodgkinson suggests that poverty should be a descriptor in the next census because, according to education research, it is at the core of educational underachievement. The four minority cultural groups with which teachers most frequently interact in the schools are African American, Hispanic American, Native American, and Asian American learners.

African American Learners

Since 1900, the African American population of the United States has remained between 10 percent and 12 percent of the total population (Forum on Child and Family Statistics, 1998). According to McAdoo (1978), the lifestyles, values, and experiences of African Americans vary, but as a group, they share the common experience of economic isolation, prejudice, and legally reinforced racism. Long-established cultural patterns and a high level of maternal employment have led to shared decision-making processes in many African American families.

An important socialization issue for African American learners is coping with racism. African American parents, in efforts to combat racism, emphasize the development of achievement motivation, self-confidence, and high self-esteem (Peters, 1981). In addition, there may be a cultural difference in their attitude toward time, which Euro-American individuals may perceive as resistance or apathy.

There are several aspects of African American culture that may lead to inappropriate identification of African American learners as having emotional/behavioral disorders. The differences in cohesiveness between the African American and Euro-American cultures may be viewed as problematic by Euro-American teachers (Hanna, 1980). Cooperation among African American learners when confronted with a task or problem, for example, may be interpreted by some teachers as "cheating."

Children who are new to a classroom negotiate interpersonal relationships and probe for common experiences with their peers. They seek cues in how to act, or what to expect from the teacher. African American learners may benefit from cooperative learning strategies because of their cultural heritage, family background, and socialization processes (Haynes & Begreyesus, 1992).

Communication patterns among some African American students may be perceived as inappropriate, resistant, or apathetic by Euro-American teachers. Some African American learners converse without constant eye contact (Allen & Majidi-Ahi, 1989), a behavior that may be interpreted as inattention by a Euro-American teacher. African American students may be more likely to verbally reinforce one another in conversation (Smith, 1981). African American children may operate in a dual system of Standard English and Black English Vernacular, and, as a consequence, carry a more demanding cognitive burden than individuals operating in a single-language system requiring fewer translations. Communication skills, such as verbal dueling and arguments, while valued among African American peers, may be viewed as aggressive and disruptive by teachers (Lynch, 1993).

Cultural differences in parental discipline may also cause a mismatch between students and their teachers. Nweke (1994) reported that though both parents of Euro-American and African American students would punish misbehavior occurring outside the home, the place and time of punishment differed. While 87.54 percent of the mothers were responsible for discipline in African American families, only 51 percent of the mothers in Euro-American families had that responsibility.

In a study of family participation in schools, Chavkin and Williams (1993) found that African American families wanted to be more involved in their children's education and to have more influence on the school. Ninety-seven percent said they cooperate with their children's teachers. These parents also showed strong interest in attending school performances, helping children with homework, and assisting in school events. These findings are in contrast to the two traditions that Harry (1992) describes which challenge the participation of African American parents. Harry maintains that, first, teachers have a deficit view of African American families, exacerbated by the second tradition, the deficit view on which special education is based. She suggests alternative roles for parents, including that of assessors (acting as official members of the assessment team), presenters of reports (providing information which becomes part of the official record), policymakers (sharing power on advisory committees), and advocates and supporters for their children and other children in their community. Supporting these alternative roles and challenging the deficit view of African American families will enhance the ability of parents to support the education of their children.

Hispanic American Learners

Hispanic Americans are persons of all races whose cultural heritage is tied to the use of the Spanish language and Latino culture (Fradd, Figueroa, & Correa, 1989). Hispanic American students may belong to any of a large number of ethnic subgroups: Mexican, Chicano, Puerto Rican, Cuban, or Central and South American.

The number of Hispanic American children has increased faster than that of any other racial and ethnic group, growing from 9 percent of all American children in 1980, to 15 percent in 1997. By 2020, more than one in five children in the United States will be Hispanic American. The poverty rate among Hispanic American families in 1986 was about two and one-half times greater than among non-Hispanic American families (Buenning, Tollefson, & Rodriguez, 1992).

Hyland (1989) describes the Hispanic American population as highly concentrated in urban areas, and highly isolated in housing and schooling. This isolation is reputedly related to linguistic skills, because Hispanic children are usually placed in classrooms or schools where children of limited English proficiency are in the majority.

Hispanic American learners may enter school with a significantly different social, economic, and cultural background than their peers who either are from, or understand, Euro-American culture (Hyland, 1989). For example, "copying" may be viewed as a legitimate activity among Hispanic American students. Copying work may be based on home socialization patterns that stress collectivity and social cohesiveness. Rather than representing low ability and lack of motivation, copying in the Hispanic American culture, may be considered a constructive approach to intellectual exchanges and the acquisition of new knowledge in a social unit composed of peers (Delgado-Gaitan & Trueba, 1985). In addition, the organization of classroom instruction may limit Hispanic American students' abilities to demonstrate their full range of competence in two languages. As a consequence, a lack of English language structural proficiency, and a lack of vocabulary in Spanish, may be interpreted by teachers as a lack of conceptual ability (Commins & Miramontes, 1989).

Native American Learners

Native Americans share a history of cultural, psychological, and physical genocide. Once estimated at ten million, the Native American population has been reduced through "cultural genocide" to fewer than two million. Rather than accepting tribally defined membership or community consensus, federal programs require one-quarter genealogically derived Native American ancestry for legal recognition as Native American to be eligible for many federal, state, and Indian nation benefits. In the United States, there are 560 federally recognized Native American entities (200 of which are in Alaska), and 60 state-recognized Native American tribes. Each of these entities maintains unique customs, traditions, social organizations, and ecological relationships (Administration for Children and Families, 1998).

Native Americans are severely economically and educationally challenged. The median income of Native Americans in 1997 was the lowest among cultural groups at $29,200 (Population Reference Bureau, 1999). Native Americans have the lowest business ownership rate, and the highest extreme poverty rate (13 percent) of all minority groups. An extreme problem for Native American youth is alcohol and drug abuse. The use of alcohol among Native American youth is three times that of youth in the population at large (Bobo, 1985).

As a consequence of efforts first to eliminate them, and, then to assimilate them, many Native Americans experience a sense of alienation from Euro-Americans (LaFramboise & Low, 1989). Responses of Native Americans to this sense of alienation have been described by Spindler and Spindler (1994) through their work with the Menominee tribe. These responses include reaffirmation, withdrawal, constructive marginality, biculturalism, and assimilation. Among the Menominee, reaffirmation was represented by a group of cultural "survivors" from the past, and a larger number of younger people who had interacted with Euro-American culture in school and the workplace. This group was trying to recreate and sustain a recognizable Native American way of life. Another group of Native Americans was so torn by cultural conflict that they could not identify with traditional Native American or Euro-American cultural symbols or groups. This group withdrew either into self-destruction through substance abuse, or by simply doing nothing about their conflict.

"Constructive marginality" was described by Spindler and Spindler as the forming of a personal culture that was instrumentally productive, but composed of several different segments, some of which were Euro-American. Among those who assimilated into Euro-American culture, two groups emerged: (a) those who were more "respectable" than most Euro-Americans and denigrated Native Americans who did not conform to the majority, Euro-American culture, and (b) those who were undifferentiated culturally from Euro-Americans, but were interested in Native American traditions in a distant way. Bicultural Native Americans were equally at home in their traditional culture and the Euro-American culture. Spindler and Spindler describe these strategies as defensive, because the self-esteem of the people is threatened.

Grimm (1992) reports several issues that challenge the identity of learners who are Native American, such as removal from the family for boarding schools and foster placements, high dropout rates (60 percent among children attending boarding school), overidentification as special education students, high incidence of alcohol and drug abuse, high suicide rates, chronic health problems, and low income.

Perhaps of greatest difficulty for Native American learners is the conflict between their traditional cooperative learning styles and the competitive setting of the school. Native American children often learn by observation rather than by displays of curiosity and verbal questioning. They tend to prefer cooperation and harmony. In school, these behaviors are perceived as a general lack of individual competitiveness and overreliance on peer structure (Brod & McQuiston, 1983). These behaviors are unacceptable to many teachers. Though cultural values may vary as related to these variables, several, potentially, may put learners in contrast to conventional school behavior. For example, the cultural expectation to comply with authority, or to have an uncomplaining attitude, may be perceived by those of an Euro-American culture as complacency, or lack of motivation. Subordinancy to the other members of the group may be inconsistent with the competitive classroom style. Silence and esteem for "the middle position" may be out of place in a classroom where the student has to request help or materials.

Asian American Learners

Asian Americans have roots in Asia, including China, Japan, and the Southeast Asian nations. Huang (1993) argues that it is difficult to generalize even within groups. Among the Vietnamese, for example, many have Chinese ancestry with a sophisticated literature culture, while the Hmong people have no written language.

Chinese family structure, according to Huang and Ying (1989), is based on Confucian ethics. Sons are more highly valued than daughters, and the first born son is perceived as the most-valued child. Fathers, removed from the everyday tasks of the family, are often figurative heads, while mothers may be the driving force in the family. The expression of emotion is highly frowned upon in Chinese American families, and the ability to suppress undesirable thoughts or emotions is highly valued. Placing group and family wishes above individual desires is highly valued (Huang & Ying, 1989).

Yamamoto and Kubota (1989) describe the Japanese American family structure as one that emphasizes the family over the individual, hierarchical relationships, conformity, and social control based on shame, guilt, and duty. Japanese culture values being "reserved," that is, not expressing one's wishes or preferences, deferring to those in authority, and repressing or internalizing emotions.

Southeast Asian refugee children and youth have spent a significant part of their lives amid violence, experiencing great personal loss, anxiety, and discontinuation of educational and health-care services. The extended family, so vital in Asian culture, is not accessible to these children and youth. Many of these families have undergone sociocultural changes, where children once viewed their parents as competent, independent individuals, now they view them as persons who acculturate more slowly than they do. Yet self-control and repression of emotions remain highly valued (Huang, 1989).

East Asians, especially Chinese, value formal schooling, and consider children's schooling directly related to the family's integrity. High achievement brings honor, while failure brings disgrace. An intense pressure to achieve may cause intergenerational conflicts, anxiety, and impaired self-esteem. As such, these cultural groups have difficulty accepting concepts such as learning disabilities and emotional/behavioral disorders. The teacher may be seen as the professional with authority over the children's schooling, and parents are not supposed to interfere with school processes (Huang, 1993).

Asian Americans, unlike other cultural, ethnic, and linguistic groups, have a positive stereotype relating to school achievement. Dao (1991) contends, however, that changes have occurred in the Asian American population that put many of these children at risk for school failure. Today, many Asian American children are from families where their life and educational experiences differ vastly from children from traditional, established Asian American families. Recent immigrant or refugee children face the triple burden of (a) learning English and a new school curriculum, (b) adjusting to a new culture, and (c) surviving in an impoverished environment. In addition, many recent refugees may have had traumatic experiences, including death, piracy, and extreme violence in their recent past, and they may not be emotionally ready to benefit from instruction.

Huang (1993) contends that Southeast Asians and Pacific Islanders may believe that several social interactions may happen simultaneously. Teachers may be irritated when Southeast Asian or Pacific Islander parents come late for an appointment without an apology, or are offended when they are inattentive to what they have to say. These teachers fail to understand that time may be seen as a simultaneous process in these cultures, rather than something that is linearly scheduled. In addition, parents may believe that in some situations, time itself can solve problems better than human intervention. In social encounters, parents may be polite or even submissive, yet when a dispute persists they may suddenly become very hostile without providing warning signals. Southeast Asians and Pacific Islanders frequently expect that Americans, who generally only pay attention to what is explicitly said, will pick up on the moods of the other conversants. In an attempt to reach closure, hearing no verbal disagreement, and not noticing the nonverbal Asian's hesitancy, American professionals may move quickly toward a resolution of the matter at hand. When the Asian American finally explodes in anger, the Westerner is surprised. In working with Asian parents, teachers should (ERIC Clearinghouse on Urban Education, 1994):

- Establish the professional's role and assume authority.
- Reach a consensus through compromise.
- Explain that involvement in the child's education is a tradition in American education.
- Provide periods of silence as opportunities for reflection on what has been said.
- Provide clear and full information, such as what is provided by, and is expected from, each participant in the discussion.
- Attend to nonverbal cues.

Students with Limited English Proficiency

Limited English proficiency poses a significant challenge for students. Rodriquez and Carrasquillo (1997), in studying Hispanic American students who had limited English proficiency and who were identified as having disabilities, found that a substantial number of the students were referred to bilingual special education programs because of academic deficits and reading and language problems. The greatest proportion of students who were referred to bilingual special education classes had been in the United States less than three years and used Spanish as their primary language. Teachers documented few interventions before referring these students to special education. A significant number of students were identified as having delayed receptive and expressive language skills and reading problems, with good achievement in mathematics. Most of the students were identified as learning disabled, and one-third were identified as "speech impaired." Echevarria (1995) suggests addressing the needs of these students by using a slower speech rate, controlling vocabulary, contextualizing instruction, providing hands-on activities, and adapting the curriculum.

Ochoa, River, and Power (1997) reported that when asked what criteria and standards they implemented to rule out environmental, cultural, and economic disadvantage in order to determine eligibility of a limited-English proficient student, school psychologists indicated that they used a variety of factors. The school psychologists indicated that they considered the student's family and home, as well as the language instruction which the student had received. These school psychologists recognized the role of appropriate assessment instruments and procedural safeguards when assessing students for whom English was not the primary language. In addition, the psychologists suggested that the students' history and experience in general education contributed to their decision making.

Assessment

Zurcher (1998) suggests that there are several factors which create a test bias for students from diverse ethnic, cultural, or linguistic groups. Bias may include language, or the nature of the illustrations provided in the text. Or, the content may not be very familiar to a particular minority group. In addition, the norming sample from which test scores were generated may not reflect students from minority groups. Yet tests persist as a major tool in identifying students with leaning disabilities or emotional/behavioral disorders.

Learners from most cultural minorities have higher rates of entering the special education referral to placement process, which increases the likelihood of their identification as emotionally/behaviorally disordered (Executive Committee CCBD, 1989). Rueda and Garcia (1997) examined educational specialists' judgments regarding how portfolio data compared to traditional standardized assessment data in terms of, (a) student competence, (b) the type and specificity of instructional activities that are derived from the data, (c) the usefulness of each type of approach, and (d) how communication is affected between the teacher and parents. Their results suggested that use of a student portfolio would lead to more numerous and more specific and detailed recommendations and decisions. In addition, portfolio data were seen as being more informative to teachers than to other assessment stakeholders, and its use led to an increased number of student strengths being identified. They concluded that portfolio assessment data may provide different decisions regarding students and instructional planning in comparison to traditional data. However, Rueda and Garcia caution that portfolio assessment may not be inherently less biased than traditional assessments. Portfolio data is still subject to interpretation because of the influence of the evaluator's prior training and beliefs. The use of any assessment tool must be considered in light of the belief system and ways that practitioners make sense of assessment information.

Gonzalez and Yawkey (1993) suggest three approaches to the assessment of children who are culturally and linguistically different, (a) the traditional psychometric model, (b) the "missionary" model of acculturation, and (c) the developmental model. The traditional psychometric model assumes the presence of innate abilities and traits genetically inherited and related to maturational and neurological factors that can be quantitatively measured. The "missionary" model uses standardized tests to demonstrate internal or racial causes for the low scores of culturally and linguistically different learners as compared to mainstream students. In this model, learners who are different are viewed as "exotic aliens" who need acculturation. The developmental assessment model, used by ethnic researchers, assumes that individual potential can be actualized or expressed differently in various sociocultural environments. These learners can only be appreciated by the uniqueness of each individual through qualitative descriptors. From this perspective, potential is not fixed and cannot be quantitatively valued. Potential is influenced by both internal and external factors.

Skiba (1989) reviewed 89 correlations between classroom observations and behavioral ratings drawn from 16 studies. He found very low correlations between what was actually observed and what was rated by teachers using formal rating scales. He suggests that there are serious problems with the validity of assessments that look for problems within the students themselves. He maintains that recognition of the "problem situation" should be used to identify and describe behavioral problems in schools.

The lack of consensus regarding the designation and description of learners identified as emotionally/behaviorally disordered extends to researchers in the field. Kavale, Forness, and Alper (1986) found in their survey of 323 studies in behavioral/emotional disorders that the research literature presents a divergent picture regarding the nature and prevalence of behavioral/emotional disorders, and reflects a lack of consensus regarding standard identification criteria. The Executive Committee of the Council for Children with Behavioral Disorders (1989) argues that until definition, classification, and measurement criteria for learners identified as behaviorally/emotionally disordered are made more objective and verifiable, assessment will continue to be highly subjective and open to multiple sources of bias. The Executive Committee offers the following recommendations for the conduct of a nonbiased, functional assessment of learners from diverse ethnic, cultural, and linguistic groups:

1. Attention should be focused on classroom and school learning environments rather than medical or mental health-based models.
2. Cultures, expectations, tolerance, learning, reinforcement history, and family situations of the learner, teacher, and administrator should be considered.
3. Attention should be focused on student and teacher behaviors and the contexts in which they occur.
4. The conditions under which behaviors are observed, taught, and required should be studied.
5. Specific, measurable, instructionally based standards for academic and social behaviors should be established.
6. An assessment of the student's current learning environment, with documentation of prereferral interventions, should be implemented prior to referral.
7. Effective and efficient instructional procedures should be applied.
8. Teaching behaviors, instructional organization, and instructional supports should be assessed.
9. The responsibility for learning or performance failure should not be placed on the student.
10. Teachers should be prepared in a functional assessment perspective that focuses on children at risk for academic and/or behavioral difficulties.
11. Professionals should be realigned toward a functional assessment perspective.

Interactions in the Classroom

In a study of student teachers, Valli (1995) recorded several experiences that had an impact on teacher-student classroom interaction. Teachers reported a "disappearance of color," and claimed that they no longer noticed what color the students were (actually, color no longer functioned as a barrier, and it ceased to signify hostility or otherness). In addition, the student teachers confronted a challenge to white privilege, where for the first time their whiteness was not a privileged skin color. In fact, because they were white, they may have been actively accused of racism. As white teachers, they did not view themselves as racialized individuals, that is, they did not regard their whiteness as a racial identify, or define themselves by color. These teachers had to admit that they, too, were people of color. The teachers found that by adding a multicultural emphasis to their teaching, they appeared more legitimate. The teachers realized that their education was Eurocentric, and that they needed to see the color of the children in order to design a multicultural curriculum. They then had to move beyond color to value multicultural curriculum for everyone. In addition, the teachers needed to establish a diverse environment, and move from the perspective of adapting the child to the classroom to the perspective of adapting the classroom to the child.

Canning (1995) offers three general strategies for working with learners from diverse cultures. First, the teacher should have an enabling attitude (open-minded, questioning, and willing to listen). Teachers should open doors to authenticity, which may require risk-taking and a willingness to be vulnerable. Teachers need to observe from the inside, as a member of one culture trying to enter another. Kea (1998) argues that teachers should acknowledge individual and critical differences enthusiastically, build relationships, observe and program for students' task orientation, and teach setting-appropriate behaviors, while valuing students' cultural experiences.

The Council for Children with Behavior Disorders presented several guidelines for providing appropriate services to learners from diverse cultures with emotional/behavioral disorders (McIntyre, 1996). These guidelines took the form of program goals and included:

- Identifying learners of diverse cultures being served in special programs who are actually demonstrating culturally based behaviors rather than emotional/behavioral disorders.
- Providing educational and treatment services to learners with emotional/behavioral disorders that are appropriate and respectful of culture.
- Implementing culturally and linguistically appropriate assessment.
- Recruiting professionals from diverse cultural groups.
- Providing preservice and inservice training that is more appropriate for meeting the needs of individuals from various cultures.
- Creating welcoming atmospheres in schools.
- Enhancing the cultural knowledge base of professionals, clients/students, and the public at large.

Gender Issues

Girls have a significantly different experience than boys. Even in playing with their fathers, there is a marked level of difference. Mann (1994) reports that fathers typically come home from work and roughhouse with their sons; the same fathers play with little girls by gathering them into their laps. In elementary schools, boys are eight times as likely to call out and demand attention, and are called on from two to twelve times more often than girls during any class period. The students most likely to receive teacher attention were, in the order of attention received, (a) white males, (b) minority males, (c) white females, and (d) minority females (Sadker, 1994).

Girls begin their school careers outperforming boys on almost every measure used. Girls' test scores begin to descend around middle school. While girls are behind boys on standardized tests which measure achievement, they are ahead when it comes to report card grades (Sadker, 1994).

Halpern (1997) believes that research that categorizes gender differences as verbal, visual-spatial and quantitative abilities is too simplistic. Gregg, Ferri, Hoy, and Stennett (in press) remind us that perceptions in the field of learning disabilities have been influenced by historical, social and political contexts, and that research has been impacted by five predominant perspectives:

- The evolutionary theory, which contends that gender differences can be attributed to development and adaptation;
- Biological theory, comprised of research focusing on genetics, hormones, and neurology;
- Social-cultural constructivism, which suggests the construction of knowledge through interactions and relationships;
- Psychobiosocial theory, in which Halpern (1997) suggests that there are variables that are both biological and social and cannot be delineated; and
- Feminist theory, which questions the idea that human experiences can be classified into binary categories (e.g. male-female; average-below average) (Gregg, Ferri, Hoy, & Stennett, in press).

From a review of multiple studies concerning gender differences in intelligence, Halpern (1997) concludes that no single finding has unanimous support. However, there is evidence to suggest that on average, there are differences between females and males. Females tend to score higher on tasks that need quick access and use of phonological and semantic information in long-term memory, generation and understanding of complex prose, fine motor skills, and perceptual speed. Males, on the other hand, tend to score higher on tasks involving changes in visual-spatial working memory, motor skills used in aiming, spatiotemporal responding, and fluid reasoning, particularly in mathematics and science. In addition, males are overrepresented in numerous low-ability groups (Halpern, 1997).

In special education, even though boys significantly outnumber girls, research has rarely focused on gender issues. The more "subjective" the diagnosis, such as "emotional/behavioral disorders" or "learning disabilities" the higher the representation of boys (American Association of University Women, 1992). In *How Schools Shortchange Girls* (AAUW, 1992), the traditional explanation for the disproportionate number of boys in special education programs that boys are born with more disabilities, is challenged by a thorough review of the literature. Medical reports on learning disabilities and attention-deficit disorders indicate that they occur almost equally in boys and girls. However, schools continue to identify many more boys than girls in these disability areas. The AAUW report suggests that girls who sit quietly are ignored, and boys who act out are placed in special education programs.

Vogel (1990) reviewed the limited body of research examining gender differences in the intellectual abilities of children with learning disabilities. Findings indicate that compared to male counterparts, system-identified females with learning disabilities, (a) function at a lower intellectual level, (b) have greater deficits in some aspects of reading and mathematics, and (c) are somewhat better in visual-motor abilities, spelling, and written language mechanics and overall written language. Further, consistent findings indicate that males with learning disabilities are superior to females with learning disabilities in mathematical reasoning. Vogel cautions that the students in this study represented a school-system-identified population that may be biased, and that generalizations can only be made about that population.

Vogel (1990) indicates that females with learning disabilities may not be identified as frequently as males, and suggests several reasons. First, there may be a mismatch between the student's problems and the expectations of the individual making the referral. Second, more males have attentional and behavioral problems, which results in more referrals and more services for males with learning disabilities. Finally, teachers may refer more boys than girls because girls do not come to the attention of teachers and parents as frequently as having attentional deficits and/or behavior problems. Further, Vogel (1990) suggests factors that may bias samples of system-identified females with learning disabilities: hyperactive and disruptive behavior, environmental and cultural expectations and values, and limited knowledge of the characteristics of females with learning disabilities.

Results of studies examining gender bias in determining eligibility for services for learning disabilities have been somewhat mixed. Gender bias in the identification of learning disabilities was not evident in a study by Clarzio and Phillips (1986); however, Leinhardt, Seewald & Zigmond (1982) did find evidence of gender bias. More recently, Payette and Clarizio (1994) examined student characteristics that might influence eligibility teams in misclassifying students as learning disabled. Misclassification referred to identification of a learning disability without a severe discrepancy, or not identifying as learning disabled when a severe discrepancy existed. The study involved 344 students in grades K–12 who were referred for learning problems; students who were referred primarily for emotional difficulties were excluded. The researchers looked at race, gender, intelligence, achievement, and grade level. Overall, there was a misclassification rate of 25 percent (a student was declared eligible without a severe discrepancy, or ineligible with a severe discrepancy). Unexpectedly, a disproportionate number of girls were granted eligibility for special education services without a severe discrepancy.

Gregg and associates (1999) suggest that in discussion and research, gender cannot be separated from ability because of their interactive effect. These researchers (1999) examined gender differences of college students with learning disabilities. Participants included 172 males and 120 females. All were given the same battery of standardized tests, including a measure of intelligence. The researchers investigated the interaction of gender and ability on cognitive, language, and achievement variables. Most measures were related to general cognitive ability. Gender was only related to the short-term memory construct on one cognitive measure, and the visual processing construct.

In their study of prevalence and incidence, Caseau, Luckasson, & Roth (1994) found that boys far outnumbered girls both among students identified and served in public schools and students identified in public schools, but receiving other mental health services. However, girls outnumbered boys among students who were not identified by the public schools, but received mental health services. In addition, girls were more likely to have serious problems of depression, family conflict, suicidal ideation, and suicide attempts. Girls had behavioral and mental health problems serious enough to warrant identification, but not of the type that would warrant identification in the public schools. The small number of girls who did receive services in the public schools exhibited externalizing behaviors (aggression, hyperactivity, delinquency) similar to those of boys. Caseau and associates suggest that services for learners with emotional/behavioral disorders in the public schools may actually serve the purpose of containment rather than treatment.

Miller (1994) found that female adolescents with emotional/behavioral disorders report a higher frequency of suicidal ideation and attempts than do male adolescents with or without emotional/behavioral disorders. His survey results indicated that females with emotional/behavioral disorders may be particularly vulnerable in terms of both suicide ideation and suicide attempts. He recommends the teaching of alternative problem-solving strategies, and facilitating the belief that adolescents can construct their futures (versus choosing suicide). Miller offers this charge to all adults who interact with adolescents, but especially teachers of students with emotional/behavioral disorders.

In reviewing issues related to gender it appears that just as learners from diverse cultures may be overidentified due to culturally specific behaviors, female learners may be underidentified because of their gender-related behaviors. Brown, Bauer, and Elgas (1996) reported that among kindergarten children with behavioral disorders, boys who followed the male communication pattern of listing facts and sequences during "sharing time" received positive teacher interactions. Girls' comments, which were more social in nature and described personal interactions around the objects they brought in for "sharing time," were judged as "off-topic" and tangential by the teacher.

Summary Points

- Due to ethnocentricity, teachers may identify individuals from diverse cultures as having learning disabilities or emotional/behavioral disorders.
- When a population to be served by special education is culturally diverse, all activities and services provided to that population must take into account its major cultural characteristics.
- Various cultural groups in programs for students identified as having learning disabilities and emotional/behavioral disorders are both over-represented and underrepresented.
- Behavior seen as adaptive by one culture may be seen as maladaptive in another.
- Girls are far less frequently served than boys in programs for students with learning disabilities or emotional/behavioral disorders.
- When compared to their male counterparts, girls with learning disabilities tend to function at a lower intellectual level, and have greater deficits in some aspects of reading and mathematics. Girls perform somewhat better in visual-motor abilities, spelling, and written language.
- Girls tend to demonstrate internalizing behaviors; boys tend to externalize.

Key Words and Phrases

African American—individuals whose ancestry can be traced to Africa

Asian Americans—individuals whose ancestry can be traced to Asia, including China, Japan, and the Southeast Asian nations

culture—a patterned way of acting, thinking, and feeling which is acquired over time and transmitted through and to members of a group

diversity—the quality or condition of being different

ethnocentricity—the belief that an individual's personal culture reflects the most appropriate behavior

Hispanic American—individuals of all races whose cultural heritage is tied to the use of the Spanish language and Latino culture including Mexican Americans, Chicanos, Puerto Ricans, Cubans, and Central and South Americans

Native American—any member of the indigenous peoples of North and South America

pluralism—the relative lack of assimilation into society

References

Administration for Children and Families. (1998). *Fact Sheet: Administration for Native Americans.* Washington, DC: Author.

Allen, L., & Majidi-Ahi, S. (1989). Black American children. In J. Gibbs and L. Huang, (Eds.), *Children of color* (pp.148–178). San Francisco: Jossey Bass.

American Association of University Women (AAUW). (1992). *How schools short-change girls.* Washington, DC: Author.

Artiles, A. J., Aquirre-Munoz, Z., & Abedi, J. (1998). Predicting placement in learning disabilities programs: Do predictors vary by ethnic group? *Exceptional Children, 64* (4), 543–559.

Artiles, A. J., Trent, S. C., & Kuan, L. (1997). Learning disabilities empirical research on ethnic minority students: An analysis of 22 years of studies published in selected refereed journals. *Learning Disabilities Research and Practice, 12* (2), 82–91.

Bobo, J. K. (1985). Preventing drug abuse among American Indian adolescents. In L. D. Gilchrist and S. P. Schinke, (Eds.), *Preventing social and health problems through life skills training.* Seattle: University of Washington School of Social Work.

Bos, C. S., & Fletcher, T. V. (1997). Sociocultural considerations in learning disabilities inclusion research: Knowledge gaps and future directions. *Learning Disabilities Research and Practice, 12* (2), 92–99.

Bowman, B. T. (1994). The challenge of diversity. *Phi Delta Kappan,* (November), 218–224.

Branch, R. C., Goodwin, Y., & Gualtieri, J. (1993). Making classroom instruction culturally pluralistic. *The Educational Forum, 58* (1), 58–70.

Brod, R. L., & McQuiston, J. M. (1983). American Indian adult education and literacy: The first national survey. *Journal of American Indian Education, 1,* 1–16.

Buenning, M., Tollefson, N., & Rodriguez, F. (1992). Hispanic cultural and the schools. In M. J. Fine and C. Carlson, (Eds.), *The handbook of family-school interventions: A systems perspective* (pp. 86–101). Boston: Allyn & Bacon.

Canning, C. (1995). Getting from the outside in: Teaching Mexican Americans when you are an "Anglo." *The High School Journal, 78* (4), 195–205.

Caseau, D. L., Luckasson, R., & Kroth, R. L. (1994). Special education services for girls with serious emotional disturbance: A case of gender bias? *Behavioral Disorders, 20,* 51–60.

Chavkin, N. F., & Williams, R. (1993). *Families and schools in a pluralistic society.* Albany, NY: State University of New York Press.

Clarizio H., & Phillips, S. (1986). Sex bias in the diagnosis of learning disabled students. *Psychology in the Schools, 23.* 44–52.

Dao, M. (1991). Designing assessment procedures for educationally at-risk southeast Asian-American students. *Journal of Learning Disabilities, 24,* 594–601, 629.

Delgado-Gaitan, C., & Trueba, H. T. (1985). Ethnographic study of participant structures in task completion: Reinterpretation of "handicaps" in Mexican children. *Learning Disability Quarterly, 8,* 67–75.

Dunn, C. W., & Tucker, C. M. (1993). Black children's adaptive functioning and maladaptive behavior associated with the quality of family support. *Journal of Multicultural Counseling and Development, 21,* 79–87.

Echavarria, J. (1995). Sheltered instruction for students with learning disabilities who have limited English proficiency. *Intervention in School and Clinic, 30* (5), 302–305.

ERIC Clearinghouse on Urban Education. (1994). *A guide to communicating with Asian American Families.* NY: Teachers College, Columbia University.

Executive Committee of the Council for Children with Behavioral Disorders. (1989). White paper on best assessment practices for students with behavioral disorders: Accommodations to cultural and individual differences. *Behavioral Disorders, 14,* 263–278.

Forum on Child and Family Statistics. (1998). *America's Children 1998.* Washington, DC: Author.

Fradd, S., Figueroa, R. A., & Correa, V. I. (1989). Meeting the multicultural needs of Hispanic students in special education. *Exceptional Children, 56,* 102–104.

Garcia, E. E. (1995). The impact of linguistic and cultural diversity on America's schools. In M. C. Wang & M. C. Reynolds, (Eds.), *Making a difference for students at risk: Trends and Alternatives* (pp. 156–181). Thousand Oaks, CA: Sage.

Garcia, S., & Yates, J. (1994). Diversity: Teaching a special population. *CEC Today, 1* (6), 1 and 10.

Gonzalez, V., & Yawkey, T. (1993). The assessment of culturally and linguistically different students: Celebrating change. *Educational Horizons, 72* (1), 41–49.

Gregg, N., Ferri, B., Hoy, C., & Stennett, R. B. (in press). Influence of gender and ability on the performance of college students with learning disabilities. *Learning Disabilities Research and Practice.*

Grimm, L. L. (1992). The native American child in school: An ecological perspective. In M. J. Fine and C. Carlson, (Eds.), *The handbook of family-school intervention: A systems perspective* (pp. 102–118). Boston: Allyn & Bacon.

Guild, P. (1994). The culture/learning style connection. *Educational Leadership,* (May), 16–21.

Halpern, D. (1997). Sex differences in intelligence: Implications for education *American Psychologist, 52,* 1091–1102.

Hanna, J. (1988). *Disruptive school behavior: Class, race, and culture.* NY: Holmes and Meyer.

Harry, B. (1992). Restructuring the participation of African-American parents in special education. *Exceptional Children, 24,* 123–131.

Haynes, N. M., & Gebreyesus, S. (1992). Cooperative learning: A case for African-American students. *School Psychology Review, 21* (4), 577–585.

Hodgkinson, H. L. (1985). *All one system.* Washington, DC: Institute for Educational Leadership.

Hodgkinson, H. L. (1995). What should we call people? Race, class, and the census of 2000. *Phi Delta Kappan, 77* (2), 173–176, 178–179.

Huang, G. (1993). *Beyond Culture: Communicating with Asian American Children and Families.* NY: ERIC Clearinghouse on Urban Education.

Huang, L. N. (1989). Southeast Asian refuge children and adolescents. In J. T. Gibbs & L. N. Huang, (Eds.), *Children of color: Psychological interventions with minority youth* (pp. 278–321). San Francisco: Jossey Bass.

Huang, L. N., & Ying, Y. (1989). Chinese American children and adolescents. In J. T. Gibbs & L. N. Huang, (Eds.), *Children of color: Psychological interventions with minority youth* (pp. 30–66). San Francisco: Jossey Bass.

Hyland, C. R. (1989). What we know about the fastest growing minority population: Hispanic Americans. *Educational Horizons, 67* (4), 124–130.

Kavale, K. A., Forness, S. R., & Alper, A. E. (1986). Research in behavioral disorders/emotional disturbance: A survey of subject identification criteria. *Behavioral Disorders, 11,* 159–167.

Kea, C. (1998). Critical teaching behaviors and instructional strategies for working with cultural diverse students. *CCBD Newsletter, 11* (5), 3–7.

Keough, B. K. Gallimore, R., & Weisner, T. (1997). A Sociocultural perspective on learning and learning disabilities. *Learning Disabilities Research and Practice, 12* (2), 107–113.

Klein, H. A. (1995). Urban Appalachian children in northern schools: A study in diversity. *Young Children, 50* (3), 10–16.

LaFramboise, T. D., & Low, K. G. (1989). American Indian children and adolescents. In J. Gibbs & L. Huang, (Eds.), *Children of color* (pp. 114–147). San Francisco: Jossey Bass.

Leap, W. L. (1981). American Indian language maintenance. *Annual Review of Anthropology, 10,* 271–280.

Leinhardt, G., Seewald, A., & Zigmond, N. (1982). Sex and race differences in learning disabilities classrooms. *Journal of Educational Psychology, 74,* 835–843.

Lynch, E. M. (1993). Negotiating status and role: An ethnographic examination of verbal dueling among students with behavior disorders. In A. M. Bauer, (Ed.), *Children who challenge the system* (29–44). Norwood, NJ: Ablex.

Mann, J. (1994). *The difference: Growing up female in America.* NY: Warner Books.

McAdoo, H. P. (1978). Minority families. In J. H. Stevens & M. Matthers, (Eds.), *Mother-child, father-child relationships* (pp. 231–245). Washington, DC: The National Association for the Education of Young Children.

McCabe, K., Yeh, M., Hough, R. L., Landsverk, J., Hurlburt, W. S., Culver, S. W., & Reynolds, B. (1999). Racial/ethnic representation across five public sectors of care for youth. *Journal of Emotional and Behavioral Disorders, 7* (2), 72–82.

McIntyre, T. (1996). Guidelines for providing appropriate services to culturally diverse students with emotional and/or behavioral disorders. *Behavioral Disorders, 21* (2), 137–144.

Matsuda, M. (1989). Working with Asian parents: Some communication strategies. *Topics in Language Disorders 9* (3), 45–53.

Miller, D. (1994). Suicidal behavior of adolescents with behavior disorders and their peers without disabilities. *Behavioral Disorders, 20* (1), 61–68.

Nweke, W. (1994). Racial differences in parental discipline practices. ERIC Document #ED388741. Reston, VA: ERIC Clearinghouse and Disabilities and Gifted Education.

Ochoa, S. H., Rivera, B. D., & Power, M. P. (1997). Factors used to comply with exclusionary clause with bilingual and limited English proficient pupils: Initial guidelines, *Learning Disabilities Research and Practice, 12* (3), 161–167.

Oswald, D. P., Coutinho, M. J., Best, A. M., & Singh, N. N. (1999). Ethnic representation in special education: The influence of school-related economic and demographic variables. *Journal of Special Education, 32* (4), 194–206.

Payette, K. A., & Clarizio, H. F. (1994). Discrepant team decisions: The effects of race, gender, achievement, and IQ on LD eligibility. *Psychology in the Schools, 31,* 40–48.

Peters, M. (1981). Parenting in Black families with young children. In H. McAdoo, (Ed.), *Black Families* (pp. 145–197). Newbury Park, CA: Sage.

Population Reference Bureau. (1998). *America's racial and ethnic minorities.* Washington, DC: Author.

Rodriquez, J., & Carrasquillo, A. L. (1997). Hispanic limited English-proficient students with disabilities: A case study example. *Learning Disabilities: A Multidisciplinary Journal, 8* (3), 169–174.

Rueda, R., & Garcia, E. (1997). Do portfolios make a difference for diverse students? The influence of type of data on making instructional decisions. *Learning Disabilities Research and Practice, 12* (2), 114–122.

Sadker, M. D. (1994). *Failing at fairness: How America's schools cheat girls.* NY: Charles Scribner's Sons.

Shon, S., & Ja, D. (1982). Asian families. In M. McGodrick, J. K. Pearce, & J. Giordano, (Eds.), *Ethnicity and family therapy* (pp. 18–27). NY: Guilford Press.

Skiba, R. J. (1989). The importance of constructive validity: Alternative models for the assessment of behavioral disorders. *Behavioral Disorders, 14,* 175–185.

Smith, E. (1981). Cultural and historical perspectives in counseling blacks. In D. W. Sue, (Ed.), *Counseling the culturally different: Theory and practice* (pp. 45–57). NY: Wiley.

Spindler, G., & Spindler, L. (1994). What is cultural therapy? In G. Spindler & L. Spindler, (Eds.), *Pathways to cultural awareness: Cultural therapy with teachers and students* (pp. 1–35). Thousand Oaks, CA: Sage.

Spradley, B. A., & McCurdy, D. W. (1984). Culture and the contemporary world. In J. P. Spradley & D. W. McCurdy, (Eds.), *Conformity and conflict: Readings in cultural anthropology* (5th ed., pp. 1–13). Boston: Little Brown.

U.S. Department of Education. (1998). Nineteenth Annual Report to Congress on the Implementation of the Individuals with Disabilities Education Act. Washington, DC: Author.

Valli, L. (1995). The dilemma of race: Learning to be color blind and color conscious. *Journal of Teacher Education, 46* (2), 120–129.

Vogel, S. A. (1990). Gender differences in intelligence, language, visual-motor abilities, and academic achievement in students with learning disabilities: A review of the literature. *Journal of Learning Disabilities, 23,* 44–52.

Yamamoto, J., & Kubota, M. (1989). The Japanese American family. In G. Powell, J. Yamamoto, & A. Morales, (Eds.), *The psychosocial development of minority group children* (pp. 231–245). NY: Brunner-Mazel.

Zurcher, R. (1998). Issues and trends in culture-fair assessment. *Intervention in School and Clinic, 34* (2), 103–106.

9 Screening to Placement

TO GUIDE YOUR READING

After completing this chapter, you will be able to answer the following questions:

- What is the role of screening in the identification of students with learning disabilities or emotional/ behavioral disorders?

- What are prereferral activities for students at-risk for learning disabilities or emotional/behavioral disorders?

- What are the referral processes used with students with learning disabilities or emotional/behavioral disorders?

- What are the assessment processes used with students with learning disabilities or emotional/behavioral disorders?

- What are the special education eligibility and placement processes applied to students with learning disabilities or emotional/behavioral disorders?

- What are the Individualized Education Plan, the Individualized Family Service Plan, and the Individualized Transition Plan, and how are these applied in services for students with learning disabilities or emotional/behavioral disorders?

◆◆ *Marcus, a recent transfer from another school outside of the district, had been disrupting his fourth grade mathematics class since the beginning of school in August. His academic work was not comparable to that of his classmates. Marcus struggled with the content of his assignments, as well as the completion of them. Ms. Villalobos, his teacher, requested help from the Glenn Middle School Student Assistance Team. Ms. Farrell, the assistant principal and chair of the team, called Marcus' teachers together to discuss the behaviors that Ms. Villalobos had been observing. In the meeting, it became apparent that Marcus's behaviors, which included taking other students' homework and putting his name on it, challenging the teachers verbally in class, and taunting students who completed their work, occurred not only during mathematics, but in science class as well. Ms. Farrell proposed that she would observe Marcus in class, and the teachers should keep daily notes on Marcus' activities during each class for two weeks. At the end of that time, the team would reconvene, and discuss potential interventions to attempt to help Marcus become more successful in his classes.*

After the two weeks of observation, Ms. Farrell reported that Marcus appeared to be "two different people." In Language Arts and Social Studies, he was an active participant, and, though sometimes boisterous, he did not miss any more assignments or homework than his classmates. In Mathematics and Physical Science, Marcus struggled with both content and behavior. In contrasting the classes, Ms. Farrell noted that Language Arts and Social Studies emphasized cooperative learning activities, exhibitions, and projects, whereas Physical Science and Mathematics were structured around individual work and written evaluations. Both Physical Science and Mathematics required computational skills; Marcus was very slow and worked tediously with computation. The team suggested allowing Marcus to use a calculator for computation when solving word problems, while continuing to work on his computation skills. Ms. Villalobos also agreed to observe Marcus in Social Studies in order to try to identify ways to evaluate his progress in ways additional to written tests. Marcus would be presented with a behavior contract which would initially emphasize more acceptable participation in the class. Ms. Villalobos thought that further accommodations would compromise the content of her class. The team agreed to give the accommodations and contract a month, and then meet again.

REFLECTION *Reflect on your own schooling. Do you remember a student entering your classroom who differed from the other students to the extent that the teachers took action? What happened with that student?*

Introduction

Up to this point, the text has concentrated on students who already have been identified as learning disabled or emotionally/behaviorally disordered. Yet many students proceed through several years of schooling before their achievement, learning style, or behavior comes to the attention of teachers. Sometimes, as in the case of Marcus, students' needs emerge when there is a change of school, or when the student moves from the primary to middle grades.

The Role of Screening in Identification

Screening is the process of identifying students who, at least on the basis of a first-level study, warrant further assessment. In screening, an entire population (for example, a class or school) of students is evaluated to determine whether individual students within the population are at risk for learning disabilities or emotional/behavioral disorders and need additional assessment (Witt and others, 1994).

As a result of screening, the learner may be classified as, (a) having no problem, (b) having a transitory problem, (c) having a problem that is a response to social and academic stressors in the school or classroom that could be altered, or (d) having a problem that is evident at school, home, and neighborhood (Long, Morse, & Newman, 1980). The result of screening is *not* to classify a learner as having a learning disability or emotional/behavioral disorder, but to identify for further study the learner who is at risk for such a problem.

Feil, Walker, and Severson (1995) suggest that learning and behavioral problems among preschool-aged children have become a priority for early childhood educators. They contend that factors such as the exponential rise in childcare utilization, increased poverty, and the incidence of child abuse have made the establishment of procedures for early identification and remediation of problem behaviors among preschool children imperative. Early identification and intervention of students assumes that behavioral and school-related problems can be prevented (Walker, Colin, & Ramsey, 1995). Remediation of behavior problems becomes more difficult as children grow older (Bower, 1981). Reid (1993) demonstrated that three-fourths of all children who show early signs of behavior problems, such as disobedience, tantrums, fighting, and stealing, move to more serious acting-out behaviors as they age. Young children with mild-to-moderate behavior problems are the most likely to be overlooked by traditional developmental screening (Beare & Lynch, 1986).

In school, teachers' judgments about students' social behavior are the primary basis for referral (Hoge, 1983). Gresham and Reschly (1988) describe a "model behavioral profile" applied by teachers when judging whether students have behavior problems. This profile encompasses behaviors that, (a) facilitate academic performance, and (b) are marked by the absence of disruptive behaviors that disturb the teacher and the classroom. In their study of teachers as judges of social competence, Gresham, Noell, and Elliott (1996) reported that teacher ratings of social skills were much more accurate in ruling out low social competence rather than identifying the presence of social incompetence. Teachers appear to base their judgments of low social competence for both boys and girls on the absence of teacher-preferred skills.

Walker, Colvin, and Ramsey (1995) suggest that screening procedures should be proactive by seeking out students who may be at risk rather than responding when students are demonstrating serious problems. In addition, the student should be evaluated by various persons in several different settings. Screening efforts, to serve the function of prevention, should take place at preschool and kindergarten levels. Though teacher nominations and rankings of behavior are helpful in initiating a screening process, additional information, such as that derived from observations, school records, and peer and parent rating scales should be used.

Rating Scales

Rating scales traditionally have been used as part of the screening process to refer students for possible special education services (Elliott, Busse, & Gresham, 1993). Elliott and associates present five issues that influence the use and interpretation of rating scales:

1. Ratings are summaries of perceptions of the relative frequency of a behavior based on observational perceptions. For example, on a specific rating scale, a teacher may rate a learner as "sometimes" demonstrating a behavior if it occurs anywhere between two and five times a day. However, there may be real differences between a student who demonstrates a behavior two times, and a student who demonstrates that same behavior five times.

2. Ratings are judgments affected by the rater's standards and by the environment. An individual's behavior may change depending on the situation, and depending on the rater's judgment of how the student is functioning.

3. The social validity, that is, the importance attributed to a behavior by significant individuals in the environment, should be recognized. A difficulty can arise when the focus becomes the tolerance of the rater for the behavior rather than the importance of the behavior to the student's functioning.

4. Several assessors of the same student's behaviors may agree only moderately. Rating scales use simple frequency counts for quantifying behaviors which may, in context, vary a great deal in frequency, intensity, and duration.

5. Rating may be related to student gender. Norms that are sensitive to gender differences must be applied when interpreting rating scales.

Table 9.1   Guidelines for the Evaluations of Behavior Rating Scales

- Is the rating scale practically useful?
- Is the content valid?
- Is each item meaningful and useful?
- Is training necessary for raters?
- Does the interpretive framework match the purpose of the raters?
- Is the rating scale reliable?
- Is there test-retest reliability?
- Is there interrater reliability?
- Is the rating scale internally valid?
- Is the rating scale externally valid?
- Can the scale be used for the purpose for which it was intended?

(Elliot, Busse, & Gresham, 1993)

Elliott and associates (1993) suggested several guidelines for the selection and evaluation of rating scales. These guidelines are summarized in Table 9.1.

Identification of a Learning Disability

The Federal Procedures for Evaluating Specific Learning Disabilities (Federal Register, USOE, 1997) define learning disabilities as a severe discrepancy between achievement and intellectual capacity in one or more areas specifically related to oral language, written language, or mathematics. Intellectual capacity and achievement are typically determined by individually administered norm-referenced tests. Nearly all the states also include a discrepancy component in their definition or criteria for determining learning disabilities (Mercer et al, 1996). Although the federal definition includes an exclusion clause (the definition does not include learning problems that are primarily the result of visual, hearing, or motor handicaps, mental retardation, emotional disturbance, or environmental, cultural or economic disadvantage), exclusion criteria are used less consistently than that of a discrepancy model (Fletcher, Francis, Shaywitz, Lyon, Foorman, Stuebing, & Shaywitz, 1998).

As described in the discussion of the definition of learning disabilities in Chapter Two, the states use various methods to determine if a discrepancy exists between intelligence and achievement. The methods are founded on the premise that the score from a norm-referenced intelligence test can predict academic success. The two most common procedures for determining the discrepancy between intelligence and achievement are the standard score comparison model, and a correction for regression (Frankenberger & Fronzaglio, 1991). A standard score model compares the standard score of the norm-referenced intelligence measure and the standard score of the achievement measure to determine if there is a significant difference between the two. A regression-based approach takes into account that when scores from intelligence tests are higher or lower than average, academic achievement cannot be predicted accurately by the intelligence quotient. The statistical phenomenon known as regression toward the mean is when students with tested intelligence quotients above the mean tend to score lower than expected on academic achievement measures, and students whose tested intelligence quotients are below average tend to score higher than expected on achievement measures (Cone & Wilson, 1981). Such an adjustment is recommended in order to prevent overidentification of children with higher tested intelligence quotients, and underidentification of children with lower tested intelligence quotients (Reynolds, 1984).

Individual states use various methods for determining discrepancies, and implement them differently. For example, a state using the standard score comparison model may specify that the intelligence quotient standard score has to be at least 20 points greater than the achievement test standard score for a severe discrepancy to exist. In other words, if the intelligence quotient is 100 and the achievement score is 85, a severe discrepancy does not exist because there is only a 15 point difference in the two scores. However, if the achievement score is 80, then there is a severe discrepancy. Another state, however, may specify a 16 point discrepancy. It would be possible for a student to be eligible for learning disabilities services in one state, and not in another.

Regardless of the formula used to calculate severe discrepancy, it is argued that intelligence quotient/achievement score discrepancy models are not viable methods to classify individuals as learning disabled (Fletcher et al, 1998). As discussed in Chapter Two, scores from norm-referenced intelligence tests may underrepresent the intelligence of students with learning disabilities (Siegel, 1989). And, based on review of large-scale studies constructed to compare discrepant groups and low-achieving groups, Fletcher and associates (1998) determined that discrepancy models do not provide good differentiation of students with learning disabilities from students with low achievement. Although the discrepancy model will identify students who have an academic or cognitive skills problem, the problem is similar to that of a student with low achievement who does not have a discrepancy between scores from norm-referenced intelligence tests and achievement tests. In addition, it is difficult to identify students in the early grades because, among young children, there is a narrow range between where students with academic problems actually perform and where they should be performing (Mather & Roberts, 1994). Fletcher and associates further point out that the average age of identification of students with learning disabilities is ten years old, and the use of the discrepancy model moves identification and intervention to later elementary years.

Because discrepancy models are viewed negatively, alternative assessment approaches are being considered. Fletcher and associates suggest that alternative approaches to identification of learning disabilities could be based on Stanovich's (1988) work distinguishing phonological-based reading problems, and reading problems due to more pervasive language impairments. They suggest that intelligence tests should not be used to determine a student's potential for learning, but should be viewed, as Kaufman (1994) suggested regarding the Weschsler Intelligence Scale for Children-III, as a type of achievement test that measures past accomplishments and predicts success in school. Further, they state that the use of achievement levels to identify learning disabilities will make it possible to focus on domain-specific factors. This notion is similar to Torgesen and Wagner's (1998) suggestion that children should be identified for special reading instruction on the basis of phonological and word-reading abilities, rather than on a discrepancy-based formula. Teachers should remember, however, that students may also have mathematics learning disabilities, and reliance on measures of reading to identify students with learning disabilities will fail to recognize those students, who also need help.

Another alternative approach to eligibility assessment using curriculum-based assessment has been proposed by Fuchs and Fuchs (1998). This model begins with two phases of assessment including, (a) assessment of the instructional environment, and (b) comparison of individual students' levels of performance and rates of improvements. If the student performance level and improvement level are significantly lower than that of peers, a third and fourth phase of assessment are employed. In the third phase, it is determined if the general education setting can, with adaptations, become an acceptable learning situation, and generate better growth. The fourth phase would determine the potential effect of special education services. Documentation required for these multiple phases is generated through curriculum-based measurement. Further discussion of curriculum-based measurement is presented later in this chapter.

Emotional/Behavioral Disorders

One example of a screening instrument for children with emotional/behavioral disorders is the Systematic Screening for Behavior Disorders (SSBD) (Walker & Severson, 1990). It is based on the assumption that teacher judgment is valid for the identification of students with emotional/behavioral disorders. The SSBD, designed for use in elementary school, includes three steps, or gates, for identification of students. The three gates are teacher rankings, teacher ratings, and direct observation in formal and informal school environments by a professional, usually the teacher. The instrument is designed to identify students who are at risk for both externalizing and internalizing behavioral disorders.

In a replication of the procedural integrity and outcomes of earlier applications of the SSBD, a state-wide study demonstrated that, (a) the SSBD has robust psychometric characteristics; (b) it can discriminate among externalizing, internalizing, and typical behavior patterns; and (c) it identifies elementary children who have serious problems with their social skills and behavior (Walker, Severson, Nicholson, Kehle, Jenson, and Clark, 1994). Walker and associates also indicated that the use of the measure was cost-effective, and generally was rated favorably by teachers and psychologists. Feil and Becker (1993) adapted the SSBD for use with preschool children. In their adaptation, teacher rankings, teacher ratings, and direct behavioral observations were employed. The resulting Preschool Screening for Behavior Problems is a three-stage, multiple-gating procedure to screen children from three- to five-years-old. Feil, Walker, and Severson (1995) reported strong interrater reliability and consistency of this screening system compared to other instruments for young children.

Another commonly used screening instrument is the Child Behavior Checklist (CBC) (Achenbach & Edelbrock, 1991). Several forms are included in this instrument: parent's report, teacher's report, and self-report. In schools, the most frequently used form of the CBC is the teacher's report. On this report, the teacher rates the student on 112 problem behaviors on a three-point scale (Not true, Somewhat or sometimes true, Very or often true). Some of the items which are rated by teachers are (a) cries a lot, (b) complains of loneliness, (c) physically attacks people, (d) seems preoccupied with sex, and (d) dislikes school. The teacher's report can be used with students from five years of age through eighteen years of age, and it generates a profile of specific problem-related factors.

Activities for At-Risk Students

Prereferral activities are strategies implemented in the general education classroom, by the general education teacher, to address the individual needs of students prior to referral for assessment for special education services. The goal of prereferral activities is to provide assistance to students with behavior problems in the general education classroom, and thus, make referral to special education unnecessary (Shea & Bauer, 1997). Such activities are *not* an initial step in the special education assessment and placement process, but are developed by general education personnel through collaborative consultation and problem solving activities. At present, prereferral activities are recommended or required in at least thirty-four states (Carter & Sugai, 1989).

Several assumptions underlie prereferral interventions (Pugach & Johnson, 1989):

- The purpose of these interventions is to avoid the classification of students as disabled.
- All educational professionals in a school, at one time or another, serve as consultants to each other, that is, consultation is multidirectional.
- Classroom teachers, given time and support, are able to solve many of their students' classroom problems without the direct intervention of specialists.
- The process of supporting students varies with the student's problem and personnel involved.

An example of a prereferral intervention with a learner who is potentially at risk for classification as emotionally/behaviorally disordered is presented in Figure 9.1 (Shea & Bauer, 1997).

Del'Homme, Kasari, Forness, and Bagley (1996), over the course of a year, examined the types of presenting problems and subsequent prereferral interventions for a large sample of elementary school students referred to a student support team. The majority of students referred had a mixture of academic and behavioral problems. They found that boys were more frequently referred for support than girls, and that the boys' referrals usually involved behavior problems. The interventions that the teachers used typically "matched" the referral problem.

The behaviors that prompt prereferral interventions tend to vary by nature or degree for children by ethnicity or gender. MacMillan, Gresham, Lopez, and Bocia (1996) reported differences among the Euro-American, African American, and Hispanic American students. Euro-American children demonstrated higher tested verbal intelligence quotients and reading achievement scores. African American children were more likely to have more problem behaviors than were Hispanic American children. Severe academic problems characterized children across all ethnic groups. Differences by gender were related to the acting-out behaviors typically exhibited by males. Differences between males and females were not reported on cognitive and achievement measures. Overall, teachers rated girls selected for prereferral intervention higher in academic competence than boys selected for prereferral intervention.

Noll, Kamps, and Seaborn (1993) studied the three-year implementation of a prereferral intervention program model for students with emotional/behavioral disorders. Each year, between 43 percent and 64 percent of the students in the program remained in the general education classroom. Between 14 percent and 22 percent were identified as having disabilities other than emotional/behavioral disorders. Between 23 percent and 39 percent were identified as having emotional/behavioral disorders, with one-half of those students being able to continue in the gen-

Louise was doing well in Mr. Raphael's fourth grade classroom until December, when her behavior changed. Louise no longer completed her homework, did not participate in games during recess, and, on two occasions, pinched children who were on "her" swing on the playground. After sending notes to Louise's mother regarding concerns about these behaviors and receiving no response, Mr. Raphael telephoned Louise's home. Louise's nineteen-year-old aunt, who was "helping out with the kids," reported that Louise's mother had entered a hospice for terminal cancer patients. Louise's father was spending a lot of time at the hospice, but "just couldn't bring himself to take the kids to visit."

Mr. Raphael met with Ms. Turner, the school principal, to discuss Louise's behavior. They agreed that an Intervention Assistance Team should be formed to address the situation. Mr. Raphael recommended that Mrs. Holts, the art teacher, with whom Louise had particular rapport, be included on the team. Ms. Turner suggested that Ms. Michael, the school counselor, and Ms. Wang, who had recently worked one of her students and her classmates through a mother's death in an automobile accident, also be included.

The team met and discussed Louise's behavior. They formulated a plan that included the following:

1. Twice-weekly meetings for Louise with the school counselor.

2. Increased informal interaction between Louise and Mrs. Holts, the art teacher.

3. Increased efforts to encourage Louise to participate appropriately during recess, while recognizing her feelings. Louise was to receive a cue such as the following: "I know it's hard to have fun when you're worried about someone. Would you like to talk about how you're feeling before you join the game?" Or, "I know you're feeling hurt and worried right now, but the rule is to keep your hands to yourself on the playground. How could you ask (child's name) to move to another swing?"

4. Review materials Ms. Wang had received from the local children's hospital regarding dealing in the classroom with death, separation, and loss.

5. Continued communication attempts with the family, recognizing that the family is in crisis, and that all contacts should be supportive rather than just reports of negative behavior.

6. Meet again in four weeks to evaluate the plan, and Louise's progress.

(Modified from Shea/Bauer, 1997)

Figure 9.1   Prereferral Intervention

eral education classroom with assistance. Noll and associates' prereferral process included a "best practice" for behavioral consultation, that is, (a) a collaborative agreement among teachers, pupil, and parents; (b) a contractual agreement with goals and specific criteria for progress evaluation; (c) built-in consequences with systematic reinforcement and loss of privilege for noncompliance; (d) self-monitoring, to encourage self-management and intrinsic control as an end result; (e) easily implemented interventions across settings and teacher/staff; and (f) a design or plan to reduce the need for external procedures through fading and delayed reinforcement strategies. An itinerant teacher was used to support general education teachers and students engaged in prereferral intervention.

The use of school-based prereferral intervention teams has been related to the increase in referrals which, after case studies, are found to qualify for special education services. These teams also provide ongoing support to classroom teachers with students not eligible for special education (Ivarie & Russell, 1992). Ivarie and Russell found concern among personnel with regards to the time available for consultation following implementation of prereferral activities. The most significant advantage described by teachers engaging in prereferral interventions was that they received immediate help when it was needed. Some students may not respond to prereferral interventions and, as a consequence are referred for special education assessment and services.

Referral Processes

Students with mild disabilities are usually identified only after failing to make progress in the general education program (MacMillan, Gresham, Bocian, & Siperstein, 1997). MacMillan and associates argue that these students come to the attention of their teachers on the basis of their educational history, psychometric measures, and observations. The students may not be identified through screening.

In addition to screening, students may be identified for assessment for special education services through the referral process. Referral is the process of soliciting and accepting nominations for assessment from others. A referral may be made by school personnel, parents, physicians, community human service agency personnel, or other persons responsible for the student's welfare (Shea & Bauer, 1987).

School referral is a two-step process. First, information is collected from all individuals who currently interact with the student in the school. The general education classroom teacher, for example, may be requested to assist in completing rating scales or checklists, or to complete information sheets. In addition, teachers document the interventions, accommodations, and resources they have used to address the issue prior to referral. This documentation is presented to the team or individual responsible for determining the appropriateness of the referral. When a Student Support Team is in place to assist the teachers in designing, implementing, and evaluating interventions, the Team is usually involved in determining whether current efforts are inadequate, and whether the student should be referred for evaluation. In other settings, a principal or special educator may be responsible for reviewing the referral information and determining its appropriateness.

If the referral is deemed appropriate, parents are invited to a conference, at which concerns of school personnel are explained, and parents are asked for permission to assess the child for special education service. A "consent for evaluation" form must be signed by the parent before evaluation can begin. If the parent does not agree to the evaluation, the school district has the right to follow due process procedures to appeal the parents' decision. When consent is granted, the multifactored evaluation proceeds.

Assessment Processes

Assessment is the process of studying the behaviors of a student to determine the nature of the problem, if in fact, there is a problem. The basic purpose of assessment for intervention is to identify needed changes in behaviors or environments, and to decide how to accomplish the goals of the needed changes (Barnett, Bauer, Barnhouse, Ehrhardt, Lentz, Macmann, & Stollar, 1997).

The Nature of Assessment

The processes used to assess students have been questioned over the past twenty years. The National Association of Early Childhood Teacher Educators, for example, urged the replacement of current questionable testing practices with procedures more compatible with the available knowledge on how young children demonstrate what they know (NAECTE, 1989). The National Center for Fair and Open Testing (1989) reported that more than a million standardized tests were administered annually to public school students.

The overriding purpose for all assessment is to gather information to facilitate decision making (Witt, Elliott, Kramer, & Gresham, 1994; Gerken, 1988). These decisions may be related to screening, eligibility and placement, student progress, programming for intervention, or program effectiveness (Salvi & Ysseldyke, 1991).

There are two general models of assessment: the medical model, and the behavioral ecological model (Witt and others, 1994). The medical model assumes that behavior which deviates from some standard is a reflection of personal disease, disturbance, disorder, or dysfunction, and that treatment must bring about change within the individual. The behavioral ecological model, on the other hand, acknowledges the impact of other people and environmental factors in the shaping of the individual's behavior. Unusual behavior is viewed as inappropriate, or maladaptive, rather than due to internal problems.

Witt and associates (1994) describe four general approaches to assessment: norm-referenced, criterion-referenced, informal, and ecological. The general assumptions, advantages, disadvantages, and questions answered by each of these approaches to assessment are presented in Table 9.2.

Table 9.2   General Approaches to Assessment

Perspective	Norm-Referenced	Criterion-Referenced	Informal	Ecological
Description	Individual performances are compared to the performance of a large, collectively representative sample, referred to as the norm	Individual performances are compared to some pre-established standard	Process is adapted to the individual child and situation	Assesses child, teacher, expectations, environment, and task
Advantages	Presents information that is easily communicated: compares to group	Identifies specific skills	Relevant to instructional process	Expands focus of assessment; recognizes complexity of behavior
Disadvantages	Information is too general; discrepancy between what is taught and what is tested; tends to promote belief that locus of problem is within the child	Difficult to establish a criterion: teachers may "teach the test"	Depends on examiner to select appropriate tests, problem solve, and interpret: values may affect recommendations	Complexity of the process; lack of adequate instruments
Question answered	How does this student compare with others his or her age?	How well does this individual perform this skill?	What seems to be contributing to the problem?	What is happening when the behavior occurs?

Appropriate assessment is grounded in the following assumptions (Witt and associates, 1994):

- Differences among students derive their meaning from the situation in which they occur.
- Tests are only samples of behavior, and should only provide support for decision making.
- Assessments are conducted to improve instruction or intervention activities.
- Individuals who are conducting assessments should be properly trained.
- No assessments are free from errors.

Assessment practices used for identifying students with learning disabilities or emotional/behavioral disorders have been criticized. Niemi and Tiuraniemi (1995) suggest that there is a lack of pedagogical value in the

In norm-referenced assessment, there may be a discrepancy between what the student has been taught and what is tested.

diagnostic reports made by psychologists concerning learning difficulties. In this forty-year longitudinal study, they reported that there were "favorite" diagnoses during specific time periods. In addition, Niemi and Tiuraniemi report a lack of positive interactions between teachers and psychologists, as they are being prepared for their professions.

Swicegood (1994) provides several recommendations for an assessment process for use with students with learning disabilities or emotional/behavioral disorders. Any assessment process should emphasize ongoing collaboration among practitioners, professionals, and students. Greater weight should be given to teacher and classroom-based assessment, with a greater reliance on informal, qualitative, and ecological methods rather than traditional "testing." Assessment should seek to describe each student's unique ecological, cultural, and linguistic personality. Information from a variety of sources and ecological contexts which confirm and corroborate decisions about eligibility and interventions should be included. Finally, it should be recognized that literacy growth, academic achievement, and social-behavioral functioning are not separate domains, but are integrated, and mutually influential.

Several trends in assessment of students with learning disabilities or emotional/behavioral disorders have emerged. These include curriculum-based measurement, functional assessment, dynamic assessment, and portfolio assessment.

Curriculum-based assessment. In curriculum-based measurement, assessment material is drawn from the student's instructional curricula (Fuchs and Deno, 1994). By using curriculum-based measurement, Fuchs and Deno argue that assessment has instructional utility. Teachers may develop their tests from their own instructional material, from material that mirrors their curriculum, or from material which represents the generalized outcomes or goals of the curriculum. In order to be useful, curriculum-based measurement must include repeated testing, and measurement should include indicators of the critical outcomes of instruction. In addition, both quantitative and qualitative descriptions of the student's performance should be included to allow teachers to determine when instructional accommodations are needed, and to formulate ideas about how to enhance instruction.

Fuchs and Fuchs (1997) suggest that curriculum-based measurement can be used to both identify problems students may be demonstrating, and to determine their eligibility for special education services. The curriculum-based measurement approach, they argue, is focused on growth and treatment enhancement. The process is comprised of three phases. First, the multidisciplinary team documents adequate classroom instruction, and the discrepancies between the student's learning and behavior and that of his or her peers. Second, prereferral interventions are designed and implemented. Third, an assessment plan specific to possible identification of the need for special education services is implemented. This assessment plan would include goals for academic growth, helping to distinguish between ineffective general education environments and unacceptable individual student learning. Such assessment plans provide information for instructional planning for the student, and evaluating relative treatment effectiveness.

Functional assessment. As part of the Individuals with Disabilities Education Act (IDEA) Amendments of 1997, local education agencies are now required to use a functional assessment to develop a behavioral intervention plan for students with disabilities when their behavior is at issue (McConnell, Hilvitz, & Cox, 1998). Functional assessment is an analytical approach for making decisions about treatment (Gable, 1996). Functional assessment is predicated on the assumption that the effectiveness of treatment increases if there is a match between the treatment and the function of the behaviors involved. Karsh, Repp, Dahlquist, and Munk (1995) suggest that this is the value of functional assessment—that treatment effectiveness increases if the treatment matches the function of the target behavior. Through functional assessment, relationships between personal and environmental events and the occurrence or nonoccurrence of a target behavior are identified (Dunlap, Kern, dePerczel, Clarke, Wilson, Childs, White, and Falk, 1993).

Blakeslee, Sugai, and Gruba (1994) describe several advantages of functional assessment. Functional assessment promotes hypothesis-driven treatment, and places more emphasis on skill building than on punishment. Because of the emphasis on skill building, it increases the probability of a positive outcome. By matching treatment to the function of the behavior, the chance of maintenance and generalization of new behaviors is increased. McConnell, Hilvitz, and Cox (1998) formulated a ten-step plan to conduct a functional assessment. This plan is presented in Table 9.3.

Dynamic assessment.   Dynamic assessment links a belief system about learning disabilities to an assessment strategy. Swanson (1995) suggests that if learning disabilities are problems in information processes, then decisions should be made at the processing level. He postulates that the reason so many students are identified as having learning disabilities is because traditional psychometric procedures fail to assess the processing potential of the student, and they don't differentiate students with learning disabilities from other students who are having difficulty achieving. He recommends that dynamic assessment be used to provide insight into information processes, and thus differentiate students with learning disabilities from other students who are having difficulty achieving.

Table 9.3   A Ten-Step Functional Assessment Procedure

1. Identify the student's behavior which should be addressed.
2. Describe the behavior in clear, specific, and detailed language. Then ask:
   a. Is this behavior important to the success of the student and others in the classroom?
   b. Does this behavior affect the student's learning?
3. Use direct observation to gather baseline information on the behavior. Collect academic information.
4. Describe the environment and the demands of the setting. Describe the physical environment, time factors, instructional expectations, and behavioral expectations.
5. Interview the teacher to gather additional information about the function of the behavior.
6. Develop a hypothesis as to the reason for the behavior.
7. Develop a behavioral intervention plan.
8. Implement the plan.
9. Collect behavioral data for at least three weeks; determine if there has been a change.
10. Conduct a follow-up meeting about the student.

(McConnell, Hilvitz, & Cox, 1998)

Most states and school districts rely on discrepancy-based formulas that include a formally tested intelligence quotient and achievement score as the primary procedure to classify children as having learning disabilities. Swanson (1995) suggests, however, that there is a problem with the integrity of the measures used. He argues that recent research has confirmed what has been known about the limitations of discrepancy scores for some time; they do not differentiate students with learning disabilities from students who are having difficulty achieving in school. Swanson suggests that dynamic assessment would provide insight into the way in which the student processes information. In dynamic assessment, the examiner attempts to modify the performance of the student in an effort to understand his or her learning potential. The result of such an assessment is a description of how the student processes information rather than a statement that he or she is unable to perform to the best of his or her ability.

Portfolio assessment.   Portfolios can provide valuable information about a student's learning and behavior. Swicegood (1994) describes the following purposes of portfolios:

- They provide a concrete display of the student's work and development.
- They provide multidimensional assessment information in a functional context, while reflecting a period of time.
- They can provide a display of the range of learning experiences or activities in which the student has engaged.
- They can encourage dialogue and collaboration between educators, and between teachers, students, and parents.

A portfolio can be linked to the student's Individualized Education Plan by including work which shows growth on objectives. Swicegood (1994) suggests that students should have as much ownership as possible in building the portfolio, and that periodic conferences should be held to hold the student accountable for growth and to evaluate and refine the objectives. In addition, periodic use of a summary sheet from the portfolio may help the teacher reflect on instructional effectiveness, as well as serve as a vehicle for communication with parents and the student.

The Use of Report Cards

A national survey of elementary and secondary general education teachers indicated that teachers find letter and number grades more helpful for students without disabilities than for those with disabilities (Bursuck, Polloway, Plante, Epstein, Jayanthi, & McConeghy, 1996). Pass/fail and checklists were reported to be more helpful for students with disabilities. General education teachers reported that they were willing to modify grading criteria for students with disability, but that grades were usually determined by scores on homework, tests, and quizzes. Bursuck and associates found, in general, that elementary school teachers communicate much more frequently with parents about grades than either middle-school or high-school teachers. Middle- or high-school teachers, however, tend to communicate somewhat more frequently with the parents of their students with disabilities than the parents of their students without disabilities. General educators assumed complete responsibility for grading students with disabilities about half of the time, whereas special and general educators worked collaboratively on grades about 40 percent of the time. In response to the question of fairness of grading adaptations only for student with disabilities, teachers responded that they wanted adaptations to be considered for all students, regardless of whether they had a diagnosed disability.

Special Education Eligibility and Placement Processes

Eligibility is the process of determining if a student meets state criteria for classification as a student with learning disabilities or emotional/behavioral disorders. Placement is the assignment of a student identified as eligible for special education services as learning disabled or emotional/behavioral disordered to specific special education and related services programs.

After the student is assessed, it is the interdisciplinary team's responsibility to determine if the student meets specific criteria for classification as emotional/behavioral disordered. The criteria for classification vary somewhat from state to state. In making this decision, the members of the team are required to take all of the available information on the student into consideration. If adequate information is not available, the team should seek additional needed information.

Placement is a responsibility of the multidisciplinary team. It is formalized at the end of the development of an Individualized Educational Plan, and is determined after the team:

- reviews all information available on the student and the environments in which the student functions;
- seeks parental evaluation of the information and determines if additional information is needed;
- analyzes the learner's academic and behavioral strengths, weaknesses, and learning style to use as a basis for educational goals and objectives;
- considers the placement alternatives in view of the student's educational goals, objectives, and learning style;
- reviews the placement selected with regard to the student's participation in general education, and its responsivity to the student's individual needs.

Since the implementation of Public Law 94-142, the placement instruments required to be used are the Individualized Education Plan, or Individualized Family Service Plan.

The Individualized Education Plan, Individualized Family Service Plan, and Individualized Transition Plan

Regardless of the specific diagnostic label assigned to a student with disabilities, the beginning point for special education services is the Individualized Education Plan (IEP). The IEP is a year-long plan of services and activities to be conducted with a learner with a disability, and, in this case, a student with learning disabilities or emotional/behavioral disorders.

The IEP is developed on the basis of the individual assessment information discussed in the previous section. The IEP is to be developed in response to the learner's individual needs. According to IDEA 97 (Section 614 (d)), the members of the IEP team include:

- the parents;
- at least one regular educator of the child, if the child is, or may be, participating in general education;
- at least one special education teacher or special education provider;
- a representative of the local education agency who is qualified to provide, or supervise, the provision of special education, is knowledgeable about the general curriculum, and is knowledgeable about the availability of the resources of the local education agency;
- an individual who can interpret the instructional implications of evaluation results;
- at the discretion of the parent or the agency, other individuals who have knowledge or special expertise regarding the child, including related services personnel as appropriate; and
- whenever appropriate, the child with a disability.

IDEA 97 (Public Law 105-17), the amendments to Public Law 94-142, have clarified the contents of the IEP to include:

- a statement of the child's present level of educational performance, including how the child's disability affects involvement and progress in the general curriculum;
- for preschool children, a statement on how the disability affects the child's participation in appropriate activities;
- a statement of measurable annual goals, including short-term objectives related to meeting the child's needs that result from the disability; how staff is enabling the child to be involved in, and progress in,

the general curriculum; and meeting each of the child's other educational needs that result from the disability;

- a statement of the special education and related services and supplementary aids and services to be provided to the child, or on behalf of the child;

- a statement of the program modifications or supports for school personnel that will be provided to enable the child to progress toward the goals, to be involved and progress in the general curriculum, to participate in extracurricular and other nonacademic activities, and to be educated and participate with other children with and without disabilities;

- an explanation of the extent, if any, to which the child will not participate with students without disabilities in general education classrooms;

- a statement of modifications in the administration of state- or district-wide assessments of student achievement that are needed in order for the child to participate in such assessment. If the IEP team determines that the child will not participate in a particular state- or district-wide assessment (or part of the assessment), a statement of the reason that assessment is not appropriate for the child; and how the child will be assessed;

- the projected date for the beginning of services and modification described in the IEP, and the anticipated frequency, location, and duration of those services and modifications;

- for students who are 14, a statement, to be updated annually, of the transition service needs of the child under the applicable components of the child's IEP that focus on the child's courses of study (such as participation in advanced-placement courses, or a vocational education program);

- beginning at age 16 (or younger, if determined appropriate by the team), a statement of needed transition services for the child, including, when appropriate, a statement of interagency responsibilities or any needed linkages;

- beginning at least one year before the child reaches the age of majority under state law, a statement that the child has been informed of his or her rights that will transfer to the child on reaching the age of majority;

- a statement of how the child's progress toward the annual goals will be measured; how the child's parents will be regularly informed, to be at least as often as parents are informed of their nondisabled children's progress toward the annual goals; and the extent to which the progress is sufficient to enable the child to achieve the goals by the end of the year (Section 614 (d) (1) (a) Public Law 105-17).

In addition, the IEP team must consider special factors related to the student, the student's functioning, and the environment in which the student functions (Section 614 d 3). When the student's behavior impedes his or her learning, or the learning of others, strategies, including positive behavioral interventions, and other supports to address that behavior, must be implemented. When students have limited English proficiency, their language needs must be addressed. For students who are visually impaired, a statement regarding Braille instruction is included, and for students who are hearing impaired, opportunities for direct communication with peers and teachers are included. Any assistive technology needed by the student is also described.

The IEP is a sequential process which answers the following questions (Ohio Department of Education, 1995):

1. What is the long-term vision or goal for this child?
2. What is the child's current functioning?
3. How far can we go toward the vision for this child this year?
4. What services will be provided to move toward that vision?
5. Where will those services be provided?

Several additional legal questions have recently emerged in the development and implementation of IEPs (Ohio Department of Education, 1995). During the IEP meeting, participation in testing and assessment programs, including statewide proficiency testing, must be discussed. If the child is between the ages of three and five, the transition from early childhood to school-age special education services must be specifically described. If the student is at least sixteen, a plan must be included for the transition from school to work and community living. All behaviors that may interfere with learning or other children's opportunity to learn must be addressed. The physical education needs of the child must be addressed. The possibility for extended school-year services should be discussed if, because of an interruption between school years, the child may be unlikely to achieve the short-term objectives.

For infants and toddlers with disabilities, described in Public Law 99-457 as individuals from birth to their third birthday, the Individualized Family Service Plan (IFSP) is developed in place of the IEP. The IFSP is reviewed semiannually and evaluated annually. It includes:

1. A statement of the infant's or toddler's present level of functioning;
2. A statement of the family's strength and needs as related to the development of the infant or toddler with disabilities;
3. A statement of the major anticipated outcomes for the infant or toddler and the family, and the criteria, procedures, and time lines used to determine the degree to which progress is being made, and whether revisions of the anticipated outcomes are necessary;

4. A description of the specific early intervention services necessary to meet the unique needs of the infant or toddler and the family;

5. The projected dates for initiation of services, and the anticipated duration of the services;

6. The name of the case manager for the service most relevant to the needs of the infant or toddler and family who is responsible for the implementation of the plan and coordination with other agencies and persons;

7. A plan for the transition of the toddler to preschool services.

Unlike the IEP, the IFSP places the emphasis for services on the family and the child as a member of the family.

IEPs for students with learning disabilities or emotional/behavioral disorders must be viewed as serious commitments to meeting the needs of the student. However, Smith (1990), after reviewing a large sample of these plans, presented evidence that a substantial number of IEPs written for students with learning disabilities and behavioral disorders failed to function as effective instructional guides.

Particular attention should be paid to supporting parents when the IEP includes transitions between educational environments or the transition to work and the community. Miner and Bates (1997) suggest that planning activities for these transitions should begin about a month before the IEP is due. Parents and students should be invited to complete a personal plan. During a home meeting, they suggest, a profile should be developed that describes the student's support system and his presence in the community. The student's preferences, gifts, and capacities should be discussed. In addition, the students desired future lifestyle should be explored. Action steps toward these goals should be reviewed, and the responsible parties should be identified. By developing this information, changes needed in the services which the student receives can be identified.

Students may also require help to actively participate in the development of their IEPs. VanReusen and Box (1994) utilized a strategy emphasizing self-advocacy, to help students participate in their IEP. Students were taught to specify their own goals, and to express their own needs. For students who learned and used this strategy, 86 percent of the goals in their IEPs were specified by the students themselves. In a comparison group of untrained students, only 13% of their goals were specified by the students.

Summary Points

- Screening is based on the assumption that behavioral and school-related problems can be prevented through early identification and intervention.

- Teachers' judgments about students' social behavior is the primary basis for referral in schools.
- Prereferral activities are designed to provide students with learning or behavior problems the assistance required in general education classrooms, making referral to special education unnecessary.
- The overriding purpose of assessment is to gather information necessary for decision making.
- Eligibility is determined by a multidisciplinary team.
- The Individual Education Plan is the placement instrument for special education.

Key Words and Phrases

assessment—the process of studying a student to determine the nature of the problem, if in fact, there is a problem

eligibility—the process of determining if a student meets specific criteria for classification as a student with a disability

Individualized Education Plan—a year-long plan of the educational services and activities to be conducted with students with disabilities

Individualized Family Service Plan—a year-long plan of services and outcomes for the family of a child with a disability who is younger than three years of age

Individualized Transition Plan—a plan to facilitate the movement of a student from home to preschool, from preschool to kindergarten, from program to program within general and special education, or from an education program to post-secondary education, training, employment, or supported employment

placement—assignment of a student with a disability to a specific special education and related services program

prereferral activities—strategies implemented in the general education classroom by the general education teacher to address the individual needs of students prior to referral for assessment for special education services

referral—the process of soliciting and accepting nominations for assessment for special education service from others

screening—the process of identifying students who, at least on the basis of first-level study, deserve further assessment

social validity—the importance attributed to the behavior of students by significant individuals in the environment

References

Achenbach, T. M., & Edelbrock, E. (1991). *Manual for the Child Behavior Checklist/4–18 and 1991 profile.* Burlington: University of Vermont.

Barnett, D. W., Bauer, A. M., Barnhouse, L., Ehrhardt, K. E., Lentz, F. E., Macmann, G., & Stollar, S. (1997). Ecological foundations of early intervention: Planned activities and strategic sampling. *Journal of Special Education 30,* 471–490.

Beare, P. L., & Lynch, E. C. (1986). Underidentification of preschool children at risk for behavioral disorders. *Behavioral Disorders, 11,* 177–183.

Blakeslee, T., Sugai, G., & Gruba, J. A. (1994). Review of functional assessment used in data-based intervention studies. *Journal of Behavioral Education, 4,* 397–413.

Bower, E. M. (1981). *Early identification of emotionally handicapped children in school (3rd ed.).* Springfield, IL: C. C. Thomas.

Bursuck, W., Polloway, E. A., Plante, L., Epstein, M. H., Jayanthi, M., & McConeghy, J. (1996). Report card grading and adaptations: A national survey of classroom practices. *Exceptional Children, 62* (4), 301–318.

Carter, J., & Sugai, G. (1989). Survey on prereferral practices: Responses from state departments of education. *Exceptional Children, 55,* 298–302.

Del'Homme, M., Kasari, C., Forness, S. R., & Bagley, R. (1996). Prereferral intervention and students at-risk for emotional or behavioral disorders. *Education and Treatment of Children, 19* (3), 272–285.

Dunlap, G., Kern, L., dePerczel, M., Clarke, S., Wilson, D., Childs, K. E., White, R., & Falk, G. D. (1993). Functional analysis of classroom variables for students with emotional and behavioral disorders. *Behavioral Disorders, 18,* 275–291.

Elliott, S. N., Busse, R. T., & Gresham, F. M. (1993). Behavior rating scales: Issues of use and development. *School Psychology Review, 22,* 313–321.

Feil, E. G., & Becker, W. C. (1993). Investigation of a multiple-gated screening system for preschool behavior problems. *Behavioral Disorders, 19* (1), 44–53.

Feil, E. G., Walker, H. M., & Severson, H. Y. (1995). The early screening project for young children with behavior problems. *Journal of Emotional and Behavioral Disorders, 1* (3), 194–202.

Fletcher, J. M., Francis, D. J., Shaywitz, S. E., Lyon, G. R., Foorman, B. R., Stuebing, K. K., & Shaywitz, B. A. (1998). Intelligent testing and the discrepancy model for children with learning disabilities. *Learning Disabilities Research and Practice, 13,* 186–203.

Frankenberger, W., & Fronzaglio, K. (1991). A review of states' criteria for identifying children with learning disabilities. *Journal of Learning Disabilities, 24,* 495–500.

Fuchs, L. S., & Deno, S. L. (1994). Must instructionally useful performance assessment be based in the curriculum? *Exceptional Children, 61* (1), 15–24.

Fuchs, L. S., & Fuchs, D. (1997). Use of curriculum-based measurement in identifying students with disabilities. *Focus on Exceptional Children, 30* (3), 1–14, 16.

Fuchs, L. S., & Fuchs, D. (1998). Treatment validity: A unifying concept for reconceptualizing the identification of learning disabilities. *Learning Disabilities Research and Practice, 13*, 204–219.

Gable, R. A. (1996). A critical analysis of functional assessment: Issues for researchers and practitioners. *Behavioral Disorders, 22* (1), 36–40.

Gerken, K. (1988). Best practice in academic assessment. In A. Thomas and J. Grimes, (Eds.), *Best Practice in School Psychology* (pp. 157–170). Washington, DC: National Association of School Psychologists.

Gresham, F. M., Noell, G. H., and Elliott, S. (1996). Teachers as judges of social competence: A conditional probability analysis. *School Psychology Review, 25*, 108–117.

Gresham, F. M., & Reschly, D. J. (1988). Issues in the conceptualization and assessment of social skills in the mildly handicapped. In T. R. Kratochwill, (Ed.), *Advances in School Psychology* (Vol. 6, pp. 203–247). Hillsdale, NJ: Lawrence Erlbaum.

Hoge, R. (1983). Psychometric properties of teacher-judgment measures of pupil aptitudes, classroom behaviors, and achievement levels. *Journal of Special Education, 17*, 401–429.

Individuals with Disabilities Education Act, IDEA 97, Pub. L. No. 105-17 §614.1-3.

Ivarie, I. J., & Russell, J. (1992). Prereferral interventions. Paper presented at the Teacher Education Division, Council for Exceptional Children, Cincinnati, OH.

Karsh, K. G., Repp, A. C., Dahlquist, C. M., & Munk, D. (1995). In vivo functional assessment and multi-element interventions for problem behaviors of students with disabilities in classroom settings. *Journal of Behavior Education, 5*, 189–210.

Kaufman, A. S. (1994). *Intelligence testing with the WISC III.* NY: Wiley.

Long, N. J., Morse, W. C., & Newman, R. G. (1980). *Conflict in the classroom (4th ed.).* Belmont, CA: Wadsworth.

MacMillan, D. L., Gresham, F. M., Bocian, K. M., & Siperstein, G. N. (1997). The role of assessment in qualifying students as eligible for special education: What is and what's supposed to be. *Focus on Exception Children, 30* (2), 1–18.

MacMillan, D. L., Gresham, F. M., Lopez, M. F., & Bocian, K. M. (1996). Comparison of students nominated for prereferral interventions by ethnicity and gender. *Journal of Special Education, 30*, 133–151.

Mather, N., & Roberts, R. (1994). Learning disabilities: A field in danger of extinction? *Learning Disabilities Research & Practice, 9*, 49–58.

McConnell, M. E., Hilvitz, P. B., & Cox, C. J. (1998). Functional assessment: A systematic process for assessment and intervention in general and special education classrooms. *Intervention in School and Clinic, 34* (1), 10–20.

Miner, C. A., & Bates, P. E. (1997). Person-centered transition planning. *Teaching Exceptional Children, 30* (1), 66–69.

National Association for Early Childhood Educators. (1989). *Resolution on testing practices.* Washington, DC: Author.

National Center for Fair and Open Testing. (1989). *Fallout from the testing operation.* Cambridge, MA: Author.

Niemi, P., & Tiuraniemi, J. (1995). Tests guide the school psychologist, not the learning problem? *Scandinavian Journal of Educational Research, 39* (2), 99–106.

Noll, M. B., Kamps, D., & Seaborn, C. F. (1993). Prereferral interventions for students with emotional and behavioral risks: Use of a behavioral consultation model. *Journal of Emotional and Behavioral Disorders, 1,* 203–214.

Ohio State Department of Education. (1995). *The Individualized Education Program: A road map to success.* Columbus, OH: Author.

Pugach, M., & Johnson, L. J. (1989). Prereferral interventions: Progress, problems, and challenges. *Exceptional Children, 56,* 217–226.

Reid, J. B. (1993). Prevention of conduct disorder before and after school entry: Relating interventions and developmental findings. *Development and Psychopathology, 5,* 311–319.

Reynolds, C. R. (1984). Critical measurement issues in learning disabilities. *Journal of Special Education, 18,* 451–476.

Salvia, J., & Ysseldyke, J. E. (1991). *Assessment.* Boston: Houghton Mifflin.

Shea, T. M., & Bauer, A. M. (1987). *Teaching children and youth with behavior disorders (2nd ed.).* Englewood Cliffs, NJ: Prentice Hall.

Shea, T. M., & Bauer, A. M. (1997). *An introduction to special education: A social systems perspective.* NY: McGraw Hill.

Siegel, L. S. (1989). IQ is irrelevant to the definition of learning disabilities. *Journal of Learning Disabilities, 22,* 468–478, 486.

Smith, S. (1990). Comparison of individualized education programs (IEPs) of students with behavioral disorders and learning disabilities. *Journal of Special Education, 24,* 85–100.

Stanovich, K. E. (1988). Explaining the differences between the dyslexic and the garden-variety poor reader: The phonological core-variable difference model. *Journal of Learning Disabilities, 21,* 590–604.

Swanson, H. L. (1995). Classification and dynamic assessment of children with learning disabilities. *Focus on Exceptional Children, 28* (9), 1–20.

Swicegood, P. (1994). Portfolio-based assessment practices: The use of portfolio assessment for students with behavioral disorders or learning disabilities. *Intervention in School and Clinic, 30* (1), 6–15.

Torgesen, J. K., & Wagner, R. K. (1998). Alternative diagnostic approaches for specific developmental reading disabilities. *Learning Disabilities Research & Practice, 13,* 220–232.

Turnbull, H. R. (1993). *Free appropriate public education: The law and children with disabilities* (4th ed.). Denver: Love.

United States Office of Education. (1977). Assistance to states for education for handicapped children: Procedures for evaluating specific learning disabilities. *Federal Register, 42,* G1082–G1085.

VanReusen, A. K., & Box, C. S. (1994). Facilitating student participation in Individualized Education Programs through motivation strategy instruction. *Exceptional Children, 60* (5), 466–475.

Walker, H. M., Colvin, G., & Ramsey, E. (1995). *Antisocial behavior in school: Strategies and best practices.* Pacific Grove, CA: Brooks/Cole.

Walker, H. M., & Severson, H. H. (1990). *Systematic screening for behavior disorders: User's guide and administration manual.* Longmont, CO: Sopris West.

Walker, H. M., Severson, H. H., Nicholson, F., Kehle, T., Jenson, W. R., & Clark, E. (1994). Replication of the Systematic Screening for Behavior Disorders (SSBD) procedure for the identification of at-risk children. *Journal of Emotional and Behavioral Disorders, 2* (2), 66–77.

Witt, J. C., Elliott, S. N., Kramer, J. J., & Gresham, F. M. (1994). *Assessment of children.* Madison, WI: Brown & Benchmark.

10 Supporting Learning and Behavior Change

TO GUIDE YOUR READING

After reading this chapter, you will be able to answer the following questions:

- What are the components of an intervention plan?
- What are several behavior management strategies that are grounded in the principles of learning, and how are these applied?
- What is positive behavioral support, and how is it applied?
- What is the role of setting events in working with students with learning disabilities or emotional/behavioral disorders?
- What are several crisis intervention strategies, and how are these applied?
- What are scaffolds, scripts, and self-regulation strategies, and how are these applied?
- What are strategies, and how are these applied?
- How can technology be used to support students with learning disabilities or emotional/behavioral disorders?

◀◆ *Jeremy, a fourth grader, was memorizing the poem he was required to recite for his cooperative learning group project. He looked out the window, and gazed at the garbage truck backing into position to empty the dumpster. When he glanced back to his paper, he noticed his "attention card" taped to the corner of his desk. He looked at his watch, and put a tally mark next to the time slot marked "10:00–10:30." He continued to work until Ms. Hanrahan told the students to re-form into their groups. Then he brought his card to Ms. Hanrahan, who said, "What do you think, Jeremy? I think you're really paying more attention to the work you're trying to complete."*

At the end of each hour, Jeremy shows Ms. Hanrahan his attention card. Each day, before he boards the bus, he records the total number of times his mind wandered off his work that day, and then enters the number on his graph. The line on the graph is slowly going down.

◀◆ *Susannah, a tenth grader, reread the question on her English examination. She knew she would need to respond with an essay; she glanced at her hand and recalled the "Fives" strategy. Thinking about what she would write, she numbered her paper one through five, leaving space to put smaller "one through fives" under each large number. She mapped her work in this way:*

1	1	What's the question asking?
	2	First thing to talk about
	3	Second thing to talk about
	4	Third thing to talk about
	5	In this paper I will . . .
2	1	First thing to talk about
	2	Detail
	3	Detail
	4	Detail
	5	Close
3	1	Second thing to talk about
	2	Detail
	3	Detail
	4	Detail
	5	Close
4	1	Third thing to talk about
	2	Detail
	3	Detail
	4	Detail
	5	Close
5	1	In this paper, I described three . . .
	2	Summarize first thing
	3	Summarize second thing
	4	Summarize third thing
	5	Close

She proceeded to put in the details and write her paper confidently.

REFLECTION *Reflect on a classroom with which you are familiar. Even during the most exciting, well-managed activity, is there one student "marching to a different drummer?" Would some individual strategy support this student?*

Introduction

Even the most skillful teacher, at times, is confronted with students who require specific help in learning new academic skills or behaviors. Individual interventions have often been behavioral in nature, emphasizing what happens before the behavior (antecedents), and events that encourage new behaviors to recur (consequences). In the social systems perspective, the developmental context of each learner must be considered. Simple linear models of antecedent–behavior–consequence do not always provide adequate information for what is happening with a learner.

A primary consideration of any effort to intervene with a student is to label the behavior, not the child (Albert, 1997). Albert argues that many teachers talk about "difficult" students, which suggests that something is inherently wrong with the child. By labeling a student "difficult," a teacher transforms a problem behavior into a personality trait. To work proactively with students, a teacher must view the behavior, not the student, as the issue to be addressed. This chapter describes ways to support learning and behavior change.

Components of an Intervention Plan

When teachers hear the words "intervention plan," they often assume that the issue is one of behavior change. However, intervention plans are written for academic, language, and social issues as well. Intervention plans help teachers and students identify what they want to change, design a way to promote the change, document whether change has occurred, and evaluate the rate and nature of the change. Applying an intervention plan is not incompatible with the social systems perspective. The systems perspective can incorporate well the problem-solving nature of intervention planning.

Though interventions are often designed from a behaviorist perspective, other ways of applying learning principles within a systems perspective are emerging. Teachers of students with learning disabilities or emotional/behavioral disorders may be applying traditional behavioral intervention plans, cognitive behavior modification plans, or comprehensive, positive behavioral supports.

Behavioral Intervention

The practitioner with a behaviorist perspective sees the problems of students with learning disabilities or emotional/behavioral disorders as problems of learning. Students who do not demonstrate desired academic skills or social behaviors are presumed either to not have the learned behaviors required to work successfully, or have learned inappropriate or nonproductive behaviors. Behaviorist practitioners are concerned with what the student does, not why the student does it. The cause of the behavior is assumed to exist outside of the individual, in antecedents and consequences. So, to change a behavior referred to as a target behavior, the practitioner manipulates the consequences the individual's behavior has on the environment (Walker & Shea, 1999).

Behavioral consequences are assumed to have a direct influence on the behavior an individual exhibits. Behavior can be changed by the systematic manipulation of its consequences. The four possible consequences of behavior are: positive reinforcement, negative reinforcement, extinction, and punishment. Table 10.1 offers several examples of behaviors and the consequences of those behaviors, the potential effects of the consequences on the repetition of the behavior in the future, and the classification of the consequence.

Two additional concepts basic to the understanding of behavioral intervention are generalization and discrimination. Generalization is the process by which a behavior reinforced in the presence of one stimulus will be exhibited in the presence of another stimulus. If generalization did not occur, each response by an individual would have to be learned in each specific situation in which it is to be applied. For example, students often generalize the behavior of raising hands for recognition. Even at a birthday party or at home, children may raise their hands when asked, "Who wants cake?" Students generalize handwriting from large pencils, to smaller pencils, or to pens without having to relearn the entire task of writing.

Through the process of discrimination, the individual learns to act one way in one situation, and another way in a different situation. Without the ability to discriminate, individuals generalize behavior to a variety of situations in which it would be inappropriate. Discrimination is

Table 10.1 Behaviors, Consequences, Potential Effects, and Classification

Behavior	Consequences	Potential Effect	Classification
Luis takes out the trash	Parents praise	Luis continues to take out the trash	Positive reinforcement
Carla makes her bed	Parents ignore, make no comments	Carla doesn't make her bed again	Extinction
Kevin, driving carelessly, dents the family car	Parents take away driving privileges for two weeks and Kevin pays for repair	Kevin drives more carefully in future	Punishment
Michael doesn't practice saxophone because it is too hard	Parents tell Michael not to practice parts that are hard	Michael practices saxophone less and less	Negative reinforcement

learned by means of differential reinforcement: A behavior is reinforced in the presence of one stimulus, but the same behavior is not reinforced in the presence of another stimulus. Students learn through discrimination that they may use loud voices on the playground, but must use quiet voices in the school building.

In the traditional behavioral intervention plan, the steps include:

- Selecting the target behavior. In this step, the practitioner identifies the behavior to be changed, states the behavior in observable or measurable terms, and determines the direction of change (increase or decrease).

- Collecting and recording baseline data. Baseline data document the level of the behavior before the intervention, and are used to determine the effectiveness of the intervention during the implementation and evaluation steps. Baseline data are also used in the selection of a reinforcement schedule to be applied during the behavior change process.

- Identifying reinforcers. The two most effective ways of identifying reinforcers are, (a) observing the individual to determine the reinforcers he or she selects when given the opportunity, and (b) asking the individual what is preferred.

- Implementing interventions and collecting and recording intervention data. Concurrent with the implementation of the intervention, the practitioner collects data on its effectiveness by means of counting and charting, as for the baseline. To be effective, the intervention must be applied consistently and persistently.

- Evaluating the effect of the intervention. By collecting and charting intervention data, the practitioner can evaluate the effectiveness of the intervention throughout the behavior change process by comparing intervention data with baseline data. If the behavior is changing in the desired direction, the practitioner may proceed as planned. However, if the behavior is not changing as projected, the practitioner must reevaluate the behavior change process: that is, the reinforcer, the intervention, and the schedule of reinforcement.

Cognitive Behavior Modification

Cognitive behavior modification (CBM) is an application of behavioral principles that emerged in response to concerns about self-management. Harris (1982) defines cognitive behavior modification as "the selective, purposeful combination of principles and procedures from diverse areas into training regimens or interventions, the purpose of which is to instate, modify, or extinguish cognitions, feelings, and/or behaviors" (p. 5).

Lloyd (1980) described several procedures that are common to those used in cognitive behavior modification, including self-assessment, self-recording, and self-management. The student is highly engaged in these procedures. These procedures often involve a sequence of designated steps, as well as monitoring and evaluating the successful implementation of the strategy or technique (Meichenbaum, 1986). The teacher first models the procedures or technique, supports the student through the learning process, and gradually turns the intervention itself over to the student. Verbalization, a key component, guides the student through the strategy. The student uses verbalization, or self-talk, which often includes such questions as "What is the problem I am confronting? What is my plan? Am I using my plan? How did I do?" (Camp & Bash, 1981).

Behavior Management Strategies

There are several behavior management strategies grounded in the principles of reinforcement. These include positive reinforcement, extinction, differential reinforcement, shaping, contingency contracting, and modeling (Walker & Shea, 1999).

Positive Reinforcement

Positive reinforcement is the process of rewarding an appropriate behavior in order to increase the probability that it will recur. The advantage of positive reinforcement is that it is responsive to the individual's natural need for attention and approval, and, thus, decreases the probability the individual will exhibit inappropriate behavior. Three guidelines should be used when applying positive reinforcement. First, the target behavior should be reinforced only after it occurs. Second, when individuals are initially learning a new behavior, they should be rewarded each time the behavior occurs. Finally, once the behavior is established at a satisfactory level, the behavior should be reinforced intermittently. Public reinforcement may be unwelcome by some students, so the practitioner should be careful to ascertain if the student is embarrassed by positive reinforcement in the presence of peers, teachers, and others. The practitioner must remain observant to determine if the reinforcers being used are in fact positively reinforcing the student.

A common classroom application of positive reinforcement is the token economy. In a token economy, immediate reinforcement is provided through tokens, which are exchanged at a later time for backup reinforcers such as items and activities. Token economies are often combined with response cost in which the student may lose tokens for inappropriate behavior. Initially, tokens are valueless; their value becomes apparent when the student understands that he or she can exchange the tokens for backup reinforcers. The properly managed token economy is effective because students are only competing with themselves; the reinforcer menu offers a variety of desirable items and activities. In addition, token economies include ways of fading the tokens as students become self-regulated and generalize productive behaviors to times when the to-ken economy cannot be implemented.

Extinction

Extinction is the discontinuation or withdrawal of the reinforcer of a target behavior that has previously reinforced or sustained it. When consistently and persistently applied, extinction results in the gradual decrease and elimination of the target behavior. Generally, behaviors that are ignored become nonfunctional and consequently stop. Extinction can be an effective means of eliminating annoying and nonproductive behaviors. Because it is a benign intervention, extinction avoids the potential for conflict between practitioner and student. Among the behaviors responsive to extinction are whining, tattling, mild tantrums, and demands for attention. It may also be applied to decrease inappropriate language, derogatory comments, meaningless questions, and annoying affectations and fads. Extinction should not be used for complex and severe behaviors that may be harmful to the individual, others, or property.

The key to applying extinction effectively is learning to completely and totally ignore the target behavior, and being consistent and persistent in its application. In many cases, when extinction is initially applied, an "extinction burst" occurs, that is, the behavior being ignored increases dramatically in frequency for a brief period of time before it decreases.

Time-out is an application of extinction. In time-out, the student is removed from an apparently reinforcing setting to a presumably nonreinforcing setting for a specific and limited period of time. Time-out can include ignoring, contingent observation, removal of materials, reduction of response-maintenance stimuli, exclusion, and seclusion (Walker & Shea, 1999).

In observational time-out or contingent observation, the student moves to the perimeter of the activity, where he or she may see and hear the activity, but not participate. Teachers may also remove the student's materials until he or she uses them appropriately. Reduction of a response-maintenance stimuli removes or reduces the stimuli necessary for a response, such as turning out the lights when the student's response is inappropriate.

Exclusionary time-out is a restrictive intervention in which the student goes to an out-of-the-way area of the classroom for a period of time. In seclusion, the student is removed to an isolation area outside of the classroom. This is an extremely restrictive intervention, must be part of the student's Individualized Education Plan, and must follow the parameters for time-out in state educational standards or regulations. Seclusion is not recommended. All time-out procedures remove the student from the opportunity to engage in other activities. The practitioner must obtain parental permission for seclusion time-out, document side effects (losing instruction time or self-injury, for example), and carefully observe and document time-out sessions. In practice, time-out is often used by the teacher as a way to remove the child rather than change the behavior; this is an unethical application of the strategy.

Lohrmann-O-Rourke and Zirkel (1998) explored the case law on time-out, and reported that recent court decisions have provided qualified support for the use of time-out. There are, however, several conditions on its use, including (a) the use of only specially designed rooms that meet state and local building and fire codes, as well as educational standards; (b) the application of time-out only when there is a documented failure of less-restrictive strategies, and the need for time-out to prevent more restrictive placements; (c) that time-out is no more than 2 to 10 minutes in length; (d) that time-out rooms allow for continuous visual and auditory monitoring; (e) that the procedures are expressly incorporated in the IEP, and written parental permission has been given; and (f) that each use of the time-out room is documented.

Differential Reinforcement

Differential reinforcement is the process of reinforcing an appropriate behavior in the presence of one stimulus and not reinforcing an inappropriate behavior in the presence of another stimulus. There are several types of differential reinforcement: (a) differential reinforcement of zero rates of behavior (DRO), (b) differential reinforcement of incompatible behaviors (DRI), and (c) differential reinforcement of lower rates of behavior (DRL). When using DRO as an intervention, the student is reinforced for not exhibiting the target behavior during a specific period of time. The student is reinforced for exhibiting appropriate behavior in other circumstances. DRO may be effectively applied for behaviors such as fighting, cursing, name calling, and talking back.

At times it is necessary, or desirable, to decrease a behavior by systematically reinforcing a behavior that is incompatible with it. For example, a student cannot be in his or her seat, and out of his or her seat, at the same time. In the DRI intervention, the practitioner will reinforce in-seat behavior and ignore out-of-seat behavior. DRL interventions are often used with habits or behaviors that do not need to be reduced either rapidly or completely. It is used to gradually reduce the behavior by progressively reinforcing lower rates of the behavior. DRL may be used with behaviors such as attention seeking, completing assignments, or handraising.

Shaping

Shaping is reinforcing successive approximations of a behavior leading to the target behavior. Shaping is usually used to establish behavior not previously, or infrequently, exhibited, and is accomplished by the consistent, systematic, and immediate reinforcement of approximations of the target behavior. During shaping, the practitioner reinforces only those behavioral manifestations that most closely approximate the target behavior. The practitioner should never reinforce lower level approximations, because it would reinforce a behavior that is the reverse of the proposed direction of change.

Shaping is similar to climbing a ladder, that is, one rung is mounted at a time, while one foot is firmly placed on the previous rung. The learner is reinforced for climbing each rung on the ascent to the top of the ladder, i.e., the target behavior. The student is reinforced only when he or she ascends to the highest rung to which he or she is capable of climbing at a particular point in the shaping process. The student is never reinforced for climbing to a rung lower than the highest one to which he or she is capable.

Contingency Contracting

A contingency contract is a verbal or written agreement between two or more individuals that stipulates the responsibilities of each concerning a specified item or activity. It is based on Premack's (1959) principle: A behavior that has a high rate of occurrence can be used to increase a behavior with a lower rate of occurrence. Some examples of contracts are:

- If you eat your lima beans, you may have some cake.
- If you complete your workbook assignment, you can have 10 minutes of free time.

An example of a written contract is presented in Figure 10.1.

November 8, 2000

Sari will write during Writing Workshop on all four days during the week in which we have Writing Workshop (Monday through Thursday). Sari will be given one verbal reminder to get out her draft and write. If Sari writes during Writing Workshop on Monday through Thursday, she will be able to help the fourth graders with art.

This contract will be reviewed after two weeks.

Sari   *Ms. Barrett*

Figure 10.1   Contingency contract

Modeling

Modeling is providing sample behavior after which the student is to pattern his or her own behavior. During modeling, the student is systematically reinforced for imitating or not imitating the model. Exposure to a model has three potential effects (Clarizio & Yelon, 1976):

- the student may acquire the behavior from the model as a new behavior;
- the student may inhibit a behavior for which the model is punished or otherwise discouraged;
- the student may approximate the model's behavior which is not necessarily "new," but which was previously learned, and is not presently exhibited.

Positive Behavioral Support

The 1997 Amendments to the Individuals with Disabilities Education Act require the use of positive behavioral support when students' behavior interferes with their learning, or that of others. Positive behavioral support does not work to eliminate the behavior, but to understand the purpose of the behavior, and replace it with a prosocial behavior that will attain the same goal for the student (Ruef, Higgins, Glaeser, & Patnode, 1998). Though the traditional emphasis on behavior change has been that of manipulating reinforcers, positive behavioral support, a system in which the environment is reconfigured to support change, has become more common (Carr, 1997). Rather than being reinforcement-based, these interventions are stimulus-based, and emphasize changing ways of interacting and events around the student to support the student in demonstrating other behaviors. Kendrick, Kurtz, Son, Gilmer, and Zeph suggest that a positive behavioral support system:

- views students as collaborators in behavior change;
- focuses on change in natural environments and in real contexts;
- regards inclusion, increased choice, and quality of life in addition to reducing the behavior;
- uses a systems approach where factors in the individual's developmental contexts are considered; and
- addresses behavior changes in a comprehensive way rather than emphasizing isolated behaviors in isolated environments.

Fox, Conroy, and Heckaman (1998) suggest three limitations in the actual practice of behavioral intervention. First, every behavioral procedure has been demonstrated as effective with some students and ineffective with others. Second, behavior changes may be lost when the intervention is re-

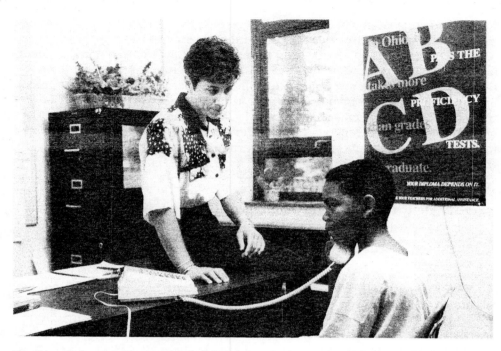

Positive behavioral support involves the student and family in the behavior change process.

moved. Third, practitioners are often confronted with the challenge of selecting one of several behavioral procedures simply from an examination of the behavior itself. Concerns have emerged regarding the lack of the relationship between assessment and the design of intervention plans. Dunlap and Childs (1996), for example, examined articles in twelve journals published between 1980 and 1993, to explore intervention research for students with emotional/behavioral disorders. In the fourteen-year period, in which 114 articles were published, only 9 articles were identified as having a clear link between assessment and intervention. Carr (1997), contrasting effectiveness of intervention designs that incorporated positive behavior supports and traditional behavioral interventions, found that the success rate of interventions based on functional assessment was almost twice that of traditional behavioral interventions. As a result of these and similar concerns, an increased emphasis on functional assessment and analysis of behaviors is emerging. Horner and Carr (1997) suggest that recently, there have been two key developments influencing the design and implementation of effective behavioral support: functional assessment and comprehensive interventions.

Functional assessment.   Functional assessment is used to gather information to maximize the effectiveness and efficiency of behavioral supports (O'Neill, Horner, Albin, Storey, and Sprague, 1990). Functional assessment is "a method for identifying the variables that reliably predict and maintain behavior" (Horner & Carr, 1997, p. 85). These variables may consist of consequences (the purpose, intent, function, motivation, or goal of the behavior, all these terms being roughly synonymous), antecedent or discriminative stimuli (the cues that trigger the behavior), and setting events (the broad context that influences the likelihood that a specific cue will trigger problem behavior). Functional assessment is performed through:

- understanding what maintains the problem behavior;
- predicting when a problem behavior will and will not occur;
- identifying ways to prevent occurrence of the problem behavior; and
- designing procedures for responding to the problem behavior when it does occur.

Fox, Conroy, and Heckaman (1998) differentiate between functional assessment and functional analysis. They suggest that in functional analysis, the teacher systematically manipulates classroom variables that may influence the behavior. In this way, he or she can form an hypotheses about factors which maintain, increase, or decrease the behavior. Horner and Carr describe the generic methods by which functional analysis is conducted. The first of these methods is to interview involved parties, asking each person to provide, (a) a physical description of the problem behavior, (b) the circumstances that predict the occurrences and nonoccurrences of the problem behavior, and (c) the reaction that the behavior evokes from others. Interviews allow for a quick review of a high number of antecedents and consequences of the behavior. However, interviews rely on subjective impressions, and have the potential for inaccuracy. A second method is descriptive observation, which can provide information about (a) the context and triggers that covary with a problem behavior; (b) the intensity, duration and form of the problem behavior; and (c) the events that follow (and presumably maintain) the problem behavior. Observations are typically collected after the interview because the interview offers the opportunity to generate more detailed information and uncover additional variables. A third method, functional analysis itself, as described earlier, is the systematic manipulation of specific variables to see whether they influence problem behavior. For example, a teacher may withdraw demands on a student, make attention contingent on the behavior, remove toys and people, provide toys and people with no demands, or provide tangible reinforcement. Ruef and associates (1998) address these issues through a series of questions:

- What challenging behaviors are causing concern?
- What events, times, or situations predict when the behavior will occur?

- What events, times, or situations predict when the behavior will not occur?
- What seems to maintain the behavior (Does the student get attention? Escape? Get a preferred item or activity?)
- What appropriate behavior could produce the same results?
- What can be learned from previous behavioral support efforts for the individual, about strategies that are ineffective, effective, or only effective for a short time?

Comprehensive intervention. Horner and Carr (1997) contend that the goal of comprehensive intervention is to produce rapid, durable, generalized reduction in problem behaviors while improving the individual's success at home, at school, in the community, or in the work environment. An intervention is comprehensive when it, (a) addresses all problem behaviors performed by an individual; (b) is driven by the functional assessment; (c) is applied throughout the day; (d) blends multiple intervention procedures (change in structure, instruction, consequences); and (e) incorporates procedures that are consistent with the values, skills, and resources of the implementors.

There are four primary ways to positive behavioral support. These involve functional communication training, curricular revision, setting event manipulations, and student choice (Horner & Carr, 1997). The first way, functional communication training, involves teaching students a specific communicative response that (a) is socially appropriate, (b) results in the same effect, and (c) is as or more efficient than the problem behavior.

Curricular revision (Horner & Carr, 1997), the second way, is used when the functional assessment suggests that the challenging behavior is maintained by avoiding certain instructional tasks. If it does, then an element of the comprehensive support plan may involve changing the curriculum. Curricular revision does not mean that difficult tasks are replaced by easier tasks. In curricular revision, instructional goals should not be compromised, but efforts should be made to define the specific features of the tasks that are aversive. Curricular revisions should be made to respond to those features.

The third way to provide positive behavioral support, the consideration of setting events, is of such importance to interventions, that it is described in detail in the following section. Student choice, the fourth strategy, reduces the likelihood that the student will be presented with challenges that elicit problem behaviors. When an activity is chosen by a student, it is less likely to evoke problem behavior than if the same activity is selected and presented by the teacher. In addition to these strategies, Ruef and associates suggest increasing the predictability of the educational environment, and appreciating positive behavior demonstrated by the student.

In terms of positive behavioral support, Koegel (1997) has identified three major variables which may produce significant gains. First, interventions implemented in the natural context appear to produce faster, more generalized, and more relevant gains than interventions in contrived or simulated settings. This implies that interventions need to occur in community settings and inclusive environments. Second, the student's family must be considered. Parents should be provided with the support needed to continue interventions in the home. Finally, pivotal behaviors (sometimes called keystone behaviors) should be the focus of intervention. These keystone behaviors produce great improvements and reduced stress in families and classrooms.

One example of the increased emphasis on positive behavioral support is the IDEA 97 provision that the Individualized Education Plan team must consider positive behavioral interventions (Turnbull, 1997). Though Turnbull suggests that this is a big step forward, the description of such interventions are limited to the school. An example of a positive behavioral support system is PASSKey.

PASSKey.   In a systems perspective, students and their behaviors must be understood in context. "Naturalistic" interventions, that is, interventions that look at the natural systems (families and classrooms), in which individuals interact rather than at individual behaviors and their contingent variables (Carta & Greenwood, 1985) are emerging as strategies to intervene with individual students, and their families. These strategies encourage generalization to other environments.

Barnett, Ehrhardt, Stollar, and Bauer (1993) describe a model for naturalistic assessment and intervention design which incorporates Planned Activities, Strategic Sampling, and Keystone behaviors (PASSKey). Through this model, significant problems are identified, and interventions are planned based on natural interactions, activities, and the realities of settings. The model is grounded in a collaborative consultation, where a consultant works directly with the teacher or parent in developing interventions.

The components of PASSKey include:

- Planned activities, which represent the goals and behaviors teachers and parents want to accomplish. These activities may include classroom routines, group instruction, riding the bus, lunch time, recess.

- Strategic sampling, which involves selecting times to observe the planned activities and targeting behaviors, as well as times to intervene.

- Keystone behaviors, which are behaviors related to desirable child and teacher behaviors; keystone behaviors are "pivotal or prerequisite" for other behaviors (Evans & Meyers, 1985). Looking for keystone behaviors is an effective strategy, because many children have multiple problem behaviors for which priorities must be set (Barnett & Carey, 1992).

The steps of PASSKey are offered as an example of the components of an intervention plan. As with any intervention plan, the steps are recycled as necessary.

The first step of PASSKey involves selecting the planned activities that are important to the teacher, parent, and child. Information is gathered on specific routines and events, and the day is described using a Waking Day Interview (Wahler & Cormier, 1970; Barnett & Carey, 1992). An example of a Waking Day Interview is presented in Figure 10.2.

As a problem setting is identified, the teacher and consultant work through a "problem solving interview" (Barnett & Carey, 1992) to clarify the concerns of the teacher. Questions in the problem solving interview may include:

- What are some specific examples of what happens in this setting? What happens right before the behavior occurs? Right after?

- How long does this behavior occur? Is it the same in other settings? Are there times when the behavior does not occur?

- What things have you tried in order to manage this behavior? How effective have they been?

- What would have to change for this child to benefit during this situation?

Once the target situation or setting has been described, strategic sampling occurs. Several strategies are used to provide more specific information concerning the behavior and the contexts in which they occur. These include real-time observations, in which the observer records meaningful and complete units of behavior and the clock time of each behavior (i.e., 1:10 p.m. Teacher says "Get out your pencils." Student says,

---

Describe the child's behavior in the following settings or situations.

On the bus:
Entering the classroom:
"Morning work":
Transitions:
Recess:
Lunch:
Seat work:
Special classes (art, music, P.E.):
Cooperative Learning Activities/Group Work:
Moving through the building:
End of day activities:

Figure 10.2   Waking Day Interview (School Setting)

Table 10.2   Antecedent, Behavior, Consequence Chart

Antecedent	Behavior	Consequence
Teacher: "Get out a pencil."	Student: "What pencil?"	Teacher: "Your pencil."
Teacher: "Your pencil."	Student: "Don't have one."	Teacher: "You need a pencil."
Teacher: "You need a pencil."	Student: "Guess you'll have to give me one."	Teacher: "Excuse me?"
Teacher: "Excuse me?"	Student: (shouting, mouthing words broadly) "Guess–you'll–have–to–give–me–one."	Class laughs.
Class laughs.	Student shrugs and shakes head.	Teacher: "I will not continue until this room is quiet."

"What pencils?"). An "ABC" chart may be used to gather more specific information. This "Antecedent–Behavior–Consequence" chart describes events in a detailed "flow of activity" manner. An example of an "ABC" chart is provided in Table 10.2.

After the problem setting is carefully described, the keystone behavior is selected. The basic strategy for selecting this behavior involves the identification of important behaviors, and the behaviors that may be linked to their development. The social validity of the behaviors should also be discussed. In the "ABC" example, the keystone behavior identified may be that the student should come prepared for class.

Scripts, which are personalized and detailed guidelines for the intervention, are then developed. A baseline is determined, and step-by-step procedures for each occasion that the intervention will be used are generated. On the script, check-off boxes are provided for the teacher, so that he or she may record the way in which the script is being followed. A script for the example behavior of not having materials for class is provided in Table 10.3.

Scripts may require modifications as they are implemented. Scripts may be refined by role-playing with another teacher, or having a peer teacher observe the intervention and provide feedback. As the script is being fine-tuned, the teacher takes data on the student's response. The stability, level, and trend of the target behavior is studied, and the script is modified as needed.

As mentioned earlier, an emerging issue in intervention design is that of functional analysis. Functional assessment is the process of identifying functional relationships between environmental events and the occurrence and nonoccurrence of a target behavior. A functional assessment consists of the methods and procedures used to identify associations

Table 10.3   Sample Script

Target behavior: James will bring his materials to class.		Dates				
Steps						
1. Teacher meets student at door and asks, "Do you have your materials?"						
2. If James says, "Yes," teacher puts checkmark on his "Earn a night without homework" card.						
3. If James says, "No," teacher provides James with a pencil that he must return at the end of class.						
4. Teacher intermittently provides check marks on "earn a night without homework" cards for students who have all materials for class.						

between behaviors and variables in the environment (Dunlap, Kern, de-Perczel, Clark, Wilson, Childs, White, & Falk, 1993). Dunlap and associates suggested that functional analysis is important to identify the behavior and environmental variables that may be directly manipulated in order to clarify the relationship. In their study, certain classroom variables did exert influence over individual students' behaviors.

A functional assessment includes identifying the problem behaviors, setting priorities, and delineating operational definitions (Demchak, 1993). Hypotheses are then developed using strategies such as structured interviews, systematic observations utilizing scatter plots, "ABC" analyses, or focus on communicative intent, and testing. Finally, the results of this assessment are linked to intervention planning.

The Role of Setting Events

In applying the systems perspective, behaviors are considered in context. One key aspect of intervention with students, then, would be to identify the things in the context that affect the intervention (Sasso, Peck, & Garrison-Harrell, 1998). Baer, Wolf, and Risley (1987) described setting events as the conditions that determine whether or not an intervention "has maximal or minimal effectiveness" (p. 319). Setting events increase or decrease the probability of interactions between student and teacher, or student and his or her peers (Repp & Karsh, 1993). For example, a teacher who has used candy effectively in a contingency contract may find that the intervention is less effective after Halloween when the students have access to brimming trick-or-treat bags. Or, a student may be less awake and less able to apply a cognitive behavior modification program when he or she has had very little sleep the previous night.

Fox and Conroy (1995) suggest that setting events have been identified in three ways. Interviews, such as the Wahler and Cormier (1970) waking day interview employed in PASSKey, have been utilized to identify the events around the occurrence of a behavior. Checklists and rating scales have also been developed. Direct observation may be used, even though many potential setting events, such as those occurring at home or on the school bus, cannot be directly observed in the classroom. Fox and Conroy suggest that practitioners use a combination of these strategies to develop a clear picture of setting events.

Because of their potential impact on interventions, practitioners should make every effort to address setting events. Gardner, Cole, Davidson, and Karan (1986) suggest three general ways of dealing with setting events. First, they suggest that the teacher can directly manipulate the occurrence of the setting event. For example, if the student is on medication for attention deficit disorder, and the intervention varies in its effectiveness as to whether or not the student receives his or her medication, the teacher can take action to insure that the medication is provided consistently. Second, the teacher can directly change the student's reaction to the setting event. For example, a student whose fighting on the school bus has an impact on his or her behavior in the morning, may be addressed by the teacher designing a program to decrease aggression. In situations where the setting events cannot be altered, Gardner and associates suggest neutralizing the setting events. Neutralizing the events occurs by modifying the curriculum and activities in which a student engages on those days in which the setting event has occurred.

Dadson and Horner (1993) presented a case study where setting events were manipulated to decrease a problem behavior. In their study, a student had difficulty with periodic verbal and physical outbursts. Through an interview and checklist, seven events were identified that seemed to affect the student's behaviors: visits to the doctor; illness; a late school bus; fewer than eight hours of sleep; a fight with a family member during the morning; a fight with a peer on the way to school; missing breakfast. The teacher then met with the student's family to determine whether the parents also felt that these events were important influences on the student's behavior. The teacher would call the student's home to inquire whether any of the setting events had occurred, and ask the bus driver if there were any events on the bus. From this data, two setting events emerged as associated with the problem behaviors: the late bus and insufficient sleep. The parents called the school on any day on which the student had less than eight hours of sleep, or if the bus was more than five minutes late. If either of these events occurred, an instructional assistant would meet the student as she entered the class and deliver lots of praise, the student was allowed to work one-on-one during the morning, the student was allowed to do one-on-one stretching instead of the exercises in which the other students engaged, and the number of opportunities was increased for the student to select the order of tasks she would perform. Though the occurrence of the setting events remained constant through the eleven months of observation, the student's behavior significantly improved.

Crisis Intervention Strategies

Teachers working with students with learning disabilities or emotional/behavioral disorders should be prepared for crisis situations. Gilliam (1993) makes several suggestions for crisis management preparation. Teachers should stay calm and send for help, if necessary. The teacher should stay out of striking range, and tell the student that the behavior needs to stop. In order to calm the situation, Gilliam urges that the teacher use as little action as possible, and refrain from counter-aggression. The student should be removed in order to calm him or herself. Once the student is calmed down, the teacher should rehearse with the student appropriate behaviors and the reasons that he or she needed to be removed from the situation.

When dealing with confrontations, Colvin, Ainge, and Nelson (1997) suggest that a comprehensive plan should be comprised of prevention, defusion, and follow-up. There are five common features of confrontational behavior:

- student displays defiant, challenging, or inappropriate behavior;
- supervising staff person reacts to the problem behavior and provides direction in opposition to the student's behavior;
- student challenges the direction by not complying, and by displaying other inappropriate behavior;
- staff person reacts to the noncompliance and presents an ultimatum;
- student takes up the challenge and the ultimatum with further defiance, and exhibits hostile and explosive behavior.

There are several ways in which teachers can defuse these situations (Colvin, Ainge, & Nelson, 1997). The teacher can focus on the task at hand to defuse minor attention-getting behavior, or present options privately in the context of a rule violation. An effort should be made to reduce the student's agitation in a demand situation. The teacher may disengage and delay responding in the presence of serious threatening behavior, waiting to confer with the student when he or she is calmer. As a means of prevention, the teacher may preteach and present choices to establish limits, and to defuse noncompliance.

Teachers who have a plan of action are more likely to remain calm in the midst of a crisis. Teachers may use life–space interviews, classroom conferencing, or behavior influence techniques when confronted with a behavioral problem. In addition, these interventions are helpful in preventing problems from developing into crises.

Life–Space Interviews

The life–space interview is a result of Redl's (1959) work with students with severe behavior problems. Life–space interviews are conducted to use life events to support change, and for "emotional first aid." When using life events to support change, the teacher helps the student become aware of (a) distorted perceptions, (b) behavioral responses, (c) hidden social and moral values and standards, or (d) reactions to the behaviors and pressures of the group. The interview is used to encourage the student to use more productive and socially acceptable ways to solve conflicts.

Teachers may use life–space interviews for emotional first aid when the student is in stress, or when the student is having a difficult time. In these situations, life–space interviews are conducted to, (a) reduce the student's frustration level, (b) support the student in emotionally charged situations, (c) restore strained communications between the teacher and the student, (d) reinforce social limits and realities, and (e) assist the student in his or her efforts to find solutions to social problems.

Morse (1980) suggested a series of stages that occur during life–space interviews. The interview usually begins as a consequence of a specific incident. The teacher encourages those involved to state their personal perception of what occurred. At this time, the teacher must determine if the incident is an isolated event, or a significant part of a recurring theme. The teacher listens to those involved in the incident as they reconstruct it. Their feelings and perceptions are accepted without moralizing or attacking. Although these individual perceptions are accepted, the teacher may suggest alternative perceptions for consideration by the student.

The interview then moves into a nonjudgmental resolution phase. Many conflicts and confrontations are resolved at this point, and the interview ends. However, if the problem is not resolved, the teacher may offer his or her view of the incident. Finally, the student and teacher develop an acceptable plan to deal with the problem, and to prevent similar problems in the future.

Classroom Conferences

McIntyre (1987) developed a method of classroom conferencing, a "long talk," applied to support the development of self-management skills. The steps in the conferencing process are:

- Meet. The teacher and student meet privately as soon as possible after the incident.
- Review. The teacher clarifies the student's perception to insure that both student and teacher are discussing a common perception. The

teacher may make corrections of the student's perception on the basis of first-person knowledge.

- Discuss respect. The teacher and student clarify what actions and feelings resulting from the incident were right and wrong, and whose rights and privileges were violated.

- Discuss typical behavior. The teacher helps the student see the problems with his or her behavior, and what is an acceptable behavior.

- Devise another response. The teacher asks the student to suggest alternative ways of responding in similar situations in the future. The teacher accepts all suggestions, writes them on paper, and asks the student to select the alternative he or she will use in the future. Teacher and student discuss the alternative's use in various situations, and its pros and cons. If the alternative selected is unrealistic, the teacher may help the student choose another.

- Reconvene. A series of conferences may occur to review student progress and performance, and engage in further planning.

Behavior Influence Techniques

Behavior influence techniques are often called "surface management techniques," because they are applied to behaviors which are not complex or deeply rooted. Long, Morse, and Newman (1980) suggest several behavior influence strategies. Several of these strategies, such as signal interference, are commonly used by effective teachers. The techniques include:

- planned ignoring, in which the teacher ignores behavior that, although not desirable, does not interfere with learning;

- signal interference, in which the teacher gestures or provides a nonverbal signal that the behavior is unacceptable and should stop;

- proximity control, in which the teacher physically moves toward the student participating in the undesirable behavior;

- interest boosting, in which the teacher injects personal interest into the activity when the student is bored or frustrated;

- tension decontamination through humor, in which the teacher provides humor in difficult situations;

- hurdle helping, in which the teacher aids the learner involved in a difficult task;

- restructuring the program, in which the teacher changes activities when students are bored or disengaged;

- support from routine, in which the teacher uses set routines to increase the likelihood of productive behavior;

- direct appeal, in which the teacher makes a direct request to stop the behavior;

- removal of seductive objects, in which the teacher removes distracting objects and returns them at the appropriate time;
- antiseptic bouncing, in which the teacher encourages the student to remove him or herself from a situation in which he or she is about to have difficulty.

Preventing Student-on-Student Aggression

Meese (1997) suggests that student conflicts are an inevitable part of classroom life. Teachers should act proactively to prevent student-on-student aggression from escalating into physical confrontation. Meese suggests that fights usually occur when students are trying to save face, defend their property and territory, test their status in the classroom, or are fearful. He offers four issues related to preventing fights among students, using the acronym RICH:

R   Rules that are clear and positive, with rewards and consequences that are consistently administered;

I   Instruction that is systematic, explicit, engaging, and emphasizes self-control and conflict resolution;

C   Classroom climate that is respectful, attractive, appealing, and safe;

H   Heed the early warning signs of conflict, respond to conflicts before they escalate.

When confronted with a physical fight, Meese suggests that teachers know and follow school, or school district, policies and procedures. The teacher should stay calm, and call for help immediately from administrators, other teachers, or security officers. Peers should be removed, and all objects that might creative injury, or be used as weapons, should be eliminated. The teacher should calmly approach the fighting students, stay out of their personal space, and attempt to create a distraction. If distraction and verbal intervention are successful, the teacher should separate the students. If distraction and verbal intervention are not successful, teachers should not step into the fight alone, but wait for assistance.

Scaffolds, Scripts, and Self-Regulation Strategies

Scaffolding is a strategy in which teachers initially provide supports and withdraw them as the student becomes increasingly successful. This technique is modeled after the scaffolding placed on a building during construction, and its systematic removal as the building becomes stable. Scaffolding is used, for the most part, to increase the communicative competence of students with learning disabilities or emotional/behavioral disorders, to increase their socially proactive behaviors.

Role-playing is an effective technique for scaffolding instruction. Anderson (1992) suggests a "Theatre Rehearsal Technique" to assist students in organizing and controlling their conversational behaviors. In these improvisational activities, students can experiment with their perceptions about social interactions, try various responses to determine what works for them, and why, and attempt to influence others to achieve their desired social consequences. Through these techniques, Anderson contends that students can learn to identify, use, and recognize relationships between thinking and acting. In a similar intervention, puppet theater may be used to help students master nonthreatening and rational solutions to issues confronting them (Caputo, 1993).

Pressley, Hogan, Wharton-McDonald, Mistretta, and Ettenberger (1967) suggest that there are several challenges to effective scaffolding. The teacher must be knowledgeable about the curriculum in general, and the students individually, in order to properly use scaffolding. Teachers must understand the problems that their students are experiencing to the extent that they can generate a variety of supports to stimulate students' thinking in appropriate directions, and away from misconceptions. Pressley and associates suggest that it takes a great deal of energy and commitment to both acquire the knowledge required to scaffold, and to carry out scaffolding, throughout the school day.

Communicative competence assumes the ability to coordinate attention toward people and objects, imitate, and play (Lieber & Beckman, 1991). In order to support young children, Lieber and Beckman suggest placing learners with more competent partners, and providing toys that encourage social interaction. In addition, teachers should observe their classroom activities and note those which encourage social exchange. Specific skills, such as initiation and responsiveness, may also need to be specifically taught to young children.

Scripts have recently emerged as specific action plans that describe intervention steps in natural language. Scripts are effective ways of addressing behavior change because they (a) provide the "how to do it" in interaction with the child, (b) increase expectations that the individual intervention can be successful, (c) provide coaching and a clear way of giving feedback, and (d) are ethnically valid because they are expressed in natural or culturally specific languages (Barnett et al, 1993).

Self-regulation is an essential skill for students with learning disabilities or emotional/behavioral disorders. Graham, Harris, and Reid (1992) contend that self-regulation, if generalized, becomes a way of proceeding for the student. Academically, learning to self-regulate allows students to become more independent, increases their task engagement, and allows them to monitor and regulate their personal performance. As students self-regulate, they are able to self-instruct, set goals, and self-monitor.

Self-regulation is, in itself, preventive discipline. Henley (1994) describes five foundations of self-regulation:

1. The student must control impulses. In school, this may mean using instructional materials, moving in unstructured space, making classroom transitions, or resisting temptation of off-limit objects.

2. The student should be able to assess social reality, accommodate classroom rules, organize learning materials, accept feedback, and appreciate feelings.

3. The student should manage group situations, maintaining composure, appraising peer pressure, participating in cooperative activities, and evaluating effects of personal behavior.

4. The student should cope with stress, adapt to new situations, manage competition, tolerate frustration, and demonstrate patience.

5. The student should solve social problems, focus on the present, learn from past experiences, recall personal behavior, and resolve conflicts.

Self-managed learners require less external control, allowing teachers to spend more time on other aspects of curriculum and instruction (DiGangi & Maag, 1992). In their efforts to analyze the interaction between self-monitoring, self-evaluation/self-reinforcement, and self-instruction, DiGangi and Maag (1992) reported that using a combination of these skills was most effective. Self-monitoring and self-evaluation/self-reinforcement, when used individually, were the least effective. The most effective component when used independently was self-instruction.

In their review of the research on self-monitoring as a behavior management technique, Webber, Schueuermann, McCall, and Coleman (1993) reported that self-monitoring was found to be successful with students of various ages and in various settings. Specifically, self-monitoring increased attention to task, positive classroom behaviors, and some social skills. In addition, inappropriate classroom behavior decreased. Self-monitoring has the additional benefit of enhancing the likelihood that positive classroom behaviors will generalize to other settings.

Instructional Strategies

An effective intervention technique that emerged from the work on self-regulation is strategies training. Derry (1990) describes learning strategies as the complete plan one formulates for accomplishing a goal. Such strategies are developed to focus attention, build a mental outline or plan, monitor comprehension, and elaborate ideas. Effective strategy use requires analyzation of the problem or task, selection of a strategy that fits the situation, monitorization of the effectiveness of the strategy, and adaptation or selection of another strategy, if necessary. Examples of strategies include:

• Rehearsal, in which students either verbally repeat, or visually reexamine, information for later retrieval;

- Transformation, using imagery or paraphrasing;
- Mnemonics, in which association is used for future retrieval;
- Organization through clustering, categorizing, or prioritizing;
- Comprehension through self-questioning or predicting.

Appropriate instruction of learning strategies is a key factor in effective implementation of appropriate strategies by students with learning disabilities. The teacher must first assess the strategies the student needs to succeed academically. The teacher must carefully plan the strategy instruction over an extended period of time. Strategy instruction cannot be done via a worksheet or a quick explanation (Scott, 1998). Strategy instruction involves selecting a strategy, and teaching it directly to the learner. The strategy in itself is taught, but the application is restricted to the task for which it is applied. Palincsar and Ransom (1988) state that students must understand the "what," "why," and "where." In other words, not only must the students know how to use a strategy, but it is crucial that they understand the relevance and the appropriate contexts for a particular strategy. Students should also be actively involved in goal setting and self-evaluation as related to strategy use (Montague, 1997).

Reid, Schmidt, Harris, and Graham (1997) suggest six steps in teaching the use of strategies:

1. The teacher assists the student in learning the prerequisite skills for the task at hand.
2. The teacher discusses the strategy with the student, motivating him or her to become an active and willing participant in learning the strategy.
3. The teacher models the strategy for the student.
4. The student memorizes the strategy.
5. The teacher supports the student as he or she uses the strategy.
6. The student uses the strategy while the student monitors his or her performance.

Strategies are useful for reading, writing, mathematics, and study skills. Examples of strategies that enhance content area learning include the following: semantic mapping, story mapping, K-W-L or K-W-L-S, and the mnemonic keyword method. Semantic mapping is a multipurpose process that guides students to access prior knowledge, connects new concepts to their prior knowledge, and generates questions regarding the targeted topic (Keefe, 1996). A story map is a worksheet with headings such as setting, problem, goal, action, and outcome to help students organize information from a story that was read, or a story to be written (Scott, 1998). The strategy known as K-W-L (Ogle, 1986) or K-W-L-S (Sippola, 1995) is an acronym for What I Know, What I Want to Know, What I Learned, and What I Still Need to Learn. This strategy can be used both pre- and post-reading. Before reading, students are directed to think about their prior knowledge and predict what information they will read about. After reading, students are directed to determine if their questions were answered, and what further research they may need to do. The mnemonmic keyword method is a technique that uses visual and auditory cues to relate vocabulary words with their definitions (McLoone, Scruggs, Mastropieri, & Zucker, 1986). In a review of research related to math instruction, Miller, Butler, and Lee (1998) determined that strategy instruction, self-regulation intervention, and manipulatives were effective for computation and problem solving.

Numerous cognitive strategies have been developed to help students learn how to acquire, organize, and retrieve information for the express purpose of enhancing their academic achievement. For example, Ledzelter and Nowacek (1999) describe these strategies for reading with adolescents:

DISSECT (for decoding): Discover the topic, Isolate ideas, Separate, Say, Examine, Check, and Try.

IT FITS (for vocabulary): Identify, Tell, Find, Imagine, Think, Study.

ASK IT (self-questioning for comprehension): Attend, Say, Keep, Identify, Talk.

Research supports the effectiveness of strategies in the area of language arts, mathematics, content areas, and study skills (Scruggs and Mastropieri, 1992; Billingsley and Wildman, 1988; Idol & Croll, 1987; Ferro & Pressley, 1991). According to Wong (1994), although the teaching of strategies has been successful, student generalization of strategies has not been successful. It has been documented that strategies must be taught to students with learning disabilities; however, commitment, motivation, and attribution training are critical elements for success (Scott, 1998). Unlike direct instruction for the purpose of mastery of discrete skills, the instruction of cognitive strategies is for the purpose of helping students learn how to obtain and utilize information about anything (Scott, 1998). Teachers must be mindful, however, that strategy instruction may not be appropriate for all students, and when strategies are taught, they must be individualized to the student's needs (Montague, 1997).

Assistive Technology

As classroom teachers employ more cooperative and group learning in their classrooms, assistive technology may become more and more important for students with learning disabilities or emotional/behavioral disorders (Bryant & Bryant, 1998). Assistive technology can range from low-level supports, such as highlighter pens, to high-technology devices such as computers (Lewis, 1998). Lewis suggests that technology can reduce various barriers to learning in the following ways:

- The print barrier may be reduced by presenting information through senses other than vision.
- The communication barrier (poor handwriting, spelling, organizational skills, and writing production) may be reduced through word processing, spelling and grammar tools, and programs to organize writing.
- The learning barrier may be reduced by providing alternatives to traditional approaches such as lecture and textbook through audiotapes, videotapes, and computers.
- Other learning barriers can be reduced by using technologies. For example, captioned films and videos can be used to enhance reading skills.

Low-technology devices. Lewis (1998) suggests that there are several low-technology devices for daily life that are readily available for students with learning disabilities or emotional/behavioral disorders. For example, handheld calculators are readily available. Students with learning disabilities or emotional/behavioral disorders qualify for books on tape. In addition, memory and organizational devices, such as telephones that are pre-programmed to call numbers, electronic organizers, calendar and time management programs, and digital and talking clocks, are becoming more and more common.

Computer-assisted instruction. Bahr, Nelson, and Van Meter (1996) explored the effects of text-based and graphics-based computer software tools on planning and organizing stories. One tool allowed students to answer story grammar questions and then type stories using the responses as a text organizer. The other tool allowed students to create graphic scenes and then type stories about the scenes. Individual differences indicated that computer-presented grammar prompts benefited students with less internal organizational skill, while students with strong organizational skills wrote more mature stories with graphics-based tools.

Word-processing programs themselves may provide support for students who have difficulty writing (Hunt-Berg & Rankin, 1994). Talking word processors, spell and grammar checkers, word cueing and prediction, and text organization are available on many word-processor systems. Using word-processing can provide struggling writers with immediate and reliable legible writing, increased fluency, efficient editing, and efficient illustration.

Hebert and Murdock (1994) contrasted computer-aided instruction output modes to support vocabulary learning for students with learning disabilities. The three output modes included no speech, synthesized speech, and digitized speech. Participants learned the vocabulary words better with the two speech output modes than the no-speech mode, though there was no evidence to indicate the superiority of one speech mode over the other.

Higgins and Raskind (1995) explored the compensatory effectiveness of speech recognition on written composition performance of postsecondary students with learning disabilities. A comparison of holistic scores on essays written with assistance, with a scribe, and with a speech-recognition system indicated that participants received higher scores on essays written with speech-recognition technology. After comparing 22 measures of fluency, vocabulary, and syntax, the authors determined that the use of longer words was a strong predictor of a holistic score, and hypothesized that the speech recognition may have "encouraged" the use of longer words. In another study investigating the effectiveness of speech synthesis, Raskind and Higgins (1995) found that speech synthesis enabled postsecondary students with learning disabilities to detect a higher percentage of errors than by having the text read aloud by another person, or with no assistance.

Videotape.   Falk, Dunlap, and Kern (1996) assessed the effects of a package consisting of self-evaluation via videotape feedback procedures on inappropriate and appropriate peer interactions of students with externalizing and internalizing behavioral problems. Students were selected from three inclusive classrooms, and all the experimental sessions included peers who did not demonstrate behavioral problems. Teachers used videotaped self-evaluation and feedback with the students regarding their interactions. The use of videotape resulted in substantial increases in appropriate interactions for students with internalizing behavioral problems, and substantial decreases in inappropriate interactions for students with externalizing behavioral problems.

Considerations of using technology.   From a 1993 international symposium on "Technology for Persons with Learning Disabilities," Raskind, Herman, and Torgesen (1995) synthesized major discussions and issues. First, it appeared that two paradigms affect opinions about how technology should be used with individuals with learning disabilities. The holistic/constructivist view stresses that technology should be used to pursue what is relevant and meaningful to an individual, and empower the individual to obtain life goals rather than academic achievement. On the other hand, the traditional scientific/empirical perspective emphasizes remediation of academics and cognitive deficits of individuals with learning disabilities. Technology can efficiently deliver sequenced instruction and practice. Thus far, it seems that the predominant purpose of technology has been remediation. Technology is often seen as an extension of the teacher. In addition, technology is also viewed as assistive when used to circumvent a deficit, rather than to alleviate it.

Another purpose of technology is assessment and diagnosis of learning disabilities. This perspective can be argued from both a good news and a bad news scenario. On the positive side, computer-assisted assessment may provide cost-effective and efficient screening, and early detection of disabilities. However, the danger lies in overreliance on a computer-based assessments that may create a "learning disability detector" based on a narrow view of learning disabilities. Other purposes for technology include information access, and the nurturing of talents in the visual arts and creative thinking. Technology has the potential of enhancing not only the educational environment, but other environments in which persons with learning disabilities or emotional/behavioral disorders function. In addition, technology may help individuals with learning disabilities develop a sense of control over their lives.

Summary Points

- Intervention plans include selecting the target behavior, collecting and recording baseline data, identifying reinforcers, implementing interventions and collecting data, and evaluating the effect of the intervention.

- Comprehensive intervention plans are grounded in the environment, and emphasize skill building.

- Positive behavioral support occurs through functional communication training, curricular revision, setting event manipulations, and choice.

- Behavior management strategies, grounded in the principles of reinforcement, are effective with students with learning disabilities and emotional/behavioral disorders.

- Setting events have a significant impact on students' behavior.

- Scaffolds, scripts, and self-regulation strategies have been demonstrated to be effective for students with learning disabilities or emotional/behavioral disorders.

- Strategies have been demonstrated to be effective in increasing academic skills and positive behaviors.

Key Words and Phrases

aversive—noxious and sometimes painful consequences of behavior

baseline—the level of the target behavior before an intervention is implemented

crisis intervention strategies—techniques applied to respond immediately to behavior problems the student is experiencing in the environment in which he or she is functioning

contingency contract—a written or verbal agreement between two or more parties that stipulates the responsibilities of both parties concerning a specific item or activity

differential reinforcement—the process of reinforcing a behavior in the presence of one stimulus, and not reinforcing the behavior in the presence of another stimulus *discrimination*—the ability to act one way in one situation and another way in a different situation

extinction—discontinuing or withholding a reinforcer from a previously reinforced behavior

functional assessment—the process of identifying functional relationships between environmental events and the occurrence or nonoccurrence of a target behavior

generalization—a learned process whereby behavior reinforced in the presence of one stimulus will be exhibited in the presence of another

intervention plan—a five-step process used in the application of individual strategies

life–space interview—here-and-now intervention built around an individual's direct life experience to enable the individual to solve the problems confronting him or her

modeling—the provision of an individual or group behavior to be imitated, or not imitated, by the individual

negative reinforcement—strengthening a behavior as a consequence of removing an already operating aversive stimulus

positive behavioral support—interventions, grounded in functional assessment, that emphasize manipulating variables in the environment to support behavior change

positive reinforcement—presentation of a desirable consequence after a behavior has been exhibited to increase the likelihood that it will recur

punishment—the addition of an aversive stimulus, or the subtraction of a pleasurable stimulus, as the consequence of behavior in order to decrease the probability that the behavior will recur

reinforcement—providing a consequence to a behavior to increase the likelihood that it will recur

sampling—selecting times to observe planned activities and behaviors, as well as times to intervene

scaffolds—supports provided to enhance student functioning, which are withdrawn as the student is successful without them

schedule of reinforcement—the pattern with which the reinforcer is presented, or not presented, in response to a target behavior

scripts—personalized and detailed guidelines for intervention

self-regulation—self-instruction, goal-setting, and self-monitoring techniques used to regulate a student's behavior

setting events—factors in the environment that determine whether or not an intervention will have maximal or minimal effectiveness

shaping—the systematic, immediate reinforcement of successive approximations of a target behavior until the behavior is established

strategy—a plan for accomplishing a goal

target behavior—the specific behavior to be changed as a result of intervention

References

Albert, L. (1997). Solutions to four behavior nightmares. *Instructor, 107* (1), 58–61.

Anderson, M. G. (1992). The use of selected theatre rehearsal technique activities with African-American adolescents labeled "behavior disordered." *Exceptional Children, 59,* 132–139.

Axelrod, S. (1983). *Behavior modification for the classroom teacher.* NY: McGraw-Hill.

Baer, D. M., Wolf, M. M., & Risley, T. R. (1987). Some still current dimensions of applied behavior analysis. *Journal of Applied Behavior Analysis, 20,* 313–327.

Bahr, C. M., Nelson, N. W., & Van Meter, A. M. (1996). The effects of text-based and graphics-based software tools on planning and organizing stories. *Journal of Learning Disabilities, 29* (4), 355–370.

Barnett, D. W., & Carey, K. T. (1992). *Designing interventions for preschool learning and behavior problems.* San Francisco, CA: Jossey-Bass.

Barnett, D. W., Ehrhardt, K. E., Stollar, S. A., & Bauer, A. M. (1993). PASSKey: A model for naturalistic assessment and intervention design. Paper presented at the National Association of School Psychologists Annual Convention, Washington, DC.

Bender, W. N. (1995). *Learning Disabilities: Characteristics, Identification and Teaching Strategies.* Boston: Allyn & Bacon.

Billingsley, B. S., & Wildman, T. M. (1988). The effects of pre-reading activities on the comprehension of learning disabled adolescents. *Learning Disabilities Research, 4,* 36–44.

Bryant, D. P., & Bryant, B. R. (1998). Using assistive technology adaptations to include students with learning disabilities in cooperative learning activities. *Journal of Learning Disabilities, 31* (3), 41–54.

Camp, B. W., & Bash, M. A. (1981). *Think aloud.* Champaign, IL: Research Press.

Caputo, R. A. (1993). Using puppets with students with emotional and behavioral disorders. *Intervention in School and Clinic, 29,* 26–30.

Carr, E. (1997). Positive behavioral support: What researchers know and what consumers want. Paper presented at the NIDRR National Behavior Management Conference, Santa Barbara, CA.

Carta, J. J., & Greenwood, C. R. (1985). Ecobehavioral assessment: A methodology for expanding the evaluation of early intervention programs. *Topics in Early Childhood Special Education, 5,* 88–104.

Colvin, G., Ainge, D., & Nelson, R. (1997). How to defuse confrontations. *Teaching Exceptional Children, 29* (6) 47–51.

Dadson, S., & Horner, R. H. (1993). Manipulating setting events to decrease problem behaviors: A case study. *Teaching Exceptional Children, 25* (3), 53–58.

Demchak, M. (1993). Functional assessment of problem behaviors in applied settings. *Intervention in School and Clinic, 29* (2), 89–95.

Derry, S. J. (1990). Remediating academic difficulties through strategy training: The acquisition of useful knowledge. *Remedial and Special Education, 11* (67), 19–31.

Deshler, D. D., & Schumaker, J. B. (1986). Learning strategies: An instructional alternative for low-achieving adolescents. *Exceptional Children, 52,* 583–590.

Di Gangi, S. A., & Maag, J. W. (1992). A component analysis of self-management training with behaviorally disordered youth. *Behavioral Disorders, 17* (4), 281–290.

Dunlap, G., & Childs, K. E. (1996). Intervention research in emotional and behavioral disorders: An analysis of studies from 1980–1993. *Behavioral Disorders, 21* (2), 125–136.

Dunlap, G., Kern., L., de Perczel, M., Clarke, S., Wilson. D., Childs, K. E., White, R., & Falk, G. D. (1993). Functional analysis of classroom variables for students with emotional and behavioral disorders. *Behavioral Disorders, 18* (4), 275–291.

Evans, I. M., & Meyers, L. H. (1985). *Educative approach to behavior problems: A practical decision model for interventions with severely handicapped learners.* Baltimore: Brookes.

Falk, G. D., Dunlap, G., & Kern, L. (1996). An analysis of self-evaluation and videotape feedback for improving the peer interactions of students with externalizing and internalizing behavioral problems. *Behavioral Disorders, 21* (4), 261–276.

Ferro, S. C., & Pressley, M. G. (1991). Imagery generation by learning disabled and average-achieving 11- to 13-year-olds. *Learning Disability Quarterly, 14,* 231–239.

Fox, J., & Conroy, M. (1995). Setting events and behavioral disorders of children and youth: An interbehavioral field analysis for research and practice. *Journal of Emotional and Behavioral Disorders, 3* (3), 130–140.

Fox, J., Conroy, M., & Heckaman. K. (1998). Research issues in functional assessment of the challenging behaviors of students with emotional and behavioral disorders. *Behavioral Disorders, 14* (1), 26–33.

Fulk, B. M. (1994). Mnemonic keyword strategy training for students with learning disabilities. *Learning Disabilities Research & Practice, 9,* 179–185.

Gardner, W. I., Cole, C. L., Davidson, D. P., & Karan, O. C. (1986). Reducing aggression in individuals with developmental disabilities: An expanded stimulus control, assessment, and intervention model. *Education and Training of the Mentally Retarded, 21,* 3–12.

Gilliam, J. E. (1993). Crisis management for students with emotional/behavioral problems. *Intervention in School and Clinic, 28,* 224–230.

Graham, S., Harris, K. R., & Reid, R. (1992). Developing self-regulated learners. *Focus on Exceptional Children, 24* (6), 1–16.

Harris, K. R. (1982). Cognitive-behavior modification: Application with exceptional students. *Focus on Exceptional Children, 15* (2), 1–16.

Hebert, B., & Murdock, J. Y. (1994). Comparing three computer-aided instruction output modes to teach vocabulary words to students with learning disabilities. *Learning Disabilities Research and Practice, 9* (3), 136–141.

Henley, M. (1994). A self-control curriculum for troubled youngsters. *Journal of Emotional and Behavioral Problems, 3* (1), 40–46.

Higgins, E. L., & Raskind, M. H. (1995). Compensatory effectiveness of speech recognition on the written composition performance of postsecondary students with learning disabilities. *Learning Disability Quarterly, 18,* 159–174.

Horner, R. H., & Carr, E. G. (1997). Behavioral support for students with severe disabilities: Functional assessment and comprehensive intervention. *The Journal of Special Education, 31* (1), 84–104.

Hunt-Berg, M., & Rankin, J. L. (1994). Ponder the possibilities: Computer supported writing for struggling writers. *Learning Disabilities Research and Practice, 9* (3), 169–178.

Idol, L., & Croll, V. J. (1987). Story-mapping training as a means of improving reading comprehension. *Learning Disability Quarterly, 10,* 214–229.

Jones, V. F. (1996). "In the face of predictable crisis": Developing a comprehensive treatment plan for students with emotional and behavioral disorders. *Teaching Exceptional Children, 29* (2), 54–59.

Keefe, C. H. (1996) *Label-free Learning: Supporting learners with disabilities.* York, ME: Stenhouse.

Kendrick, M., Kurtz, A., Son, K., Gilmer, D., & Zeph, L. (1998). A new way of thinking about positive supports. *Counterpoint, 19* (2), 1, 12–13.

Koegel, R. (1997). Intensive early intervention for children with autism. Paper presented at the NIDRR National Behavior Management Conference, Santa Barbara, CA.

Ledzelter, S., & Nowacek, E. J. (1999). Reading strategies for secondary students with mild disabilities. *Intervention in School and Clinic, 34* (4), 212–219.

Lewis, R. B. (1998). Assistive technology and learning disabilities: Today's realities and tomorrow's promises. *Journal of Learning Disabilities, 31* (1), 16–26.

Lieber, J., & Beckman, P. J. (1991). Social coordination as a component of social competence in young children with disabilities. *Focus on Exceptional Children, 24* (4), 1–10.

Lloyd, J. W. (1980). Academic instruction and cognitive behavior modification: The need for attack strategy training. *Exceptional Education Quarterly, 1* (1), 53–63.

Lohrmann-O-Rourke, S., & Zirkel, P. A. (1998). The case law on aversive interventions for students with disabilities. *Exceptional Children, 65,* 101–123.

Long, N. J., Morse, W. C., & Newman, R. G. (1980). *Conflict in the classroom* (4th ed.). Belmont, CA: Wadsworth.

McIntyre, T. (1987). Classroom conferencing: Providing support and guidance for misbehaving youth. *Teaching: Behaviorally Disordered Youth, 3,* 33–35.

McLoone, B., Scruggs, T. E., Mastropieri, M. A., & Zucker, S. F. (1986). Memory strategy instruction and training with learning disabled adolescents. *Learning Disabilities Research, 2,* 45–53.

Meese, R. L. (1997). Student fights: Preventive strategies for preventing and managing student conflicts. *Intervention in School and Clinic, 33* (1), 26–29, 35.

Montague, M. (1997). Cognitive strategy instruction in mathematics for students with learning disabilities. *Journal of Learning Disabilities, 30* (2), 164–177.

Morse, W. C. (1980). Worksheet in life space interviewing. In. N. J. Long, W. C. Morse, & R. G. Newman, (Eds.), *Conflict in the classroom* (4th ed.). Belmont, CA: Wadsworth.

Ogle, D. (1986). K-W-L: A teaching model that develops active reading of expository text. *The Reading Teacher, 39,* 564–570.

O'Neill, R. E., Horner, R. H., Albin, R. W., Storey, K., & Sprague, J. R. (1990). *Functional analysis of problem behavior: A practical assessment guide.* Pacific Grove, CA: Brooks/Cole.

Palincsar, A., & Ransom, K. (1988). From the mystery spot to the thoughtful spot: The instruction of metacognitive strategies. *Learning Disabilities Research and Practice, 3,* 784–789.

Pressley, M., Hogan, K., Wharton-McDonald, R., Mistretta, J., & Ettenberger, S. (1996). The challenges of instructional scaffolding: The challenges of instruction that supports student thinking. *Learning Disabilities Research and Practice, 11* (3), 138–146.

Raskind, M. H., & Higgins, E. (1995). Effects of speech synthesis on the proofreading efficiency of postsecondary students with learning disabilities. *Learning Disability Quarterly, 18,* 141–158.

Raskind, M. H., Herman, K. L., Torgesen, J. K. (1995). Technology for persons with disabilities: Report on an international symposium. *Learning Disability Quarterly, 18,* 175–184.

Redl, F. (1959). The concept of life space interview. *American Journal of Orthopsychiatry, 29,* 1–18.

Reid, R., Schmidt, T., Harris, K. R., & Graham, S. (1997). Cognitive strategy instruction: Developing self-regulated learners. *Journal of Emotional and Behavioral Problems, 6* (2), 97–102.

Repp, A. C., & Karsh, K. G. (1990). A taxonomic approach to the nonaversive treatment of maladaptive behavior of persons with developmental disabilities. In A. C. Repp & N. N. Singh, (Eds.), *Perspectives on the use of nonaversive and aversive interventions for persons with developmental disabilities* (pp. 333–438). Sycamore, IL: Sycamore.

Ruef, M. B., Higgins, C., Glaeser, B. J. C., & Patnode, M. (1998). Positive behavioral support: Strategies for teachers. *Intervention in School and Clinic, 34* (1), 21–32.

Sasso, G. M., Peck, J., & Garrison-Harrell, L. (1998). Social interaction setting events: Experimental analysis of contextual variables. *Behavioral Disorders, 24* (1), 34–43.

Scott, K. (1998). Cognitive instructional strategies. In W. N. Bender, (Ed.), *Professional issues in learning disabilities: practical strategies and relevant research findings.* Austin: Pro-Ed.

Scruggs, T. E., & Mastropieri, M. A. (1992). Classroom applications of mnemonic instruction: Acquisition, maintenance, and generalization, *Exceptional Children, 58,* 219–229.

Sippola, A. E. (1995). K-W-L-S, *The Reading Teacher, 48,* 542–543.

Swanson, H. L. (1989). Strategy instruction: Overview of principles and procedures for effective use. *Learning Disability Quarterly, 12,* 3–13.

Torgesen, J. K. (1975). Problems and prospects in the study of learning disabilities. In E. M. Hetherington & O. Hage, (Eds.), *Review of Child Development Research,* (Vol. 5). University of Chicago Press.

Torgesen, J. K. (1977). The role of non-specific factors in the task performance of learning disabled children. A theoretical assessment. *Journal of Learning Disabilities, 10,* 27–35.

Turnbull, H. R. III, (1997). A model state and federal statute on the use of positive behavioral support. Paper presented at the NIDRR National Behavior Management Conference, Santa Barbara, CA.

Wahler, R. G., & Cormier, W. H. (1970). The ecological interview: A first step in outpatient child behavior therapy. *Journal of Behavior Therapy and Experimental Psychiatry, 1,* 279–289.

Walker, J. E., & Shea, T. M. (1999). Behavior Management: A Practical Approach for Educators (7th ed.). Columbus, OH: Prentice Hall–Merrill.

Webber, J., Scheuermann, B., McCall, C., & Coleman, M. (1993). Research on self-monitoring as a behavior management technique in special education classrooms: A descriptive review. *Remedial and Special Education, 14* (2), 38–56.

Wong, B. Y. L. (1994). Instructional parameters promoting transfer of learned strategies in students with learning disabilities. *Learning Disability Quarterly, 17,* 110–120.

11

Supporting Learning and Behavior Change: Class and School-Wide Interventions

TO GUIDE YOUR READING

After reading this chapter, you will be able to answer the following questions:

- What characteristics of teacher stance support learning among students with learning disabilities or emotional/behavioral disorders?

- What classroom structures and management strategies are effective with students with learning disabilities or emotional/behavioral disorders?

- What school-wide structures support students with learning disabilities and emotional/behavioral disorders?

◆ *It was not until after the December holiday break that Tara was referred to the teacher assistance team. Ms. Stacy, her teacher, had left the fourth-grade classroom on maternity leave. Ms. Halbard, her replacement, explained to the students, on her first day, that things would be very different while she was the teacher. Ms. Halbard, concerned about the students' performance on the state proficiency test, increased the number of drills and practices on addition, subtraction, multiplication, and division facts. Because she wanted the students to do well on the reading section of the test, Ms. Halbard used comprehension workbooks, which included reading passages about three or four paragraphs long, followed by a series of questions. Students' performances and progress on these materials in both mathematics and reading were charted on the wall in the room.*

Tara, by now identified as having learning disabilities, was becoming more and more withdrawn. Because her Individualized Education Plan indicated that she should use a calculator to check her computation, and because her scores on the state proficiency test in mathematics would not be documented, Ms. Halbard did not include Tara's name on the "Basic Facts Achievement Chart" displayed in the classroom. With her short-term memory difficulties, Tara was slow to complete the comprehension workbooks; she needed to look back into the reading selections several times in order to accurately answer the questions. Tara had been able to cope in Ms. Stacy's literature-based reading sections, having participated in the discussions in a lively manner, but the current reading structure did not provide her with a way to show her strengths.

Ms. Halbard was becoming more frustrated with Tara, whose achievement was declining. She requested that the Student Assistance Team help in her effort to meet her teaching goals, and to assist her in helping Tara find academic success in her classroom.

REFLECTION *Have you had a similar experience? If you had a teacher leave at midterm, did the changes in the classroom create difficulties for you in subjects in which you had previously done well? What strategies did you use to cope with the new situation?*

Introduction

In this chapter, several topics related to group interventions are examined. First, teacher stance as it relates to the prevention and amelioration of learning disabilities or emotional/behavioral disorders is presented, including a discussion on facilitative versus controlling teacher stance, and authoritarian teacher stance. In the next section, classroom structure and other management strategies that are effective with students with learning disabilities and emotional/behavioral disorders are introduced. The chapter concludes with a discussion of the inclusion of students with learning disabilities and emotional/behavioral disorders in the general education classroom and school.

Characteristics of Teacher Stance

A teacher's stance encompasses his or her personal posture toward self and others, as well as his or her theoretical orientation, and instructional and management strategies (McGee, Menolascino, Hobbs, and Menousek, 1987). Teacher stance has a significant effect on students' social perceptions of their teacher, their classmates, and themselves. Evertson and Weade (1989) described the efficacy of a teacher stance that elicited and supported student participation. The effective teacher provided explicit rationales for activities, set and followed consistent routines for classroom interaction, and maintained sensitivity to students' needs in relation to the difficulty level of the lesson content.

The teacher's role in "facilitating learning" has emerged in qualitative studies conducted in general education classrooms. Rogers, Weller, and Perrin (1987) described that the interactions of an "excellent" facilitative teacher are characterized by extended conversations with the students. The teacher's interactions were described as natural, spontaneous, sensitive, and individualized. Through facilitation, the teacher becomes less constraining, and monitors the students' responses more carefully.

More specific contrasts between the communicative styles of facilitative and directive teachers were provided by Mirenda and Donellan (1986). Facilitative teachers initiated fewer topics, and they initiated those topics through indirect questions, statements, or comments. Direct questions were rarely used to extend topics. Rather, statements, encouragements, and expansions were used.

Story (1985) reports that facilitative teachers provided for positive and close physical relationships, being on the same eye level when in discussion with students, and touching the student to emphasize encouragement or enthusiasm. Verbal interactions were marked by encouragement, humor, and clarification strategies.

The "curriculum of control," often used to describe classrooms of students with emotional/behavioral disorders, is in stark contrast to facilitative teaching. As Nichols (1992) suggests, a controlling stance tends to generate the behaviors that placement in programs for students with emotional/behavioral disorders is designed to ameliorate. Nichols contends that when teachers are having problems they rarely smile; successful teachers look at their students when they talk to them, or quietly exchange everyday pleasantries. Morse (1994) agrees, noting that a common thread among gifted teachers is knowing their students, and having a deep empathy for the stress in their lives.

Dayton-Sakori's (1997) observations of struggling readers suggest that teachers tend to control the learning situation with the struggling reader as a passive participant, while allowing the excellent readers to be in control. For example, during one-on-one instruction with students in a reading clinic, teachers talked, wrote, handed out materials, took pencils out of pencil cases, opened and held books open, turned pages, erased mistakes, manipulated materials, posed questions and carried the discussions. The students looked away, leaned back, played with a pencil, did not touch the reading materials, did not read, write or talk. Teachers of struggling readers controlled the materials to a greater extent than teachers of excellent readers. Excellent readers and their teachers shared the reading experience through discussion of the text and text structure. In addition, the heads of the good readers were up, and they made eye contact. Struggling readers, on the other hand, were bent over and had little interaction with the text or with the teacher. Excellent readers securely held their books with both hands, while struggling readers may have kept the book open with one hand or with a thumb. Excellent readers freely moved the materials to accommodate their position, while struggling readers twisted their bodies and heads without moving the book to a more appropriate position. The emotions from excellent readers were drawn from what they were reading; however, the emotions of the struggling readers indicated how they felt about reading. In general, the excellent readers demonstrated control over the reading experience; the struggling readers were uninvolved and were not in control. Dayton-Sakari (1997) cautions teachers not to do the work for the students, and to be conscious of who is in control of the learning situation. In other words, teachers must not only give up control, but should teach students who have learned to be passive how to take control.

Kohn (1993) argues that there are three alternatives to control: managing content, collaborating with students, and providing them with choice. In managing content, he suggests that teachers look at what the students are being asked to do; if a student does not comply with a request, consider the nature of the request. Collaboration involves mutual problem solving. In collaboration, teacher and student come to a mutual understanding of what constitutes appropriate and inappropriate behavior. Kohn suggests that explanation is the most limited version of collaboration, and is the very least that is owed to a child. The more the student feels his or her view is solicited and taken seriously, the fewer problems there will be to deal with.

Teachers of students with emotional/behavioral disorders must project a stance which supports the reintegration of their students into general education. Schechtman, Reiter, & Schanin (1993) reported that teachers who viewed efforts to integrate students with disabilities into the classroom as a personal and professional challenge were more likely to have favorable attitudes toward including those individuals. A teacher's stance held greater significance in an individual's successful reintegration into general education than the amount of external school support the teacher received. Rock, Rosenberg, and Carran (1995) indicate that a "positive reintegration orientation" was also significant to the success of students with emotional/behavioral disorders in less restrictive settings.

A constructivist stance has been proposed as a way to support students with learning disabilities (Harris and Graham, 1996; Mercer, Jordan, & Miller, 1996), and is applicable to students with emotional/behavioral disorders. Constructivism does not define teaching methods, rather, it is a philosophy about teaching and learning (Harris & Graham, 1996). In constructivism, students are seen as active, self-regulating learners who construct knowledge in developmentally appropriate ways within social contexts. Learning begins with the student's prior knowledge and experiences, and understanding is recognized only when students participate fully in learning (Harris & Graham, 1996). Learning is socially situated, and is enhanced in functional, authentic contexts. In constructivist classrooms, teachers try to facilitate and assist the construction of powerful knowledge rather than to explicitly provide knowledge and information (Tharp & Gallimore, 1988).

Harris and Graham (1996) suggest that in constructivist classrooms, explicit, focused, and, at times, isolated instruction needs to be provided as needed by individual children. However, this instruction should be integrated into the larger learning context. They suggest that ideally, integrated, coherent instruction is based in learning communities that are educationally purposeful, open, caring, and joyful. In these learning communities, teachers' decisions are based on ongoing assessment that includes students' cognitive and metacognitive abilities, skills, knowledge and prior experiences, and individual characteristics. In these ideal settings, students are provided whatever level of support they need to acquire and personalize powerful strategies, develop fluency and automaticity in skills and strategies, and develop concepts.

Though constructivism originally emphasized implicit instructional strategies, recent interpretations of constructivism have expanded to include explicit instruction (Mercer, Jordan, & Miller, 1996). Mercer, Jordan, and Miller (1996) suggest that constructivist settings put specific demands on students. These demands include that students must:

- have sufficient prior knowledge to construct new and appropriate meaning from understanding connections between prior learning and new information;
- attend to teacher presentations, teacher–student interactions, and student–student interactions;
- use cognitive and metacognitive processes to acquire, remember, and construct new knowledge in a way that is authentic to their lives;
- be active participants in their own learning;
- engage in group discussions to solve problems;
- recognize their own learning characteristics, develop a sense of the strategies they use, and maintain a proactive attitude about learning.

Mercer and associates suggest that though constructivism has been identified with implicit practices, the constructivist continuum includes both explicit and implicit teaching. Explicit teaching may be needed immediately to help students with learning disabilities or emotional/behavioral disorders, whereas implicit teaching may be supportive of more mature students.

Mercer and associates suggest that there are several applications of a constructive continuum of instruction that may be applied. The authentic contexts for learning, including the school context, family/community context, and futuristic context may be used to increase student participation and motivation. Teachers may provide activities that move from concrete, to representational, to abstract supports. Rather than using a "drill and skill" perspective, a strong understanding of basic concepts can reduce the need for memorization. Explicit modeling can be used to "paint pictures" for students in such a way that understanding is insured, and implicit modeling can be used by having the teacher practice what is taught. Mnemonics may also be useful to support students by helping them remember procedures, and also by helping the teacher organizing thinking aloud while modeling a process.

Constructivism can be used to support classroom management as well as instruction according to Dollard, Christenssen, Colucci, and Epanchin (1996). In constructive classroom management, an emphasis is on building caring relationships, and utilizing techniques which establish dialogue among teachers and students. They suggest that interventions such as instruction in problem solving, self-management, conflict resolution, and self-assessment may be employed in constructivist classrooms. In addition, students can be supported through "cognitive restructuring," a method to help students manage their stress.

Effective Classroom Structures and Management Strategies

This section discusses classroom structures and other management strategies. More specifically, social skills curricula, cooperative learning structures, and the learning environment, i.e., the antecedents of effective management are presented. Among the strategies discussed are procedures, rules, space and facilities, schedules, cueing, and transitions.

Social Skills Training

Students with learning disabilities or emotional/behavioral disorders are often viewed by peers, teachers, parents, and others as socially incompetent. Students with learning disabilities may have problems in establishing satisfactory peer relationships (Sale & Carey, 1995), or dealing with negative peer judgments.

Students with emotional/behavior disorders may engage in behavior excesses, such as cursing, shouting, arguing, and disrupting. They either have not had the opportunity to learn or, given the opportunity, have not learned appropriate social skills (Carter and Sugai, 1989). Bryan and Bryan (1997) suggest that these students have problems in social skills information processes, including encoding social skills, interpreting them, identifying a response, deciding on a response, and enacting that response.

Fad (1990) identified three behavioral domains essential to students with behavior problems if they are to function effectively in the general education classroom: peer relationships, work habits, and coping skills. To learn these skills, Fad suggests, (a) identifying and assessing a student's present level of skill, (b) setting priorities among the skills to be learned, (c) selecting effective instructional methods to teach the skills, and (d) evaluating and conducting follow-up assessment of the skills learned.

Social skills training is designed to help students increase their awareness and understanding of personal emotions, values, and attitudes through educational activities (Edwards and O'Toole, 1985; McGinnis, Sauerbry, and Nichols, 1985). These activities lead to improvement of the student's interpersonal problem-solving skills.

Three primary assessment techniques for evaluating students' social functioning are peer reports, behavior rating scales, and observational techniques (Vaughn, LaGreca, & Kuttler, 1999). Peer reports can provide insightful information because children observe other children in environments where adults are not present. Sociometrics, or peer nominations and peer ratings, are useful methods for obtaining peer reports (Vaughn et al., 1999). A common sociometric technique is peer nomination of those who are liked or disliked (Polloway & Patton, 1997). Likert-type peer ratings typically ask each student to rate classmates with regard to a certain criterion such as how much a student is liked (Vaughn et al., 1999; Polloway & Patton, 1997). Vaughn and associates (1999) caution that the stem used for rating scales should be selected carefully. For example, "How much do you like," may elicit a very different response from, "How much would you like to work with," or, "How much would you like to play with." Responses to these stems may depend on a variety of variables such as if the target student prefers to work alone, is a slow worker, or has motor difficulties. Peer acceptance does not necessarily provide information regarding friendships. However, reciprocal friendships can be determined by having students identify their "best friend" in the peer nomination process (Vaughn et al., 1999).

Self-report measures, such as questionnaires, rating scales, and checklists may be used to glean information regarding a student's perception of his or her behavior (Polloway & Patton, 1997). The Social Skills Rating System (Gresham & Elliott, 1990) obtains parallel parent, teacher, and student self-reports in the areas of cooperation, assertion, responsibility, empathy, and self-control. Participants are asked to rate the importance of each behavior. Polloway and Patton (1997) caution that such an assessment relies on the raters' memories and that it cannot be determined if the identified problem behaviors are due to social deficits or motivational problems, unless several raters complete an assessment.

Finally, for the purpose of assessment, a student can be directly observed in a natural social function setting. Advantages of such an approach are, (a) the observation is conducted in conjunction with the environment, and (b) there is a reduction of teacher or parent bias. The major disadvantage of observation as an assessment technique is that it is time-consuming (Vaughn et al., 1999).

There are several social skills training programs available in the literature. The practitioner must give careful consideration to the appropriateness of a particular program for the students with whom it is to be applied. Schumaker, Pederson, Hazel, and Meten (1983) suggest five questions for teachers to address when selecting a social skills curriculum:

- Does the curriculum promote social competence?
- Does the curriculum respond to the learning characteristics of the students with whom it is to be applied?
- Does the curriculum target the social skills deficits of the students with whom it is to be applied?
- Does the curriculum provide training in situations, as well as in skills?
- Does the curriculum include instructional methodologies found to be effective with the population of students with whom it is to be applied?

Carter and Sugai (1989) developed a comprehensive procedure for the selection and analysis of a social skills curriculum. They describe several programming issues which should be considered. First, they suggest that training take place in groups, yet be individualized to meet the needs of the students. Individualization may occur through varying levels of teacher assistance, reinforcers, accuracy criteria, and examples selected. The program should require little additional training for the teacher, and it should be affordable. The curriculum must provide for student assessment, progress monitoring, and maintenance and generalization training. Carter and Sugai have designed a useful curriculum analysis checklist and decision making grid.

Two important issues in social skills programming are maintenance and generalization. To increase the likely occurrence of maintenance and generalization, teachers should use multiple instructors, and instruct in multiple settings. Responses should be varied so that they will be maintained in the natural environment. In addition, a variety of instructional strategies should be applied, including modeling, direct instruction, placing students in settings with other students who exhibit appropriate behavior, rehearsal and practice, shaping, prompting and coaching, and positive practice.

Nelson (1988) notes that research indicates that a social skills curriculum does promote the acquisition of socially appropriate behaviors by students with disabilities. However, there is little research evidence that social skills instruction is effective over time and across settings. Zaragoza, Vaughn, and McIntosh (1991) analyzed 27 studies on the effects of social skills training on school-aged children. They were somewhat optimistic with respect to the effects of social skills interventions with students identified as emotionally/behaviorally disordered. When compared with non-participants, the participants felt better about themselves, and their teachers and parents felt better about them. In the majority of the studies, peers' feelings about the students with emotional/behavioral disorders did not change. Further, while social behavior may change as a result of individual programs, Melich and McAninch (1992) point out that they may not improve peer's acceptance of the student. Therefore, additional strategies that consider the student's environment should supplement the skills training. For example, nontarget peers and teachers should be involved so that they notice and are receptive to change in the target student's social behavior.

Sabornie and Beard (1990) suggest that instruction in social skills for students with mild disabilities should be based on an individual assessment of needs. If the learner needs instruction, then that instruction should be structured and frequent. They suggest two approaches to instruction in social skills: (a) manipulation of antecedents and consequences of students' social behavior, and (b) application of a "packaged" curriculum. Armstrong and McPherson (1991) suggest that instruction in social skills is most effective when it is a collaborative home–school or parent–teacher–student activity. Such cooperation will facilitate generalization of learned skills. Several social skills training curricula are described in Table 11.1.

Bryan and Bryan (1997) suggest a curriculum approach to teach social information processing which they refer to as "Amazing Discoveries." Amazing Discoveries is comprised of a series of hands-on experiences that introduce students to the scientific study of human behavior, how beliefs and feelings influence behavior, how others influence behavior, and how people influence each other through communication. In each activity, students learn both about science and human behavior. Bryan and Bryan suggest that through this curriculum-based approach students can acquire the social information processing knowledge and skills that are the core of social competence.

A similar approach to teaching prosocial behaviors is described by Warger and Rutherford (1997). In their program, instructional strategies usually employed in academic areas are used to teach prosocial behavior in the classroom. Teachers target social skills, teach skills, and

Table 11.1 Social Skills Curricula

Program	Target Population	Skills
A Social Skills Program for Adolescents (ASSET) Hazel, Schumaker, Sherman, & Sheldon-Wildgen, 1981).	Adolescents with learning disabilities	Positive and negative feedback: accepting negative feedback; resisting peer pressure; problem solving; negotiation, following instructions; conversation
Cognitive-Behavioral Program (LaGreca et al., 1980, 1981, 1989)	Low-accepted elementary school students; has been adapted for students with learning disabilities	Greeting others; showing positive affect; joining others; extending invitations; participating in conversation; sharing; providing positive feedback
Interpersonal Problem Solving (Amish et al., 1988)	Students with behavior problems	Determine problem; goal; solutions; consequences and implementation of appropriate solution
Mutual Interest Discovery (Fox, 1989)	Students with learning disabilities	Peer acceptance
PALS: Problem Solving and Affective Learning Strategies (Vaughn et al., 1986)	Students between four and eight years of age	Small group and whole group
Skillstreaming the Elementary School Child: A Guide for Teaching Prosocial Skills (McGinnis et al., 1984)	Elementary school students	Prosocial skills for classroom, making friends, dealing with feelings, alternatives to aggression, dealing with stress
Skillstreaming the Adolescent: A Structured Learning Approach to Teaching Prosocial Skills (Goldstein et al., 1980)	Adolescents	Prosocial skills in classroom survival, making friends, dealing with feelings, alternatives to aggression, dealing with stress
Social Skills for Daily Living Program (Schumaker, Hazel, & Pederson, 1989)	Adolescents with disabilities	Thirty social skills
Strategic Problem Solving Approach (Vaughn et al., 1999) FAST and SLAM (McIntosh, Vaughn, & Bennerson, 1995)	Students with learning disabilities who are not well accepted	FAST: problem-solving process; SLAM: accept and appropriately respond to negative feedback
Think Aloud: Increasing Social and Cognitive Skills: A Problem Solving Program for Children (Bash, et al., 1985)	Elementary students, Grades 1–6	Dealing with social conflicts
The Walker Social Skills Curriculum: The ACCEPTS Program (Walker et al., 1983).	Students with disabilities	Skills for transitions into less restrictive settings

evaluate the success of their intervention. They begin with basis social-interactions skills such as listening, following directions, asking questions, communicating information, and waiting turns. Additional skills are related to responsibility (sharing, cooperating, caring, helping), respect (understanding another point of view, accepting individual differences, tolerance, disagreeing appropriately), and conflict resolution (problem solving, accepting feedback, mediation, compromising). Direct teaching is used, with modeling, practice, social reinforcement or feedback, and self-monitoring.

Efforts to address the social learning needs of students with learning disabilities or emotional/behavioral disorders have ranged from the in-depth curriculum suggested by Bryan and Bryan (1997), to playing "monopoly"-like board games (Wiener & Harris, 1997). However, in their meta-analysis of the research involving social skills instruction for students with learning disabilities, Forness and Kavale (1996) reported disappointing effects of social skills training. They offered five possible causes for this lack of progress. First, instruction in social skills training was usually thirty hours or less. In many studies, the social skills being assessed, and those being trained, did not match. Most of the studies used social skills training programs with no clear rationale, and little pilot testing. The disappointing results could also be related to the controversy over the origin of social skills problems for use with students with learning disabilities. Finally, they suggest that there may be only a subset of students identified as learning disabled who respond to social skills instruction.

Self-determination, the ability to identify and act upon one's own life goals (Rivera & Smith, 1997), has been identified as an important component of social skills. Students need to be able to express their needs and their goals. Curricula for explicit "self-determination" skills have been developed for transition programs. Self-determination skills may include self-awareness, self-advocacy, self-efficacy, decision-making, independent performance, self-evaluation, and adjustment (Martin & Marshall, 1995). See Table 11.2 for examples of self-determination curricula.

Cooperative Learning Structures

Cooperative learning structures have evolved from earlier descriptions of group activities. At present, cooperative learning structures involve cooperative teaching and student-cooperative teams, as well as the more traditional cooperative group activities.

Cooperative teaching refers to the educational approach in which general and special educators jointly teach academically and behaviorally heterogeneous groups of students in general education classrooms (Bauwens, Hourcard, & Friend, 1989). Cooperative teaching is proactive. In cooperative teaching, students with academic and/or learning difficulties im-

Table 11.2   Self-Determination Curricula

Program	Target Population	Skills
Steps to Self-determination Curriculum (Field & Hoffman, 1992)	Adolescents with parents and community members as support	Knowing yourself, valuing yourself, planning, acting, experiencing outcomes, learning
Learning with PURPOSE (Serna & Lau-Smith, 1994, 1995)	Students with mild/moderate disabilities; at risk for failure in school and community; and in general education classroom	Social skills, self-evaluation skills, self-direction skills, networking skills, collaboration skills, persistence and risk-taking skills, stress management
ChoiceMakers (Martin & Huber-Marshall, 1995)	Students with disabilities who can participate in IEP meetings	Choosing goals, expressing goals, taking action, self-awareness, self-advocacy, self-efficacy, decision-making, independent performance, self-evaluation, adjustment

mediately receive instruction, or curricular modifications. Bauwens and associates describe three basic implementation options of cooperative teaching:

- complementary instruction, in which the general education teacher maintains the primary responsibility for teaching the specific subject matter in the instructional program, while the special educator assumes primary responsibility for the student's mastery of academic survival skills;

- team teaching, in which, at various times, each of the teachers assumes primary responsibility for specific types of instruction or portions of the curriculum; and

- supportive learning activities, in which the general education teacher maintains responsibility for delivering the essential content of instruction, while the special educator is responsible for developing and implementing supplementary and supportive learning activities; both teachers are present and cooperatively monitor essential content and supplementary activities.

Cooperative teaching also may be structured in teams rather than pairs. A teaching team is an instructional arrangement of two or more members of the school or greater community who distribute among themselves planning, instructional, and evaluation responsibilities for the same students, on a regular basis, for an extended period of time (Thousand &

Villa, 1990). Teams provide students with support from a variety of adults, all of whom are engaged in group problem solving (Vandercook & York, 1990). Flicek, Olsen, Chiverse, Kaufman, and Anderson (1996), for example, provide a model of a classroom comprised of six students with learning disabilities, three students with emotional/behavioral disorders, and nineteen students without disabilities who were taught cooperatively by a general education teacher, a special education teacher, and three teaching assistants. Cooperative teaching allows general and special educators to complement each other. Most general educators are skilled in large group management and content, whereas special educators have expertise in analyzing and adapting instructional materials and strategies, and developing Individualized Education Plans (Bauwens, Hourcade, & Friend, 1989).

Three barriers to the implementation of a cooperative teaching structure have been identified by Bauwens and associates. First, there is a significant amount of time needed for planning as a team. Second, there must be cooperative working relationships. Finally, teachers initially perceive teaming as increased work; however, eventually they assume specific responsibilities based not only in their own area of expertise, or area of interest, and their concern regarding work load decreased. In Flicek and associates' cooperative teaching classroom, teaching ratings indicated that the problem behaviors of students with emotional/behavioral disorders were within a normative level by the last two months of the academic year.

According to Gartner and Lipsky (1990), student cooperative teaming provides unique opportunities for the improvement of all students. Using class-wide tutoring teams, Gartner and Lipsky reported an increase in students' opportunities to respond, and to have those responses affirmed or corrected. Student cooperative teams were small and heterogenous (four to five students of varying ability levels) who used game formats for reviewing weekly instructional content. The cooperative goal structures were used in conjunction with systematic instructional strategies, and the daily posting of the teams' performance. In these groups, the students' "job" is to help their teammates learn the weekly content using materials, questions, and answers provided by the teachers. Students take turns acting as tutor, while their remaining teammates are tutees. Roles are then switched.

Cooperative learning structures offer ways for organizing social interaction in the classroom (Kagan, 1989). Cooperative learning structures are independent of content, and can be used across almost any subject area. Kagan contrasts cooperative learning with traditional teaching through the following example. In traditional teaching, the teacher usually asks a question, the students who wish to respond raise their hands, the teacher calls on one student, and the student attempts to state the correct answer. In a cooperative classroom, the teacher would form two groups. The teacher would have the students number off within their groups, and then ask a question. The teacher would ask the students to "put their heads together" to make sure that everyone on the team knows the answer. The teacher then calls a number, and the students with that number can raise their hands to respond. This is a cooperative structure because if any student knows the answer, the ability of each student is increased. High achievers share answers because they know their number might not be called and they want their group to do well. Lower achievers listen carefully because they know their number may be called. Several of Kagan's structures for cooperative learning are presented in Table 11.3.

Learning Environment

Variables related to the learning environment (antecedents to effective instruction) are discussed in this section. Among the variables that are discussed are rules, schedules, transitions, cueing, procedures, and curricular issues.

An effective program is planned and organized to facilitate instruction and management. Prior to the beginning of any school day, or year, the practitioner must take into consideration a broad range of factors to en-

Table 11.3 Sample Cooperative Learning Structures

Structure	Description	Functions
Round Robin	Students are in small groups; each student shares something with classmates	Expressing ideas and opinions; equal participation
Corners	Teacher presents four alternatives; each student moves to a corner of the room. Students discuss within their corners, then listen to and paraphrase ideas from other corners	Seeing alternatives; respecting different points of view
Pairs Check	Students work in pairs within groups of four. Within pairs, students alternate—one solves a problem and the other coaches. After every two problems, the pair checks to see if they have the same answer as other pairs.	Practice; helping; praising
Co-op Co-op	Students work in groups to produce a particular group product to share with the whole class; each student makes a particular contribution to the group	Learning and sharing complex materials with multiple sources; presentation skills

(Kagan, 1989)

hance the probability that learning will occur. The teacher must develop procedures for individual, small, and whole group activities, beginning and ending the school day or instructional period, transitions, housekeeping, interruptions, visitors, fire drills, and various other planned and unplanned activities.

McQuillan, DuPaul, Shapiro, and Cole (1996) contrasted three ways of evaluating academic and behavioral performance in the classroom. These three strategies involved:

- Teacher-evaluation, in which token points were awarded on a variable-interval schedule, based on the teacher's evaluation of each student's behavior. Points were exchanged for back-up reinforcers during three exchange periods in the school day, or saved for more costly reinforcers.

- Self-evaluation, whereby students used a form to rate adherence to classroom rules on a six-point scale. The teacher and students each evaluated at the same time, and, if the student's score matched the teacher's, the student received a bonus point. If ratings were within one point, the student was allowed to keep the number of points he or she earned. If ratings differed by more than one point, the student earned no points.

- Group-evaluation, in which students rated the group's overall adherence to classroom rules on a six-point scale. The group rating was determined by the average of the individual ratings and rounded to the nearest whole number. If the score was within one point of the teacher's rating, the group received those points. If they matched, the students received a bonus point. If they differed by more than one, no points were rewarded.

Data indicated that students significantly improved their academic performance when either the self- or group-evaluation procedures were implemented.

Rules

According to Joyce, Joyce, and Chase (1989), a rule is "the specification of a relation between two events and may take the form of instruction, direction, or principle." Teachers use various kinds of rules to organize instruction and conduct. Rules are usually designed to apply to those activities and occurrences that are not governed by classroom and non-classroom procedures.

Rules should be few in number. They should be brief and understandable to the students and positively stated. They should communicate expectations rather than prohibitions. Rules are best developed through the collaborative efforts of students and teacher (Thorson, 1996). When students are involved in developing rules, the rules become "our rules" rather than "the teacher's rules." When rules are set collaboratively, they may be changed only through discussion and consensus (Cheney, 1989).

Rules should be posted in a highly visible location in the classroom and reviewed frequently (Blankenship, 1986). During the initial weeks of the school year, rules should be reviewed daily. Teachers should give students repeated examples of the behaviors that a student demonstrates when following the rules. The function of a rule is to encourage appropriate behavior and prevent inappropriate behavior. Teachers are responsible for enforcing rules with fairness and consistency (Reith and Evertson, 1988).

Four or five rules are more than adequate to govern classroom behavior. They should be general in nature—but not so general as to be meaningless. Examples of rules are:

- Be polite and helpful.
- Keep your space and materials in order.
- Take care of classroom and school property.

Some practitioners have certain highly specific rules. Examples are:

- Raise your hand before speaking.
- Leave your seat only with permission.
- Only one person in the restroom at a time.

Joyce, Joyce, and Chase (1989) remind teachers that students whose behavior is rule-governed (under control of reinforcers) may become insensitive to environmental conditions that make rule-following inappropriate. To prevent the development of environmental insensitivity due to rule-following, they suggest that students (a) be exposed to contingencies incompatible with specific rules, (b) be provided various tasks for meeting the objective of the rule, (c) be exposed to natural contingencies for appropriate behavior, and (d) be overtly aided to make transitions from rule-governed behaviors that were in effect in previous environments.

Schedules

A schedule is the order in which activities are planned to occur. Rosenshine (1977) found that student learning increases when teachers allocate considerable time for instruction and maintain a high level of task engagement. To develop an effective schedule, two important variables are considered: allocated time and engaged time (Shea and Bauer, 1987). Englert (1984) describes allocated time as the amount of time scheduled for a specific subject or activity. Engaged time is the amount of time students actually participate in the scheduled subject or activity. The literature indicates that generally half of the typical school hour is allocated to instruction, and most students are engaged only 70 to 80 percent of that time (Hollowood, Salisbury, Rainforth, & Palombaro, 1995). To increase engaged time, teachers must plan the schedule with care, begin and end activities on time, facilitate transitions from activity to activity, and assign scheduled activities as a first priority rather than engaging in spontaneous, alternative activities.

Scheduling is a dynamic process—a continuous and creative activity (Gallagher, 1988). Schedules must be revised throughout the school year in response to emerging student needs and changing behaviors, as well as the demands of the curriculum. The two most important kinds of scheduling are overall program scheduling and individual program scheduling.

Schedules are based on individual and group priorities. After the practitioner determines priorities, available time, personnel, materials and equipment must be fitted into those priorities. Shea and Bauer (1987) suggested the step-by-step process for schedule development presented in Table 11.4.

The Premack (1965) principle is often used in developing schedules. The Premack schedule is based on the presumption that behaviors that occur frequently and freely can be used as reinforcers for less frequently occurring behaviors. To apply this principle to scheduling, the teacher first marks each period of time with a plus (+) or a minus (−). The plus denotes behaviors that naturally occur at a high frequency level, and the minus sign denotes those that generally do not. It is suggested that the

Table 11.4   Schedule development process

1. Using each student's individualized education program or personal records as a data base, complete a 3x5 card for each goal for each student. On the card, write the student's name, current level of functioning, and short-term objectives with reference to the goal.

2. Group students by sorting cards by goals and functional levels.

3. Choose a specific schedule format. Reproduce the format on a standard sheet of paper. In the left-hand column, write the time periods available for scheduling.

4. Write the "given" activities (lunch, recess, art, music, speech therapy, physical education) on the schedule. Resource teachers must write the "givens" imposed by other teachers' schedules. Write the times needed for transitions. Write the times needed for data recording, communicating with others, and preparing for instruction.

5. Write group activities on the schedule. Adjust these until there are no conflicts with other scheduled activities.

6. Review and discuss the proposed schedule with others serving the students (general education teachers, special education teachers, therapists, parents, instructional specialists) to minimize conflicts.

7. Establish procedures for reevaluating the schedule.

day begin and end with + activities. The following is a partial Premack schedule.

+9:00	Free time to play and interact quietly
−9:10	Return to seats for individual study during attendance, lunch count, and so on
+9:15	Circle or sharing time
−9:35	First reading group, individual study for others
+9:55	Transition time, drinks, restroom
−10:00	Second reading group, individual study for others
+10:20	Recess

Block scheduling is a strategy often used in inclusive settings to re-structure the distribution of school resources, such as staff, space, and time (Snell, Lowman, & Canady, 1996). When working in blocks, students with disabilities are assigned to their grade level; assignments are balanced so that no teacher receives significantly more students with disabilities than another. Snell and associates also suggest that students with more extensive needs be assigned to teachers who had volunteered to have them, and those who had fewer students overall.

In a sample morning block, four base homeroom teachers, two special education teachers, two instructional assistants, and support staff are assigned to a grade or set of grades. Students work with teachers in small, teacher-directed groups; activities may include writing lab, working on reading comprehension, language arts, or the reading-writing connection. When students are not working in teacher-directed groups, they attend the Extension Center. In the Extension Center, all students receive enrichment and support, including journal writing, reading, library use, computer, group projects, cooperative learning, English as a second language, counseling, speech, or tutoring. The Extension Center is staffed by a variety of people, including special educators, Title I teachers, tutors, or support staff.

Another variable to be considered when developing schedules is the length of time of the activity periods. As a rule, it is more effective to begin the school year with brief activity periods, and gradually lengthen them as the year progresses; the students then learn the schedule and become more quickly involved in the learning process.

Transitions

Transitions are the movement from one activity to another. According to Rosenkoetter and Fowler (1986), transitions are complex activities that frequently result in classroom disruptions. They should be carefully planned to minimize the loss of instructional time. Effective transitions teach students self-management skills.

In a study of 22 classes (15 general and 7 special education) for young children (4- and 5-year-olds), Rosenkoetter and Fowler (1986) found that, on average, 18 percent of the school day was devoted to transitions. Special and general education classes differed with regard to the management of transitions. General education teachers used more cues than special education teachers. Special teachers used children's names as cues; general education teachers used group names. Individual cues in the general education classroom were rare; when special education teachers used group cues, they would follow with individual cues. Special teachers employed one- and two-step directions; regular teachers employed three- and four-step directions. Special teachers often used proximity control. It was noted that in special education class, children frequently were not held responsible for their materials, and were not taught group movement.

According to Shea and Bauer (1987), teachers may use the following activities to facilitate transitions:

- Model appropriate transition behaviors;
- Signal or cue the beginning and ending of activities;
- Remediate transition difficulties such as slowness and disruptiveness;
- Observe student performance during transitions and, if the student is having difficulties, repeat the rules and practice until they are firmly established behaviors;
- Reinforce quick and quiet transitions.

Buck (1999) presents a series of questions to facilitate students during transitions. He suggests that teachers ask themselves:

1. Have I clearly defined the kind of behavior I expect during transitions?
2. Have I communicated these expectations clearly?
3. Have I assessed the way students appear to understand my expectations?
4. Have I assessed the extent to which the students' behavior matches my expectations?
5. Have I assessed the degree to which the behavior of certain students varies from those of other students?
6. Have I periodically restated my expectations?
7. Have I provided periodic feedback to students regarding their behavior in relation to my expectations?

Cueing

Cueing is the process of using symbols to communicate essential messages between individuals. The use of cueing reduces interruptions of ongoing activities, and the symbols facilitate structure and provide routine

(Legare, 1984; Olsen, 1989). Cueing is a proactive, preventive behavior management intervention (Slade and Callaghan, 1988). Various cues or help signs can be used in the classroom. Such cues are most effective if developed collaboratively by the students and teacher at the beginning of the school year. Among the many cues that may be implemented are the following:

- Students place a sign or flag in a holder at their work station when assistance is needed;
- Students write their names on the chalkboard when assistance is needed;
- Students take a ticket (as in the supermarket deli) when assistance is needed;
- Students use a cardboard symbol, such as the letter "R" for restroom, "P" for pencil, "W" for water, in place of frequently asked questions;
- Teacher uses traffic signals to control noise levels (red = too loud, yellow = caution, green = noise level OK);
- Teacher turns lights off and on to signal the beginning and ending of activities.

In addition, teachers may wish to use body language, hand signals, smiles and frowns, and schedules as cues. The design and use of cues in the classroom is only limited by the imagination of the teacher and students. Of course, cues should not be used in lieu of appropriate verbal communication.

Procedures

The teacher is responsible for developing a variety of classroom and non-classroom procedures designed to facilitate instruction and appropriate behavior (Walker and Shea, 1995; Emmer, Evertson, Clements, and Worsham, 1997; Evertson, Emmer, Clements, and Worsham, 1997).

Procedures should be established to facilitate the care of students' desks and storage areas. They are established for the number of students permitted in various areas of the room at one time, and for the use of the pencil sharpener, reference materials, and other shared items. Procedures for the use and care of common and personal instructional materials must be developed, and procedures should be made with regard to students' and teachers' personal space and possessions.

Procedures are needed for the use of nonclassroom space and facilities such as restrooms, drinking fountains, offices, library, media rooms, resource rooms, and other areas. The movement of individual students and groups within the school building, and of students leaving the classroom must be regulated. Playground activity guidelines must be developed to facilitate fair play, safety, and maximize enjoyment. Special procedures are frequently needed for the lunchroom because of the large number of students in the facility, and the limited time and space available.

The practitioner must also develop procedures for a variety of individual, small group, and whole group activities. Policies should be developed for the conduct of discussions, the answering of questions during class, talking among students, out-of-seat behavior, and so on. Students are instructed about the cues and prompts the teacher will use to attain student attention. Procedures are developed for making assignments to work groups, assigning home study, distributing supplies and materials, turning in work, and returning work, and completing missing assignments. Students should know what they are expected to do when they have completed assignments and have unscheduled time available.

During small group activities, students should know the cues the teacher uses to begin and end, what materials to bring to group, and behavioral expectations. Students who are not in a particular small group must know what is expected of them during other students' small group activities. Students working individually must know how to obtain their work, where they are to work, what work to do, how to signal for assistance, and what to do when their work is completed.

It is wise to establish standard procedures for beginning and ending the school day and each period. Students should know the procedures for reporting after an absence, tardiness, and early dismissal. Procedures should be established for the selection and duties of classroom helper, and such activities should be shared by all of the students. Finally, procedures are needed for expected conduct during interruptions and delays, fire, tornado or earthquake drills, and other infrequent and unplanned occurrences.

Structuring Instruction

In his review of over 180 intervention studies, Swanson (1999) reports that class-wide use of direct instruction and strategy instruction are related to the best predicted success for students with learning disabilities. He identified several components of classroom instruction that are important to increasing positive outcomes. These components include:

- careful sequencing of skills;
- drill-repetition and practice-feedback;
- breaking information into smaller units and then synthesizing the parts into a whole;
- teachers' asking of process and content-related questions;
- monitoring the processing demands of the tasks, carefully sequencing them from easy to difficult;
- using technology;
- using small groups with high levels of teacher interaction;

- supplementing teacher and peer involvement with homework;
- reminders to use strategies and ongoing modeling of problem solving.

An additional emphasis should be on using class-wide efforts to increase students' planning and self-regulation. Troia, Graham, and Harris (1999) reported that providing direct instruction in planning, where students learn to set goals, brainstorm ideas, and sequence their ideas, increased students' written responses. Instruction included a variety of procedures for inducing thoughtful application of the planning strategies. Such planning strategies have been successful in inclusive classrooms where general education teachers provided instruction to all students, including those with learning disabilities (DeLaPaz, 1999).

Specific teaching practices have also been related to class-wide mathematics instruction for students with learning disabilities. Miller, Butler, and Lee (1998) found that students benefited from step-by-step processes to guide their thinking and performance. The use of manipulatives and drawings were effective for instruction in both computation and word problems. Several interventions were particularly helpful, including providing students adequate time to respond, pausing during lectures, and the use of goals structures to increase motivation and achievement.

One serious issue in structuring instruction to support students with emotional/behavioral disorders relates to the paucity of research in this area (Gunter & Denny, 1998). Gunter and Denny (1998) suggest that teachers should monitor the rate of correct responses made by students with emotional/behavioral disorders in order to assess their academic performance. They found, unfortunately, that teachers of students with emotional/behavioral disorders often fail to provide enough information to students regarding the material and tasks being studied so that they can respond correctly. Gunter and Denny urge teachers to provide students with the information needed to respond correctly, and to increase their rates of praise to students responding accurately. The results of a study of teacher instructional behavior by Wehby, Symons, Canale, and Go (1998) concurred with Gunter and Denny's findings. They argue that successful teachers include instructional sequences that promote high rates of academic engagement and high levels of student responding. This creates a classroom environment where independent seatwork is limited, and social interactions are encouraged. In practice, teachers often attend to inappropriate behavior and ignore appropriate behavior (Wehby, Symons, Canale, & Go, 1998).

Arts Curriculum and Classroom Management

As described in the last chapter, the past decade has seen a shift in the manner in which behavior problems are perceived and managed; the new approach avoids punishment procedures, and, instead, seeks to produce desired change through individualized rearrangements of the environmental context, and development of effective repertoires of behavior. Dunlap, White, Arcadia, Wilson, & Panacek (1996) reported that individualized curricular adjustments produced substantial benefits to students in terms of their prosocial behaviors. Curricular modification emerged as a proactive intervention.

Visual arts, music, dance, and drama are art forms that have been used successfully with students with disabilities, particularly students with emotional/behavioral disorders. Numerous programs using the arts have been given credit for enhancing students self-expression, self-esteem, and social skills (King & Schwabenlender, 1994; Mills, 1987; Natale, 1996). Carrigan (1994) describes a Swiss-based program called "Paint Talk" that utilizes spontaneous painting to reduce emotional episodes and provide an alternative means of communication. In addition, the "Paint Talk" seemed to enhance self-expression and self-esteem.

An art-centered approach may contribute to the development of literacy (Anderson, 1994; Keefe, 1996). An arts workshop utilizing visual arts, music, dance/movement and drama, as described by Keefe (1996), gives students alternative entry points into learning. During the first weeks of the workshop, students are introduced to the arts. The next stage provides students with more in-depth exposure and demonstration of the art forms. After students have been exposed, teachers design instructional time around, (a) art talk, (b) work time, and (c) artist on stage. During art talk, the teacher shares, gives an explanation, and so on. Next, the students have time to work on individual projects. Finally, students share their finished artwork or perform during the designated "Artist on Stage."

Dramatics appears to have been particularly useful in facilitating social and emotional development, along with a sense of community (Bernstein, 1985; Jackson & Bynum, 1997). The benefits of drama for students with emotional difficulties may result from the collective experience of drama. For example, dramatization allows individuals to understand how they are more like one another rather than different (Bolton, 1985). Bernstein (1985) describes the Spolin Theater Games. These games develop physical awareness and interaction with the environment through group problem solving. As a result, the dramatic experience creates a harmony and mutuality that results in a sense of community. A key element in the success of this program is the role of the teacher as facilitator rather than director (Bernstein, 1985). Dramatics is particularly useful with culturally diverse students with emotional/behavioral disorders because they are able to learn skills needed for positive social interaction, "without shedding culturally significant behaviors" (Jackson and Bynum, 1997, p. 165).

Increasing attention has been paid to using literature and the arts with students with learning disabilities or emotional/behavioral disorders. Boswell and Mentzer (1995) describe the use of creative movement in the presentation of poetry. Through a program in which students listen, then explore movement to poetry, students are presented the opportunity to increase their appreciation of poetry, and to release excess tension through movement. DeGeorge (1998) uses literature to present aspects of friendship to students with learning disabilities. Kahn (1996) suggests using clay to improve self-image, increase task orientation, improve decision-making and problem-solving skills, delay gratification and develop patience, and increase handling failure and success positively.

School-Wide Structures

In his discussion of schools and students with disabilities, Knight (1998) suggests that a strong mental model about schools exists. This is illustrated by how little schools have changed in the past fifty years. Several implications arise when schools are viewed as learning organizations. Helping schools evolve into learning organizations, he contends, begins with educators reviewing their own implicitly held internal pictures about how schools should work. If the work of schools is to transfer knowledge, then practitioners should be able to translate research into knowledge that is applicable to the immediate concerns of the classroom teacher. Schools must become collaborative work structures in which authentic communication is an essential part of daily practice. Schools must also have a shared vision, and be a place where teachers feel they have authentic ownership, and feel empowered. Leaders are partners rather than patriarchs. The primary emphasis of the school as a learning organization is to give students competency to adapt to a mutable, unknowable future. He concludes that schools should confront their own learning disabilities, and invent better ways for teachers to learn.

Students are not particularly happy with current discipline structures in schools. In his report on student discussions of discipline, Thorson (1996) reports that students cry out for freedom from rote enforcement and standard procedures. He indicates that students believe that good educational practice and honest communication would avert many situations, and solve many problems without the need for punishment. Students admit freely that their youth and inexperience lead them to make foolish mistakes, and that they look to teachers and administrators for advice and counseling. In the study, Thorson found that the lack of meaningful interaction with adults was a major complaint of students.

Most discussions of school-wide programs involve school-wide discipline plans rather than school-wide learning plans. McLane, Burnette, & Orkwis (1997) contend that school-wide behavior management systems typically have the following common features:

- total staff commitment to managing behavior, regardless of the approach;

- clearly stated expectations and rules;
- clear consequences and procedures for rule-breaking behaviors;
- instruction in self-control and/or social skill strategies; and
- a plan to address the needs of students who demonstrate persistent, challenging behaviors.

Lewis (1997, 1999) describes "Effective Behavioral Support" as a system of school-wide processes and individualized instruction designed to prevent and decrease problem behavior and maintain appropriate behavior. In this system, teams develop the school-wide plan by clarifying the needs of the school, developing a team focus with shared ownership, selecting practices that have a sound research base, developing an action plan that establishes staff responsibilities, and monitoring behavioral support activities. In Effective Behavioral Support, Lewis suggests that first and foremost, faculty and staff must agree that school-wide behavior management is a top priority.

Another emerging model for school-wide behavior management involves plans that teach and support prosocial behaviors and identify school-wide responses. In Project DESTINY (Cheney, Barringer, Upham, & Manning, 1995), schools evaluate the use of their resources and de-

School-wide behavior management includes teaching prosocial behaviors.

velop school-wide management plans. In addition, school-wide social skills training programs are implemented, and classroom environments are structured to support cognitive and social development. In the model, behavior support teams are established, and crisis prevention and intervention strategies for students with serious problems are implemented. Family support networks, including community agencies, are developed.

Another example of a school-wide plan is presented by Nelson, Crabtree, Marchand-Martella & Martella (1998). This model emphasizes direct intervention approaches within and across all school settings, and relies heavily on teaching students acceptable behaviors. The school-wide plan has three interrelated components: (a) ecological arrangement of common areas of the school, such as hallways and the cafeteria; (b) establishing clear and concise behavioral guidelines or expectations for common area routines; and (c) supervising the common area routines to prevent disruptive behavior from occurring, and responding effectively when it does occur. School-wide management strategies include catching disruptive behavior early, and the use of a designated "Think Time" classroom. In Think Time, the student is given a precise request about the inappropriate behavior, given time to think over the request, and then debriefed. Afterward, the student rejoins the class.

Mendler (1997) emphasizes that systems should move beyond traditional models of discipline that coerce the student into short-term compliance. Rather, discipline plans should be developed to encourage students to learn new strategies for success in school and in life. Effective discipline, he argues, requires methods that focus on addressing these questions:

- Is dignity or humiliation elicited by the method?
- Is obedience demanded, or responsibility developed?
- Is the method effective?

School Suspension

School suspension is frequently discussed regarding students with learning disabilities or emotional/behavioral disorders. Farner (1996) described how staff in one school developed proactive discipline procedures that increased mutual respect throughout the school. The new discipline system had two primary components. First, a computerized, honor-level discipline system was put in place that emphasized student responsibility. Second, proactive discipline procedures were adopted that replaced a punitive system by focusing on meaningful consequences, rewards for appropriate behavior, and helping students take responsibility for their actions.

Morgan-D'Atrio, Northup, LaFleur, and Spera (1996) studied the use of suspension in a large, urban high school. Their results documented a high frequency of disciplinary referrals and suspensions, and poor corre-

spondence between the school's disciplinary policy and the discip
actions taken. In conducting individual assessments of students'
and academic behavior, Morgan-D'Atrio and associates documented
incidence of academic and social problems, as well as adjustmen
lems, among students with recurrent suspensions. The students v
recurrent suspensions were a fairly heterogeneous group, with
problems. Suspension was used on the premise that exclusion from the
classroom and school was a punishment. Though suspension is a punishment for some students, it was almost a relief for those who are frequently suspended.

Summary Points

- The teacher's stance has a significant impact on interactions within the classroom.
- Social skills curricula may support students in developing the peer re-lationships, work habits, and coping skills required in general educa-tion classrooms.
- Effective programs facilitate instruction through managing variables within the learning environment, including rules, schedules, transi-tions, cues, and procedures.

Key Words and Phrases

allocated time—the amount of time scheduled for a specific subject or activity

collaborative consultation—consultation in which the special educator and general educator work as a team to develop interventions for students with disabilities

constructivism—a philosophy about teaching and learning in which the student is viewed as an active, self-regulated learner who constructs knowledge in a social context

cueing—the process of using symbols to communicate essential messages between individuals

engaged time—the amount of time students are actually participating in a subject or activity

levels system—an organizational framework within which various behavioral management interventions are applied in an effort to change behavior

rules—the specification, in the form of an instruction, direction, or prin-ciple, of a relationship between two events

schedule—the order in which activities are planned to occur

self-control—the capacity to direct and regulate personal action (behavior) flexibly and realistically in a given situation

social skills curriculum—an intervention designed to help students increase their awareness and understanding of personal emotions, values, and attitudes through educational activities and, as a consequence, improve their interpersonal problem-solving skills

teacher stance—personal posture towards self and others, including theoretical orientation and instructional and management strategies

transitions—the movement from one activity to another

References

Amish, P. L., Gesten, E. L., Smith, J. K., Clark, H. B., & Stark, C. (1988). Social problem-solving training for severely emotionally and behaviorally disturbed children. *Behavioral Disorders, 13,* 175–186.

Anderson, F. E. (1992). *Art for all the children: Approaches to art therapy for children with disabilities.* Springfield, IL: Charles C. Thomas Publisher.

Bash, M. A. S., & Camp, B. W. (1985). *Think aloud: Increasing social and cognitive skills: A problem-solving program for children.* Champaign, IL: Research Press.

Bauwens, J., Hourcade, J. J., & Friend, M. (1989). Cooperative teaching: A model for general and special education integration. *Remedial and Special Education, 10* (2), 17–22.

Bernstein, B. (1985). Becoming involved: Spolin theater games in classes for the educationally handicapped. *Theory Into Practice, 24,* (3), 219–222.

Blankenship, C. S. (1986). Managing pupil behavior during instruction. *Teaching Exceptional Children, 19,* 52–53.

Bolton, D. (1985). Imaginary gardens with real toads. Reading and drama in education. *Theory into Practice 24,* (3) 193–198.

Boswell, B. B., & Mentzer, M. (1995). Integrating poetry and movement for children with learning and/or behavioral disorders. *Intervention in School and Clinic, 31* (2), 108–113.

Bryan, T., & Bryan, J. (1997). A curriculum approach to teaching social information processing: Amazing discoveries. *Learning Disabilities: A Multidisciplinary Journal, 8* (3), 133–143.

Buck, G. H. (1999). Smoothing the rough edges of classroom transitions. *Intervention in School and Clinic, 34* (4), 224–227.

Carrigan, J. (1994, Winter). Paint talk: An adaptive art experience promoting communication and understanding among students in an integrated classroom. *Preventing School Failure,* 34–37.

Carter, J., & Sugai, G. (1989). Social skills curriculum analysis. *Teaching Exceptional Children, 22* (1), 36–39.

Cheney, C. O. (1989, August). First time in the classroom? Start off strong! *Exceptional Times,* 4.

Cheney, D., Barringer, C., Upham, D., & Manning, B. (1995). Project DESTINY: A model for developing educational support teams through interagency networks for youth with emotional or behavioral disorders. *Special Services in the Schools, 10* (2), 57–76.

Dayton-Sakari, M. (1997). Struggling readers don't work at reading: They just get their teachers to! *Intervention in School and Clinic, 32* (5), 295–301.

DeGeorge, K. L. (1998). Friendship and stories: Using children's literature to teach friendship skills to children with learning disabilities. *Intervention in School and Clinic, 33* (3), 157–162.

DeLaPaz, S. (1999). Self-regulated strategy instruction in regular education settings: Improving outcomes for students with and without learning disabilities. *Learning Disabilities Research and Practice, 14,* 92–106.

Dollard, N., Christenssen, L., Colucci, K., & Epanchin, B. (1996). Constructive classroom management. *Focus on Exceptional Children, 29* (2), 1–12.

Dunlap, G., White, R., Arcadia, V., Wilson, D., & Panacek, L. (1996). The effects of multi-component, assessment-based curricular modifications on the classroom behavior of children with emotional and behavioral disorders. *Journal of Behavioral Education, 6* (4), 481–500.

Edwards, L. L., & O'Toole, B. (1985). Application of self-control curriculum with behavior disordered students. *Focus on Exceptional Children, 17* (8), 1–8.

Emmer, E. T., Evertson, C. M., Clements, B. S., & Worsham, M. E. (1997). *Classroom management for secondary teachers* (4th ed.). Boston: Allyn and Bacon.

Englert, C. S. (1984). Measuring teacher effectiveness from the teacher's point of view. *Focus on Exceptional Children, 17,* 1–14.

Evertson, C. M., & Weade, R. (1989). Classroom management and teaching style: Instructional stability and variability in two junior high English classrooms. *Elementary School Journal, 89,* 379–393.

Evertson, C. M., Emmer, E. T., Clements, B. S., & Worsham, M. E. (1997). *Classroom management for elementary teachers* (4th ed.). Boston: Allyn and Bacon.

Fad, K. (1990). The fast track to success: Social-behavioral skills. *Intervention in School and Clinic, 26,* 39–43.

Farner, C. D. (1996). Proactive alternatives to school suspension. *Journal of Emotional and Behavioral Problems, 5* (1), 47–51.

Field, S., & Hoffman, A. (1992). *Steps to self determination* (field-test version). Detroit: Wayne State University, College of Education, Developmental Disabilities Institute.

Flicek, M., Olsen, C., Chiverse, R., Kaufman, C. J., & Anderson, J. A. (1996). The combined classroom model for serving elementary students with and without behavioral disorders. *Behavioral Disorders, 21* (3), 241–248.

Forness, S. R., & Kavale, K. A. (1996). Treating social skill deficits in children with learning disabilities: A meta-analysis of the research. *Learning Disabilities Quarterly, 19,* 2–13.

Fox, C. L. (1989). Peer acceptance of learning disabled in the regular classroom. *Exceptional Children, 56,* 50–59.

Gallagher, P. A. (1988). *Teaching students with behavior disorders* (2nd ed.). Denver: Love.

Gartner, A., & Lipsky, D. K. (1990). Students as instructional agents. In W. Stainback & S. Stainback, (Eds.), *Support networks for inclusive schooling* (pp. 81–98). Baltimore: Brookes.

Goldstein, A. P., Spafkin, R. P., Gershaw, N. J., & Klein, P. (1980). *Skillstreaming the adolescent: A structured learning approach to teaching prosocial skills.* Champaign, IL: Research Press.

Goldstein, A. P., Spafkin, R. P., Gershaw, N. J., & Klein, P. (1983). Structured learning: A psychoeducational approach for teaching social competencies. *Behavioral Disorders, 8* (3), 161–170.

Gresham, F. M., & Elliott, S. N. (1990). *Social skills rating system.* Circle Pines, MN: American Guidance Service.

Gunter, P., & Denny, R. K. (1998). Trends and issues in research regarding academic instruction of students with emotional and behavioral disorders. *Behavioral Disorders, 24* (1), 44–50.

Harris, K. R., & Graham, S. (1996). Constructivism and students with special needs: Issues in the classroom. *Learning Disabilities Research and Practice, 11* (3), 134–137.

Hazel, J. S., Schumaker, J. B., Sherman, J. A., & Sheldon-Wildgen, J. B. (1981). ASSET: A social skills program for adolescents. Champaign, IL: Research Press.

Hollowood, T. M., Salisbury, C. L., Rainforth, B., & Palombaro, M. M. (1995). Use of instructional time in classrooms serving students with and without severe disabilities. *Exceptional Children, 61* (3), 242–253.

Jackson, J. T., & Bynum, N. (1997). Drama: A teaching tool for culturally diverse children with behavioral disorders. *Journal of Instructional Psychology, 24,* (3), 158–167.

Joyce, B. G., Joyce, J. H., & Chase, P. N. (1989). Considerations for the use of rules in academic settings. *Education and Treatment of Children, 12,* 82–92.

Kagan, S. (1989). The structural approach to cooperative learning. *Educational Leadership, 217,* 12–15.

Kahn, V. (1996). Shaping up with clay therapy. *Teaching Exceptional Children, 28* (3), 73–74.

Keefe, C. H. (1996). *Label-free learning:* Supporting learners with disabilities. York, ME: Stenhouse.

Knight, J. (1998). Do schools have learning disabilities? *Focus on Exceptional Children, 30* (9), 1–14.

Kohn, A. (1993). *Punished by rewards: The trouble with gold stars, incentive plans, A's, praise, and other bribes.* NY: Houghton Mifflin.

La Greca, A. M., & Mesibov, G. B. (1981). Facilitating interpersonal functioning with peers of learning disabled children. *Journal of Learning Disabilities, 14,* 197–199, 238.

La Greca, A. M., & Santogrossi, D. A. (1980). Social-skills training: A behavioral group approach. *Journal of Consulting and Clinicalm Psychology, 48,* 220–228.

La Greca, A. M., Stone, W. L., & Noriega-Garcia, A. (1989). Social skills intervention: A case of a learning disabled boy. In M. C. Roberts & C. E. Walker, (Eds.), *Case studies in clinical child/pediatric psychology* (pp. 139–160). NY: Guilford.

Legare, A. F. (1984). Using symbols to enhance classroom structure. *Teaching Exceptional Children, 17,* 69–70.

Lewis, T. J. (1997). *Responsible decision making about effective behavioral support.* Reston, VA: ERIC Clearinghouse on Disabilities and Gifted Education.

Lewis, T. J. (1999). Effective behavior support: A systems approach to proactive schoolwide management. *Focus on Exceptional Children, 31* (6), 1–24.

Martin J. E., & Huber-Marshall, L. 1995. Choice makes a comprehensive self-determination transition program. *Intervention in School and Clinic, 30* (3), 147–156.

McGee, J. J., Menolascino, F. J., Hobbs, D. C., & Menousek, P. E. (1987). *Gentle teaching.* NY: Human Science Press.

McGinnis, E., Sauerbry, L., & Nichols, P. (1985). Skillstreaming: Teaching social skills to children with behavior disorders. *Teaching Exceptional Children, 17* (3), 160–167.

McGinnis, E., Goldstein, A. P., Spafkin, R. P., & Gershaw, N. J. (1984). Skillstreaming the elementary school child: A guide for teaching prosocial skills. Champaign, IL: Research Press.

McIntosh, R., Vaughn, S., & Bennerson, D. (1995). FAST social skills with a SLAM and a RAP: Providing social skills training for students with learning disabilities. *Teaching Exceptional Children, 28* (1), 37–41.

McLane, K., Burnette, J., & Orkwis, R. (1997). School-wide behavioral management systems. *Research Connections in Special Education, 1* (1), 1–8.

McQuillan, K., DuPaul, G. J., Shapiro, E. S., & Cole, C. L. (1996). Classroom performance of students with serious emotional disturbance: A comparative study of evaluation methods for behavior management. *Journal of Emotional and Behavioral Disorders, 4* (1), 162–170.

Mendler, A. (1997). Beyond discipline survival. *Journal of Emotional and Behavioral Problems, 67* (1), 41–44.

Mercer, C. D., Jordan, L., & Miller, S. P. (1996). Constructivistic math instruction for diverse learners. *Learning Disabilities Research and Practice, 11* (3), 147–156.

Miller, S. P., Butler, F. M., & Lee, K. (1998). Validated practices for teaching mathematics to students with learning disabilities: A review of literature. *Focus on Exceptional Children, 31* (1), 1–24.

Mirenda, P., & Donellan, A. (1986). Effects of adult interaction style versus conversational behavior in students with severe communication problems. *Language, Speech, and Hearing Services in the Schools, 17,* 126–141.

Morgan-D'Atrio, M., Northup, J., LaFleur, L., & Spera, S. (1996). Toward prescriptive alternatives to suspension: A preliminary evaluation. *Behavioral Disorders, 21* (2), 190–200.

Morse, W. C. (1994). The role of caring in teaching children with behavior problems. *Contemporary Education, 66* (3), 42.

Nelson, C. M. (1988). Social skills training for handicapped children. *Teaching Exceptional Children, 20,* 19–23.

Nelson, J. R., Crabtree, M., Marchand-Martella, N., & Martella, R. (1998). Teaching good behavior in the whole school. *Teaching Exceptional Children, 30* (4), 4–9.

Nichols, P. (1992). The Curriculum of control: Twelve reasons for it, some arguments against it. *Beyond Behavior, 3* (2), 3–5.

Olson, J. (1989). Managing life in the classroom: Dealing with the nitty gritty. *Academic Therapy, 24,* 545–553.

Polloway, E. A., & Patton, J. R. (1997). *Strategies for teaching learners with special needs.* Upper Saddle River, NJ: Merrill.

Premack, D. (1965). Reinforcement theory. In D. LeVine, (Ed.), *Nebraska symposium on motivation.* Lincoln: University of Nebraska Press.

Reith, H., & Evertson, C. (1988). Variables related to the effective instruction of difficult-to-teach children. *Focus on Exceptional Children, 20,* 1–8.

Rivera, D. P., & Smith, D. D. (1997). *Teaching students with learning and behavior problems.* Boston: Allyn & Bacon.

Rock, E. E., Rosenberg, M. S., & Carran, D. T. (1995). Variables affecting the reintegration rate of students with serious emotional disturbance. *Exceptional Children, 61* (3), 254–268.

Rogers, D. L., Waller, C. B., & Perrin, M. S. (1987). Learning more about what makes a good teacher good through collaborative research in the classroom. *Young Children, 34,* 34–39.

Rosenkoetter, S. E., & Fowler, S. A. (1986). Teaching mainstreamed children to manage daily transitions. *Teaching Exceptional Children, 19,* 20–23.

Rosenshine, B. (1977). Review of teaching variables and student achievement. In G. D. Borich and K. S. Fenton, (Eds.), *The appraisal of teaching: Concepts and process.* Menlo Park, CA: Addison Wesley.

Sabornie, E. J., & Beard, G. H. (1990). Teaching social skills to students with mild handicaps. *Teaching Exceptional Children, 23* (1), 35–38.

Sale, P., & Carey, D. M. (1995). The sociometric status of students with disabilities in a full-inclusion school. *Exceptional Children, 62,* 6–19.

Schechtman, Z., Reiter, S., & Schanin, M. (1993). Intrinsic motivation of teachers and the challenge of mainstreaming: An empirical investigation. *Special Services in the Schools, 7* (1), 107–121.

Scheuermann, B., & Webber, J. (1996). Level Systems: Problems and solutions. *Beyond Behavior, 7* (2), 12–17.

Scheuermann, B., Webber, J., Partin, M., & Knies, W. C. (1994). Levels systems and the law: Are they compatible? *Behavioral Disorders, 19* (3), 205–220.

Schumaker, J. B., Hazel, J. S., & Pederson, C. S. (1989). *Social skills for daily living.* Circle Pines, MN: American Guidance Service.

Schumaker, J. B., Pederson, C. S., Hazel, J. S., & Mayen, E. L. (1983). Social skills curricula for mildly handicapped adolescents: A review. *Focus on Exceptional Children, 16* (4), 1–16.

Serna, L. A., & Lau-Smith, J. A. (1994–1995). Learning with PURPOSE: Instruction manuals for teaching self-determination skills to students who are at-risk for failure. Unpublished manuals. Honolulu: University of Hawaii.

Shea, T. M., & Bauer, A. M. (1987). *Teaching children and youth with behavior disorders* (2nd ed.). Englewood Cliffs, NJ: Prentice Hall.

Slade, D., & Callaghan, T. (1988). Preventing management problems. *Academic Therapy, 23,* 229–235.

Smith, S. W., & Farrell, D. T. (1993). Levels system use in special education: Classroom intervention with prima facie appeal. *Behavioral Disorders, 18* (4), 251–264.

Snell, M., Lowman, D. K., & Canady, R. L. (1996). Parallel block scheduling: Accommodating students' diverse needs in elementary schools. *Journal of Early Intervention, 20* (3), 265–278.

Story, C. M. (1985). Facilitator of learning: A micro-ethnographic study of the teacher of the gifted. *Gifted Child Quarterly, 29* (4), 155–158.

Swanson, H. L. (1999). Instructional components that predict treatment outcomes for students with learning disabilities: Support for a combined strategy and direct instruction model. *Learning Disabilities Research and Practice, 14,* 129–140.

Tharp, R. G., & Gallimore, R. (1988). *Rousing minds to life: Teaching, learning, and schooling in social context.* NY: Cambridge University Press.

Thorson, S. (1996). The missing link: Students discuss school discipline. *Focus on Exceptional Children, 29* (3), 1–12.

Thousand, J. S., & Villa, R. A. (1990). Sharing expertise and responsibilities through teaching teams. In W. Stainback & S. Stainback, (Eds.), *Support networks for inclusive schooling* (pp. 151–166). Baltimore: Brookes.

Troia, G. A., Graham, S., & Harris, K. R. (1999). Teaching students with learning disabilities to mindfully plan when writing. *Exceptional Children, 64* (2), 235–252.

Vaughn, S., La Greca, A. M., & Luttler, A. F. (1999). The why, who, and how of social skills. In W. N. Bender. (Ed.), *Professional issues learning disabilities: Practical strategies and relevant research findings.* Austin: ProEd.

Vaughn, S., Levine, L., & Ridley, C. (1986). PALS: Problem-solving and affective learning strategies. Chicago: Science Research Associates.

Walker, H. M., McConnell, S., Homes, D., Todis, B., Walker, J., & Golden, N. (1983). *The Walker social skills curriculum: The ACCEPTS program.* Austin: ProEd.

Walker, J. E., & Shea, T. M. (1999). *Behavior management: A practical approach for educators* (7th ed.). Englewood Cliffs, NJ: Prentice Hall.

Warger, C. L., & Rutherford, R. B., Jr. (1997). Teaching respect and responsibility in inclusive classrooms: An instructional approach. *Journal of Emotional and Behavioral Problems, 67* (1), 171–175.

Wehby, J. H., Symons, F. J., Canale, J., & Go, F. J. (1998). Teaching practices in classrooms for students with emotional and behavioral disorders: Discrepancies between recommendations and observations. *Behavioral Disorders, 24* (1), 51–56.

Wiener, J., & Harris, P. J. (1997). Evaluation of an individualized, context-based social skills training program for children with learning disabilities. *Learning Disabilities Research and Practice, 12,* 40–53.

Zaragoza, N., Vaughn, S., & McIntosh, R. (1991). Social skills interventions and children with behavioral problems: A review. *Behavioral Disorders, 16* (4), 260–275.

12 Accommodating Students in Inclusive Settings

TO GUIDE YOUR READING

After completing this chapter, you will be able to answer the following questions:

- What strategies facilitate inclusion for students with learning disabilities or emotional/behavioral disorders?
- What are roles for teachers in inclusive settings?
- What accommodations can be made for students with learning disabilities or emotional/behavioral disorders?
- How do students with learning disabilities or emotional/behavioral disorders fare in inclusive settings?

◆◀ *Christopher was sitting in his usual seat in his tenth grade Physical Science classroom. He was "front and center," as called for by his Individualized Education Plan. The teacher was lecturing from overheads, pointing out the role of "significant numbers" in measurement. While looking up at the screen, Christopher followed along with a note and study guide that his teacher had provided to him at the beginning of the week. As she proceeded through the lecture, Christopher filled out the outline provided, looking both at the study guide and the overheads. The teacher moved over toward Christopher, and put her hand on his desk. After calling on another student, she requested a response from Christopher, who responded calmly, knowing from her signal (her hand on his desk) that she was going to call on him soon. At the "two-minute warning," as the students were packing up their books, Christopher pulled out a sheet, circled whether or not he felt he stayed with the class, kept his hands quiet, and spoke appropriately. He then took the sheet up to the teacher, who circled her evaluations of his participation in the class and returned it to him. As the bell rang, Christopher joined the other students in the hall and moved to his next class.*

REFLECTION *Review the case of Christopher. Is Christopher identified as having learning disabilities and emotional/behavioral disorders? What accommodations were in place that supported his successful inclusion in Physical Science? What do you think would happen if these accommodations were not in place?*

Introduction

In this chapter, it is presumed that all classrooms are inclusive. A classroom may have

- learners from diverse cultural, ethnic, or linguistic groups, including African American, Asian American, European American, Hispanic American, Appalachian, and Native American, and all of the ethnic, religious, and cultural subgroups that these larger groups encompass;

- learners who vary in their ways of interacting, including males and females, learners with various challenging behaviors, and learners with identified emotional/behavioral disorders;

- learners who vary in their learning styles and rates, including all of the various mode preferences (auditory, visual, and kinesthetic), learners who are academically gifted or challenged, learners identified as having learning disabilities, and learners identified with mental retardation and developmental disabilities;

- learners who vary in their ways of gaining access to the environment, including any of a wide range of physical, health, visual, hearing, or communicative issues (Bauer & Shea, 1999).

As you proceed through the chapter, remember that students with learning disabilities or emotional/behavioral disorders, in inclusive settings, contribute to the already existing diversity in the classroom. "Inclusive" doesn't just pertain to disability, rather, it pertains to the wide range of abilities, interests, issues, and needs that are reflected in any classroom.

Strategies to Facilitate Inclusion

Issues of self-efficacy face both teachers and learners. If a teacher perceives himself or herself as able to meet the needs of the learners assigned to his or her classroom, then that teacher will find ways to meet those needs. The problem is not the child, but the context in which the child is attempting to function.

Children construct their own knowledge as a result of their interaction with the social and physical environments. The role of the teacher, from the constructivist perspective, is to function as one who is capable of and responsible for learning about the children within his or her care. The teacher uses this knowledge to construct practices that are developmentally appropriate for the individual children in particular contexts (Mallory & New, 1994). Bloom, Perlmutter, and Burrell (1999) contend that constructivism involves attending to and capitalizing on the social context of the classroom by creating a sense of community. In this community, every child gains a sense of belonging. The classroom is structured so that each child is actively engaged in problem solving, conflict resolution, and learning to self-manage his or her behavior.

In this role, the teacher engages in what is becoming known as "critical pedagogy." The teacher incorporates into the teaching and learning process the students' experiences and background knowledge, and creates authentic tasks that are meaningful to the students, and reflect students' interests. The teacher places emphasis on meaning rather than on form, and on creativity and divergent thinking rather than on correctness. The teacher interacts and dialogues with students rather than directs instruction, and assesses students by contrasting students' unassisted performances with their assisted performances on authentic tasks. To function effectively in a critical pedagogical classroom, teachers need to be well informed of the community history, the history of the cultural group with whom they are working, and community resources, including individuals as well as community centers, that can provide information and support both to themselves and to their students (Goldstein, 1996).

Students with disabilities are more and more frequently included in general education. Using the *Annual Report(s) to Congress*, McLeskey, Henry, & Hodges (1998) analyzed data related to placement settings of students ages 6–17, from 1988–89 through 1994–95. McLeskey and associates report the following changes in placement settings:

- sixty percent more students were educated in general education classes;
- sixteen percent fewer students were served in resource rooms;

- five percent more students were educated in separate classes;
- twenty percent fewer students attended separate day schools, residential facilities, or were taught in home or hospital settings.

McLesky and his colleagues (1998) speculate that the increase of general education classroom placement may be a result of moving students with mild disabilities from resource settings into the general education classrooms, along with the increase of students identified as having learning disabilities. Because of the increase of students with disabilities, particularly students with learning disabilities, who receive the majority of their education in the general education classroom, it is important to be aware of the impact this has on both the teachers and the students.

According to the *Twentieth Annual Report to Congress,* in 1995–96, more than 95 percent of students with disabilities ages 6 through 21 attended school with nondisabled peers. A total of 45.4 percent were classified as being educated in regular classes, meaning they were removed from regular classes to receive special education and related services for less than 21 percent of the school day. An additional 28.7 percent were in the resource room category, meaning they received special education and related services outside the regular class for 21 to 60 percent of the school day. About 22 percent of the students with disabilities were in the separate class category, meaning they were served outside the regular class for more than 60 percent of the school day. A total of 4.4 percent of students with disabilities ages 6–21 did not attend schools with nondisabled peers. Rather, they attended separate day schools, residential facilities, or received home or hospital services.

Schwartz (1996) contends that the goal of inclusion is more than about measured behaviors; it is about belonging and participating in a community of one's peers, and being supported to succeed in an accepting, yet challenging environment. The goals of inclusive settings are (Stainback & Stainback, 1990):

- meeting the unique educational needs of all students within the same classroom;
- helping all students feel welcome and secure through the development of friendships and/or peer supports;
- challenging every student to go as fast and as far as possible to fulfilling his or her potential;
- developing and maintaining a positive classroom atmosphere that is conducive to learning for all students;
- arranging the physical and organizational characteristics of the classroom to accommodate each student;
- providing each student with the ancillary services he or she needs to succeed.

Tomlinson (1995) provides several rules of thumb for differentiating instruction within inclusive classrooms. Teachers should be clear on key concepts and generalizations or principles that give meaning and structure to the topic, chapter, unit, or lesson being planned. All lessons should be engaging, and should emphasize critical thinking. In addition, there should be a balance between student-selected and teacher-assigned tasks and work arrangements.

Tomlinson provides several strategies for managing an inclusive classroom:

- have a strong rationale for differentiating instruction based on student readiness and interest;
- allocate slightly shorter time to a task than the attention span of the students who are working on the task;
- use an anchor activity (an activity linked to the instruction to which the students can return independently, to free up time for more individualized assistance); begin by teaching the whole class, then have half the class work on an anchor activity while the other half engages in different content-based activities;
- create and deliver instructions carefully;
- have a home base, where each student has a specific place with the materials he or she needs; beginning and ending classes or lessons from a home base enables students to use materials more effectively;
- design a way for students to get help when the teacher is occupied;
- give students as much responsibility for their learning as possible.

Vandercook and York (1990) indicate that in the inclusive classroom, there should be clear understandings among adults, adults and students, and among students. The goals for including the student should be evident to all involved, and the roles of all support persons should be very clear. Students should be empowered to be active participants in the classroom, with support personnel doing things with, instead of for, individual students.

Many strategies to facilitate inclusion are grounded in good teaching and common sense. As a result of a study of thirteen schools, Pearce (1996) suggests that teachers develop classroom rules, and focus on the structure of activities in their classroom. She suggests that teachers ask for help, using special educators and specialists to adapt the curriculum for all students. Teachers should be explicit with their students in regards to their expectations for participation in inclusive classrooms. Through the use of cooperative learning, peer tutoring, and other group work strategies, students should be helped to develop friendships. Finally, she suggests that teachers should learn when to change course and try something new to support student learning.

Developing social relationships among students in inclusive settings is a challenge. In an analysis of the efforts of general education teachers to facilitate social interactions in their inclusive classrooms, Salisbury, Gallucci, Palombaro, and Peck (1995) identified five themes. First, cooperative learning groups were helpful; they decreased competition among students. Collaborative problem solving was also helpful, as teachers worked with the students to capitalize on discussions of interpersonal issues that, if solved by an adult alone, may yield less understanding and social knowledge. Peer tutoring and roles for each student were essential to developing social relationships, as was structuring time and opportunity for the students to make connections on their own.

As more students with learning disabilities or emotional/behavioral disorders are included in general education classrooms, the use of instructional assistants to support those students has significantly increased. Giangreco, Edelman, Luiselli, and MacFarland (1997) described several key issues in the use of instructional assistants as a strategy to support inclusion. When instructional assistants are assigned to students rather than the classroom at large, significant problems arise relating to the assistant's physical proximity to the student. Giangreco identified several problems related to instructional assistant's proximity:

- Teachers demonstrated less ownership and responsibility for working with the student, allowing the assistant to determine how to help the student participate.

- Instructional assistants sometimes separated the student from his or her classmates, lining up the student last, or waiting until other students departed.

- Students became dependent on the assistants.

- The presence of an instructional assistant interfered with typical student-to-student interactions.

- Other students may be distracted by the instructional assistant.

- Instructional assistants presented instruction in a limited number of ways, rather than having the student participate with the class in the varied instructional activities presented by the teacher.

Giangreco and associates suggest that instructional assistants should be assigned to classrooms rather than to individual students. In addition, the need for close physical proximity of the instructional assistant to the student should be agreed upon by teachers, students, and parents. The role of the classroom teacher and school staff related to the instruction of the student should be very clear.

In view of the challenges of using instructional assistants effectively, natural classroom supports have emerged. Supports that occur naturally in the environment are more likely to help maintain behaviors that can then generalize to other environments (Barnett & Bauer, 1992). Peers are one of the primary sources of natural supports. Hanline (1993) provides the example of encouraging social interactions. She suggested a teacher's saying to a peer who is playing with clay, "Can Louise have some of those pies you're making?" Through modeling interactions, the teacher can further the social interactions of the students with learning disabilities or emotional/behavioral disorders. In some situations, the teacher may need to interpret the behavior of students as meaningful by, for example, making statements such as, "We can tell it's Louise's paper because she put an 'L' on it," or, "When Mark is waving his hands like that, he's excited." Hanline also encourages teachers to answer students' questions about students with disabilities as they occur. When a student asks, "Why does Michael hit when he wants stuff?" the teacher could reply, "Michael does not have many words yet, so the way he gets things is by hitting. When he hits, say, 'No hitting, Michael.'" With learning disabilities, additional challenges emerge because the student is generally very much like his or her peers, until a specific task is required.

Functioning in inclusive settings demands significant effort and work. There is a particular bias against students who demonstrate undesirable behaviors. Schumm and Vaughn (1992) reported that general education teachers were willing to serve students with disabilities in their classrooms as long as these students did not exhibit emotional/behavioral disorders. General education teachers were willing to make adaptations while students were taking tests, or working on instructional assignments. However, these teachers cited budgetary factors, accountability, access to equipment and materials, and the physical environment of the classroom as barriers to planning for students with disabilities. They cited class size, lack of teacher preparation, problems with students with emotional/behavioral disorders, and limited instructional time as factors that inhibit planning for students with disabilities.

Roles for Teachers in Inclusive Settings

As inclusive classrooms become more common, new roles emerge for teachers. Some teachers have discovered that using a constructivist perspective allows them to recreate their classrooms so that a more diverse group of students can feel a sense of belonging. Teachers are able to foster a sense of belonging, and a sense of caring for each other, by using rituals and ceremonies, reading aloud stories that highlight the importance of caring, helping children to develop self-management behaviors, helping students develop problem-solving skills, helping students see the possibilities for success, creating clear and shared expectations, fostering an attitude that mistakes facilitate learning, and creating a physical environment that promotes structured, but active, learning (Bloom, Perlmutter & Burrell, 1999). Each of these is an important characteristic of an inclusive classroom.

Ferguson, Meyer, Jeanchild, Juniper, and Zingo (1992) describe an "inclusion facilitator" who works as a broker (locating resources and matching them in a way which will not deter the formation of natural supports), an adaptor (developing and suggesting accommodations), and a collaborator (working closely with other teachers.) The three kinds of support which emerged for the inclusion facilitator included, (a) teaching support, both in the planning of teaching and actually teaching; (b) prosthetic support, having strategies to support what was happening in the classroom; and (c) interpretive support, providing explanations regarding the individual's disability, learning styles, and strengths.

The roles teachers assume in working with students with disabilities may be tempered by their assumptions about learning and students. Simmons, Kameenui, and Chard (1998) reported five conclusions regarding teachers' perceptions of factors that influence learning for students with learning disabilities. Teachers believed that:

- a great deal of responsibility for learning resides within and is determined by the student;
- the quality and design of published materials have little influence on student learning;

Teachers often collaborate in inclusive settings.

- commercial language arts programs are inadequate and require modification;
- most teachers have declarative knowledge of lesson inadequacies and some procedural knowledge of how to correct inadequacies;
- teachers are confident about their practices, and their ability to modify the inadequacies of materials.

In inclusive settings, teachers often act as team members, working collaboratively with other professionals. Coben, Thomas, Sattler, and Morsink (1997) explored the challenges of working both collaboratively with others and with consultants. The primary limitation they identified across team models was related to the perceived roles of special educators and general educators. Specifically, special educators were perceived as the consultant, and general educators were perceived as being in need of assistance. Rather than the traditional helper/helpee roles, Coben and associates propose an interactive teaming model in which all team members collaborate to provide direct and indirect services to students, share knowledge and expertise, and, as appropriate, "teach" each other their skills. Various team members become the "expert" depending on the problem being solved.

Accommodation

When general education teachers were asked how they adapted their classrooms for inclusion, two areas emerged: (a) structural arrangements, and (b) instructional arrangements (Ysseldyke, Thurlow, Wotruba, & Nania, 1990). In structural arrangements, teachers reported that they used another adult in the room, but did not vary their groupings. The most frequent methods of instruction were direct instruction, followed by cooperative groups, discovery learning, and independent work. The two most common instructional adaptations were (a) holding the student accountable for his or her performance and quality of work, and making students accountable for working to the best of their abilities, and (b) altering instruction so that the students could experience success.

In another study of adaptations, Fuchs and Fuchs (1998) report that there is little evidence that teachers routinely adapt instruction. In addition, few changes are made as a result of student difficulty. The most common adaptations reflect teachers' reducing their expectations for students. In response to these concerns, Fuchs and Fuchs developed methods to extend general education strategies for students with learning disabilities. They found that conventional general education classes, even with special education support, may not provide adequate specialized adaptations for students with learning problems. Routine adaptations can be enhanced with ongoing assessment information and peer-assisted learning strategies. However, the percentage of students with learning disabilities who benefited from these enhancements was smaller than the percentage of other students who had difficulty with achievement and profited from the enhancements. Not all students with learning disabilities benefitted from the adaptation. Fuchs and Fuchs reported that some general educators can meet the challenge of specialized adaptation. Some specialized adaptations reflect reliance on the same strategies even though there is a lack of effectiveness.

Content area subjects may present unique challenges for students with learning disabilities or emotional/behavioral disorders. Mastropieri and Scruggs (1992) suggest that science instruction may be one content area appropriate for inclusion. Science teachers need to be aware of effective strategies to meet the challenges of the science classroom. Specific challenges include: textbooks with extended reading assignments, vocabulary, whole-class lectures, and group activity-based lessons (Munk, Bruckert, Call, Stoehermann, & Radandt, 1999). Munk and colleagues (1999) summarized empirically validated strategies that enhance the performance of students with learning disabilities on textbook-based instruction and recall and active academic responding. Strategies to enhance textbook use include: (a) prioritization of material with regard to what portion should be mastered and what can be presented as an overview or skipped; (b) preteaching vocabulary; (c) paraphrasing key passages; (d) providing study guides, graphics, and organizers; and (e) providing supplemental audiotapes. Further, performance during instruction can be enhanced with mnemonics, guided notes, response cards, and cooperative learning groups.

In their study of general education teachers' perceptions of test adaptations, Gajria, Salend, and Hemick (1994) reported that the majority of the teachers are aware of test adaptations, but may not use them because they are perceived as ineffective, difficult, or a threat to the academic integrity of their tests. Further, these respondents indicated they were more likely to use modifications that were applicable to all students. They were less likely to use modifications specific to individual students such as dictating responses, or taking tests in another location.

As Schumm and Vaughn (1992) reported, teachers have particular concerns about students who demonstrate behaviors that vary from the behaviors of their peers. In general education classrooms, students with learning disabilities may demonstrate difficulties in interactions, which may generate negative attitudes and judgments in others (Bryan, 1991). Students identified with emotional/behavioral disorders, by definition, have difficulty in interactions. However, as stated earlier, good teaching practices can address many of these concerns. If we relate the actions of teachers to what is known about learning, several implications evolve (Herman, Aschbacher, and Winters, 1992):

- If knowledge is constructed, then teachers should encourage divergent thinking and multiple correct responses, critical thinking, and various ways of self-expression.

- If learning isn't a linear progression of discrete skills, then teachers should engage students in problem solving and critical thinking.

- If students vary in learning style, attention span, memory, learning rate, and strengths, then teachers should provide choices in tasks, provide opportunities to reflect, revise, and rethink, and include concrete experiences.

- If students learn better when the goals and criteria for evaluation are clear, then teachers should engage students in defining goals and provide opportunities for self-evaluation and peer review.

- If students are to know how and when to use their knowledge and manage their own learning, then teachers should provide real-world opportunities, and engage students in self-evaluation.

- If motivation, effort, and self-esteem affect learning, then students should be encouraged to see the connection between effort and results.

- If learning is a social process, then teachers should consider group products and processes.

Social Functioning in Inclusive Settings

Vaughn, Elbaum, and Schumm (1996) reported data on the social functioning of students in the second, third, and fourth grades who participated in an inclusive classroom for an entire school year. The social functioning of students identified as learning disabled, low achieving, and average/high achieving was assessed at the beginning and end of the school year. The results of this study suggested that students with learning disabilities were less well liked, and more frequently rejected, than the average/high-achieving students. Although students' overall self-worth did not differ by achievement group, the student with learning disabilities demonstrated significantly lower academic self-concept scores than others. The students with learning disabilities did not differ from others on ratings of loneliness. They demonstrated increases in the number of within-class reciprocal friendships from fall to spring.

Vaughn, Elbaurm, Schumm, and Hughes (1998) investigated the social functioning of students with learning disabilities, low- to average-achieving students, and high-achieving students in two types of inclusive settings: co-teaching and consultation/collaborative. The co-teaching setting included a general education teacher and special education teacher who co-taught in the same classroom for the entire day. Although each assumed similar roles, the general education teachers tended to use whole-class instruction more frequently, while the special education teacher taught individuals or small groups more frequently. In the consultation/collaboration setting, the general education teachers were assigned a part-time teaching assistant and a special education teacher for one to two hours a day during Language Arts and Mathematics. The special education teacher led lessons, demonstrated adaptation, and worked with small groups of students and individual students with learning disabilities. In addition, the teachers had a formal 30-minute per week coplanning time. Social outcomes of the students were determined through measures of peer acceptance and reciprocal friendships, self-concept, friendship quality, and teacher perceptions of social skills. Compared to the co-teaching setting, students with learning disabilities in the consultation/collaboration setting demonstrated more positive outcomes on friendship quality and peer acceptance, and some increase in the number of reciprocal friendships from fall to spring. Additionally, the results indicated that students from all groups in the consultation/collaboration setting performed well socially. Researchers observed that a climate of high acceptance and high expectations for all students existed in the consultation/collaboration settings. In the co-teaching settings, it was observed that there was high acceptance, but high expectations were not always present. Interviews with teachers in the co-teaching settings indicated they were overwhelmed by the number of low-achieving students in their classes. The researchers suggested that more research is needed concerning the effect of clustering students with learning disabilities disproportionately in general education classrooms.

Farmer and Farmer (1996) provided an in-depth description of classroom social networks in an inclusive setting. The classrooms that they studied had well-defined social structures in which students affiliated with others who were similar to them on salient personal and social characteristics. Students with disabilities were well-integrated into their classrooms' social structure. Each classroom contained distinct clusters that occupied three roles within the classroom. The clusters were (a) prosocial, (b) antisocial, and (c) shy. The social behavior and personality of students with emotional/behavioral disorders appeared to vary substantially based on available affiliation partners. Farmer and Farmer concluded that the composition of students in a classroom appeared to affect the possible positions any individual would hold within the structure.

In a setting in which separate classes for students with learning disabilities were closed, and teachers of students with disabilities worked collaboratively with two or more general education teachers, Waldron and McLeskey (1998) reported that, in inclusive settings, when compared to separate settings, more students with mild learning disabilities made progress in reading in comparison to that made by their general education peers. In addition, students with severe learning disabilities made comparable progress in reading and mathematics regardless of the setting. Each student's program was built upon the general education program, providing "very good general education," instead of attempting to replicate special education in the general education classroom.

The academic outcomes of high-achieving, low-to-average-achieving, and students with learning disabilities in full-time placements in third through sixth grade general education classes were examined by Klingner, Vaughn, Hughes, Schumm, and Elbaum (1998). Teachers of these classes received a year-long professional development program that focused on literacy development and targeted instructional practices that (a) demonstrated effectiveness in general education classrooms with students with learning disabilities, (b) promoted literacy learning, (c) were multilevel, and (d) did not require extraordinary expenditures. Academic outcomes were measured by standardized and informal measures. All high-achieving students, and most students with learning disabilities, showed gains over the year. Compared to students with learning disabilities, fewer low-to-average-achieving students improved, and very poor readers made no progress. The researchers concluded that very poor readers need both in-class support and daily intensive, one-on-one instruction.

Martinez (1995) emphasizes working with general education students about including students with learning disabilities or emotional/behavioral disorders in their classrooms. In the first phase, he suggests that the special educator visit the class to talk about disabilities, how they affect children, and some of the tools used in teaching special education students. In this first phase, students are encouraged to ask their questions, and simulation activities may be conducted. In the second phase, the general education students visit the special education program and are provided opportunities to discuss their observations and ask questions. In the third phase, the general education students and special education student interact in a culminating activity.

Summary Points

- Increasing numbers of students with learning disabilities or emotional/behavioral disorders are being served in general education classrooms.
- Many strategies to support inclusion are grounded in good teaching and common sense.
- Inclusive classrooms require new roles for general and special education teachers.

Key Words and Phrases

anchor activity—an activity linked to instruction to which the student can return independently, to free up time for more individualized assistance

home base—a specific place where each student has the materials he or she needs for learning; a place to begin and end activities/lessons *inclusion*—the philosophy that all students, regardless of disability, are a vital and integral part of the general education system; special needs services addressing the Individualized Education Plan goals and objectives of students with disabilities are rendered in the general education classroom

inclusion facilitator—a support person who serves as a broker (locating resources and matching them to student needs in a way that will not deter the formation of natural supports), an adaptor (developing and suggesting accommodations), and a collaborator (working closely with other teachers)

natural supports—the least intrusive and least contrived supports available

References

Barnett, D. W., & Bauer, A. M. (1992). *Designing interventions for young children: A model of service delivery for Ohio* (Grant Proposal). Cincinnati: Ohio Department of Education, Division of Early Childhood.

Bauer, A. M., & Shea, T. M. (1999). *Inclusion 101: How to teach all learners.* Baltimore: Paul H. Brookes.

Bloom, L. A., Perlmutter, J., & Burrell, L. (1999). The general educator: Applying constructivism in inclusive classrooms. *Intervention in School and Clinic, 34* (3), 132–136.

Bryan, T. (1991). Social problems and learning disabilities. In B. L. Y. Wong, (Ed.), *Learning about learning disabilities* (pp. 195–229). San Diego: Academic Press.

Coben, S. S., Thomas, C. C., Sattler, R. O., & Morsink, C. V. (1997). Meeting the challenge of consultation and collaboration: Developing interactive teams. *Journal of Learning Disabilities, 30* (4), 427–432.

Farmer, T. W., & Farmer, E. Z. (1996). Social relationships of students with exceptionalities in mainstream classrooms: Social networks and homophily. *Exceptional Children, 62* (5), 431–450.

Ferguson, D. L., Meyer, G., Jeanchild, L., Juniper, L., & Zingo, J. (1992). Figuring out what to do with the grownups: How teachers make inclusion work for students with disabilities. *Journal of the Association for Persons with Severe Handicaps, 17,* 218–226.

Fuchs, L., & Fuchs, D. (1998). General educators' instruction adaptation for students with learning disabilities. *Learning Disability Quarterly, 21,* 23–33.

Gajria, M., Salend, S. J., & Hemrick, M. A. (1994). Teacher acceptability of testing modifications for mainstreamed students. *Learning Disabilities Research & Practice, 9* (4) 236–243.

Giangreco, M. F., Edelman, S. W., Luiselli, T. E., & MacFarland, S. Z. C. (1997). Helping or hovering? Effects of instructional assistant proximity on students with disabilities. *Exceptional Children, 64,* 7–18.

Goldstein, B. S. C. (1996). Critical pedagogy in a bilingual special education classroom. In M. S. Poplin & P. T. Cousin, (Eds.), *Alternative views of learning disabilities: Issues for the 21st Century* (pp. 145–167). Austin, TX: ProEd.

Hanline, M. F. (1993). Inclusion of preschoolers with profound disabilities: An analysis of children's interactions. *Journal of the Association for Persons with Severe Handicaps, 18,* 28–35.

Herman, J. L., Aschbacher, P. R., & Winters, L. (1992). *A practical guide to alternative assessment.* Alexandria, VA: Association for Supervision and Curriculum Development.

Klingner, J. K., Vaughn, S., Hughes, M. T., Schumm, J. S., & Elbaum, B. (1998). Outcomes for students with and without learning disabilities in inclusive classrooms. *Learning Disabilities Research & Practice, 13* (3) 153–161.

Mallory, B. L., & New, R. S. (1994). Social constructivist theory and principles of inclusion: Challenges for early childhood special education. *Journal of Special Education, 26,* 322–337.

Martinez, T. (1995). Building a bridge with special students. *Instructor, 105* (1), 44–46.

McLeskey, J., Henry, D., & Hodges, D. (1998). Inclusion: Where is it happening? *Teaching Exceptional Children, 31* (1) 4–10.

Munk, D. D., Bruckert, D. T., Call, T. S., & Radandt, E. (1999). Strategies for enhancing the performance of students with LD in inclusive science classes. *Intervention in School and Clinic, 34,* 73–78.

Pearce, M. (1996). Inclusion: Twelve secrets to making it work in your classroom. *Instructor, 106* (2), 81–84.

Salisbury, C. L., Gallucci, C., Palombaro, M. M., & Peck, C. A. (1995). Strategies that promote social relations among elementary students with and without severe disabilities in inclusive schools. *Exceptional Children, 62* (2), 125–137.

Schumm, J. S., & Vaughn, S. (1992). Planning for mainstreamed special education students: Perceptions of general classroom teachers. *Exceptionality, 3,* 81–98.

Schwartz, I. S. (1996). Expanding the zone: Thoughts about social validity and training. *Journal of Early Intervention, 20* (3), 204–205.

Simmons, D., Kameenui, E. J., & Chard, D. J. (1998). General education teachers' assumptions about learning and students with learning disabilities: Design of instruction analysis. *Learning Disability Quarterly, 21,* 6–21.

Stainback, S., & Stainback, W. (1990). Facilitating support networks. In W. Stainback & S. Stainback, (Eds.), *Support networks for inclusive schooling* (pp. 25–36). Baltimore: Paul H. Brookes.

Tomlinson, C. A. (1995). *How to differentiate instruction in mixed-ability classrooms.* Alexandria, VA: ASCD.

United States Department of Education. (1998). Twentieth Annual Report to Congress on the Implementation of the Individuals with Disabilities Education Act. Washington, DC: Author.

Vandercook, T., & York, J. (1990). A team approach to program development and support. In W. Stainback & S. Stainback, (Eds.), *Support networks for inclusive schooling* (pp. 95–112). Baltimore: Paul H. Brookes.

Vaughn, S., Elbaum, B. E., & Schumm, J. S. (1996). The effects of inclusion on the social functioning of students with learning disabilities. *Journal of Learning Disabilities, 129* (6), 594–608.

Vaughn, S., Elbaum, B. E., Schumm, J. S., & Hughes, M. T. (1998). Social outcomes for students with and without learning disabilities in inclusive classrooms. *Journal of Learning Disabilities, 31* (5) 428–436.

Waldron, N. L., & McLeskey, J. (1998). The effects of an inclusive school program on students with mild and severe learning disabilities. *Exceptional Children, 64* (3), 395–405.

Ysseldyke, J. E., Thurlow, M. L., Wotruba, J. W., & Nania, P. (1990). Instructional arrangements: Perceptions from general education. *Teaching Exceptional Children, 22* (4), 4–8.

13 Adolescents and Adults with Learning Disabilities or Emotional/Behavioral Disorders

TO GUIDE YOUR READING

After you complete this chapter, you will be able to answer the following questions:

- What are the unique characteristics and issues of adolescents and adults with learning disabilities?

- What are some of the issues related to vocational education and employment for students with learning disabilities or emotional/behavioral disorders?

- What are some of the issues related to postsecondary education for students with learning disabilities or emotional/behavioral disorders?

- What are some of the issues related to transition from school to work and community for students with learning disabilities or emotional/behavioral disorders?

- What supports are available for adolescents and adults with learning disabilities or emotional/behavioral disorders?

◆ *Ryan was a small, thin, twelve-year-old when he was identified as having a learning disability and emotional/behavioral disorders. Before his identification during sixth grade, he had passed his classes with the help of a tutor hired by his upper-middle class family. In addition, Ryan had weekly counseling sessions and monthly visits with a psychiatrist to monitor his medication for Attention Deficit Hyperactivity Disorder. Ryan's achievement continued to decline, even though he received accommodations and individualized assistance. When Ryan was fourteen, he was hospitalized for two weeks for depression, and, after he was considered stable with medication to manage the mood disorder, he was released back to school. At that time, Ryan discovered his love for animals, and became a constant volunteer at a local animal shelter.*

Ryan's freshman year in high school was extremely challenging. The transition from middle school to the large, multi-building campus was difficult for Ryan, and, when he started receiving frequent tardy slips for being late to his classes, he began cutting those classes. Ryan began to use marijuana, and subsequently moved on to using cocaine; his parents sent him to live with his grandfather in a small town in an attempt to remove him from the drug culture. Ryan enjoyed living on the small farm, and he especially enjoyed working with the animals. He joined 4-H, and he seemed to be making progress at school. However, when he turned sixteen and obtained his driver's license, he started hanging out with a group of kids who gathered in isolated areas and used alcohol. After he drove his grandfather's pick-up into a tree while he was under the influence of alcohol, he was sent back to his parents.

When he was 17 years old, Ryan faced the same high school that had earlier been so difficult for him. Ryan and his family decided he should get a job and begin working on his GED. By staying at home, and working in an area away from school, Ryan's family hoped that he would stay away from his drug-using friends. He refused to return to Al-a-teen, or Alcoholics Anonymous, because he felt that he was not really an alcoholic. Ryan got a paying job at a veterinarian's office, and enjoyed his work. His plan was to complete his GED and work on an associate degree in veterinarian technology. He turned his paycheck over to his parents to make sure he wouldn't buy drugs or alcohol. They gave him a daily allowance to cover lunch, a few indulgences, and transportation.

It wasn't long, however, until Ryan began using his daily allowance to buy alcohol. He missed days at work, and was fired when his attendance became inconsistent. He began to shoplift, and, one day, walked into a convenience store and grabbed money out of an open register while the clerk was giving another customer change. The clerk grabbed a pistol under the counter and shot Ryan. Ryan is now in the hospital, facing charges of robbery.

◆ *Megan finally decided to take a big step and enroll in a graduate education class. Sitting in the first class, her stomach began to "tangle in knots" as she listened to the professor discuss the requirements for the class. Her self-doubts were increasing. Why did she ever think she could handle a graduate class? Her undergraduate degree had been a struggle. From the time she began taking her first freshman classes, it took her eleven years to get her undergraduate education degree. She started and quit five times. She enrolled in four institutions, two of which were community colleges. She changed her major three times.*

Finally, she felt as though she had achieved some success. She was a special education teacher in an urban district where teacher shortages were high.

She often wondered if she would have been hired if the district had not been so desperate for teachers. On the other hand, Megan felt good about herself as a teacher. She could relate very well to her middle-school students. She could put herself in their place, because she had been there. She had been identified as having a learning disability when she was in the fourth grade. She had struggled to keep up with her peers since kindergarten, but she was a "sweet little girl" who tried hard, and teachers were willing to help her and ignore some of · her apparent learning problems. But, by the middle of third grade, she had difficulty coping with the curriculum demands, and her behavior changed dramatically. No longer was she a "sweet little girl"; her behavior became aggressive. Finally, she was referred for special education services and was identified as learning disabled.

Through her flashback of past struggles and conquests with academics, Megan decided she could succeed in this graduate class just as she had done before—by expending an extraordinary amount of time and energy. She still had a few decisions to make. Would she need accommodations? If so, would she be willing to ask for them? Finally, she was still trying to decide if she should continue "passing," or disclose to her professor that she had a learning disability.

REFLECTION *Consider the case of Ryan, and reflect on your own high school experiences. What challenges would confront someone with learning disabilities? With emotional/behavioral disorders? What supports would be necessary for someone like Ryan? What about Megan? Is graduate study appropriate for an individual with her skills?*

Introduction

Generally, students do not "outgrow" learning disabilities or emotional/behavioral disorders. The outlook for students with learning disabilities or emotional/behavioral disorders may not be very positive as they approach adulthood. Narratives of individuals with learning disabilities present themes of isolation, undervaluing, and perceived oppression (Reid & Button, 1995). The National Adolescent and Child Treatment Study indicated that students identified as having emotional/behavioral disorders had serious problems in many domains, and the problems remained serious for these students at the end of the study (Greenbaum, Dedrick, Friedman, Kutash, Brown, Lardieri, and Pugh, 1996). In their review of the National Longitudinal Transition Study of Special Education Students with Disabilities, Browning, Dunn, Rabren, and Wheatstone (1995) reported that the transition outcomes for students have been disappointing, with school leavers entering what they refer to as segregated, dependent, and nonproductive lives. Teachers and parents rated students' skills in academics, language, social skills or effort lower than the students themselves, with teachers and parents perceiving students as having an overestimation of their ability (Stone, 1997).

Characteristics and Issues of Adolescents and Adults

According to Gerber (1994), conceptualizing learning disabilities as a life-span issue requires us to take a developmental perspective. However, most research concerning students with learning disabilities or emotional/behavioral disorders has been conducted during the school-age years, which last approximately 12 to 13 years. Research for individuals during their school career may not be generalizable to adult years, because development during school-age years is rapid and temporally compact, while a span of adulthood can be upward to 60 years. Developmental theorists (e.g., Buhler, Gouled, and Levinson) divide adulthood into phases, with adulthood beginning around 16 to 17 years of age. From a developmental perspective, adulthood is not a unitary construct, but rather a dynamic and complex stage that changes according to societal demands, transition, and relative stability (Gerber 1994).

In 1987, the Joint Committee on Learning Disabilities called for more research concerning adults with learning disabilities. For the most part, however, the research has focused on service delivery: transition from school to work, college services, rehabilitation services, adult literacy, assessment, and employment (Gerber, 1994). Most studies have been done with college-age subjects whose ages are usually not more than 30 years. High school follow-up studies typically focus on individuals in their early 20s. Few studies have included subjects who are 40 years or older (Gerber 1994). Therefore, as we discuss the characteristics of adolescents and adults with learning disabilities and emotional/behavioral disorders, it is important to keep in mind the ages of the populations that have been studied, and the limitations of generalizing the results.

Adolescents

Describing the results of a qualitative study, Barga (1996) reported that students with learning disabilities experienced labeling, stigmatization, and gatekeeping throughout their school years. In order to address these challenges, students relied on benefactors, self-improvement techniques, or strategies and management skills. However, students also reported that they devoted energy to avoid disclosing their disability, and created tension by "passing" as students without identified disabilities.

Academic Issues of Adolescents

In terms of writing, Wong (1997) reported that adolescents with learning disabilities have little awareness of the need to plan and revise. Their production problems are so extensive that it takes a long time to produce a small amount of writing. The adolescents' poor awareness of text structure, the writing process, and their own cognitive processes in writing has a deleterious effect on their writing. Students had little understanding of paragraph or story structure.

Shokoohi-Yekta studied whether increased course work in high school for students with learning disabilities enhanced performance on the American College Testing (ACT) entrance examination. Subjects included almost four thousand students with learning disabilities who took the ACT in 1991, with extended time or special test administration procedures. Three additional associated categories of students were included: attention deficit disordered, developmental arithmetic disordered, and dyslexic. These subjects were combined with the group of students with learning disabilities for a total sample of almost 9,000 students. About 79,000 students without learning disabilities also took the ACT. The results indicated that examinees with learning disabilities received lower ACT scores and earned fewer credits for the basic areas of study in high school. Overall, the number of credits earned for mathematics in high school appeared to be the best indicator of the ACT mathematics score for both groups. For English and Science, however, high-school average seems to be a better predictor. Considering all variables investigated, the group with learning disabilities was found to be less predictable with respect to ACT performance.

It is difficult to look at academic achievement in isolation. In a study of scholastic competence, Hagborg (1999) reported that students with learning disabilities who demonstrated adequate scholastic competence demonstrated greater measured self-worth than their peers who were not judged adequate in scholastic competence. Hagborg suggests that nonacademic success also bolsters scholastic competence. Though students with learning disabilities may have a history of school problems, they can achieve a sense of adequate academic self-concept.

Parental Expectations and Perceptions

Misano and Hodap (1996) used the National Education Longitudinal Study of 1988 eighth-grade students to examine the effects of child disability on parental educational expectations. They found that the type of disability did not significantly impact parental expectations. Rather, school performance, parent education, and race were found to influence parents' educational expectations for students with and without disabilities. Parents of children with and without disabilities were found to have similar expectations for the children's educational attainment. When the student's age was addressed statistically (students with disabilities were slightly older than those without), parental expectations were found to be slightly higher for the group with disabilities.

In a study to identify the needs of students with disabilities as they complete their final year of high school, Maliam and Love (1998) found that students who are ultimately involved in their educational programs had a better sense of the daily instructional process than did their parents. Students had more intimate knowledge of their job and life experiences. These students were able to express a direct working knowledge of the demands, successes, and challenges of their jobs. Maliam and Love report that parents of young people who left high school special education may have idealistic expectations in the areas of academics and social skills. Parents reported that their sons and daughters always needed more academic instruction and more social skills training. Students, on the other hand, reported that their attained skills were appropriate for their jobs. Parents were also more concerned regarding the future needs of their sons and daughters, whereas students were concerned with their current jobs. Whereas parents were concerned about their sons and daughters surviving on their own, students were more motivated to leave their parental household.

In comparing students with and without learning disabilities, Sabornie (1994) found no difference regarding self-confidence among students. When rated by teachers, students with learning disabilities were identified as more lonely, less proficient in integration, more likely to be victimized, and less likely to participate in activities, yet did not vary from their peers without identified disabilities in self-concept. In another comparison study, Geisthardt and Munsch (1996) reported that students with and without learning disabilities are similarly affected by stressful school events. They used the same coping strategies, even though students with learning disabilities reported a higher rate of class failure, relied more heavily on avoidance, and used fewer peers for support when they had academic and interpersonal problems.

Adults

The 1998 National Organization on Disability/Louis Harris and Associates Survey of Americans with Disabilities (1998) reported that Americans with disabilities continue to lag well behind other Americans in many aspects of life. Large gaps exist between the lives of adults with disabilities and other adults with regard to employment, education, income, frequency of socialization, and other quality of life issues. In addition, most of these gaps show little evidence of narrowing since the 1994 and 1986 surveys, and, in some cases, the gaps between variables in the lives of people with and without disabilities have widened. Employment remains the area of greatest challenge to individuals with disabilities. Only 30 percent of working age adults with disabilities are employed full or part time, compared to eighty percent of individuals without disabilities. Working age adults with disabilities are no more likely to be employed today than they were a decade ago, nor has the income gap between adults with and without disabilities narrowed. One in three adults with disabilities lives in households with less than $15,000 annual income. One in five adults with disabilities fails to complete high school, compared with only one in ten adults without disabilities.

Gaps in frequency of socializing, entertainment, and access to transportation and health care contributed to significant differences in life satisfaction, with only about one in three Americans with disabilities saying that they are very satisfied with life in general, compared to six out of ten Americans without disabilities. Though the proportion of persons with disabilities who are very satisfied had not declined since the 1994 poll, the proportion who feel that their disabilities have prevented them from reaching their full abilities as a person has increased considerably during the same time period.

Changes in the population of individuals with disabilities may have had some impact on the results of the survey. Adults with disabilities are more likely today than in the past to say that their disability is very or somewhat severe, that they are unable to work because of their disability, that their disability prevents them from "getting around," and that they need help from another person in work, school, or housework. If the population of individuals with disabilities has indeed become more severely disabled, there is a real danger that the gaps between the lives of individuals with and without disabilities will not only persist, but will widen.

On a positive note, a clear majority of Americans with disabilities believe that life has improved for people with disabilities over the past decade. Two out of three feel that things have gotten much better, or somewhat better, over the past ten years, and majority feel that access to public facilities, quality of life, public attitudes toward people with disabilities, how the media portray people with disabilities, and access to public transportation have improved since the 1994 survey.

In terms of adults with learning disabilities, Weller, Watteyne, Herbert, and Crelly (1994) suggest that many adults with learning disabilities use a "maladaptive" strategy of ignoring their disability and hiding their weaknesses. Yet many young adults with learning disabilities are independent, socially responsible, and successful individuals. In their study of social status and interpersonal behaviors, Weller and Associates found that factors such as acceptance of the disability, proficiency with pragmatic language, setting appropriate goals, and persistence in meeting goals may attribute to success. The problems that individuals with learning disabilities experienced as adolescents continue into adulthood. The most frequently mentioned characteristics regarding strengths and limitations include oral language, reading, written language, mathematics, study skills and attentional difficulties (Vogel, 1998). Based on input from adults with learning disabilities enrolled in a college setting, Vogel (1985 as cited in Vogel, 1998) identified some of the areas of greatest difficulty including concentrating in a noisy environment (reported by 72 percent), reading comprehension, spelling, grammar, and mathematics skills (62 percent), language issues such as punctuation and capitalization, writing compositions, recognizing misspelled words, and reading in front of a group (52 to 55 percent), difficulties with multiplication (45 percent), and keyboarding (33 percent).

According to Vogel (1998) the prevalence of learning disabilities among the adult population has been determined through estimates and self-reports. Estimates of prevalence rates of adults with learning disabilities have come from specific educational and workplace training environments, and have ranged from 10 percent to more than 50 percent. The percentage of adults who self-reported learning disabilities increased from 1.6 percent in 1985, to 3 percent in 1994 (Vogel, 1998). Using a nationally representative sample of postsecondary institutions, 2.6 percent of the students were documented to have learning disabilities. However, the prevalence of learning disabilities among students ranged from .5 percent in highly selective institutions, to 10 percent in open admissions colleges (Vogel, 1998).

The first national data base on adults with learning disabilities in the United States was compiled using the National Adult Literacy Survey, developed by the National Center for Education Statistics in conjunction with the Education Testing Service. The survey included, (a) direct assessment of literacy skills and activities; (b) language background; (c) educational and work experience, (d) health problems, and (e) disabilities, if any (Vogel, 1998). This survey was administered during a one-hour, in-home interview of a nationally representative random sample of approximately 25,000 individuals, at least sixteen years old, with the final target sample consisting of approximately 15,000 men (48 percent) and women (52 percent). Through a series of questions, 392 adults (3 percent) reported they had a learning disability, with a higher percentage of men (56 percent) reporting such than women (44 percent) (Vogel, 1998; Vogel & Reder, 1998a). However, when the participants were segmented according to literacy skills and years of school completion, the prevalence rate of learning disabilities among those with the poorest literacy skills was between 10 and 15 percent. There was no significant difference in incidence of self-reported learning disabilities between the African American and non-African American participants (Vogel & Reder, 1998b). A continuum of learning disabilities, from mild to severe, emerged from the data. The mean literacy score for women with learning disabilities was 15 points higher than for men with learning disabilities. This data contradicts other studies in which women with learning disabilities had significantly more severe reading disabilities, and poorer academic achievement skills, than male peers.

Vogel and Reder (1998a) make three points: (a) individuals still considered themselves as having a learning disability even though they had acquired a high level of literacy proficiency, (b) the high percentage of individuals who self-reported learning disabilities receiving scores at the lowest level underscores the persistence of literacy problems throughout the adult life, and (c) there seems to be no contribution of gender to literacy acquisition.

Mental Health Issues

The self-perceptions of fifty college students with identified learning disabilities and fifty without identified learning disabilities were studied by Cosden and McNamara (1997). The students with learning disabilities reported lower levels of scholastic competence and intellectual ability. Both groups were similar in their perceptions of global self-worth, and the importance placed on academics. Both groups related perceptions of global self-worth to perceptions of scholastic competence, cognitive ability, vocational skills, physical appearance, and social acceptance. More social acceptance and support from campus organizations were reported by students with learning disabilities. Whereas students with learning disabilities related support from organizations to their self-esteem, students without identified learning disabilities associated self-esteem with support from instructors.

The comorbity (co-occurrence) of emotional problems and learning disabilities has often been discussed. Though individuals with learning disabilities tend to be more anxious and depressed than their counterparts, there is wide variation in depression and anxiety among students with learning disabilities. Morrison and Cosden (1997) put forward two hypotheses about the wide variation of emotional adjustment. First, some subtypes of learning disabilities may present a high level of risk for depression and other emotional problems. Second, depression and anxiety may be the result of high levels of frustration, lack of control, and predictability that results from having such a disability.

Depression and anxiety appeared to be a significant problem among adults with learning disabilities according to Hoy, Gregg, Wisenbaker, Manglitz, and Moreland (1997). In addition to the results of their comparison of students with and without learning disabilities, Hoy and associates highlighted common themes from the students that focused on outcomes for adults with learning disabilities. They reported the following:

- Learning disabilities affect academic, vocational, and emotional health; these challenges continue and increase over time.
- Individuals with learning disabilities may demonstrate anxiety that has an impact on their daily life.
- Poor social skills among adults with learning disabilities may result in poor self-concept rather than cognitive processing problems.
- The emotional stress caused by growing up with learning disabilities may result in dropping out of secondary or postsecondary institutions.

Though it is often assumed that individuals with learning disabilities are more prone to substance abuse, Maag, Reid, and Vasa (1994) stated that the reported prevalence for alcohol use for students with learning disabilities was not higher than that of their peers without identified disabilities. The reported prevalence of tobacco and marijuana use, however, was proportionally higher for adolescents with learning disabilities.

Graduation

Graduating from secondary school is a challenge for many persons with learning disabilities or emotional/behavioral disorders. Oswald and Coutinho (1996) examined, state-by-state, the nature of variations in high school completion rates, and the impact of state-level child disability demographics and economic factors on the reason for exiting school for youth with emotional/behavioral disorders. High numbers of students identified as having emotional/behavioral disorders, high per capita income, in schools with high per pupil revenue were positively correlated with the exit by diploma rate. The percentage of the student population reporting their race as white was inversely related to exit by certificate. When the basis of exit was a certificate of attendance rather than a diploma, approximately half of the variance in state school completion was accounted for by ethnicity (percentage white), per pupil revenue, and residence in the Northeast or South. Almost one-third of the variation in school completion by diploma was accounted for by the rate of identification as emotionally/behaviorally disordered and per capita income. States in the highest quartile for per capita income and per pupil revenue accounted for the differences in rates of graduation by diploma.

Using telephone surveys, Murray, Goldstein, and Edgar (1997) determined the employment, postsecondary education, and parenting status of a cohort of graduates with and without learning disabilities. Results for employment rates indicated that graduates with learning disabilities were employed with a frequency similar to that of their peers without identified disabilities. However, 40 percent of the students identified with learning disabilities failed to graduate from high school.

In a further study of the National Longitudinal Transition Study (NLTS) database, Rylance (1997) explored predictors of graduating from versus dropping out of high school for 664 youths identified as having emotional/behavioral disorders. Almost 50 percent of the sample dropped out of high school. Participation in school-based counseling and vocational education were two factors significantly associated with high school graduation. Razeghi (1998) reported that one of the key indicators for dropping out was having repeated one or more grades in school. Students who repeated one grade were 50 percent more likely to leave school, and those who repeated two grades were 90 percent more likely to drop out of school than those students completing grades on schedule. In addition, students who left high school had poor grades, poor attendance, and limited participation in extracurricular activities. Young men who dropped out often experienced discipline problems and conflict with authority, and young women frequently became pregnant or married. A large proportion of the students who left school early were from economically challenged homes or single-parent households.

Gender Issues

The relationship of teenage motherhood to learning disabilities or emotional/behavioral disorders was studied by Rauch-Elnekave (1994). The majority (56 percent) of the girls in her sample tested one or more years below grade level in total reading and total language, and 36 percent scored two or more years below level in total reading on the CATS prior to their pregnancy. The girls' mathematics performance was stronger, with 36 percent scoring one or more years below grade level, and 20 percent scoring two or more years below grade level. Only two of the students had undergone testing and were receiving special education services. Another student was found to have been well below grade level throughout her school career, with significantly impaired verbal skills. She tested two standard deviations below the mean on a standardized IQ test, but had never been tested for learning disabilities because no teacher nor parent had ever requested it. The challenges confronting these girls had an impact on their babies, who were at risk for developmental delays and weaknesses in language and cognitive skills.

The long-term postschool outcomes of girls and boys with emotional/ behavioral disorders also differ. According to Levine and Edgar (1995), a serious problem confronting girls with regard to their participation in postsecondary education and employment was becoming pregnant and parenting. Parenting had a significant impact on the ability of girls to participate in postsecondary education programs. Benz and associates (1998) also found that women with disabilities are less likely than young men to be engaged productively in postschool employment and education activities. They reported that three factors predicted better outcomes: (a) student self-esteem at time of exit from school, (b) continuing instructional needs in personal-social skills, and (c) continuing instructional needs in vocational skills. Young women who experienced early parenting responsibilities, or who came from a family with a low annual household income were less likely to be engaged in productive work and educational activities. Young women were more likely to be productively engaged when they and their parents agreed on the student's postschool work and education goals.

Vocational Education and Employment

Federal and state laws have had a significant role in shaping vocational education for students with disabilities (Levinson, 1994). With these mandates, there has been an increase in school-based vocational assessment, vocational rehabilitation programs, and transdisciplinary vocational assessment for students with disabilities. Evers (1996) reports that studies published between 1985 and 1993 revealed a significant relationship between vocational courses or employment while in school and postschool employment. Evers suggests that vocational education for individuals with disabilities will continue to evolve as curricula becomes more consistent with demands in the workplace, and as school-to-work transition systems are implemented.

One of the issues related to vocational preparation of students with learning disabilities is that of eligibility. In their study related to definitions and eligibility criteria for adolescents and adults with learning disabilities, Gregg, Scott, McPeek, and Ferri (1999) found that while students were being served by vocational rehabilitation services in school, the state's special education definition was applied to determine eligibility. However, if services were sought outside of the school system, vocational rehabilitation departments used psychologists, and applied definitions from the Diagnostic and Statistical Manual of the American Psychological Association (DSM-IV). The differences between that definition and those used in schools could make students who may profit from the services ineligible.

Barriers to finding and maintaining employment are consistently encountered by students with emotional/behavioral disorders according to Schelly (1995). Their problems with verbal and nonverbal communication may be demonstrated by the ordeal of going through the interview process, poor posture, limited eye contact, voice tone, facial expressions, inappropriate dress, hairstyles, or jewelry. The students avoid risk-taking experiences, and lack follow-through in job seeking. Because of their fear of increased responsibilities and pressures, they may sabotage the situation. Students with emotional/behavioral disorders also have difficulties following instructions, and problems staying on task, accepting feedback, planning ahead, and demonstrating socially acceptable work behavior.

Positive changes, however, are occurring for students with emotional/behavioral disorders. Frank and Sitlington (1997) compared outcomes of students identified as having emotional/behavioral disorders for the classes of 1985, and 1993. They found that students from the class of 1993 demonstrated better outcomes than students from the class of 1985 in several areas, but graduates with emotional/behavioral disorders did not experience outcomes equal to those of their classmates without disabilities. Sixty-eight percent of the 1993 students were employed, whereas only fifty-four percent of the 1985 students were employed. However, in another study, Malmgren, Edgar, and Neel (1998), found that employment for students with emotional/behavioral disorders remained significantly lower than that of their peers.

Wiener (1995) argues that students with learning disabilities should not be coddled, because less than 200 percent effort is not accepted in the real world. He contends that in classrooms for adolescents, everything must be related to the real world. Assignments should be given clearly, and students should be given time deadlines and requirements to complete them. If work is not completed accurately, it should be returned. Wiener reported that when this standard was applied, parents, students, and other teachers were upset and shocked that an 85 percent correct rate was not acceptable, and that students were held accountable.

An additional option for students with learning disabilities or emotional/behavioral disorders is state vocational rehabilitation programs. Federal monies are provided to each state to run a vocational rehabilitation program, with guidelines provided by the federal government. Referral systems are typically in place for each school district to request services for individual students. However, school districts may not have adequate information to appropriately access these services, or to relay this information to the families. Dowdy (1996) suggests that one of the main goals of vocational rehabilitation is to educate families that a learning disability is a lifelong disability. He contends that some schools are guilty of just presenting goals to get students with learning disabilities out of high school, and not providing goals to prepare them after graduation. High school curriculum must produce outcome-oriented results in postsecondary education, vocational training, integrated employment, continuing adult services, independent living, and/or community participation. The use of vocational rehabilitation services may be of significant help to students with learning disabilities or emotional/behavioral disorders.

Several supports for adolescents and adults with emotional/behavioral disorders as they seek employment were suggested by Schelly (1995). The use of a functional community assessment, where strengths, interests, barriers, and support strategies are identified, is recommended. Volunteer short-term work trials, hands-on experience, and specific behavioral support may be helpful. Students with emotional/behavioral disorders may also need a modified form of supported employment; a consultant could help to educate employers, facilitate problem-solving and effective communication, and provide behind-the-scenes support. Students may need specific help in career skills preparation, with an experiential community-based career skills curriculum. Finally, the student, employer, and employment consultant may need to sign a problem-solving agreement to facilitate open communication among all parties, and to allow everyone to plan ahead. Schelly suggests that natural consequences should be allowed to occur. If the students continually act out, or refuse to take steps to correct their disruptive behavior, the best option may be the natural consequence of losing their job.

Gender and Employment

When males with learning disabilities graduate from high school, their outcomes are far more positive than females (Goldstein, Murray, & Edgar, 1998). Goldstein and associates report that male graduates with learning disabilities, when compared with females with learning disabilities and their nonidentified peers, had the highest average earning and employment hours per week in early postgraduation years. However, in later postgraduation years this changed, probably when the individuals without learning disabilities completed college. Female graduates with learning disabilities, however, had the lowest earnings and worked the least number of hours each week. Levine and Edgar (1994) hypothesize that

Job experience while in school is one factor that contributes to a better postschool outcome.

some of the discrepancy between males and females may be due to females dedicating their time to parenting rather than employment outside the home.

Doren and Benz (1998) report that young women with disabilities are more likely to experience poorer postschool employment outcomes than young men with disabilities. Their findings indicated that two factors predict better outcomes for both young men and young women with disabilities: (a) having two or more job experiences while in high school, and (b) having used the self–family–friend network to find their postschool job. Females who came from a family with a low household annual income, who had low self-esteem at the time of exit from high school, and who fit both these characteristics were much less likely to be competitively employed out of school than females who did not fit these characteristics.

The finding that young women with disabilities were less likely to be competitively employed than young men with disabilities was also reported by Fulton and Sabornie (1994). The young women with disabilities who did hold jobs were more likely than young men to, (a) work in lower status occupations, (b) work fewer hours per week, (c) earn lower wages per hour, (d) hold jobs that offered few or no benefits, and (e) experienced greater job instability.

Americans with Disabilities Act

The Americans with Disabilities Act (ADA) has had a significant impact on the employment of students with learning disabilities or emotional/behavioral disorders. However, Anderson, Kazmierski, and Cronin (1995) suggest that accommodations for individuals with learning disabilities or emotional/behavioral disorders are not as readily accepted as those for individuals with visible physical disabilities. They suggest that an unwillingness to generate accommodations may be due to a general tendency to view physical disabilities in a more positive light than other disabilities, a limited experience, and a lack of knowledge. Anderson and associates present a list of skills which support students in seeking employment and using the American with Disabilities Act appropriately. These skills are presented in Table 13.1.

Postsecondary Education

Several variables have emerged as predictive of postsecondary education for students with disabilities. Halpern, Yavonoff, Doren, and Benz (1996) counted all forms of postsecondary education or training as participation, including programs designed specifically for people with disabilities. They reported that significant predictors of participation were:

- high scores on a functional achievement inventory;
- completing instruction successfully in certain relevant areas;

Table 13.1 Skills for Students Seeking Employment

Students should be able to:

- demonstrate self-advocacy and self-determination
- articulate their strengths and weaknesses
- anticipate difficult tasks and generate solutions
- understand the requirements of the Americans with Disabilities Act and their rights under the law
- recognize appropriate modifications for various types of job tasks
- accept and act on suggestions for improvement in their work
- use negotiation
- locate employment and advocacy resources in the community
- demonstrate good general work habits
- participate fully in transition planning at the secondary level
- participate in paid employment or training situations prior to leaving secondary school

(Anderson and associates, 1995)

- participating in transition planning;
- parent satisfaction with instruction received by the student;
- student satisfaction with instruction received;
- parent perception that the student no longer needed help in certain critical skill areas.

Four challenges that often emerge for students with disabilities when they make the transition from school to college or other postsecondary institutions were described by Garten, Rumrill, and Serebreni (1996). They report that, in post-secondary programs, there is (a) a decrease in teacher–student contact, (b) an increase in academic competition, (c) a change in personal support network, and (d) a loss of the protective public school environment. Many skills become necessary for a successful transition to postsecondary education. In terms of general adjustment, students need to be able to act as self-advocates, to handle frustration, to be able to solve social problems, to demonstrate social interactions similar to other students in college, and to identify and maintain mentor relationships. Academically, adolescents need help in preparing for college entrance examinations, general test-taking, career awareness, goal setting, academic remediation, learning strategies, and developing a plan for the transition to college. There should also be linkages and orientation to the post-secondary program. The possibility for a specific orientation and support group, including a buddy system, is discussed.

Several issues related to students with learning disabilities who are attending universities are illustrated in the "Guckenberger case" (Elswit, Geetter, & Goldberg, 1999). Elswit and associates relate that during the early 1990s, Boston University was perceived as a supportive environment for students with learning disabilities. Because of that perception, "self-identified" applicants with learning disabilities increased. During the spring and summer of 1995, the provost was critical of the impact of the learning disabilities "movement" on the educational process, and requested that all recommended accommodations be sent to the provost's office for review. After reviewing several files, he concluded that criteria for learning disabilities and accommodations were unclear, and that the documentation was poor. As a result, he prescribed standards for further accommodations, and indicated that evaluations had to be conducted within three years of the request for accommodations. Students were notified that their requests for accommodations were denied, or that they needed to be re-evaluated to document their learning disability. A lawsuit was filed asserting that the university had violated state and federal laws, breached its contract with students with learning disabilities, caused emotional distress, and created a hostile learning environment. The university was found to have violated federal law because sufficient prior notice was not provided to students regarding the policy change. The policy for re-evaluation every three years was upheld. In addition, the court ruled that the university does not have to modify degree requirements to provide course substitutions for students with learning disabilities.

Siegel (1999) argues that the *Guckenberger v. Boston University* case is grounded in a fundamental issue of learning disability. Postsecondary institutions must decide whether a student who requests accommodations truly has a learning disability, though the field of learning disabilities itself does not provide clear guidelines. In addition, course substitution may be considered a reasonable accommodation; yet, under the Americans with Disabilities Act, an institution can refuse to provide a reasonable accommodation if it results in a fundamental alteration of an academic program. For example, it was deemed that a substitute for the foreign language requirement would alter the program of a Bachelor of Arts degree at Boston University (Wolinsky & Whelan, 1999).

Greenbaum, Graham, and Scales (1996) interviewed adults who had attended the University of Maryland over a 12-year period and had received services for students with learning disabilities while at the university. The students were primarily from upper-middle class homes with positive family support. Thirty-five of the 49 adults who agreed to participate were currently employed, mostly in professional, technical, or managerial positions. After being hired, 26 were still unwilling to reveal their disability, and only ten indicated that accommodations or adjustments for their disability had been made. Over half of the adults were still living at home, and all were involved in social activities such as going to movies, going out to eat, and going to bars. These adults reported that an effective family support system was an important influence on their lives. Most of the adults reported that their learning disability affected them in their strategies for coping, taking extra time to complete assignments, asking for additional help, and carefully monitoring their own work. Adults who were employed indicated that disclosure of their learning disability during the job application process would lead to not being hired. Greenbaum and associates suggest that these findings indicate that we need to increase our efforts to empower persons with learning disabilities by helping them become more aware of their rights, and how to exercise these rights in an effective and thoughtful manner.

In another study with the same population of adults with learning disabilities, Greenbaum, Graham, and Scales (1995) indicated that the adults reported several potential barriers to their success. They reported that too much socializing and a lack of motivation posed problems for them. In addition, the responses of their instructors to the disability, who often operate with a lack of understanding or cooperation from faculty and administration, were problematic. Greenbaum and associates stated that disability-related services need to be improved and advertised widely to students. Support or social groups should be developed for students with learning disabilities. Greenbaum and associates also urged families to carefully investigate schools before they enroll their children.

Other researchers have also studied successful adults with disabilities. Witte, Philips, and Kakela (1998), comparing graduates with and without learning disabilities, reported graduates with learning disabilities required significantly more time to complete their degrees, and showed significantly lower grade-point averages. In addition, graduates with learning disabilities perceived themselves as receiving significantly less pay and fewer promotional opportunities, and reported less total job satisfaction than graduates without identified learning disabilities. The majority of this group did not disclose their learning disability in the work setting, and only 5 percent mentioned the status of their special needs, or requested accommodations. However, no significant salary differences between the groups were found. In a single-case study, Kershner, Kirkpatrick, & McLaren (1995) reported that the successful adult with whom they worked knew his limitations and purposefully controlled his environment. His successful business was perhaps the result of the creation of a management team, with each person fulfilling a function that the case-study subject was unable to complete himself.

Transition from School to Work and Community

The 1997 Amendments of the Individuals with Disabilities Education Act require that transition services be considered for all students 14 years of age or more. A statement related to transition services must be included in the Individualized Education Program (IEP). This statement should include a commitment by any participating agency to provide the transition services described. However, the school district remains responsible for ensuring that the student receives a free, appropriate public education (Missouri Department of Elementary and Secondary Education, 1999).

Transition services should be coordinated and designed to meet specific goals. Bullis and Cheney (1999) indicate that transitions services could include postsecondary education, vocational training, supported employment, continuing and adult education, adult services, independent living, or community participation. These coordinated activities should be grounded in the students' needs, taking into account student preferences and interests. Transition plans should include instruction, community experiences, the development of employment, and adult living objectives. If appropriate, they should also include acquisition of daily living skills and functional evaluation.

It is a myth that students with learning disabilities, who have been educated in general education classrooms, can make it on their own and don't need transition service (Dunn, 1996). In addition to being required by law, they are needed by the students. However, in their evaluation of the transition components that were documented in Individualized Education Programs, Grigal, Test, Beattie, and Wood (1997) found that though the transition components complied with IDEA's mandates, they lacked many of the essential elements reflective of best practices in transition. This raises the issue of "paper compliance" regarding transition plans.

In her report of the status of transition planning for students with learning disabilities, Dunn (1996) reported that over half of the transition goals involved competitive employment, with fewer goals of vocational training (32.4 percent), or college attendance (27.8%). Traditional planning for the students with learning disabilities was completed primarily by the secondary school personnel without the involvement of other professionals. Parents, however, reported that their children who had been out of secondary schools up to five years needed services in vocational assistance, life skills training, tutoring/reading/interpreting, or personal counseling. The reported need was greater than the services received. Dunn suggested that transition planning must be individualized for students with learning disabilities. In addition, a wide variety of services for vocational preparation should be included, with structured job seeking and supported placement. Follow-up and support services, including academic remediation and support, should be included. In addition, there should be an emphasis on helping the student with learning disabilities understand his or her disability, and in developing self-determination skills.

Clark (1996) concurs that transition plans have not been reflective of students' needs. He contends, however, that there should be a "transition-referenced" assessment process involving students and parents. This assessment should be ongoing, and address questions such as "Who am I?" And, "What do I want from life, now and in the future?" This assessment information should be organized for easy access in transition planning. In addition, Clark suggests that someone in the school should take primary responsibility for soliciting and coordinating assessment for transition activities.

The challenges of transition have also generated concerns about the nature of secondary education for students with disabilities. Sitlington (1996) suggests that students need help in learning how to maintain a home, and how to become appropriately involved in the community. Students should be supported in developing satisfactory personal and social relationships. Maag and Katsiyannis (1998) indicate that providing transition services to students with emotional/behavioral disorders has been particularly challenging because their interaction problems often result in poor outcomes such as leaving school, unemployment, or incarceration. Key to transition planning for students with emotional/behavior disorders is social skills instruction. In addition, the transition plan should identify, establish, and maintain linkages with community agencies and businesses. Sample (1998) described six transition practices that are linked to positive postschool outcomes for students with emotional/behavioral disorders: (a) vocational intervention, (b) paid work experience,

(c) social skills training, (d) interagency collaboration, (e) parent involvement, and (f) individual planning.

The adult members of the IEP team must support the student's participation in his or her transition plan. Thoma (1999) suggests that the
adults should hold high expectations for the student and prepare him or
her for the transition planning meeting. The student should participate
in decisions about who should participate, and when and where the meeting should be held. She urges adults to expand their own ideas about
what is possible for the student, and involve community members as participants in the transition planning team.

Student self-determination is the foundation of transition planning for
young adults with learning disabilities or emotional/behavioral disorders
(Morningstar, Kleinhammer-Tramill, & Lattin, 1999). The best practices
include individualized planning, involvement of family and support networks, a focus on community outcomes, and interagency collaboration.
Professionals have specific responsibilities to the student and family during transition planning. These responsibilities include asking family members how they want to be involved and respecting this level of involvement. Professionals should view extended family members as potential
contributors to transition planning, and they should help families and the
student connect with appropriate adult services.

Adolescent and Adult Supports

In their ethnographic study of 71 adults with learning disabilities, Reiff,
Gerber, and Ginsberg (1996) identified specific themes which have significant implications for teachers of students with learning disabilities.
The ongoing emphasis was to address accomplishments rather than
deficits. They suggested that students should be taught strategies to anticipate problems. Internal skills, including the desire to succeed, should
be oriented toward realistic goals and reframing, i.e., helping students
learn about themselves while discovering and nurturing strengths and
acknowledging and responding to weaknesses. In terms of external manifestations of success, these successful adults argued that schools should
teach persistence. Individuals with learning disabilities should choose
work and other environments that maximize the potential for their individual strengths and minimize the effects of their weaknesses. They should
enjoy what they do. These adults argued that success requires original-
ity, and that, as adults, they should make use of and develop their own
interpersonal support systems.

Curriculum

Ellis (1997; 1998) contends that though accommodations may be designed
to ensure the success of an adolescent with learning disabilities in content area classes, watering down the curriculum may, in fact, decrease

the opportunities that the student has for learning. Ellis (1997) proposes that teachers focus on "big ideas." They should promote elaboration, relate content to real world contexts, and integrate thinking skills and strategies into the curriculum. Ellis (1998) urges teachers to "water up" the curriculum, which would foster a sense of competence and confidence, an "attack" attitude about challenging tasks, willingness to take risks, and a sense of personal potency. He suggests that more time should be spent on student reflection and active participation, with an emphasis on developing social responsibility and collaboration among students. Teachers should provide intensive and extensive instruction targeting critical areas of need.

Self-Advocacy

Students with learning disabilities must be able to serve as their own advocates as adults (Skinner, 1998). Self-advocacy is essential to success. In a study of successful adults with learning disabilities, Reiff, Ginsberg, and Gerber (1996) found that successful adults had all undergone a process whereby they gained or regained a sense of control in their lives. These adults had made a conscious decision to take charge of their lives. One of the primary needs for adolescents and adults with learning disabilities or emotional/behavioral disorders is self-advocacy skills. Self-advocacy is "the ability to recognize and meet the needs specific to one's learning disability without compromising the dignity of oneself or others" (Brinckerhoff, 1994, p. 229). Self-advocacy is comprised of three interrelated skills: (a) knowledge of what you want, (b) knowledge of what you are legally entitled to, and (c) the ability to effectively achieve your goals. Brinckerhoff (1994) describes a self-advocacy seminar which includes:

* describing learning disabilities in plain language;
* rights under the law;
* the basics of self-advocacy;
* determining reasonable accommodations in the classroom;
* independence versus dependence issues;
* strategy instruction and self-advocacy role-playing;
* self-advocacy role-playing and direct application.

The reported aspirations of students with learning disabilities lends credence to the argument that self-advocacy is essential for individuals with learning disabilities as adults. Rojewski (1996a), using the National Education Longitudinal Study of 1988, found that adolescents with learning disabilities who aspired to a high school diploma or less, and those who aspired to an advanced college degree, espoused lower occupational aspirations than did their peers without disabilities. Females with learning disabilities were particularly at high risk for setting limits on their occupational futures (Rojewski, 1996b).

In a follow-up study on self-determination, it was found that students who addressed self-determination were more likely to have achieved more positive adult outcomes, including being employed at a higher rate, and earning more per hour, than their peers who did not demonstrate self-determination (Wehmeyer & Schwartz, 1997).

One move toward self-determination is IDEA's mandate that students with disabilities be involved in the development of their transition plans. Field (1996) recommends to teachers that they encourage self-determination in a variety of ways. Teachers can model active self-determination, and provide opportunities to students to make choices. In addition, teachers can assist students in developing more accurate attributions of their strengths and weaknesses, and can use behavioral strategies as needed. Self determination, Field indicates, requires service providers to take on a more consultative and facilitative role, in which the service provider is a partner rather than an expert.

Time management may pose a particular problem for adolescents with learning disabilities. Poor time management skills reflect poorly upon these students in tardiness, gauging the amount of time it takes to complete a task, and organizing their efforts. Manganello (1994) suggests that teachers work with adolescents specifically on ways to manage their time. Direct instruction and modeling are needed regarding using the calendar, referring to a watch or clock, developing a sense of time, punctuality, and "discovering where time goes."

Summary Points

- Students with learning disabilities or emotional/behavioral disorders typically continue to demonstrate their disability throughout their life.
- Parents of children with or without disabilities have similar expectations for their children's adult outcomes.
- Graduating from high school remains a challenge for many students with learning disabilities or emotional/behavioral disorders.
- The Americans with Disabilities Act has been a significant support in the increased employment of individuals with learning disabilities or emotional/behavioral disorders.
- Self-advocacy is essential for students with learning disabilities or emotional/behavioral disorders.

Key Words and Phrases

comorbidity—the co-occurrence of two disabilities

self-advocacy—the ability to recognize and meet the needs specific to one's learning disability without compromising the dignity of oneself or others

self-reported learning disabilities—learning disabilities that are identified by individuals rather than documented by the referral, evaluation, and classification process

References

Anderson, P., Kazmierski, S., & Cronin, M. (1995). Learning disabilities, employment discrimination, and the ADA. *Journal of Learning Disabilities, 28,* 196–204.

Barga, N. K. (1996). Students with learning disabilities in education. Managing a disability. *Journal of Learning Disabilities, 29* (4), 413–421.

Benz, M. R., Dorne, B., & Yovanoff, P. (1998). Cross the great divide: Predicting productive engagement for young women with disabilities. *Career Development for Exceptional Individuals, 21,* 3–16.

Brinckerhoff, L. C. (1994). Developing effective self-advocacy skill in college-bound students with learning disabilities.

Browning, P., Dunn, C., Rabren, K., & Whetstone, M. (1995). Postschool outcomes for students with disabilities: A U.S. synopsis. *Issues in Special Education & Rehabilitation, 10* (1), 33–40.

Bullis, M., & Cheney, D. (1999). Vocational and transition intervention for adolescents and young adults with emotional or behavioral disorders. *Focus on Exceptional Children, 31* (7), 1–24.

Clark, G. M. (1996). Transition planning assessment for secondary-level students with learning disabilities. *Journal of Learning Disabilities, 29* (1), 79–92.

Cosden, M., & McNamara, J. (1997). Self-concept and perceived social support among college students with and without learning disabilities. *Learning Disability Quarterly, 20,* 2–12.

Doren, B., & Benz, M. R. (1998). Employment inequality revealed: Predictors of better employment outcomes for young women with disabilities in transition. *The Journal of Special Education, 31* (4), 425–442.

Dowdy, C. (1996). Vocational rehabilitation and special education: Partners in transition for individuals with learning disabilities. *Journal of Learning Disabilities, 29,* 137–147.

Dunn, C. (1996). A status report on transition planning for individuals with learning disabilities. *Journal of Learning Disabilities, 29,* 17–30.

Ellis, E. S. (1997). Watering up the curriculum for adolescents with learning disabilities. *Remedial and Special Education, 18* (6), 326–346.

Ellis, E. S. (1998). Watering up the curriculum for adolescents with learning disabilities—Part 2. *Remedial and Special Education, 19* (2), 91–105.

Elswit, L. S., Geetter, E., & Goldberg. (1999). Between passion and policy: Litigating the Guckenberger case. *Journal of Learning Disabilities, 32,* 292–304.

Evers, R. B. (1996). The positive force of vocational education: Transition outcomes for youth with learning disabilities. *Journal of Learning Disabilities, 29* (1), 69–78.

Field, S. (1996). Self-determination instructional strategies for youth with learning disabilities. *Journal of Learning Disabilities, 29* (1), 40–52.

Frank, A. R., & Sitlington, P. L. (1997). Young adults with behavioral disorders—before and after IDEA, *Behavioral Disorders, 23* (1), 40–56.

Fulton, S. A., & Sabornie, E. J. (1994). Evidence of employment inequality among females with disabilities. *Journal of Special Education, 28,* 149–165.

Garten, B. C., Rumrill, P., & Serebreni, R. (1996). The higher education transition model: Guidelines for facilitating college transition among college-bound students with disabilities. *Teaching Exceptional Children, 29* (1), 30–33.

Geisthardt, C., & Munsch, J. (1996). Coping with school stress: A comparison of adolescents with and without learning disabilities. *Journal of Learning Disabilities, 29* (3), 287–296.

Gerber, P. J. (1994). Researching adults with learning disabilities from an adult-development perspective. *Journal of Learning Disabilities, 27* (1), 6–9.

Goldstein, D. E., Murray, C., & Edgar, E. (1998). Employment earnings and hours of high school graduates with learning disabilities through the first decade after graduation. *Learning Disabilities Research and Practice, 13* (1), 53–64.

Greenbaum, B., Graham, S., & Scales, W. (1996a). Adults with learning disabilities: Educational and social experiences during college. *Exceptional Children, 61* (5), 460–471.

Greenbaum, B., Graham, S., & Scales, W. (1996b). Adults with learning disabilities: Occupational and social status after college. *Journal of Learning Disabilities, 29,* 167–173.

Greenbaum, P. E., Dedrick, R. F., Friedman, R. M., Kutash, K., Brown, E. C., Lardieri, S. P., & Pugh, A. M. (1996). National adolescent and child treatment study (NACTS): Outcomes for children with serious emotional and behavioral disturbance. *Journal of Emotional and Behavioral Disorders, 4* (3), 130–146.

Gregg, N., Scott, S., McPeek, D., & Ferri, B. (1999). Definitions and eligibility criteria applied to the adolescent and adult population with learning disabilities across agencies. *Learning Disability Quarterly, 22,* 213–223.

Grigal, M., Test, D. W., Beattie, J., & Wood, W. M. (1997). An evaluation of transition components of individualized education programs. *Exceptional Children, 63* (3), 357–372.

Hagborg, W. J. (1999). Scholastic competence subgroups among high school students with learning disabilities. *Learning Disability Quarterly, 22,* 3–10.

Halpern, A. S., Yavonoff, P., Doren, B., & Benz, M. R. (1996). Predicting participation in postsecondary education for school leavers with disabilities. *Exceptional Children, 62* (2), 151–164.

Hoy, C., Gregg, N., Wisenbaker, J., Manglitz, K., & Moreland, C. (1997). Depression and anxiety in two groups of adults with learning disabilities. *Learning Disability Quarterly, 20,* 280–291.

Kershner, J., Kirkpatrick, T., & McLaren, D. (1995). The career success of an adult with a learning disability. *Journal of Learning Disabilities, 28,* 121–126.

Levine, P., & Edgar, E. (1994). An analysis by gender of long-term postschool outcomes for youth with and without disabilities. *Exceptional Children, 61* (3), 282–300.

Levine, P., & Nourse, S. W. (1998). What follow-up studies say about postschool life for young men and women with learning disabilities: A critical look at the literature. *Journal of Learning Disabilities, 31,* (3) 212–233.

Levinson, E. (1994). Current vocational assessment models for students with disabilities. *Journal of Counseling and Development, 73,* 94–101.

Louis Harris and Associates. (1998). *The 1998 National Organization on Disability/Louis Harris & Associates Survey of Americans with Disabilities Executive Summary.* Washington, DC: Author.

Maag, J. W., Irvin, D., Reid, R., & Vasa, S. F. (1994). Prevalence and predictors of substance use: A comparison between adolescents with and without learning disabilities. *Journal of Learning Disabilities, 27* (4), 223–234.

Maag, J. W., & Katsiyannis, A. (1998). Challenges facing successful transition for youths with E/BD. *Behavioral Disorders, 23* (4), 209–221.

Maliam, I. M., & Love, L. L. (1998). Leaving high school: An ongoing transition study. *Teaching Exceptional Children, 30* (3), 4–10.

Malmgren, K., Edgar, E., & Neel, R. S. (1998). Postschool status of youths with behavioral disorders. *Behavioral Disorders, 23* (4), 257–263.

Manganello, R. E. (1994). Time management instruction for older students with learning disabilities. *Teaching Exceptional Children, 26* (2), 60–62.

Misano, L. L., & Hodap, R. M. (1996). Parental educational expectations for adolescents with disabilities. *Exceptional Children 62* (2), 515–523.

Missouri Department of Elementary and Secondary Education, Division of Special Education. (1999). *Issues in education: Transition, school to post school activities. Technical Assistance Bulletin, January, 1999.* Jefferson City, MO: Author.

Morningstar, M. E., Kleinhammer-Tramill, P. J., & Lattin, D. L. (1999). Using successful models of student-centered transition planning and services for adolescent with disabilities. *Focus on Exceptional Children, 31* (9), 1–19.

Morrison, G. M., & Cosden, M. A. (1997). Risk, resilience, and adjustment of individuals with learning disabilities. *Learning Disabilities Quarterly, 20,* 43–60.

Murray, C., Goldstein, D. E., & Edgar, E. (1997). The employment and engagement status of high school graduates with learning disabilities through the first decade after graduation. *Learning Disabilities Research and Practice, 12* (3), 151–160.

National Education Goals Panel. (1991). The national goals report: Building a nation of learners. Washington, DC: U.S. Printing Office.

Oswald, D. P., & Coutinho, M. J. (1996). Leaving school: The impact of state economic and demographic factors for students with serious emotional disturbance. *Journal of Emotional and Behavioral Disorders, 4* (2), 114–125.

Rauch-Elnekave, H. (1994). Teenage motherhood: Its relationship to undetected learning problems. *Adolescence, 29* (113), 91–103.

Razeghi, J. A. (1998). A first step toward solving the problem of special education dropouts: Infusing career education into the curriculum. *Intervention in School and Clinic, 33* (3), 148–156.

Reid, D. K., & Button, L. J. (1995). Anna's story: Narratives of personal experience about being labeled learning disabled. *Journal of Learning Disabilities, 28* (10), 602–614.

Reiff, H. B., Gerber, P. J., & Ginsberg, R. (1996). What successful adults with learning disabilities can tell us about teaching children. *Teaching Exceptional Children, 29* (2), 10–16.

Reis, S. M., New, T. W., & McGuire, J. M. (1997). Case studies of high-ability students with learning disabilities who have achieved. *Exceptional Children, 63* (4), 463–479.

Rojewski, J. W. (1996a). Educational and occupational aspirations of high school seniors with learning disabilities. *Exceptional Children, 62* (5), 463–476.

Rojewski, J. W. (1996b). Occupational aspirations and early career-choice patterns of adolescents with and without learning disabilities. *Learning Desirability Quarterly, 19,* 99–116.

Rylance, B. J. (1997). Predictors of high school graduation or dropping out for youth with severe emotional disorders. *Behavioral Disorders, 23* (1), 5–17.

Sabornie, E. J. (1994). Social-affective characteristics in early adolescents identified as learning disabled and nondisabled. *Learning Disabilities Quarterly, 17,* 268–279.

Sample, P. L. (1998). Postschool outcomes for students with significant emotional disturbance following best-practice transition services. *Behavioral Disorders, 23* (4), 231–242.

Schelly, C. (1995). *Vocational support strategies for students with emotional disorders.* Reston, VA: ERIC Clearinghouse on Disabilities and Gifted Education.

Shokoohi-Yekta, M. (1994). Effects of increased high school graduation standards on college entrance examination performance of students with learning disabilities. *Learning Disabilities Research and Practice, 9* (4), 213–218.

Siegel, L. S. (1999). Issues in the definition and diagnosis of learning disabilities: A perspective on Guckenberger v. Boston University. *Journal of Learning Disabilities, 32,* 304–320.

Sitlington, P. L. (1996). Transition to living: The neglected component of transition programming for individuals with learning disabilities. *Journal of Learning Disabilities, 29* (1), 31–39, 52.

Skinner, M. E. (1998). Promoting self-advocacy among college students with learning disabilities. *Intervention in School and Clinic, 33* (5), 278–283.

Speckman, N. J., Herman, K. L., & Vogel, S. A. (1993). Risk, and resilience in individuals with learning disabilities: A challenge to the field. *Learning Disabilities Research and Practice 8* (1) 59–65.

Stone, C. A. (1997) Correspondences among parent, teacher, and student perceptions of adolescents' learning disabilities. *Journal of Learning Disabilities, 30* (6), 660–669.

Thoma, C. A. (1999). Supporting student voice in transition planning. *Teaching Exceptional Children, 31* (5), 4–9.

Vogel, S. A. (1998). Adults with learning disabilities: What learning disabilities specialists, adult literacy educators, and other service providers want and need to know. In S. A. Vogel and S. Reder, (Eds.), *Learning Disabilities, Literacy, and Adult Education* (pp. 5–28). Baltimore: Paul H. Brookes.

Vogel, S. A., Hruby, P., & Adelman, P. B. (1993). Educational and psychological factors in successful and unsuccessful college students with learning disabilities. *Learning Disabilities Research & Practice, 8* (1) 35–43.

Vogel, S. A., & Reder, S. (1998a). Educational attainment of adults with learning disabilities. In S. A. Vogel and S. Reder, (Eds.), *Learning Disabilities, Literacy, and Adult Education* (pp. 43–68). Baltimore: Paul H. Brookes.

Vogel, S. A., & Reder, S. (1998b). Literacy proficiency among adults with self-reported learning disabilities. In C. Smith, (Ed.), *Literacy for the twenty-first century: Research, policy, practices, and the National Adult Literacy Survey.* Praeger: Westport, Conn.

Wehmeyer, M., & Schwartz, M. (1997). Self-determination and positive adult outcomes: A follow-up study of youth with mental retardation or learning disabilities. *Exceptional Children, 63* (2), 245–255.

Weller, C., Watteyne, L., Herbert, M., & Crelly, C. (1994). Adaptive behavior of adults and young adults with learning disabilities. *Learning Disability Quarterly. 17,* 282–295.

Wiener, C. S. (1995). Employers do not accept 85%. *Teaching Exceptional Children. 28* (1), 10–11.

Witte, R., Philips, L., & Kakela, M. (1998). Job satisfaction of college graduates with learning disabilities. *Journal of Learning Disabilities, 31* (3), 259–266.

Wolinsky, S., & Whelan, A. (1999). Federal law and the accommodation of students with LD: The lawyers' look at the BU decision. *Journal of Learning Disabilities, 32* (4), 286–292.

Wong, B. Y. L. (1997). Research on genre specific strategies from enhancing writing in adolescents with learning disabilities. *Learning Disability Quarterly, 20,* 140–159.

14

Prevention and Early Intervention of Learning Disabilities and Emotional/Behavioral Disorders

TO GUIDE YOUR READING

After reading this chapter, you will be able to answer the following questions:

- What is prevention?
- What is the role of early intervention for young children at risk for learning disabilities or emotional/behavioral disorders?
- What is the role of conflict resolution in the prevention of learning disabilities or emotional/behavioral disorders?
- What is the role of family intervention in the prevention of learning disabilities or emotional/behavioral disorders?
- What is the role of violence prevention in schools?
- What preventive efforts can teachers engage in that are related to contemporary social problems?

◀◀ *Robert, a premature baby, was of very low birth weight. Because he had respiratory distress, he remained hospitalized for three months. Before he left the hospital, Robert's parents were put in contact with their school district's early intervention services. As soon as he was physically stable, and settled in his home with his two older brothers, Robert's parents began a home-based program with him. Robert received monthly visits from an occupational therapist who assisted with his feeding problems. A physical therapist assisted his parents in the development of Robert's physical skills. When he reached two years of age, a communication specialist began to work with the family. By the time Robert entered an inclusive preschool, he was communicating his needs well, and was beginning to demonstrate basic concepts. Though his fine motor skills appeared delayed, and his processing was not as rapid as his peers, Robert actively joined in and participated with the other children. His parents were pleased with the results of all the work that they, and all their professional and personal supporters, did to assure Robert's success.*

REFLECTION *Robert received early intervention services which significantly increased the potential for positive outcomes in his life. Reflect on children who do not receive such services. What is their potential? What are the possible outcomes from not receiving early intervention services?*

Introduction

"**A**t-risk" may not be a precise category, but it does represent a set of dynamics that could place an individual in danger of negative future events (McWhirter, McWhirter, McWhirter, & McWhirter, 1998). McWhirter and associates describe "at-risk" as a continuum, ranging from minimal risk, where an individual has favorable demographics (positive family, school, and social interaction, and limited stressors), through high risk (negative family, school, and social interaction, numerous stressors, negative attitudes and emotions, and skill deficiencies), to imminent risk (the development of gateway or threshold behaviors and activities). A large number of at-risk children are inner-city children who live in poverty and are exposed to the challenges of inner-urban life. Agencies may also be at fault, compounding the problem by engaging in "turfism" rather than providing integrated services to children and families (Fredericks, 1994).

The issue of "hope" is an important one for learners who are at-risk. Curwin (1994) has two basic suggestions for instilling hope in these learners. First, students must believe they are competent in the subjects they are learning. Teachers should help students gain confidence by achieving at least one meaningful learning goal each day. Second, learning tasks should not be too easy; simple tasks can be perceived by students as condescending, babyish, and not worth doing.

Prevention

Prevention is the effort engaged in to keep learning disabilities and emotional/behavioral disorders from occurring. The most commonly used definition of prevention describes three levels of activity: primary, secondary, and tertiary (Caplan, 1964). Primary prevention focuses on the population at large. It is concerned with eliminating the causes of learning disabilities or emotional/behavioral disorders, and reducing the incidence of the development of learning disabilities or emotional/behavioral disorders. Secondary prevention, in Caplan's structure, is aimed at reducing the duration of cases of individuals with learning disabilities or emotional/behavioral disorders. The goals of secondary prevention are to reduce the intensity and/or duration of learning disabilities or emotional/behavioral disorders in order to prevent more serious disabilities in the future. Tertiary prevention is directed at reducing the likelihood that individuals with learning disabilities or emotional/behavioral disorders will develop more serious problems. Its aim is to reduce the residual effects of these disabilities.

A strong rationale for prevention is provided by Apter (1982). First, mental health services are expensive, and with increased incidence of learning and behavioral problems, as well as increased medical costs, these services are becoming even more expensive. In addition, mental health care is not always effective, nor it is universally available. The mental health system has too few professionals to serve the needs of the community. An additional concern with regard to prevention is that mental health services have a history of reaching too few people, too late.

Currently, two major prevention-focused programs are being developed: (a) programs related to reducing stress in the schools and community, and (b) programs related to building individual capacity to withstand stress. Community prevention efforts include support to families, community education, and the utilization of community strengths. Individual efforts include supporting the development of competence in children, identifying and building on the specific strengths of each child, providing basic social behaviors to each child, and building competence in individual adults (Apter, 1982).

The issue of prevention of learning disabilities is quite complex. Keough and Sears (1991) suggest that inferences about outcomes and indicators of risk for learning disabilities vary depending on when end-point information is gathered. In other words, conclusions from short-term studies may be very different than those from long-term studies. They contend that the length of time and beginning and end points of prevention studies clearly influence the nature of findings about contributors to developmental risks. In younger children, for example, medical conditions are powerful contributors to outcomes if follow-up is conducted when the children are young, but environmental conditions become increasingly influential as children grow older (Aylward, 1988). For children with learning disabilities, designation as "at-risk" does not necessarily mean that the child will remain at-risk, and apparently intact preschoolers may become at-risk during the school years (Keough and Sears, 1991).

Prevention of behavior problems is a primary means of managing behavior. Curwin and Mendler (1988) suggest that there are several stages of prevention: (a) increasing teacher self-awareness, (b) increasing student self-awareness, (c) expressing genuine feelings, (d) discovering and recognizing an alternative, (e) motivating students, (f) establishing social contracts within the class, and (g) implementing social contracts. Curwin and Mendler feel that by providing structure and direction, as well as demonstrating flexibility, teachers can prevent many learning and behavior problems. In their emphasis on prevention, they assert that teachers should use a problem resolution process that includes individual student contracts to prevent behavior problems. These contracts should begin with a discussion of preventive procedures with the student, and develop a mutually agreeable plan for problem resolution. Teachers and students then monitor the plan and revise it as necessary.

Early Intervention for Young Children Who Are At-Risk

Early intervention has both a legal and a colloquial definition. Legally, early intervention is services provided to infants and toddlers (birth through three years of age) and their families in response to the mandates of the Individuals with Disabilities Education Act (IDEA). These early intervention services are provided through the implementation of an Individualized Family Service Plan (IFSP). Colloquially, early intervention is used to refer to services provided to families before their children attain school age. Regardless of the definition used, the goal of early intervention is to optimize the learning potential and daily well-being of the child, and his or her family (Dunst, Trivette, & Deal, 1988).

Ramey and Ramey (1992) found significant long-lasting (through age twelve) differences between children who received intensive early intervention and a control group that did not receive services. Significantly fewer of the children receiving care failed a grade, or had tested intelligence quotients of more than one standard deviation below the mean.

Kauffman (1989) suggests that the strongest predictor of appropriate behavior in children is the quantity and quality of caregiver supervision. Zirpoli and Melloy (1997) suggest several other variables related to the development of appropriate behavior in young children. Consistency, they indicate, is significant in that it builds understanding and expectations between a child and his or her caregivers.

The educational environment may also have an influence on the behavior of young children. Variables in the environment related to the behavior of young children include (Zirpoli, 1995):

- Social density or the number of children in the setting. Crowded settings are related to reduced responsiveness on the part of caregivers.
- Physical layout. The setting should be safe, and the design of the setting should limit the number of young children in each area.
- Appropriate use of materials, including calming materials and activities, as well as stimulating materials and activities.
- Effective scheduling, including routines, short time segments, active play and group times, as well as passive and quiet activities.
- Staffing qualifications and ratios.

In a demonstration project, the Community Integration Project, Bruder (1993) found eight characteristics of effective service delivery within early childhood programs. First, there should be a program philosophy for inclusive early childhood services, i.e., an inclusive school is a place where everyone belongs, is accepted, and is supported by his or her peers in the course of having his or her individual educational needs met (Stainback & Stainback, 1990). Second, a consistent and ongoing system for family involvement should be in place. Services should be based on the premise that the family is the enduring and central force in the life of the child, and as such, services should be responsive to the lifestyles, values, and priorities of the family. The concerns, resources, and priorities of families must be documented. Third, a system of team planning and program implementation should be in place using transdisciplinary teams, in which members share roles, and cross professional services boundaries systematically, communicating on a regularly planned basis. Fourth, there should be a system of collaboration and communication with other agencies that provide services to young children with disabilities and their families. Fifth, each child should have a well-constructed Individualized Education Plan, or Individualized Family Service Plan, that dictates instructional content. Individualized goals should be functional and imbedded within daily activities and routines. Sixth, an integrated delivery system of educational and related services is needed. By capitalizing on the child's interests, preferences, and actions, emphasis is placed on the child's initiations rather than on individual service provider's choices; interventions, then, encourage the acquisition of generalizable and functional skills. Seventh, there should be a consistent and ongoing system for training and staff development. Finally, a comprehensive system for evaluating the effectiveness of the program should be in place.

Tension between early childhood education and early childhood special education professionals has been ongoing. Bredekamp (1993) suggests that the tension may be grounded in misconceptions about developmentally appropriate practice. She raises the point that according to the National Association for the Education of Young Children, developmentally appropriate means both age-appropriate and individually-appropriate. In addition, the almost exclusive use of teacher-directed instruction is not appropriate for any children because it denies them the opportunity for social interaction. She argues that programming must be individually appropriate: a program must assess and plan for children's individual needs and interests. In addition, Bredekamp specifies six elements of best practice in early childhood special education that could be better integrated within the early childhood education knowledge base. These elements are summarized in Table 14.1.

Guidelines to support both individual and developmental appropriateness in early intervention programs for young children with disabilities are provided by McCormick and Feeney (1995). They suggest that expected intervention outcomes should be modified only if it is clear that the child cannot accomplish the outcome even partially, or at a less sophisticated level, without some modification. When alternative activity arrangements are necessary, the modifications should be as rich and varied as the activities provided for typically developing peers. Alternative activity arrangements should not interfere with ordinary routines, promote dependence, or call attention to the child. They suggest that activities and materials that promote the development of age-appropriate social and communication skills should be a high priority. Finally, toys and materi-

Table 14.1   Components of Best Practice in Early Childhood Special Education

1. Individually appropriate practice. Early childhood education strongly values the individual child, but has been less systematic in ensuring that the individual child's needs are met in relation to program goals.

2. Early intervention. Early intervention should be conducted through interactive teaching, and a continuum of possible teaching behaviors from nondirective to directive, with the mediating behaviors of facilitating, supporting, and scaffolding in the middle.

3. Family-centered services. As the child is perceived less at-risk, focus on family weakness in early childhood programs.

4. Advocacy. Early childhood educators need to join in advocacy for young children with special needs.

5. Transition. Transition is a challenge due to inappropriate practices in kindergarten and primary grades.

6. Interdisciplinary approaches. Collaboration is needed in early childhood education.

(Bredekamp, 1993)

als provided for children with disabilities should be appropriate for their chronological age.

In inclusive early childhood education settings, Cavallaro, Haney, and Cabello (1992) suggest using strategies which capitalize on the developmental opportunities available within integrated preschool settings without compromising child choice. These strategies include:

1. Attention and responsiveness to children, responding to both the children's interests and their intent.

2. Environmental structuring strategies, including selecting materials to facilitate engagement and interaction, structuring activities to promote interaction, providing choices, maintaining adult proximity, and facilitating peer proximity.

3. Adult mediation strategies, including questioning, encouraging, and commenting; behavioral metacognitive, and reflective modeling; responsive prompting; fine tuning; and feedback.

4. Peer mediation strategies, including modeling and peer mediated training.

Using a social-communicative perspective, Kaiser and Hester (1997) propose a model for early intervention suggesting that environmental factors and parent and child characteristics can contribute to the development of conduct disorders in early childhood. Environmental stressors associated with poverty, parent characteristics (including poor parenting strategies), and child characteristics (including deficits in communication skills) appeared to be factors that affect parent–child interactions in ways that contribute to the development of conduct disorders. Early intervention for these children should involve parent training, direct intervention with children, and support for maintaining behavior changes and transitions.

The National Center for Learning Disabilities (1998) suggests that early intervention can make a significant difference for young children with learning disabilities. However, with the challenges in identifying learning disabilities at an early age, they urge parents to give priority to their child's medical issues. Unevenness in development may indicate a potential problem, as may variations from age-peers in language, motor skills, social interventions, self-help skills, or attention.

McCarthy, Harris, and Reeves (1997) explored ways in which each of the fifty states serve preschool children who are identified as having specific learning disabilities, the impact of the preschool-specific or noncategorical labels, and the quantitative criteria used for eligibility. All of the states indicated that preschool children with learning disabilities would receive services in their preschool programs. Twenty-four states used the learning disabilities label; the others did not use a label. Forty-two states reported that preschool children with specific learning disabilities would probably be served under a noncategorical label such as developmentally delayed, or "preschool child with a disability." Most of the states used the IDEA definition of learning disabilities, though seven states modified the federal definition to specifically address young children. All states reported using clinical judgment to determine eligibility, and a majority of states used quantitative criteria such as standard deviation below the mean, percentage delay, months delay below chronological age, or a combination of these factors.

McCarthy and associates (1997) reported a continued debate over the existence of learning disabilities in preschool children. Some of the states modify the federal definition to specifically address young children, and emphasize the definitional components of listening, thinking, and speaking. Some states stressed developmentally appropriate assessment. Other states emphasized academic discrepancies. The Learning Disabilities Association of American (1999) advises that parents should consider their preschool child's skills and discuss them with the family physician. They submit that preschoolers who (a) knock things over, bump into doors, or fall out of chairs; (b) overreact, or underreact, to stimuli; (c) have difficulty manipulating toys, avoid puzzles or blocks, or appear clumsy; (d) have difficulty focusing, distinguishing shapes and colors, remembering what they see, or ordering and sequencing what they see; or (e) are disorganized and disheveled may indeed be at risk for learning problems. Variation from peers in one or two behaviors is not an issue; consistent problems within a group of behaviors may be an indication that the child has learning disabilities (Coordinated Campaign for Learning Disabilities, 1997). If parents have concerns, the Learning Disabilities Association of America urges them to speak with their physician and school districts. Cicci (1995) however, cautions that visits with pediatricians are often brief, and parents may choose to consider a more in-depth evaluation if they have concerns about their child's early development.

Behavioral problems among preschool children have become a priority for early childhood educators according to Feil, Walker, and Severson (1995). Factors such as the exponential rise in childcare utilization, increasing poverty, and the incidence of child abuse have made the establishment of procedures for early identification and remediation of problem behaviors among preschool children imperative.

Among young children, teachers should avoid viewing the child's behavior as "misbehavior." Gartrell (1995) recommends that the behavior should be viewed as a "mistake," and describes three levels of "mistaken" behavior in young children. First, there is "strong needs mistaken behavior," in which the child is at the social-emotional survival level. Though his or her behavior may be at times nonsocial, or even anti-social, the teacher must intervene nonpunitively, work to build a positive relationship, seek more information about the child, and generate a coordinated individual guidance plan with other adults. Second, there is "socially influenced mistake behavior." For example, if one child would say. "Hi, Dumbo!" other children might join in. The goal is then to help each child to be autonomous rather than following social influence. The third type is "experimental mistaken behavior." The child, learning about the world, tries a behavior in order to observe the teacher's reaction. The teacher may step back and allow the student to learn from experience, reiterate guidelines, and offer a more desired alternative behavior.

Conflict Resolution in Prevention

Conflict, a condition of disagreement or disharmony, has a negative connotation. Johnson and Johnson (1996), however, argue that conflicts are both inevitable and desirable if they are managed constructively. They contend that conflicts have value in that they:

1. Focus attention on problems which need solutions;
2. Clarify a student's identity and values;
3. Highlight patterns of behavior which are not successful;
4. Help students understand other students and their values;
5. Strengthen relationships by increasing confidence that participants can resolve disagreements;
6. Resolve the small tensions that occur when interacting with others;
7. Release anger, anxiety, insecurity, and sadness;
8. Clarify students' commitments;
9. Stimulate students to action.

Johnson and Johnson (1996) describe their "Teaching Students to be Peacemakers Program" as a school-wide cooperative effort. There are six steps in a twelve-year spiral program in which students learn increasingly sophisticated negotiation and mediation strategies. The steps in the program are: (a) develop a cooperative context, (b) teach students to recognize when conflict is and is not occurring, (c) instruct students in concrete and specific strategies for negotiating agreements, (d) instruct in the application of concrete and specific mediation strategies, (e) initiate the peer mediation program, and (f) continue the program on a weekly basis from the first through the twelfth grade.

Disruptive behaviors may occur more often when students are asked to complete tasks, or perform when they do not have the skills necessary for success (Denny, DePaepe, Gunter, Jack, & Shores, 1994). Occurrences of disruptive behavior, in this study, decreased dramatically when direct instruction and feedback were provided. Teachers, however, supplied information that the students needed in order to complete the tasks only about 20 percent of the time.

Family Intervention in Prevention

Historically, blame for learning problems or emotional/behavioral disorders has been placed on family factors (Terkelsen, 1983). As a result, prevention efforts often focus on the family. Family interventions include strategies to target family interactions and change the behavior of family members.

In terms of learning disabilities, Keough and Sears (1991) argue that little attention is paid to the developmental contexts of children. In addition, little attention is paid to their strengths. Consideration of protective factors and strengths when planning efforts on behalf of children with learning disabilities and their families, they maintain, will maximize the potential power of interventions.

Patterson (1986) describes a model of interaction for families engaged in aversive behavior patterns. In these families, interaction sequences of relatively trivial behaviors were the learning base for family members' high-amplitude aggressive behaviors. Escape-avoidance behaviors (attack, counterattack, positive outcome) may occur hundreds of times a day. Children move from being noncompliant to physically assaultive, beginning with behaviors such as whining, yelling, and temper tantrums, as a substitute social skill. As other family members begin to use these skills in response, the likelihood of violent behavior increases. As the child becomes more skillfully coercive, he or she becomes even more difficult to discipline. Presumably, training parents to use more effective discipline would reduce this behavior.

Family-focused interventions for students at-risk for learning disabilities or emotional/behavior disorders vary depending on family structure, family interaction patterns, and other family characteristics (Lambie & Daniels-Mohring, 1993). Lambie and Daniels-Mohring suggest seven different types of intervention that may support prevention:

1. Emotional support, which may simply involve listening (Lambie, 1987). In emotional support, the professional provides the family with a sense of being understood and cared about.

2. Resource identification, which may include making information about rights, procedures, and services available.

3. Technical assistance, including suggestions for management strategies.

4. Referral to counseling, therapy, medical or financial services.

5. Normalization, which helps parents view children's behavior as within normal limits.

6. Reframing, which offers an alternative interpretation of behavioral events to change the meaning of the behavior in the family.

7. Contextualization, in which professionals help families interpret behavior through the context in which it occurs.

In a study by Soderlund, Epstein, Quinn, Cumblad, and Petersen (1995), parents reported persistent needs even though their general feelings about the services that they had received were positive. They indicated that they needed additional information about community services, needed to be able to find recreational activities, and needed assistance in locating transition programs and alternative schooling for their children.

Hanson and Carta (1995) contend that children and their parents who live with the constant stress of exposure in their home environments are likely to feel helpless and frustrated. Special educators should recognize that the problems children and their families face do not come from a single cause, so, single interventions will probably not be effective. Families need more than school-based interventions. Teachers should also recognize that it may be difficult to enlist these parents and caregivers as partners. They are so overwhelmed with meeting basic needs that they cannot respond to the specific developmental needs of their children. Families living with a multitude of stressors may find it difficult to follow through with plans or programs for their children.

In supporting children and their families, Hanson and Carta suggest that professionals:

- provide opportunities for positive caregiving transactions, establish positive and mutually satisfying relationships with one another to prevent or relieve stress;
- shift focus from deficits to emphasis on individual and family strengths;
- recognize and encourage informal sources of support;
- provide comprehensive, coordinated services;
- recognize the need to offer families a broad spectrum of services;
- deliver flexible, usable services; and
- cross professional boundaries, avoid "turfism," and overcome bureaucratic limitations.

Some families are so overwhelmed that their children may be either voluntarily or involuntarily removed and placed in substitute care. Smucker, Kauffman, and Ball (1996) indicate that a high percentage of children in foster care receive special education services. However, little is known about the academic and social problems found among this population. Searches of school archival records and brief interviews with school personnel were used to obtain measures of school-related problems of four groups of students: (a) those receiving both foster care and special education for emotional/behavioral disorders, (b) foster care only, (c) special education only, or (d) neither. Children in foster care with emotional/behavior disorders were found to exhibit more school-related problems. Children in either foster care or special education exhibited fewer problems.

The American Public Welfare Association (1993) reported estimates of the number of children receiving foster care at two points during fiscal year 1990: 363,000 children at the start of the year, and 406,000 children at the end of the year. During that fiscal year, there was an 11.8 percent increase of children in substitute care, compared with a growth in the general child population of .36 percent. In the United States, 5.4 of every 10,000 children were in foster care at the end of Fiscal Year 1990.

A large number of children in foster care receive special education services. Hill, Hayden, Lakin, Menke, and Amado (1990) concluded that the prevalence of disabilities among children and youth in foster care is about twice that among school-age children as a whole. Goerge, Voorhis, Grant, Casey, and Robinson (1992) reported that 30 percent of the children in foster care in Illinois were placed in special education. Of this group, more than half (i.e., about 54 percent of children in foster care) were identified as having emotional/behavioral disorders as their primary disability. Similarly, Sawyer and Dubowitz (1994) found that almost 30 percent of the children in Baltimore city schools who were in the care of extended family members due to neglect or abuse by their parents were receiving special education services.

Children in foster care are placed in special education about three times more often than children in the general population (Goerge and associates, 1992; Sawyer & Dubowitz, 1994). Goerge and associates (1992) also found that children in foster care were identified as having emotional/behavioral disorders about 14 times more frequently than children not in foster care. Reasonable estimates based on the best available prevalence studies indicated that about 3 to 6 percent of the general child population could be considered to have emotional/behavioral disorders requiring special education services (Kauffman, 1993); the prevalence reported by Goerge and associates is roughly three to five times greater among children in foster care.

The unavailability of appropriate support services in schools, and the lack of collaborative intervention planning among children services agencies and professionals has placed serious limitations on the application of effective interventions across settings, as well as the merger of interventions across settings (Knitzer, 1993). To provide supports, Eber, Nelson, and Miles (1997) propose the use of school-based wraparound programs.

"Wraparound" is an approach that involves an unconditional commitment to blend and create services for children, their teachers, and their families (Eber, Nelson, & Miles, 1997). The wraparound process encourages service planners to think differently about the needs of students and their families, as well as how services can be provided to meet those needs effectively. A unique feature of wraparound is that one integrated plan addresses the needs of the student during and beyond the school day. Wraparound plans include comprehensive services blended across agencies to address needs in more than one life domain.

An important characteristic separating wraparound plans from other types of student plans is that they are driven by needs rather than by the parameters of programs currently available. In contrast to the traditional practice of evaluating student needs on the basis of available educational placements and existing program components, services are analyzed and employed according to their usefulness in meeting student needs. Services are not based on a categorical model, but are accessed or created on the basis of the specific needs of the student, family, and teacher. The child and family team consists of persons who know the student best, and who can provide active support to the student, family, and teacher. Extended family members, neighbors, family friends, and mentors are frequently participants in child and family teams. For students served in special education, the school-based portion of the wraparound plan is translated into an Individualized Education Program (IEP). The school plan addresses all components of the school day where proactive supports and interventions are needed. It is for students with comprehensive needs that involve both home and community settings. The school-based wraparound plan is an integrated part of the broader wraparound plan that addresses other life domains.

A major issue in wraparound plans is that supports and services are provided in the natural environment. Available resources are used creatively to meet unique needs. Professionals build interventions on the strengths that exist in the student, teacher, and family. Services are based on normalization, i.e., the needs of all persons of like age, grade, gender, community, and culture. Wraparound services are evaluated on the basis of significant and accountable measures, and outcomes are generated by parents, teacher, and child expectations. The team providing wraparound services is committed to unconditional care; it assumes responsibility for changing the plan to make it work for the student.

Parent programs can also have a significant impact on student outcomes. Trembly, Pagini-Kurtz, and Vitaro (1995) studied the effects of a two-year program which included a home-based parent training component and a school-based social skills program. Students were followed to mid adolescence. Results indicated that a significantly greater percentage of treated students remained in an age-appropriate regular classroom through the end of elementary school, and that the treated students reported significantly less delinquent behaviors at yearly assessment. The preventive program appeared to have a significant long-term effect on the social development on the students.

School Violence Prevention

Violence has increased significantly in the past ten years. Curwin (1994) argues that violence is now more random and senseless when compared to violence in the past. In response to this change, Curwin suggests that students be actively taught alternatives to violence, making effective choices, and modeling expressions of anger, frustration, and impatience.

The role of television viewing in violent behavior in children has been implicated for many years. Gadow and Sprafkin (1993) conducted a ten-year study of television-viewing habits, aggressive acts, and a "viewing skills curriculum." They reported that children with emotional/behavioral disorders viewed relatively large amounts of violent material, preferred aggressive characters, and were more likely to believe that fictional content was true. However, it was not more likely for them to behave aggressively following aggression-laded viewing. Though students did increase their knowledge of television viewing following the implementation of a "viewing skills curriculum," their actual viewing behavior did not change.

Brendtro and Long (1994) suggest that a conflict cycle is at work among individuals engaged in violence. They posit that a stressful situation evokes an irrational belief in an individual, such as "everyone is against me." In turn, these irrational, biased beliefs trigger feelings of distress, such as fear or anger. These feelings drive defensive behavior, such as aggression. The individual's aggressive behavior then provokes reciprocal reactions from the adult, i.e., counter aggression.

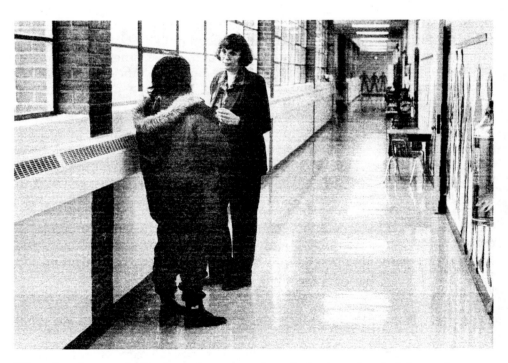

When teachers are effective at empowering students, school violence is decreased.

In order to break this cycle, Brendtro and Long suggest primary prevention activities, such as preventing broken relationships, teaching children self-discipline, and teaching conflict resolution. In early intervention, both children and parents should be targeted for mentoring, and they should be encouraged to disengage from punitive cycles. School bullying should be addressed. Social bonds should be restored through fostering attachment, achievement, and autonomy.

The more effective teachers are at empowering students, the less violence the students will initiate (Haberman, 1994). Haberman suggests that students experiencing poverty have a lack of trust, making them suspicious of adults' motives and actions. In addition, violence is present in their daily lives. A sense of hopelessness characterizes the urban life of older children and adults who live in poverty, as well as a frustration with the many bureaucracies with which they must engage. The culture of authoritarianism, which pervades poverty, leads to frustration, which is expressed as violence.

Habermann suggests that if the harshest punishments available to teachers and schools can be ignored or even laughed at by students, then teachers are unjustified in believing they can coerce, force, demand, or require students to comply and learn. He contends that most teachers do not know alternatives to coercive teaching; they were either never taught these alternatives in their preparation, or they were personally socialized through power relationships. A teacher's strength is an inner quality demonstrated by an ability to share authority with children whom most people are unwilling to trust. Teachers must self-analyze their prejudices, and treat everyone with respect and dignity.

A contrasting view is that of "getting tough with violence." Kauffman (1994) proposes that schools should provide effective consequences to stop aggressive behavior early. Students' access to instruments of aggression should be restricted. In addition, teachers should use effective instructional strategies. However, Skiba and Peterson (1999) describe a "dark side" of zero tolerance. They contend that rigid adherence to harsh and extreme measures does not necessarily avert school violence. In their review of the literature, they found that schools with no reported crime were less likely to have a zero tolerance policy than those that reported incidence of serious crime. In addition, African American students are overrepresented among those who are corrected by means of corporal punishment and expulsion, and underrepresented among those corrected by the use of milder disciplinary alternatives. Further study suggests that inequitable treatment may also be linked to socioeconomic status.

Zero-tolerance programs frequently apply suspension and expulsion as strategies. However, the National Association of Child Advocates (1998) argues that teachers, administrators, and students alike related that student suspension and expulsion is more often a reward than a punishment. Suspending or expelling students makes the problem worse by

Table 14.2   Recommendations for Decreasing Violence in Schools

- Provide prenatal and early childhood programs for at-risk populations.
- Expand parent educational and family support programs.
- Provide violence prevention programs such as conflict resolution and peer mediation.
- Provide and integrate family support services that affect children including school, child care, and health care.
- Restrict everyone's access to guns—reform the gun industry, with stronger criminal liabilities for illegal sales. Educate families about the risk of maintaining firearms at home. Enforce zero tolerance for gun possession at school.
- Reduce instances of violence presented to the public as entertainment.
- Encourage the use of effective alternatives to incarcerations for youth, when appropriate, and the use of effective rehabilitation programs.
- Expand interventions that place caring adults in the lives of young adults.
- Prevent teen pregnancy through outreach programs, including outreach to young males.
- Support programs that reduce violence in families by making homes safer for all family members.

National Summit on Youth and Violence (1994)

pushing out those students who need to be in school the most. They suggest (a) in-school suspension, (b) peer mediation, (c) community service and work-related obligations, (d) restitution, (e) mandatory parent attendance at school, (f) voluntary substance abuse counseling or testing, and (g) student, family, or parent counseling.

The National Summit on Youth and Violence (1994) generated several recommendations for decreasing violence in schools. These recommendations are summarized in Table 14.2.

Preventive Efforts Related to Contemporary Social Problems

Effective discipline may, in itself, prevent behavior problems. Smith and Rivera (1995) suggest several principles for effective discipline. The climate of the school and classroom should be positive, and a foundation for a positive learning environment should be in place. Prevention rather than reaction should be emphasized, that is, schools should be proactive rather than reactive. Collaborative relationships with parents and other professionals to deal with disciplinary concerns and promote a positive learning climate should be established. Interventions should match the behavior problems, and an evaluation system should be in place to frequently monitor student progress.

Jones (1993) suggests that building an effective plan for a school addresses just five questions:

- Does the plan treat students with dignity?
- Does the response to student behavior include an educational component, such as teaching students new skills?
- Does the program require and support an environmental analysis?
- Is the response to rule violation clear to everyone?
- Is there a sequential response to rule violation?

Suicide

Though teachers and parents often think of students with emotional/ behavioral disorders as being at risk for suicide, students with learning disabilities should also be considered at-risk. Among students with learning disabilities, self-perceived social acceptance has been found to be related to depression (Heath & Wiener, 1996). Students with learning disabilities, in a study by Stanley, Dai, and Nolan (1997) demonstrated lower self-esteem than their peers with emotional/behavioral disorders, though both groups reported mild depression. Among elementary school-aged children who attempted suicide, or reported considering suicide, self-esteem, academic failure, and learning disabilities were issues of critical concern (1990). Students with learning disabilities are considered at risk for severe depression and suicide (Huntington & Bender, 1993).

Most school-based suicide prevention programs deal with identifying signs of depression and suicidal ideation. Prevention efforts attempt to help students to be successful in school, and work on emotional growth and achieve personal potential (Putnam, 1995). McGee and Guetzloe (1988), however, make several suggestions regarding working with a student who may be suicidal:

- Always consider suicide threats or gestures as serious.
- Convey to the student that you consider suicide threats as serious; do not make the student feel guilty.
- Encourage the student to use social support systems including parents, friends, school personnel, or a counseling center.
- Recognize that to an adolescent the loss of a romantic relationship may represent the end of any hope for a loving relationship.
- Remove anything in the immediate environment that could be used as a weapon.
- Mention events that may be coming up to elicit their interest.
- Make sure that students have the telephone number of a crisis center, suicide hotline, or an appropriate member of school staff.

- Tell the student that you cannot keep their suicidal statement secret.
- Ask the student for a commitment that he or she will not harm himself or herself, and that if he or she feels any kind of suicidal impulse, he or she will call a teacher, a counselor, or hotline worker.

Drug and Alcohol Use and Abuse

Putnam (1995) describes several programs which are available for the prevention of alcohol and other drug use. "Students Against Drunk Driving" (SADD), for example, is a club to promote the abstinence from alcohol and other drugs by peers and parents, particularly when the individual plans on driving. Individuals write a "contract for life" in which the individual agrees to call for help or transportation in situations where they have been drinking and need to go home. SADD uses strategies such as posters, presentations, and speakers. "Just Say No Clubs" also advocate the abstinence from alcohol and other drugs, as well as training in how to say no to peers and supporting each others' abstinence. Adventure-based programs, including canoeing, camping, mountain climbing, sailing, and hiking may also be used to fill the adolescent's need for adventure and risk-taking behaviors without the use of alcohol or other drugs. Mini-courses and wellness days, as well as activities to increase positive school climate, are also used to prevent drug and alcohol use.

Adolescent Pregnancy

Approximately one million American adolescent girls become pregnant each year. Of these girls, approximately one-third have abortions, one in seven have a miscarriage, and slightly over half have children. According to the Children's Defense Fund (1997), the annual cost of adolescent motherhood, plus the costs of other disadvantages faced by adolescent mothers, may be between 13 and 19 billion dollars.

The National Campaign to Prevent Teen Pregnancy, which began in 1996, aims to reduce teen births through enlisting the media, supporting state and local actions, and disseminating information on effective programs. The campaign identified several likely causes of the high pregnancy rates among American teens, including the lack of negative consequences for male partners, the absence of forceful messages that teens should not be parents, mass glorification of sex, influences of childhood sexual abuse, sexual exploitation by older men, earlier onset of puberty, lack of accessibility to family planning, and insufficient information about sexuality and contraception. Prevention programs emphasize the need to provide comprehensive youth development programs and education on sexuality and contraception.

Summary Points

- Prevention is usually described at three levels of activity: primary, secondary, and tertiary.
- Two major prevention-focused programs include (a) reducing stress in the community, and (b) building individual capacity to withstand stress.
- Early Intervention can make significant, long-lasting differences in the lives of young children with learning disabilities or emotional/behavioral disorders.
- Providing students with opportunities and training to mediate their own conflicts increases their ability to self-regulate and self-monitor.
- Family intervention efforts vary depending on family characteristics.
- Students must be actively taught alternatives to violence.
- Through effective discipline and installing hope, teachers can mitigate the impact of contemporary social problems on their students.

Key Words and Phrases

at-risk—a set of presumed dynamics that could place an individual in danger of negative future outcomes

conflict—a disagreement or disharmony

conflict resolution—activities used to generate an answer or solution to a disagreement or disharmony

early intervention—services provided to infants and toddlers, birth through age three, and their families

family intervention—strategies that target family interactions to change the behavior of family members

prevention—efforts engaged in to keep learning disabilities or emotional/behavioral disorders from occurring

primary prevention—prevention efforts aimed at the population at large

secondary prevention—prevention efforts to reduce the intensity and/or duration of problems in the future

tertiary prevention—prevention efforts directed at reducing the likelihood that problems will become more serious

turfism—guarding areas of professional expertise and services from encroachment by others

violence prevention—efforts aimed at decreasing the engagement of individuals in aggressive activities

wraparound—a needs driven process for creating and providing services for individual children and their families

References

American Public Welfare Association. (1993). *Characteristics of children in substitute care and adoptive care.* Washington, DC: Author.

Apter, S. (1982). *Troubled children, troubled systems.* NY: Pergamon.

Aylward, G. P. (1988). Issues in prediction and developmental follow-up. *Developmental Behavior and Pediatrics, 9* (5), 307–309.

Bredekamp, S. (1993). The relationship between early childhood education and early childhood special education: Healthy marriage or family feud? *Topics in Early Childhood Special Education, 13* (3), 259–273.

Brendtro, L. K., & Long, N. J. (1994). Violence begets violence: Breaking conflict cycles. *Journal of Emotional and Behavioral Problems, 3* (1), 2–7.

Bruder, M. B. (1993). The provision of early intervention and early childhood special education within community early childhood programs: Characteristics of effective service delivery. *Topics in Early Childhood Special Education, 13* (3), 19–37.

Caplan, G. (1964) *Principles of preventive psychiatry.* NY: Basic Books.

Cavallaro, C. C., Haney, M., & Cabello, B. (1992). Developmentally appropriate strategies for promoting full participation in early childhood settings. *Topics in Early Childhood Special Education, 13* (3), 293–307.

Children's Defense Fund. (1997). *The state of American children yearbook 1997.* Washington, DC: Author.

Cicci, R. (1995). *Getting ready for school: The preschool years.* NY: York Press.

Coordinated Campaign for Learning Disabilities (1997). *Early Warning Signs of Learning Disabilities.* Washington, DC: Author.

Curwin, R. L. (1994). Teaching at-riskers how to hope. *The Education Digest, 60* (2), 11–15.

Curwin, R. L. (1995). A human approach to reducing violence in schools. *Educational Leadership, 52* (5), 72.

Denny, R. K., DePaepe, P. A., Gunder, P. L., Jack, S. L., & Shores, R. E. (1994). A case study of the effects of altering instructional interactions on the disruptive behavior of a child identified with SBD. *Education and Treatment of Children, 17,* 435–444.

Dunst, C. J., Trivette, C., & Deal, A. (1988). *Enabling and empowering families: Principles and guidelines for practice.* Cambridge, MA: Brookline Books.

Feil, E. G., Walker, H. M., & Severson, H. H. (1995). The early screening project for young children with behavior problems. *Journal of Emotional and Behavioral Disorders, 1* (3), 194–202.

Fredericks, B. (1994). Integrated service systems for troubled youth. *Education and Treatment of Children, 17,* 387–416.

Gadow, K. D., & Sprafkin, J. (1993). Television "violence" and children with emotional and behavioral disorders. *Journal of Emotional and Behavioral Disorders, 1* (1), 54–63.

Gatrell, D. (1995). Misbehavior or mistaken behavior? *Young Children, 50* (5), 27–34.

Goerge, R. M., Voorhis, J. V., Grant, S., Casey, K., & Robinson, M. (1992). Special education experiences of foster children: An empirical study. *Child Welfare, 71,* 419–437.

Haberman, M. (1994). Gentle teaching . . . in a violent society. *Educational Horizons,* Spring, 131–135.

Hanson, M. J., & Carta, J. J. (1995). Addressing the challenge of families with multiple risks. *Exceptional Children, 62* (3), 102–212.

Heath, N. L., & Wiener, J. (1996). Depression and nonacademic self-perceptions in children with and without learning disabilities. *Learning Disability Quarterly, 19* (1), 34–44.

Henley, M. (1994). A self-control curriculum for troubled youngsters. Journal of *Emotional and Behavioral Problems, 3* (1), 40–46.

Hill, B. K., Hayden, M. F., Lakin, K. C., Menke, J., & Amado, A. R. N. (1990). State-by-state data on children with handicaps in foster care. *Child Welfare, 69,* 447–462.

Huntington, D. D., & Bender, W. N. (1993). Adolescents with learning disabilities at risk? Emotional well-being, depression, suicide. *Journal of Learning Disabilities, 26* (3), 159–166.

Johnson, D. W., & Johnson, R. T. (1996). Peacemakers: Teaching students to resolve their own and schoolmates' conflicts. *Focus on Exceptional Children, 28* (6), 1–11.

Jones, V. (1993). Assessing your classroom and school wide management plan. *Beyond Behavior, 4* (3), 9–12.

Kaiser, A. P., & Hester, P. P. (1997). Prevention of conduct disorders through early intervention: A social-communicative perspective. *Behavioral Disorders, 21* (3), 117–130.

Kauffman, J. M. (1993). *Characteristics of emotional and behavioral disorders of children and youth* (5th ed.). NY: Merrill/Macmillan.

Kauffman, J. M. (1994). Violence and aggression of children and youth. *Preventing School Failure, 38,* 8–9.

Keogh, B. K., & Sears, S. (1991). Early identification of learning disabilities. In B. Y. L. Wong, (Ed.), *Learning about learning disabilities* (pp. 485–503). San Diego, CA: Academic Press.

Lambie, R., (1987). *Working with families of children with handicaps.* Richmond: Virginia Department of Education.

Lambie, R., & Daniels-Mohring, D. (1993). *Family systems within educational contexts.* Denver: Love.

Learning Disabilities Association of America. (1999). *Early childhood intervention pamphlet.* Pittsburgh, PA: Author.

McCarthy, J. M., Harris, M. J., & Reeves, K. K. (1997). Specific learning disabilities in preschool children: Shifting paradigms in the middle of the stream. *Learning Disabilities Research and Practice, 12,* 146–150.

McCormick, L., & Feeney, S. (1995). Modifying and expanding activities for children with disabilities. *Young Children, 50* (4), 10–17.

McGee, K., & Guetzloe, E. (1988). Suicidal emotionally handicapped students: Tips for the classroom teacher. *The Pointer, 32,* 7–10.

McWhirter, J. J., McWhirter, B. T., McWhirter, A. M., & McWhirter, E. H. (1998). *At risk youth: A comprehensive response* (2nd ed.). Pacific Grove, CA: Brooks/Cole.

National Association of Child Advocates. (1998). Why school suspension and expulsion are not the answer. *Reclaiming Children and Youth: Journal of Emotional and Behavioral Problems, 7* (2), 87–90.

National Center for Learning Disabilities. (1998). Understanding early warning signs. *Exceptional Parent, 28* (5), 52.

National Summit on Youth Violence. (1994). Breaking the cycle of violence. Bloomington, IN: National Educational Service Foundation.

Nelson, R. E., & Crawford, B. (1990). Suicide among elementary school-aged children. *Elementary School Guidance and Counseling, 25* (2), 123–128.

Putnam, M. L. (1995). Crisis intervention with adolescents with learning disabilities. *Focus on Exceptional Children, 28* (2), 1–24.

Ramey, C. T., & Ramey, S. L. (1992). Effective early intervention. *Mental Retardation, 30,* 337–345.

Sawyer, R. J., & Dubowitz, H. (1994). School performance of children in kinship care. *Child Abuse and Neglect, 18,* 587–597.

Skiba, R., & Peterson, R. (1999). The dark side of zero tolerance. *Phi Delta Kappan, 80* (5), 372–376.

Smith, D. D., & Rivera, D. P. (1995). Discipline in special education and general education settings. *Focus on Exceptional Children, 27* (5), 1–14.

Smucker, K. S., Kauffman, J. M., & Ball, D. W. (1996). School-related problems of special education foster-care students with emotional or behavioral disorders: A comparison to other groups. *Journal of Emotional and Behavioral Disorders, 4* (1) 30–39.

Soderlund, J., Epstein, M. H., Quinn, K. P., Cumblad, C., & Petersen, S. (1995). Parental perspectives on comprehensive services for children and youth with emotional and behavioral disorders. *Behavioral Disorders, 29* (3), 157–170.

Stainback, S., & Stainback, W. (1990). *Support networks for inclusive schooling.* Baltimore: Brookes.

Stanley, P. D., Dai, Y., & Nolan, R. F. (1997). Differences in depression and self-esteem reported by learning disabled and behavior disordered middle school students. *Journal of Adolescence, 20* (2), 219–222.

Terkelsen, K. G. (1983). Schizophrenia and the family: Adverse effects of family therapy. *Family Processes, 22,* 191–200.

Tremblay, R. E., Paginani-Kurtz, L., Masse, L. C., & Vitaro, F. (1995). A bimodal preventive intervention for disruptive kindergarten boys: Its impact through mid-adolescence. *Journal of Consulting and Clinical Psychology, 63* (4), 560–568.

Zirpoli, T. J. (1995). *Understanding and affecting the behavior of young children.* Upper Saddle River, NJ: Prentice-Hall.

Zirpoli, T. J. (1997). *Behavior management: Applications for teachers and parents.* Upper Saddle River, NJ: Prentice Hall.

Index